Practical Reason, Aristotle,
and Weakness of the Will

Minnesota Publications in the Humanities, Volume Four

A series of books published with
the financial assistance of the Graduate School
and the College of Liberal Arts of
the University of Minnesota.

Practical Reason, Aristotle, and Weakness of the Will

Norman O. Dahl

University of Minnesota Press   *Minneapolis*

Copyright © 1984 by the University of Minnesota
All rights reserved.
Published by the University of Minnesota Press,
2037 University Avenue Southeast, Minneapolis, MN 55414
Printed in the United States of America

Library of Congress Cataloging in Publication Data

Dahl, Norman O.
    Practical reason, Aristotle, and weakness of the
will.

    (Minnesota publications in humanities; v. 4)
    Bibliography: p.
    Includes index.
    1. Aristotle — Ethics.   2. Ethics — History.
3. Reason — History.   I. Title.
B491.E7D33 1984   171'.3   83-14845
ISBN 0-8166-1245-5
ISBN 0-8166-1246-3 (pbk.)

To my father,
and in memory of
my mother

Contents

Acknowledgments

Work on the topic of this book began in the fall of 1971 when I was on leave from the University of Minnesota to study Greek philosophy at Harvard University. It started with what was supposed to be a paper on Aristotle on weakness of the will. When a section on practical reason grew longer than the length intended for the original paper, I discovered that I was embarked on a larger enterprise. The expansions and revisions that followed spanned two sabbatical leaves from the University of Minnesota and were supported on more than one occasion by a research grant from the University of Minnesota. While I was on sabbatical leave in 1981-82, the Philosophy Department of Pacific Lutheran University was kind enough to provide me with office space and secretarial help. All of this I happily and gratefully acknowledge.

Throughout the various stages of this work I have benefited from the comments of a number of people, including Allen Buchanan, Cynthia Freeland, Vicki Harper, Charles Barry Hoffmaster, Richard Kraut, James Lesher, Terrance McConnell, Fred Miller, Sandra Peterson, and an anonymous referee. During a sabbatical leave at Oxford University in 1974-75 Justin Gosling, David Pears, and Michael Woods were kind enough to read large portions of a second draft. Their comments and suggestions helped me avoid a number of mistakes. During this same time I also profited greatly from a series of discussions with David Charles and Troels Engberg-Pedersen. I am also thankful to William Hanson, who took time to read a complete third draft and provide me with his comments on it. Parts of various stages of this manuscript were read to philosophy departments at the University of Minnesota, the University of Nebraska, Pacific Lutheran University, Reed College, the University of Washington, and to meetings of the Pacific and Western Division of the American Philosophical Association. I am grateful to all those who commented on those occasions.

Two debts deserve special acknowledgment. The first is to Thomas Nagel, who first helped me see the importance of the existence of practical reason for ethics, and whose suggestions in a series of lectures on Aristotle's ethics at the University of California, Berkeley in 1965-66 provided the basis for parts of what I have argued in this book. The second is to the late G. E. L. Owen, who first drew my attention to the virtues of Aristotle, and whose own work set a standard of excellence to try to live up to. His encouragement and criticism of the first two drafts of this manuscript were of immeasurable help.

Of course, none of those whom I have mentioned should be taken to have endorsed what I argue for in this book, least of all Professors Nagel and Owen. Professor Nagel may well be surprised to see what has become of some of his suggestions, and I know that I resisted more than one of the changes that Professor Owen urged on me. Besides, anyone who knew Professor Owen knew that were he to have written on the topic of this book, all other scholars would have had to thoroughly rethink their own views.

Vicki Field, Debbie Florian, Ruth Anne Ruud, Paula Sotirin, and Shirley Zurmuhlen all had a hand in various stages of the preparation of this manuscript, and Carl Brandt was kind enough to prepare the General Index. I gratefully acknowledge their help.

My thanks also to my wife, Pat, without whose work not even the second draft of this manuscript would have been written.

Practical Reason, Aristotle, and Weakness of the Will

Introduction

One of the central problems in recent moral philosophy is the apparent tension between the "practical" or "action-guiding" side of moral judgments and their objectivity. The most natural way of accounting for the practical side of moral judgments is to adopt *internalism*,[1] a position according to which motivation is essential to moral obligation. According to internalism, necessarily if a person has (or recognizes, accepts, or assents to) an obligation, then he or she has a motive to fulfill that obligation. But, since what motivates a person seems to vary from agent to agent, taking motivation to be essential to obligation seems to eliminate the objectivity of judgments of obligation.[2] Whatever one may say constitutes a person's obligation, it will always be open to someone else to deny that it does, arguing that that person or another lacks the requisite motivation under similar circumstances. On the other hand, if one adopts *externalism*, the view that there is no necessary connection between obligation and motivation, one can allow for the objectivity of judgments of obligation, but, since these judgments are no longer essentially tied to motivation, they seem to lose their practical force.

This tension would not exist if *practical reason* existed (if reason played a substantial role in producing motivation) *and* if judgments of obligation were based on the demands of practical reason (if the recognition of obligation were one of the areas in which practical reason operated). If both of these conditions were met, then judgments of obligation would be both practical and objective—practical since practical reason would guarantee an essential connection between obligation and motivation, and objective since practical reason

3

would provide a motivation invariant over all (rational) agents. However, if one is to argue for both of these conditions, one must be able to indicate just what practical reason is, how one knows it exists, and just what the connection is between practical reason and moral obligation. It seems unlikely that one will make much headway in answering these questions unless one recognizes at least some of the details of alternative views about what it is for practical reason to exist, and what its connection with morality is. At least one such account of the connection between morality and practical reason exists (Nagel, 1970), and it is part of the purpose of this book to furnish another. I shall argue that Aristotle admits the existence of practical reason, that the considerations he would offer in support of its existence are plausible ones, and that the ethical theory that rests on his conception of practical reason, whether it is by itself wholly adequate or not, deserves to be taken seriously.

Aristotle is a natural place to begin an investigation of practical reason and its connection with ethics, because Aristotle's conception of *phronēsis* (practical wisdom) seems to be the first recognition of a uniquely practical form of knowledge, and *phronēsis* clearly plays a central role in Aristotle's ethical theory. However, when one begins to investigate Aristotle's views on the existence of practical reason, an interesting problem arises. In a number of passages, what Aristotle says implies that practical reason exists and that its scope is sufficiently broad to provide a basis for ethics. But when one looks at the role that Aristotle allows reason to play in the production of motivation and action, his position seems to be identical with Hume's. Hume correctly draws the conclusion from his view that there is no such thing as practical reason. The problem is whether Aristotle did provide an adequate foundation for acknowledging the existence of practical reason. Did he really share Hume's view on the role that reason plays in action, or does Aristotle take two incompatible positions on this topic? I shall argue that Aristotle did consistently allow for the existence of practical reason. He did provide an account of the role that reason plays in action that is sufficient to allow for practical reason; he did not share Hume's view on the realtion between reason and action; and he takes only one position on this topic.

The central question in whether Aristotle's ethics is based on practical reason is what role Aristotle allowed reason to play in the acquisition of ends. When the question is put in this way, one discovers that commentators' discussion of Aristotle on practical reason and its connection with his ethics has a history that stretches back at least to the nineteenth century, the effect of which has been that, for the most part, current opinion does not recognize practical reason as playing a central role in Aristotle's ethics. Julius Walter

(1874) argued that according to Aristotle reason has nothing to do with the ends of action, and largely through his influence on Burnet (1904) it is this view that for the most part was accepted by English scholars. Although Richard Loening (1903) argued against Walter, his arguments seem to have had little effect. Jaeger (1948) also advocated the view that Aristotle allowed reason to have no influence on the acquisition of ends. More recently, D. J. Allan (1953) repeated the arguments of Loening against the prevailing view, but his discussion is too short to be entirely convincing.[3] Allan did convince Gauthier (1958), but until just recently more typical of prevailing opinion was either Walsh's (1963) view that two strands of thought occur in Aristotle on practical reason, one that allows reason to play a role in the acquisition of ends and one that does not, or that of Fortenbaugh (1975), who sides with Walter against Loening and Allan. J. Donald Monan (1968) did follow Allan's position, but essentially added no new arguments for it. Although Ando (1971) did offer new arguments for Aristotle's admission of practical reason, a number of them seem to me to be doubtful. In the last few years, attempts have been made to show the extent of Artistotle's commitment to practical reason, the most detailed of which is John Cooper's (1975).[4] However, even these, I think, do not acknowledge the full extent to which Aristotle's ethics is based on practical reason.

Those who are unaffected by classical scholarship also have seemed unable to appreciate Aristotle's views on reason and action. The reason for this, I think, is that having read Hume or others who share Hume's view on reason and action, they come prepared to read such a view into Aristotle. It will be part of the purpose of this book to show the extent to which Aristotle's ethics does rest on practical reason, and to argue for this in the detail that it deserves.

A second topic that has occupied the attention of contemporary moral philosophers is weakness of the will—the failure to do what one knows one ought to do.[5] Aside from its intrinsic interest, weakness of the will has an important connection with the attempt to base ethics on practical reason. If practical reason exists and one of the areas in which it operates is the recognition of what one ought to do, then weakness of the will will be puzzling in the sense that it will always stand in need of an explanation. If practical reason exists and is operative in the recognition of what one ought to do, then anyone who knows what he or she ought to do will have a motive to do it. Failure to act in the face of this motive will require an explanation. Furthermore, if on one's theory of practical reason the motivation to act as one ought turns out to be a relatively strong one, it will be tempting to deny the existence of weakness of the will. However, since it seems to be a fact that weakness of the will does exist, a criterion of adequacy for any attempt to base ethics on practical reason will be that it explain how genuine cases of weakness of the will are possible.

Again, Aristotle's work is a natural place to begin a discussion of weakness of the will, and, again, when one investigates Aristotle's position on weakness of the will, an interesting problem arises. At first sight, Aristotle seems to deny the possibility of genuine cases of weakness of the will, because he seems to deny that people can recognize that they are in a position to act on their knowledge of what to do and fail to act on it. However, some passages appear to be incompatible with this denial. Did Aristotle really deny the possibility of weakness of the will, or was he inconsistent in his views about weakness of the will? If he did deny the possibility of weakness of the will, what led him to this denial? Was it his position on practical reason? If so, then it looks as if his position fails to meet the criterion of adequacy mentioned above. If, however, his position on practical reason allows for weakness of the will, then why did Aristotle end up denying its possibility? If he did *not* deny its possibility, then how is the admission of its possibility compatible with his position on practical reason? I shall argue that, despite appearances to the contrary, Aristotle did allow for genuine cases of weakness of the will and that he was not inconsistent in his views about weakness of the will. Since part of the evidence for this will come from Aristotle's position on practical reason, it will turn out that his position on practical reason does meet the criterion of adequacy mentioned above.

Thus, although what follows is primarily a historical discussion of Aristotle on practical reason and weakness of the will, the discussion has a philosophical point as well. If I am right, Aristotle has presented one alternative on how to base ethics on practical reason, one that deserves to be taken seriously, in part because it meets at least one important criterion of adequacy.

Before beginning the discussion of Aristotle on practical reason and weakness of the will I should mention two assumptions about the development of Aristotle's thought. First I assume that the *Nicomachean Ethics* (NE) is later than the *Eudemian Ethics* (EE), and that the "common books" (Books V, VI, and VII of NE) are common and do belong to the *Nicomachean Ethics*. This assumption is certainly controversial,[6] but I don't think it matters a great deal if I am wrong. The bulk of the evidence that I shall cite comes from the "common books," and most of those who date the *Eudemian Ethics* later than the *Nicomachean Ethics* take the "common books" to belong to the *Eudemian Ethics*. The most I would have to admit if I am wrong is that I should have looked more to the *Eudemian Ethics* for ancillary evidence. (Also, if the arguments I give are correct and the *Eudemian Ethics* is later than the *Nicomachean Ethics*, then the doctrines of a number of parts of the *Nicomachean Ethics* cohere much better with that part of the *Eudemian Ethics* that includes the "common books" than might otherwise be expected.) The second assumption is that the doctrines found in Aristotle's later psychological works (especially *De Anima*) are consistent with the psychological doctrines found in his ethical writings, so that one can interpret what Aristotle says in his ethical works on the basis of what he says in his psychological works.[7]

Unless otherwise specified, all translations are those of the Oxford translation.

Part One

Practical Reason and Aristotle

CHAPTER 1

A Statement
of the Problem

Part of the purpose of this book is to argue that Aristotle provides an example of one who attempts to base ethics on the existence of practical reason. The interest of such an attempt is that if it is successful it provides a way of reconciling two apparently opposing sides of moral judgments, their "practical" side and their objectivity. However, before one can determine whether Aristotle, or anyone else, provides such an example, two questions must be answered. What is it for practical reason to exist? And what must the scope of practical reason be for it to provide an objective basis for ethics? In this chapter I shall try to answer these two questions, and, on the basis of these answers, raise a problem about whether Aristotle's ethics does rest on the existence of practical reason.

I. The Nature of Practical Reason

What is it for *practical reason* to exist? I shall say that practical reason exists if and only if, strictly speaking, actions, passions, motives, intentions, etc. can be said to be *rational* or *irrational*. However, to say this provides little understanding of what it is for practical reason to exist unless one knows what the conditions are under which, strictly speaking, actions and passions can be said to be rational or irrational. Perhaps the easiest way to discover what these conditions are is to look at Hume's denial of the existence of practical reason (Hume [1964], pp. 413-18, pp. 456-59).

Hume's explicit view is that no action is rational or irrational because reason by itself is impotent to motivate anyone to act. The

11

only function reason has is to discover deductive relationships (relations between ideas) and matters of fact, particularly cause and effect relationships. In the fulfillment of neither of these roles does reason by itself excite anyone to do anything. Passions are what move people to act, and the only thing contrary to a passion is another passion. Since reason by itself can not produce a passion, reason can not be contrary to a passion, nor can a passion be contrary to reason. Therefore, "Tis not contrary to reason to prefer the destruction of the whole world to the scratching of my finger," ([1964], p. 416). That is, no passion (and therefore no action) is rational or irrational.

Hume seems to accept the following thesis about the conditions under which practical reason exists,

(i) Practical reason exists if and only if reason by itself motivates people to act.

On this thesis passions will be rational if they accord with the motivation produced by reason itself and irrational if they are contrary to it. Actions will be rational if they would be done by one acting on the motivation produced by reason itself, irrational if they are contrary to what would be done by someone acting on such a motivation. However, since reason by itself does *not* move people to act, actions and passions are neither rational nor irrational. Hume allows that in a secondary sense actions or passions can be said to be irrational if they are based on false or irrational judgments, but these actions are irrational *only* in a *secondary* sense. If, for example, I fear some distant object because I mistakenly believe it to be a wild animal, then my fear might be called irrational. Or if I stand in line because I mistakenly believe that by doing so I will be able to buy some tickets I want, then, in a sense, my standing in line might be said to be irrational. However, *strictly speaking* it is my *judgment* that the distant object is a wild animal, or my *judgment* that I can obtain the tickets I want by standing in line, that is irrational in these cases, (if indeed anything is irrational). *Strictly speaking* my fear of the distant object and my standing in line are neither rational nor irrational.[1]

One might argue that (i) is too strong a condition for the existence of practical reason, arguing that Hume is just perverse in refusing to say in all strictness that passions and actions based on false judgments can be irrational. Being based on a false judgment, one might argue, at least sometimes *is* sufficient for the irrationality of a passion or action. After all, had it not been for the false judgment one wouldn't have had the passion. Although I think (i) is too strong as a condition for practical reason, I think there is something correct in Hume's refusal to accept this as a ground for saying that passions can be irrational. His refusal rests on a position which, if correct, would make it improper to describe any passion as rational or irrational. However, if one looks at the position more closely, one will see that it requires Hume to adopt a stronger thesis about the connection between reason and motivation than that required by (i). This in turn will lead one to see that a weaker condition exists than (i) for the existence of practical reason.

Hume's refusal to say that even passions based on false judgments can be irrational rests on the thesis that if passions (or actions) are to be irrational, they must be capable of being *contrary to* reason. If reason's only task is the discovery of things capable of truth or falsehood, it looks as if something could be contrary to reason only if it were capable of truth or falsehood. Since passions are not capable of truth or falsehood, it looks as if they cannot be contrary to reason. Given that passion is what moves one toward or away from various objects, it looks as if only something that could exert a similar effect could be contrary to passion. Since reason on no occasion exerts any such influence, reason cannot be contrary to a passion. When a passion is based on a false judgment, there is nothing about the passion that is false, and there is nothing about the judgment that moves one to avoid the object of the passion. Thus, only a judgment can be contrary to reason, not a passion. If we *say* that a passion based on a false judgment is irrational, then we are (or should be) simply saying that it is based on an irrational judgment. A passion is simply the wrong sort of thing to be irrational ([1964], pp. 413-17, pp. 458-59).

If this is the basis of Hume's denial of the existence of practical reason, then it requires him to maintain something stronger than that reason *by itself* never moves anyone to act. It requires him to say that reason does not have *any* influence on the production of motivation; it does not contribute to or account for even *part of* any motivation. If it did make such a partial contribution, then it too would be the sort of thing, like passion, that can produce motivation, and, thus, could be contrary to passion.

Hume seems at least partially aware of this, for when considering a case like the one in which I stand in line to buy some tickets he says,

> But 'tis evident in this case that the impulse *arises* not from reason, but is only *directed* by it. 'Tis from the prospect of pain or pleasure that the aversion or propensity arises towards any object: And these emotions *extend* themselves to the causes and effects of that object, as they are pointed out to us by reason and experience. ([1964], p. 414, emphasis mine)

It is, of course, difficult to know exactly how to distinguish an impulse's being *directed by* reason's discovery of certain means, from desire for the means *arising* from such a discovery,[2] but this distinction together with Hume's talk about emotions "extending themselves" to certain causes, does suggest that it is the desire for the end alone that causes the desire for the means. This seems confirmed by Hume's saying that when a passion is based on a false judgment and the falsity of the judgment is discovered, the passion immediately ceases to exist ([1964] pp. 416-17). If a desire for an object arises *solely* because a desire for an end is directed toward it by reason, then one would expect the desire for the object to cease should reason cease to direct the desire for the end toward it. If the desire were to persist, it is difficult to see how Hume could account for it without admitting that reason does influence or aid in the production of motivation.[3] Hume summarizes what he thinks he has shown by saying,

> I have prov'd, that reason is perfectly inert, and can never either prevent or produce any action or affection. ([1964], p. 458)

Shortly afterwards he says,

> Reason is wholly inactive, and can never be the source of so active a principle as conscience, or a sense of morals. ([1964], p. 458)

However, whether Hume recognized it or not, his argument does commit him to denying reason any active role in the production of motivation. Even if reason did not by itself produce any motivation, if it together with desire produced a motivation that singly neither of them could produce, reason would still be the sort of thing that could move people to act. If it is that sort of thing, then it can be contrary to a passion, and passions can be said to be rational or irrational. If it is not that sort of thing, then Hume is correct in denying that strictly speaking passions are rational or irrational, including passions based on false judgments.

What this means is that (i) is too strong as a statement of the conditions for the existence of practical reason. Of course, if reason does by itself move people to act, then practical reason exists,[4] but practical reason also exists if reason *co-produces* motivation. Furthermore, it would be too weak just to say that practical reason exists if one wouldn't have had certain motivations had one not reasoned in certain ways. As an attempt at providing a statement of the conditions for the existence of practical reason that satisfies all of the above I suggest,

> (ii) Practical reason exists if and only if, in an appropriate sense of 'necessity' weaker than that of logical necessity, there are circumstances in which necessarily if a person's reason operates corrrectly he or she will have certain motivations, the motivations he or she would have not being necessitated by the circumstances themselves.

For the present I shall take the appropriate sense of necessity to be causal necessity. (ii) allows for the existence of practical reason if reason by itself moves people to act, for in those circumstances in which reason does move people to act, it will be causally necessary that people have certain motivations. (ii) also allows for the existence of practical reason if reason co-produces motivation together with desire, for, taking these desires as part of the circumstances, it will be causally necessary that if reason operates in the presence of these desires certain motivations will be produced. (ii) does not, however, allow practical reason to exist when it is only true that one wouldn't have had certain motivations if one hadn't reasoned in certain ways. For example, the latter could be true when it wasn't causally necessary that if one hadn't reasoned in certain ways one wouldn't have had certain motivations.

To illustrate (ii) and further clarify the conditions under which practical reason can exist, let us return to the case in which a person desires the means to some already desired end. How does such a desire arise? There are at least four possibilities. The first is that in a sense the desire for the means is already contained in the desire for the end, for to have a desire for a certain end just is to be disposed to want or desire the means.[5] If this is the account of how a desire for the means arises, then I think that such a desire provides no grounds for the existence of practical reason. This accords with the results one gets from applying (ii), for even though on such an account it is necessary that one who has a desire for an end and recognizes means to that end will desire the means, the necessity is logical necessity. (ii) requires the necessity to be weaker than logical necessity.

The second possibility is that it is logically possible for someone to desire an end but not desire the means to that end, and that when people do desire means to ends they have, the desire for the means is caused (e.g., through some principle of association) by the desire for the end. Of course, the desire for the means would not have occurred if reason had not allowed the person to recognize the means as means to the end, but according to the second possibility, reason's recognition of the means is an *initial* condition rather than a *causal* condition of the desire for the means.[6] It is this position that I am inclined to think Hume held, for I interpret his distinction between reason's *directing* the desire for an end to certain means and the desire for those means *arising* from reason as the distinction between reason being an initial condition and its being a causal condition of the desire for the means. Whether or not this is right, I think it is clear that on this account the desire for the means provides no grounds for the existence of practical reason. One gets the same conclusion by applying (ii), for even though there are certain circumstances (including the desire for the end) in which it is causally necessary that if reason recognizes the means to the end, a motive to pursue the means will be produced, given that reason's recognition of the means is only an initial condition of the motive, the motive will be causally necessitated by the circumstances (including the desire for the end) alone. According to (ii), this is not enough for the existence of practical reason.

A third possibility is that it is logically possible for a person to desire an end but not desire the means to that end, and that when a person does desire the means to an end, it is because he has a general desire to pursue means to ends that he has. This general desire together with the desire for the end causes the desire for the means. Reason's recognition of the means is again only an initial condition of the production of this desire. For reasons similar to those given just above, on this account the desire for the means provides no grounds for the existence of practical reason. Again, the application of (ii) yields the same result.

The fourth possibility is that although it is logically possible for a person to desire the end without desiring the means, it is reason's recognition of the means that produces the desire for the means. On this account reason's recognition of the means is a causal and not an initial condition of the desire for the means. If this is the way the desire for the means arises, then I think practical reason does exist. Its existence also follows according to (ii). Whether or not one is entitled to say that in these circumstances reason *by itself* produces the desire for the means, it is at least true that reason along with the desire for the end co-produces the desire for the means. In some circumstances (including the desire for the end) it is causally necessary that if reason recognizes the means, a motive to pursue the means will result. And since reason is a causal condition of the production of that motive, the motive is not causally necessitated by those circumstances themselves.[7]

Although a good deal more needs to be said before one would have a completely adequate account of the conditions under which practical reason exists, I think I have said enough to show why one should prefer (ii) to (i) as a statement of these conditions. This is important, since I think that if one is to find Aristotle admitting the existence of practical reason, it will be on the basis of something like (ii) rather than (i).

Before proceeding, I should point out what some might feel is a defect in the foregoing discussion, and indicate how it can be removed if it is thought necessary to do so. The discussion so far has talked as if wants, desires, etc.—the sorts of things mentioned in explanations of actions—are causes of motives or actions. One might argue, however, that reasons are not causes, that they stand in their own special noncausal relation to the actions they explain.[8] As a result, the foregoing discussion is beside the point. Whatever the relation is between reason and motivation which, if it holds, allows actions and motives to be rational or irrational, it is not a causal one. That this does not show that the foregoing discussion is beside the point can be seen as follows. Suppose the relation between reasons and actions is not a causal one, but a special relation of its own, call it *rationalization*. One can still adopt the foregoing as an account of the conditions under which practical reason exists, replacing causal talk with talk about rationalization. Practical reason will exist if reason rationalizes or co-rationalizes motives or actions in the way that desires sometimes do. To apply (ii), one simply has to take the sense of necessity in question to be one appropriately tied to rationalization. In what follows, though, I shall continue to talk about practical reason in terms of reason's causing or co-causing motivation.

II. The Scope of Practical Reason

If what I have said in Section I is correct, then practical reason could exist if reason just played a causal role in the production of desires for means to already existing ends. However, if this were the only role that reason played in producing motivation, the existence of practical reason would be of little interest to one concerned with the attempt to base ethics on practical reason. If the existence of practical reason is to provide an objective foundation for morality, there must be some way of saying that whatever morality says one ought to do is something that would be rational for anyone to do and irrational for anyone not to do, and that whatever morality says that one ought not to do would be irrational for anyone to do. In this section I shall outline certain conditions under which the existence of practical reason would provide such a foundation for morality. They may not be the only conditions under which the existence of practical reason would provide such a foundation, but they are a plausible set of conditions, and I think they are the conditions one must look to to determine whether Aristotle's ethics is based on practical reason.

The first condition is that reason can play a role in the acquisition of ends. If practical reason were limited to the production of desires for means to already existing ends, then unless there were ends that everyone pursued, one could not support the claim that something ought to be done by arguing that it would be rational for anyone to do and irrational not to do. As long as ends can vary from person to person, any action put forward as something that ought to be done could fail to be a means to someone's ends, and hence fail to be something that would be rational for anyone to do. Given that it is unlikely that there will be ends shared by everyone unless reason itself plays a role in their acquisition, a plausible condition for practical reason's providing an objective basis for morality is that reason can play a role in the acquisition of ends. It should be pointed out that there are at least two ways in which reason might play this role. First, reason operates on already existing ends, redirecting or making them more determinate and, in a sense, helping create new ends. For example, if someone has his own happiness as an end, reason could redirect this end, putting constraints on when it is pursued, so that the person acquires a new end, the desire to pursue his happiness only when it is compatible with a like amount of freedom for others to pursue their happiness. Or, second, a person might have an indeterminate conception of her own happiness, and reason could lead her to pursue a more determinate conception of her own happiness. On the second way, reason does not operate on already existing ends, redirecting them or making them more determinate; rather, it helps one to acquire new ends "from scratch."

It will not be enough for reason just to play a role in the acquisition of ends. The correct exercise of reason can not lead to any and every end that someone might have, nor can it lead to incompatible ends.[9] If the correct exercise of reason could lead to the acquisition of any end, then any action could turn out to be rational. But then the rationality or irrationality of certain actions could not be the basis for picking out some actions as ones that anyone ought to do and others as ones that anyone ought not to do. Nor could the correct exercise of reason lead to the acquisition of incompatible ends, for this would leave open the possibility that two incompatible actions would both be rational to do and irrational not to do. If this were possible, it is difficult to see how one could argue that certain actions ought to be done and that any alternative to them ought not to be done on the grounds that the actions that ought to be done are rational and that alternatives to them are irrational.[10]

As a third condition I suggest that the correct exercise of reason can lead to a certain harmony or ordering among the ends that it leads one to acquire. This is designed to deal with the possibility of two or more ends, each of which is sometimes rational to pursue, coming in conflict with one another.[11] If morality is objective, then in any situation there should be a uniquely correct answer to the question of how one ought to behave.[12] If this objectivity is to be founded on the existence of practical reason, then the correct answer to how one ought to behave must in some way depend on the correct exercise of practical reason. The possibility of two or more rational ends coming in conflict with one another threatens this foundation in at least two ways. First, it leaves open the possibility that in such a situation there are two incompatible actions each of which ought to be done, and hence that there is not a uniquely correct answer to the question of how one ought to behave in this situation.[13] Second, it leaves open the possibility that whatever one would rely on to decide which of the incompatible actions ought to be done, it has nothing to do with the rationality of actions. On this possibility morality could turn out not to be objective, if whatever one relied on was itself incompatible with the objectivity of morality. And if morality did turn out to be objective, the objectivity of moral judgments could depend on something other than practical reason. These difficulties would be avoided if sufficient harmony or order existed among the ends that reason leads one to acquire, to insure that no such conflict could occur. This could come about in one or more of three ways. First, those ends that are rational to pursue and irrational not to pursue never come in conflict with one another.[14] Second, where it looks as if two rational ends conflict with one another, it turns out that each conflicting end is rational to pursue but not irrational not to pursue. What would be irrational would be the pursuit of neither of the conflicting ends. That is, there is a kind of indeterminacy in what reason would lead one to do in certain circumstances; on some occasions, rational action is compatible with more than one specific action. Third, in cases where it looks as if two rational ends conflict, reason aids in establishing an ordering among ends that allows one to decide which among the competing ends is the best to pursue. Finally, there could be a combination of all three of these ways. Some ends that reason leads one to acquire never come in conflict with one another; other ends are just one among a number of ends which it would be rational to pursue, no specific end being determined by practical reason; still others would be susceptible of a kind of rank ordering that allows one to determine which among them is rational to pursue when they conflict with one another. Which of these, or which combination of these, one adopts will depend on how plausible it is to say that the ends associated with morality can come in conflict with one another, to what extent morality displays a certain indeterminacy, and to what extent it is plausible to say that the ends associated with morality are susceptible to a rank ordering. Whatever one says, though, I think it is plausible to say that if practical reason is to provide an objective foundation for morality, then the correct exercise of reason can lead to a certain harmony or order among the ends that it leads one to acquire.

The fourth condition is one that seems to guarantee the satisfaction of the other three: that there is a single end that the correct exercise of reason can lead one to acquire, every other rational end being related to it as a means or a part of it. If this condition holds, then reason can play a role in the acquisition of ends. Since on this condition the correct exercise of reason leads to a single end, every other rational end being a means or a part of it, if this single end is consistent, it looks as if the correct exercise of reason will lead only to certain ends and not to incompatible ends. Finally, if this fourth condition is satisfied, it looks as if the relation of every other rational end to this single end will provide at least part of the basis for the harmony or order among ends required by the third condition. If one were looking for a candidate for such an end in Greek thought, an obvious candidate would be *eudaimonia* (happiness or well-being), where *eudaimonia* is understood as having some specific content.

III. Does Aristotle's Ethics Rest on Practical Reason?

Does Aristotle admit the existence of practical reason, and, if he does, is its scope sufficiently wide to allow it to provide an objective foundation for ethics? If it is not already obvious, 'practical reason' as I have been using it does not correspond directly to Aristotle's use of 'practical reason' *(nous praktikos)* in either *De Anima* (433a15 ff) or in the *Nicomachean Ethics* (1143a35 ff). Nor does it correspond to such terms as 'practical wisdom' *(phronēsis),* or 'opinion' *(doxa)* as the latter is used in practical matters. All of these, if they have any connection with what I have called practical reason, will at best encompass part of it.[15] The question I am concerned with can not be answered simply by showing that Aristotle had a use for expressions like *'nous praktikos'* or *'phronēsis'.* It will be answered by discovering whether Aristotle allowed reason to play a role in motivation and action that conforms to thesis (ii) in Section I and satisfies the three or four conditions set out in Section II.

There are passages that strongly suggest that Aristotle did or would have admitted the existence of practical reason, and that he did or would have admitted that its scope was sufficient to allow it to provide a basis for ethics. In NE Bk. I Aristotle's final account of *eudaimonia* is that *eudaimonia* is rational activity in accord with virtue (1098a12-18). The good man, the one who has achieved *eudaimonia,* is one who engages in rational activity *well.* This seems to mean that he is one who acts rationally as opposed to irrationally. In Ch. 13 of Bk. I Aristotle considers what parts of the soul "share in a rational principle," and says that moral virtue is concerned with those parts that do share in such a principle. He goes on to say that there is a part of the soul that shares in a rational principle that "urges them aright and towards the best objects" (1102b16-17). He also maintains that the possession of practical wisdom *(phronēsis)* implies that one has the right ends (1142b38). And in *De Anima* Aristotle criticizes those who would split the soul into a rational element and an irrational element, putting desire only in the latter, by claiming that there is a rational form of desire (432b5 ff). All of this strongly suggests that Aristotle would admit the existence of practical reason. He does seem to want to say that actions can be rational or irrational, and he does seem to want to say that on occasions reason carries along with itself a kind of motivation. There is a part of the soul that shares in a rational principle and "urges" men to act in certain ways, there is a state of wisdom achievable in part by the exercise of reason that insures that one has certain ends, and there is desire in the rational part of the soul.

It also suggests that the scope of practical reason is sufficient to provide an objective basis for ethics. Since a part of the soul shares in a rational principle that urges people "aright and towards the best objects," and since *phronēsis,* the excellence of reason in its practical role, insures that one has the right ends, it looks as if Aristotle is saying that the correct exercise of practical reason will lead one to have certain ends, the ends that a good person would have. As long as a good person would not have incompatible ends, it looks as if the correct exercise of reason will not lead to incompatible ends. And if the ends of a good person have the kind of harmony or order mentioned in the third condition in Section II, then it looks as if this condition will be satisfied as well. It also looks as if Aristotle would admit that the fourth condition is satisfied. Aristotle does talk about *eudaimonia* as the end of human activity (e.g. 1097b20-21), and, as we have seen, he describes *eudaimonia* in terms of rational as opposed to irrational activity. If all other good ends either contribute to or constitute *eudaimonia,* then it looks as if Aristotle would say that there is a single end to which all other good ends are related as means or parts, an end which would be achieved by rational as opposed to irrational action. Thus, there is textual evidence for saying that Aristotle did admit the existence of practical reason and that its existence provides an objective foundation for ethics.

However, in some passages in Aristotle the actual account of the role that reason plays in action and desire seems to be much closer to the account that Hume gives. In Bk. III of NE where Aristotle discusses deliberation, the most obvious place in which reason plays a role in action, Aristotle says that deliberation is always about means and never about ends (1112b13, 1112b34-35). And despite Aristotle's statement in Bk. VI that one who possesses *phronēsis* has the right ends, he also seems to say in Bk. VI that *phronēsis* does not provide one with the right ends, but that something else, virtue *(aretē),* does (1144a7-9). Both of these passages strongly suggest that reason's only role in motivation and action is to discern means to already existing ends. If in this role reason only *directs* the desire for the end to certain means, the desire for the means not *arising* from reason, then the view put forward seems to be identical with Hume's. Even if reason does play an active role in the production of the desire for means, as long as reason has nothing to do with ends, the view will be close enough to Hume's to prevent practical reason from providing a basis for ethics.

There seem, then, to be two strands in Aristotle's thought about practical reason and its relation to ethics. On the one hand, he seems to admit its existence and to allow it a sufficient scope to provide a basis for ethics. On the other hand, he either denies its existence or limits its scope in such a way that it can not provide a basis for ethics. In the light of this, what is one to say? Did Aristotle admit the existence of practical reason in a way that allows it to provide a basis for ethics, or did he only talk that way? Did Aristotle share with Hume the view that reason has nothing to do with ends, or did he really allow reason to play a role in their acquisition? Or was Aristotle inconsistent, maintaining both that reason does and does not play a sufficiently strong role in the production of motivation to provide a foundation for ethics? It is this problem that will be the main concern of the first part of this book.

CHAPTER 2

Aristotle and Hume: A Preliminary Contrast

As I have already indicated, I shall be arguing that Aristotle did admit the existence of practical reason and that his ethics is based on the existence of practical reason. I shall put forward the argument as a response to one who is convinced that the Humean position on practical reason and its relation to ethics is correct. He is one who recognizes passages in which Aristotle *says* that there is a specifically rational form of motivation and in which Aristotle *says* that this motivation urges one to act rightly, but he regards this as just so much talk, because when he finds Aristotle actually spelling out the role that reason plays in action, he does not find anything that allows reason to play a central role in Aristotle's ethics. Reason's only role is to identify objects for already existing desires and to discover means for already existing ends. This is only to be expected, for reason does not play any other role. Whether or not its playing this role is sufficient for practical reason, it is certainly not sufficient to provide a basis for ethics. To convince such a person that Aristotle did base ethics on practical reason, one will have to come up with a detailed argument that Aristotle did provide a role for reason other than identifying objects for already existing desires and discovering means to already existing ends, and one will have to show exactly how reason plays this role.

Although casting one's argument as a response to such a person is unfair to Aristotle, unfair because in doing so one refuses to take a large part of what Aristotle says at face value, doing so will be useful for at least two reasons. Casting the argument in this way approximates a bias that a good many twentieth-century readers of Aristotle have, a bias they have acquired either through contact with the scholarship mentioned in the Introduction, or by reading Hume or others who share Hume's view and coming prepared to read this view into Aristotle. Bringing this bias out in the open will permit counteracting it. Second, if one can come with an answer to someone who holds such a Humean view, one will have the strongest grounds possible for saying that Aristotle did base his ethics on practical reason.

The argument against such a Humean critic will be built up slowly. I shall begin with a preliminary comparison of Aristotle and Hume over that part of Aristotle's psychology of action which seems closest to Hume's. I shall argue that even here their views seem to diverge. This should make one at least pause before asserting with any degree of confidence that Aristotle shared Hume's views on practical reason. Next I shall look at the more or less direct textual evidence for saying that, according to Aristotle, reason plays a role in the acquisition of ends. I shall argue that in at least three passages Aristotle says that reason plays a role in the apprehension of ends, and that in a fourth passage he says that this occurs through "induction." I shall sketch a way in which such an induction can play a role in the acquisition of ends. Although the sketch contains some details for which no direct textual evidence exists, I shall argue that they are required by what Aristotle has said and that they do not import anything foreign to Aristotle. At this stage of the argument I think I have at least shown that there is room in Aristotle's psychology of action for reason to play a role in the acquisition of ends. In Chapter 4, I turn to less direct evidence for the position I attribute to Aristotle. I shall argue that there are a number of passages in which what Aristotle says is puzzling on a Humean picture of practical reason, but which become intelligible on the position I attribute to Aristotle. These passages suggest that the textual support for the position I attribute to Aristotle is much broader than one might at first think. Finally, I shall look at those passages that seem most strongly to support a Humean interpretation of Aristotle on practical reason, and I shall argue that not only do they not support such an interpretation, but they fit much better with the position I attribute to Aristotle. With this I hope the last resistance on the part of my Humean critic will vanish.

The present chapter is devoted to a preliminary contrast between Aristotle and Hume over that part of Aristotle's psychology of action which seems closest to Hume. I shall argue that even here their views seem to diverge. The account of Aristotle is drawn primarily from Bk. III of *De Anima.*

I. Action as a Result of Appetite

What is it that makes animals, including men, move? According to Aristotle, motion only occurs in animals with sense perception, but sense perception itself is not sufficient for motion (*De Anima* 432b18-20); imagination is also required. Imagination is that part of the soul that produces emotion (427b15-23, 433b27-31), and it is required to perceive an object as pleasant or painful.[1] When such a perception occurs, motion also occurs (431a8-9). That which moves an animal is the faculty of desire *(orexis)* (433a22, 433b28). Desire has an object as an end, and this object is something perceived as good or bad. In *De Anima* this is said to involve perceiving it as pleasant or painful (431a8-10, 431a14-16). Desire is capable of error, since imagination is capable of error (428a18), and, therefore, the object or end of desire may be either the good or the apparent good (433a26-28). Desire in its primary form contains no deliberative element (434a13).

Thus, the most primitive form of action, according to Aristotle, is when an animal acts simply because it perceives a present object as pleasant or painful. For example, an animal drinks because it is thirsty. To be thirsty is in part to be disposed to perceive drink as pleasant. If an animal drinks because it is thirsty, when it perceives something as drink, it perceives the drink as pleasant, and pursues it. What is the most primitive form of action, then, is an action where the agent, if asked for an explanation, would respond by citing a present desire. ("Why did you drink that?" "I was thirsty. I wanted something to drink, and there it was.")

II. Action as a Result of Desire and Deliberation

Obviously the above will not do to explain all action, and Aristotle recognizes this, for he maintains that, in a sense, there are two sources of movement, mind *(nous)* and desire *(orexis)* (433a9-16). This may seem puzzling, since Aristotle also says that what moves is a single faculty, the faculty of desire *(orexis)* (433a22). As outlined above, desire in its primary form contains no deliberative element, no element of mind. However, there is no inconsistency here, for according to Aristotle desire *(orexis)* has at least three forms—appetite *(epithumia)*, passion *(thumos)*, and rational desire *(boulēsis)*—some of which involve mind and some of which do not (*De Motu* 701a39, *De Anima* 414b2-3). What was mentioned above as the primary form of desire might just as well have been referred to as *epithumia*. Besides this primary form of *epithumia*, there is also a form of desire that involves a faculty of mind, a faculty Aristotle calls calculative imagination (433a23-25).[2]

In contrast to the case discussed above, the object of a desire resting on calculative imagination is typically distant in time.[3] Mind calculates by means of thoughts or images and pronounces some future object to be pleasant or painful (431b7-9). However, simply imagining a future object as pleasant or painful is not enough for a person to act from such a desire. The object must be something that can be brought about (or avoided) by action (433a28-29). This means that action from such a desire involves deliberation, for deliberation is concerned with means that can be brought about by action.[4] If there is more than one set of means, deliberation determines which of these is easiest or best (NE 1112b16-17). Finally, in order for a person to act from such a desire, he or she must be aware that the means for pursuing or avoiding the object are at hand. This means that action from such a desire involves perception, for whether or not means are at hand is a matter for perception (NE 1113a2).[5]

Borrowing and amplifying an example of Aristotle's, what seems to be involved in action from a desire resting on calculative imagination is something like the following. Suppose I see the leaves turning and calculate that winter is coming on, bringing with it cold weather. I also calculate that given the present state of my wardrobe I will be cold, a state I imagine to be painful. I recognize that I need a covering to keep me warm in the winter. I know that a coat is a covering, and I also recognize that in my present circumstances the easiest way for me to get a coat is to make one. I see that material for a coat is lying about, so I set about making a coat to forestall being chilled by winter weather.

III. The Practical Syllogism

Before going further, it will be useful to take up a much debated topic in Aristotle, the practical syllogism. Aristotle's remarks on the practical syllogism are scattered throughout *De Anima*, the *Nicomachean Ethics,* and *De Motu Animalium,* and examples of practical syllogisms can be found in these three works and in the *Metaphysics*.[6] The practical syllogism consists of two sorts of premises and a conclusion. One kind of premise, the major premise, is concerned with what is good, and the other kind of premise, the minor premise, is concerned with what is possible (*De Motu* 701a23-25).[7] Aristotle's examples of practical syllogisms give as major premises not only ones that set out certain things as good, but also ones that set out certain things as wanted or needed. This is not incompatible with the statement that major premises are about the good, for as we have seen, the object of desire is either the good or the apparent good. The minor premises in Aristotle's examples set out means for achieving what is aimed at in the major premise, or they indicate that one is in a position to achieve what is aimed at in the major premise. The final minor premise indicates that means are at hand or that one is in a position to achieve the good aimed at, and is grasped by perception (NE 1112b38-1113a2, 1142a27-28). Aristotle's examples fit the statement that minor premises are about the possible, for in NE Aristotle defines things that are *possible* as "things that might be brought about by our own efforts" (1112b26-27). The conclusion of a practical syllogism seems to be an action (*De Motu* 701a13 ff, NE 1147a27-29).[8]

What does a syllogism with these parts amount to? Is it part of a theory about the validity of practical inference? Is it a stylized description of what goes on when a person acts or makes a decision? Or is it a model for explaining actions? Answering these questions is complicated by other questions that arise in connection with the practical syllogism. Does the presence of both kinds of premises in a practical syllogism *necessitate* the conclusion, or the *drawing* of the conclusion? If so, how? And what kind of necessity is this? When a practical syllogism is operative, must the one in whom it is operative by fully conscious of all the premises, or can some of them be implicit? Is the conclusion of a practical syllogism really an action, or is it a judgment expressing a decision, resolution, or intention to act?

There is a way of showing, without having to answer all of these questions, at least part of what Aristotle had in mind when he talked about the practical syllogism. Following a number of commentators (e.g., Allan [1955], Hardie [1980], Santas [1969]), I propose taking the practical syllogism to be at least in part a model for explaining action on the basis of desire. The main reason for this is the parallel that exists between the parts of the practical syllogism and the elements present in action on the basis of desire as it has been set out so far. The major premise indicates what the object of desire is. The minor premises set out those features discovered by deliberation. And the final minor premise sets out the results of perception, something needed for any action from desire. The conclusion, viewed for the time being as an action, is that which results or is done from desire.

As an illustration of this parallel, the two examples of action on the basis of desire offered in Sections I and II are exact counterparts of two of Aristotle's examples of practical syllogisms in *De Motu Animalium*.

I want to drink, says appetite, this is drink, says sense or imagination or mind; straightway I drink (701a32-33).

I need a covering, a coat is a covering: I need a coat. What I need I ought to make, I need a coat: I make a coat. And the conclusion I must make a coat is in action. And the action goes back to the beginning or first step. If there is to be a coat, one must first have B, and if B then A, so one gets A to begin with. (*De Motu* 701a18-22)

In the first example the major premise, 'I want to drink,' sets out an object of appetite; the only minor premise indicates that means for securing this object are at hand; and the conclusion is the action done from appetite.[9] In the second example, the major premise 'I need a covering' sets out an object of desire, a covering. The minor premises, indicating that the best means at hand for securing this object are making a coat, are expressed in a compressed way, together with an intermediate conclusion. The conclusion is the action of beginning to make a coat. These examples do support taking the practical syllogism to be a model for explaining actions done from desire.

Accepting this allows one to have some understanding of what a practical syllogism is without having to answer all of the questions raised above. One needn't take the agent to be fully aware of all the premises that explain his action, for often an agent will mention in an explanation of his action something which he did not specifically run through in his mind before acting. However, if one decides that Aristotle did require the agent to be aware of all of the premises of a practical syllogism before he could be said to have acted on it,[10] one can simply restrict the scope of the actions that are to be explained by the model. Nor does one have to indicate what kind of necessity, if any, is involved in the practical syllogism. One can simply say that it is whatever kind necessity is implied by the relation between a desire and an action done from that desire. If the practical syllogism turns out to be more than a model for explaining actions, if, for example, it is also part of a theory about the validity of practical inference, there may be other applications of the practical syllogism in which another kind of necessity is involved (even "logical necessity"), but this can simply be set aside for the time being. One can also treat the conclusion of a practical syllogism as an action without being committed to its being an action. Using the practical syllogism as a model for explaining actions, one will always have an action on hand to be explained and thus to be taken as the conclusion of the syllogism that explains it. And even if ultimately the conclusion is not an action but, for example, a decision, the practical syllogism can still be used to explain actions, for, having acted on a decision, an explanation of the decision will provide an explanation of the action. In fact, if the practical syllogism plays more than one role, as a model for explaining actions and as part of a theory of practical inference, one can understand how Aristotle could talk about the conclusion of a practical syllogism as both an action and as something like a proposition. Each way of talking would be appropriate to a different role played by the practical syllogism.[11]

In adopting the above position, I have not followed the recent arguments of John Cooper ([1975], Ch. 1 Section 2, Appendix), who allocates a much more restricted role to the practical syllogism than I have. According to Cooper, the practical syllogism is *not* the vehicle for expressing what goes on in deliberation. Deliberation results in a specific judgment or decision (in most cases a *prohairesis*) about a specific *kind* of action, not about a specific act. The practical syllogism is limited to the implementation of this kind of decision into action. Its major premise sets out the results of deliberation, that a specific kind of action is to be done. Typically, it does not contain demonstratives or pronouns. Its minor premise indicates by demonstratives or pronouns that persons or objects of the kind mentioned in the major premise are present. The conclusion is the action that immediately follows.

I do not have the time to do justice to Cooper's arguments for his position. Like many arguments of the present work, they gain their strength from the way they tie together diverse passages and parts of Aristotle's thought. As a result, his position on practical reason is best thought of as part of a quite general position, one which would be best compared as a whole with the general position that emerges from this work. However, I think that there is at least an initial reason for preferring the broader picture I have suggested over Cooper's narrower view. Cooper's view does not fully fit all of Aristotle's examples.[12] Therefore I shall continue to operate with this broader picture of the practical syllogism.

There is an important consequence of taking the practical syllogism in the way I have suggested, and that is that knowledge of or possession of a major premise implies a motivation for what is said in the major premise to be good. This follows from treating the major premise as setting out an object of desire. Again, the main reason for this is the strong parallel that exists between the parts of the practical syllogism and Aristotle's explanation of action from desire as it has been presented so far.

IV. A Preliminary Contrast

Taking just what has been said so far, is there any reason for thinking that Aristotle's views on the existence and scope of practical reason differ from Hume's? At first sight, Aristotle's views seem quite close to Hume's especially if we neglect any difference between their respective views of the means-end relationship. According to Aristotle, reason (if it is construed broadly enough to include perception and imagination) seems to play two roles: first, to identify by perception or calculative imagination objects for already existing desires, and second, to discover by deliberation means for securing the object of some already existing desire. This view seems very close to Hume's. Are there any important differences between them? Two questions have to be answered here. First, does Aristotle's account of action from desire provide any evidence that he believed in the existence of practical reason? Second, if he did, is there any evidence that he acknowledged that it is involved in anything other than identifying objects or discovering means for already existing ends? I shall begin with the first question.

We have already seen that one could admit the existence of practical reason simply on the basis of reason's role in the production of the desire for means to already existing ends. What is Aristotle's view on how such a desire arises? What is his view on the corresponding question of how the desire for an object arises when it has been identified by calculative imagination as an object of an already existing desire? Chapter 1 set out four ways in which one might explain how a desire for means arises, and only one of them provided grounds for the existence of practical reason. A similar list of explanations could be given for how the desire arises for something identified as an object for an already existing desire. Which of these would Aristotle have accepted?

At least two sets of remarks suggest that Aristotle regarded reason as a co-producer of desire and, thus, that he would have accepted an explanation of the desires in question that implies the existence of practical reason. The first is his criticism of those who would divide the soul into two or three parts, at *De Anima* 432b5-8. He says that if one pays attention to the faculty of desire, one will see that the soul cannot be split into an irrational part and a rational part, desire occurring only in the irrational part, for desire is found in both of these "parts." The calculative faculty is in the rational part of the soul and desire is found in the calculative part of the soul. Thus, there is desire in the rational part of the soul. Yet other species of desire are found in the irrational part of the soul. On a Humean view, however, the soul should be divided into two parts, one appetitive and irrational and the other rational and nonappetitive. Even though reason may direct antecedently existing desires to their appropriate objects, what moves a person is desire and not reason. Aristotle's refusal to accept such a division suggests that, at least for desires arising from calculation, he would regard reason as at least their co-producer.

The second set of remarks is his saying at 433a9-10 and at 433b18-20 that mind is a source of movement, while at the same time saying that there is a single faculty of motion, desire (433a22-23). This makes sense if mind is a co-producer of desire. Mind will be a source of motion if it co-produces desire, but it will not be a separate source of motion because it only *co*-produces desire. Indeed, Aristotle seems to have something like this in mind when he says,

> As it is mind is never found producing movement without appetite (for wish is a form of appetite; and when movement is produced according to calculation it is also according to wish). (433a23-25)

However, all of this would be quite puzzling if Aristotle held a Humean position on practical reason. On such a position Aristotle should have concluded from the fact that mind does not produce movement without desire, not only that there is a single faculty of movement (desire), but that mind is *not* a source of movement. His failure to do so suggests that he did not hold a Humean position on practical reason.

However, if one's main concern is the extent to which the existence of practical reason provides an objective basis for Aristotle's ethics, this difference between Aristotle and Hume, even if granted, will not be enough. It arises only over reason's role in discovering means for already existing ends and in identifying objects for already existing desires. If the existence of practical reason is to provide an objective basis for Aristotle's ethics, then Aristotle must allow reason to play a role in the acquisition of ends. In particular, the existence of practical reason should satisfy the three or four conditions set out in Chapter 1 Section II. Is there any evidence that Aristotle thought that the existence of practical reason satisfies these conditions?

There are two passages that can be read as saying that he would, although the considerations in favor of reading them in this way are hardly decisive. At NE 1112b16-17 Aristotle says about those who deliberate,

> They assume the end and consider how and by what means it is to be attained; and if it seems to be produced by several means they consider by which it is most easily and best produced.

At *De Anima* 434a6-9 Aristotle says,

> For whether this or that shall be enacted is already a task requiring calculation; and there must be a single standard to measure by, for that is pursued which is *greater*. It follows that what acts in this way must be able to make a unity out of several images.

The NE passage says that where there is more than one means, deliberation will involve a decision as to which of these is the best and easiest. The *De Anima* passages implies that where there is more than one object thought to be pleasant or good, one must determine according to a single standard which of the objects is greater, this being the object pursued in action.[13] The question is how this determination of the greatest end or the best and easiest means takes place. Does it essentially involve the exercise of reason? If so, will this involve the satisfaction of any of the conditions set out in Section II of Chapter 1?

The first thing to note about the NE passage is that the decision as to which means to pursue is not determined solely by considerations about the most efficient way to secure some end. It also involves what we would call moral considerations.[14] Thus, Aristotle does seem to be talking about the kind of conflict among ends involved in the third condition in Section II of Chapter 1. Second, the determination of the greatest end or the best means does involve the exercise of reason. Determination of the best means is by deliberation, an exercise of reason, and calculation is required for the determination of the greatest end. The question is whether this exercise of reason involves anything more than is involved in the discovery of means or the identification of objects for already existing ends.

There are two explanations according to which this exercise of reason does *not* involve anything other than what is involved in the discovery of means and the identification of objects for already existing ends. The first is that the determination of the greatest end and of the easiest and best means is accomplished by seeing what the consequences of various alternatives are and which of them one desires most. I determine that A is a better means to E than B, because I recognize that A leads to C as well as E, while B leads to D; and I desire A, C, and E more than I desire B, D, and E. I estimate that a future pleasure X is greater than a future pleasure Y because I recognize that X leads to Z while Y does not; and I desire X and Z more than I do Y without Z. On this explanation there are no grounds for thinking that any of the conditions in Section II of Chapter 1 are satisfied. On this explanation the determination of which means is best or which ends are greatest is ultimately a matter of the strength of one's desires, and the strength of one's desires is not due to some special exercise of reason.

The second explanation is similar to the first except that the determination of the greatest end or the best means is based on certain special desires or feelings. As Hume would put it, I determine that A is a better means to E than B if, for example, I recognize that A is or leads to something that I have a feeling of approval toward when I take an impartial point of view, whereas B is or leads to something that I have a feeling of disapproval toward when I take an impartial point of view. In a sense, these feelings of approval and disapproval just are my judgment that A is better than B. Similarly, my determination of which of two ends is greater would also be based on impartial feelings of approval or disapproval toward those ends and/or things connected with them. Since these feelings do not arise through any special exercise of practical reason, this explanation again would provide no grounds for saying that the scope of practical reason includes anything other than the discovery of means or identifying objects for already existing ends. Of course, Aristotle would not describe such judgments in terms of impartial feelings of approval or disapproval, but he might still offer a similar explanation based on feelings or dispositions associated with virtue, feelings or dispositions acquired by habit or training and not through any exercise of reason.

If one reads either one of these two explanations into the NE and *De Anima* passages, then these passages provide no grounds for thinking that the scope of practical reason is wide enough to provide a basis for ethics. However, if one reads either one of these explanations into these passages, it is important to recognize that that is just what one is doing: one is reading them in. There is no specific textual basis in either of the passages for either of these two explanations.

In fact, there is some reason for *not* reading either of the above two explanations into at least the *De Anima* passage, although the reason rests on a passage whose connection with the *De Anima* passage is tenuous enough that one may question its relevance. In the *De Anima* passage, Aristotle refers to a *single standard* against which whatever is estimated is measured. At NE 1113a16-33 Aristotle says,

That wish (*boulēsis*) is for the end has already been stated; some think it is for the good, others for the apparent good. Now those who say that the good is the object of wish must admit in consequence that that which the man who does not choose aright wishes for is not an object of wish (for if it is to be so, it must also be good; but it was, if it so happened, bad); while those who say the apparent good is the object of which must admit that there is no natural object of wish, but only what seems good to each man. Now different things appear good to different people, and, if it so happens, even contrary things.

If these consequences are unpleasing, are we to say that absolutely and in truth the good is the object of wish, but for each person the apparent good; that that which is in truth an object of wish is an object of wish to the good man, while any chance thing may be so to the bad man, as in the case of bodies also the things that are in truth wholesome are wholesome for bodies which are in good condition, while for those that are diseased other things are wholesome — or bitter or sweet or hot or heavy, and so on; since the good man judges each class of things rightly, and in each the truth appears to him? For each state of character has its own ideas of the noble and the pleasant, and perhaps the good man differs from others most by seeing the truth in each class of things, being as it were the norm and measure of them.

There is certainly the strong suggestion here that there will be a single standard of good which can be applied to all men only if there is a natural object of desire. And there is also the strong suggestion that there is such a natural object of desire. If Aristotle's reference to a single standard in De Anima was intended to refer to a standard based on such a natural object of desire, then there is reason for *not* reading the above two explanations into the De Anima passage, for on these two explanations the object of desire is the *apparent* good. Determining what is best simply on the basis of what one desires most or on whether one has certain feelings, is determining what is best on the basis of what appears to be good. Since what is desired most or what is the object of these feelings can vary from person to person, on these explanations there will be no single standard of good applicable to all men.

If, on the other hand, there is a natural object associated with the desires or feelings involved in the determination of the greatest end or best means, something that if it were the object of those desires or feelings would make the judgments based on them correct, then there would be a single standard applicable to all men. Furthermore, if it were the correct exercise of reason that allowed one to apprehend this natural object of desire and to acquire it as the object of one's own desires, one would be well on the way to showing that the correct exercise of practical reason is involved in the acquisition of specific ends that allow one to determine what to do when ends conflict with one another. That is, one would be well on the way to showing that the conditions mentioned in Chapter 1 for practical reason's providing an objective basis for ethics were satisfied.

Of course, to maintain that it is the correct exercise of practical reason that allows one to acquire the natural object of desire as one's own object of desire is also to read into NE 1113a16-33 something that is not explicitly in the text. And taking NE 1113a16-33 as a basis for understanding Aristotle's reference to a single standard in De Anima 434a6-9 is itself open to question. Certainly nothing I have said would convince my Humean critic. However, all I want to maintain here is that even where Aristotle's explanation of action from desire seems closest to Hume's, there is good reason to doubt that their views are exactly the same. There is good reason for thinking that Aristotle did admit the existence of practical reason; and there is some reason for reading into Aristotle a position on the scope of practical reason that allows it to provide an objective basis for ethics. One should at least pause before asserting that Aristotle shared Hume's view on practical reason and its relation to ethics.

CHAPTER 3

Reason and General Ends

Although what has been said so far might cause my Humean critic to pause, it would not cause him to pause too long. As it stands, the case for saying that Aristotle based his ethics on practical reason is weak. To convince my Humean critic, one will have to show more than that it is possible to read into a passage or two a view according to which practical reason provides a basis for ethics. One must show that Aristotle actually left room for reason to play the role in the acquisition of ends needed to provide a basis for ethics, and one must show exactly how it plays this role. Furthermore, one should show that the recognition of this role is not confined to a few passages. Finally, one should be able to deal with those passages that seem to support a Humean interpretation of Aristotle.

In this chapter I shall try to provide a foundation for meeting these demands by looking at the most direct textual evidence there is for saying that reason plays a role in the acquisition of ends. In an argument with my Humean critic it is important to begin with as direct textual evidence as possible, for the more one has to read something into the text, the more my Humean critic will feel entitled to read it out. In subsequent chapters I shall argue that the position argued for in this chapter is not confined to the passages that are discussed here, and I shall argue that the passages that seem to support a Humean interpretation of Aristotle do not really do so.

There is an important feature of the overall argument of this and the next two chapters that should be noted at this time. And that is that the argument is in a sense cumulative. Although for the most part earlier stages of the argument will be put forward on the basis of considerations independent of later stages,[1] later stages of the argument provide additional support for what has been argued for earlier. As a result, the full argument for the theses argued for in this chapter will not be completed until the end of Chapter 5.

There is more to Aristotle's psychology of action than has been discussed so far, although what has been left out has not been given the explicit attention by Aristotle that it deserves. What has been left out is an account of action from general principles or ends. People act not only to pursue or avoid relatively specific objects that they believe to be good or bad (like a coat or a covering); they also act because they believe that certain sorts of things are good or bad for everyone (for example, health). In short, they act on general principles. To put the point in terms of the practical syllogism, there are practical syllogisms whose major premises are universal, and we have yet to look at what is involved when a person acts from such a major premise.[2] If reason played or could play an essential role in the acquisition of general principles, and if one could spell out just what that role was, one would be well on the way to seeing whether the existence of practical reason does provide an objective basis for Aristotle's ethics.

This further account of action from desire is also needed to fill in the discussion of action from rational desire *(boulēsis)* and choice *(prohairesis)*. In *De Anima, boulēsis* is described as a form of desire involving the calculative faculty (432b5), and on the basis of what has been said so far it looks as if this is just the kind of desire based on calculative imagination that was discussed in Chapter 2. At NE 1113a11-12, *prohairesis* is defined as deliberate desire of things in our own power, so that it looks as if action from *prohairesis* will also be action from a desire based on calculative imagination. It will be action from the desire that results from deliberation about means for satisfying such a calculative desire. However, Aristotle says that an incontinent person acts from appetite but *not* from *prohairesis* (NE 1111b14-15), and yet Aristotle says that an incontinent person can act from deliberation (NE 1142b18-20). Furthermore, Aristotle says that *prohairesis* can't exist without moral character (NE 1139a33-35), something that involves a fixed disposition to aim at what one takes to be good. As it has been set out so far, acting from a desire based on calculative imagination doesn't require such a fixed disposition. How is one to reconcile these remarks?[3] The answer is that acting from *boulēsis* and *prohairesis* involves more than acting from desires based on calculative imagination and deliberation. It involves acting on a conception of what is good for human beings. That is why, for example, the incontinent person can act from deliberation but not from *prohairesis*. Such a person acts contrary to what his or her conception of the good is. To act from *boulēsis* and *prohairesis*, then, is to act from what I have called general ends.

How, according to Aristotle, does one acquire general ends? I shall argue that, at least in part, the answer is similar to the answer to how one acquires universal premises for theoretical syllogisms. Reason in the form of *nous* helps one to acquire first principles through a kind of induction.

Before arguing for this, I want to forestall an obvious objection. Aristotle makes it clear that the ends we have are a result of habit and/or training. For morally good people, "virtue makes us aim at the right mark," (NE 1144a7-8), and virtue is something acquired by habit and/or training (NE 1103a23-35, 1103b21-26). As it is with good people, so it is with others. The ends that people have are a result of habit or training. Nowhere in this these remarks is there any mention of reason. Why isn't it clear at the outset that reason does *not* play a role in the acquisition of ends? To forestall this objection all that needs to be said is that the acquisition of ends by habituation is not incompatible with their being acquired through an exercise of reason. Habituation need not be "mindless." It can be guided by reason, including an inductive use of reason. Whether it is so guided is, of course, what is at issue.

But what evidence is there for thinking that according to Aristotle reason does play a role in the acquisition of ends, let alone via some inductive inference? In this chapter I shall discuss four passages that bear on this question. I shall first discuss three passages in which I think Aristotle says that reason plays a role in the apprehension of ends, two from the *Nicomachean Ethics* and one from the *Metaphysics.* I shall then go on to discuss a passage in the *Nicomachean Ethics* in which Aristotle treats the role of *nous* in practical matters and in which I think Aristotle says that universal ends are acquired by a kind of induction. I shall argue that it really is the acquisition of ends that Aristotle is talking about, and I shall sketch an account of just how induction can play a role in the acquisition of ends. Although the sketch that I shall give reads something into Aristotle, I shall argue that this is inevitable. I argue that what I have read in (or something like it) is required by what Aristotle has said, and I shall defend it against the objection that it brings with it elements that are foreign to Aristotle.

I. Reason Apprehends the Ends of Action

At NE 1139a21-26 Aristotle says,

What affirmation and negation are in thinking, pursuit and avoidance are in desire; so that since moral virtue is a state of character concerned with choice, and choice is deliberate desire, therefore both the reasoning must be true and the desire right, if the choice is to be good, and the latter must pursue just what the former asserts.

Aristotle seems to be saying here that reason does apprehend the ends of action, for he seems to be saying that in order for a choice to be good, desire must pursue what reason has told it to pursue, viz., an appropriate end. My Humean critic would be quick to point out that this passage is ambiguous. It can also be read as saying that desire must pursue the means that reason has discovered for it. Given what Aristotle has said elsewhere, he might argue, this latter reading is preferable. The familiar passages in which Aristotle says that deliberation is about means and not ends (NE 1112b13, 1112b34-35), and that practical wisdom is concerned with means and not ends (NE 1145a5-6) suggest that reason has nothing to do with ends. Besides, almost immediately after 1139a21-26, Aristotle says that intellect (dianoia) itself moves nothing. This would be surprising if reason did apprehend the ends of action.

A complete answer to this objection can only come after a detailed examination of passages like NE 1112b13 and 1144a6-9,[4] but the following will do for now. Even if Aristotle does say that deliberation is about means and not ends, he does not say that reason's only role in action is deliberation. What is at issue is whether it also plays a role in the apprehension of ends. And even though Aristotle does say that practical wisdom is concerned with means, these remarks are balanced off by his claim that one cannot have practical wisdom without virtue (NE 1144a36-37, 1145a1-2). This suggests that practical wisdom does carry with it the apprehension of the right ends.[5] Finally, when Aristotle says at 1139a35 that intellect itself does not move anything, what he has in mind is intellect in its theoretical employment. He goes on to contrast intellect that moves nothing, not with desire, but with practical intellect, intellect that aims at an end. And what he says about practical intellect does suggest that it moves people to act. In fact, one of the points that Aristotle wants to make in this part of Bk. VI is that both reason and desire are necessary to account for choice and for good action. This certainly fits with a view that reason along with desire determines what the ends of rational desire are.

However, one might argue that at most this shows that the reading I have suggested is no worse than that of my Humean critic; it doesn't show that it is any better. There are, however, additional considerations that favor the reading I have suggested. What Aristotle says at 1139a24-26 is that both the reasoning must be true and the desire *(orexis)* right, if the choice *(prohairesis)* is to be good, and the latter *(orexis)*[6] must pursue just what the former asserts. Since desire must pursue what reasoning asserts, the question of whether reasoning is concerned with ends or means is the question of whether the desire being talked about here is for means or for the end.

That Aristotle uses the term *'orexis'* itself suggests that this desire includes a desire for the end.[7] If it were desire only for means it would have been more natural for Aristotle to use *'prohairesis'*, since *prohairesis* is defined as deliberate desire for means. The same thing is suggested by the analogy that Aristotle draws at the beginning of the passage. As Kenny points out ([1979], pp. 92-93), affirmation and denial can be viewed either as specific forms of decisive thought (judgment), or as specific outcomes of a more general kind of preliminary thinking that leads to judgment. What Aristotle says at 1139a21-22 is that pursuit and avoidance are to desire *(orexis)* as affirmation and denial are to *thinking (dianoia), not* judgment. Thus, at line 22, *orexis* should be taken as a more general form of desire including the desire for ends, *not* as the decisive form of desire *prohairesis*. This same general use of *'orexis'* seems to be carried over at line 25.[8] Indeed the passage would have an odd implication if at line 25 desire were just desire for means. 1139a24-26 suggests that desire may fail to pursue what reason asserts, and that this is one of the things that will make a *prohairesis* bad. But nowhere does Aristotle acknowledge the possibility of a bad *prohairesis* resulting from desire's failure to pursue means that reason has discovered.[9] If, however, desire is for an end, then Aristotle has marked off a condition for a bad *prohairesis*. Desire's failure to pursue ends that reason has asserted are appropriate will result in a bad *prohairesis*.[10] Desire, thus, is for ends, not just means.

Despite its ambiguity, 1139a21-26 should be taken as saying that reason does play a role in the apprehension of ends.

The second passage in which I think Aristotle affirms such a role for reason is NE 1142b31-34, where Aristotle says,

> If then it is characteristic of men of practical wisdom to have deliberated well, excellence in deliberation will be correctness with regard to what conduces to the end of which practical wisdom is the true apprehension.

Again, Aristotle seems to be saying that reason apprehends the ends of action, for he seems to be saying that practical wisdom provides a person with a true apprehension of the end. Again, my Humean critic would point out that the passage is ambiguous. The antecedent of 'of which' can be taken as either 'the end' or as 'what conduces to the end', and taking it in the latter way accords to practical wisdom only the capacity to determine the correct means to already given ends.

He would point out that commentators have traditionally taken this latter reading, citing as grounds the passages mentioned above in which Aristotle says that practical wisdom is concerned with means.[11]

Again, however, not only are these passages balanced off by others, a further consideration favors the reading I have suggested. 1142b31-34 occurs at the end of a discussion of what sort of correctness is implied by deliberative excellence (*euboulia*). One of the points made is that the correctness is not that involved in cleverness (*deinotēs*), because cleverness is compatible with arriving at something evil (1142b18-22). Immediately preceding this passage Aristotle says,

> Excellence in deliberation in the unqualified sense, then, is that which succeeds with reference to what is the end in the unqualified sense, and excellence in deliberation in a particular sense is that which succeeds relatively to a particular end (1142b29-31).

The main focus of this discussion is that excellence in deliberation is something that allows one to achieve the right end. Given this focus, what point would there be in Aristotle concluding the discussion by saying that if a man of practical wisdom deliberates well, *euboulia* will be correctness with regard to means that practical wisdom discovers, if practical wisdom discovers only means? The main focus of the preceding discussion would have been dropped and nothing would have been added. It was already quite clear that *euboulia* allows one to discover appropriate means. On the other hand, if Aristotle is saying that practical wisdom gives one the true apprehension of ends, then not only has the main point of the preceding discussion been carried on, there is a sense in which one can understand why *euboulia* is correctness in deliberating about the right end. *Euboulia* is the correctness in deliberation involved in practical wisdom, and practical wisdom gives one the true apprehension of ends. Although the margin may not be great, the balance of evidence seems to favor a reading that implies that reason plays a role in the apprehension of ends.

The third passage is *Metaphysics* 1072a24-30,

> And since that which is moved and moves in intermediate, there is some-which moves without being moved, being eternal, substance, and actuality. And the object of desire and the object of thought move in this way; they move without being moved. The primary objects of desire and of thought are the same. For the apparent good is the object of appetite, and the real good is the primary object of rational wish. But desire is consequent on opinion rather than opinion on desire; for the thinking is the starting point.

Here Aristotle seems to consider and reject a Humean account of the relation between reason and desire, for he seems to rule out the view that reason only directs antecedently existing desires toward certain objects when he says that desire is consequent on opinion rather than opinion on desire. Since *thinking* is the starting point of action and desire, it looks as if reason would play a role in the apprehension of ends.

Again my Humean critic might argue that there is an alternative, more plausible reading, arguing that the passage should be read in connection with *De Anima* 433a15-20 where Aristotle says that what is last in the process of thinking is the beginning of action. What is last in the process of thinking is the discovery of means, and the thought that particular means are at hand is the beginning of the desire for and the pursuit of those means. However, thought about means is a result of a desire for the end (*De Anima* 433a8-20). Taking the thinking mentioned at *Metaphysics* 1072a30 to be that which begins movement, Aristotle's remark at 1072a29 that desire is consequent on opinion rather than vice versa becomes the perfectly correct point that the desire for means is consequent on the thought that they are means rather than vice versa. Nothing is said about thinking being a starting point for a desire for some end.

However, this interpretation of 1072a24-30 cannot be correct. At 1072a27-28 Aristotle says that the primary objects of thought and desire are the same, and that the apparent good is the object of appetite and that the real good is the primary object of rational desire. Desires whose objects are the apparent or real good are desires whose objects are ends. Since Aristotle says that the objects of thought and desire are the same, the objects of thought that Aristotle is talking about are not means but ends. Aristotle *is* saying that thinking is the starting point for desires about ends, and thus that reason does play a role in the apprehension of ends.

Thus, in at least three passages Aristotle says that reason can determine what ends one should be aiming at.

II. Universal Ends Acquired by Induction: The Role of *Nous* in Practical Affairs

Even if I am right about the three passages discussed above, this would not convince my Humean critic. He already admits that there are passages in which Aristotle talks as if practical reason exists and provides a basis for ethics. He can simply add these passages to his list. What he argues is that this talk is unsupported by any account of how reason plays a role in the acquisition of ends. Without such an account, he will continue to dismiss these passages as just so much talk.[12] There is, however, a passage in which Aristotle does seem to provide an indication of how reason plays a role in the acquisition of ends, NE 1143a35-b5. In it he seems to say that universal ends are acquired by a kind of "induction." As Ross translates the passage, it runs as follows.

> And intuitive reason (nous) is concerned with ultimates in both directions, for both the first terms and the last are objects of intuitive reason and not of argument, and the intuitive reason which is presupposed by demonstrations grasps the unchangeable and first terms, while the intuitive reason involved in practical reasoning grasps the last and variable fact (tou eschatou kai endechomenou), i.e., the minor premis (kai tēs heteras protaseōs). For these variable facts are the starting points for the apprehension of the end, since the universals are reached from particulars (et tōn kath' hekasta gar ta katholou); of these therefore we must have perception, and this perception is intuitive reason (nous).

This passage is, however, notoriously difficult, so much so that it deserves a detailed discussion of its own. I have devoted an appendix to just such a discussion,[13] and one will find the full argument for my interpretation of the passage there. What follows is a summary of some of the main points of that argument.

Two major problems arise in trying to interpret 1143a35-b5. The first is reconciling Aristotle's apparent reference to an inductive grasp of universal ends with what Aristotle says *nous* grasps in practical reasoning. On the face of it Aristotle seems to be saying that *nous* plays a role in an inductive grasp of universal ends. *Nous* is said to grasp through perception the starting points for an end, and this is likened to the way in which universals depend on particulars. However, on Ross's translation, what Aristotle says *nous* grasps is the final minor premise of a practical syllogism (1143b2-3). If Aristotle is saying that *nous* is involved in an inductive inference *to* ends, why would he say that *nous* grasps something that is part of a noninductive inference *from* ends?[14]

The second problem is explaining why Aristotle would bring in *nous* at all when he is talking about the perception of particulars involved in practical reasoning. Three chapters earlier (1142a24-31) Aristotle contrasted *phronēsis* with *nous* on the grounds that the former deals with particulars that are grasped through perception, whereas *nous* grasps what is universal and first in scientific knowledge. Why should he apparently reverse his position now and admit that *nous* is involved in the perception of particulars involved in practical reasoning?

These difficulties and others have led commentators to suggest a wide variety of accounts of what is going on in this passage. The most important one for present purposes is one that denies that the passage contains any reference to an inductive inference to ends. It is just such an interpretation that my Humean critic would seize on.

When Aristotle says that *nous'* grasp of the starting points for an end is like the way in which universals depend on particulars *(ek tōn kath' hekesta gar ta katholou)*, he doesn't mention a specific dependency relation. One can take the dependency relation to refer to the way securing universal ends depends on pursuing particular means. Adopting a particular means is a starting point for securing a universal end. Read in this way, there is no problem in reconciling what *nous* grasps with the way universals depend on particulars. What *nous* grasps, particular means, are just what universal ends depend on. Why isn't this the way 1143a35-b5 should be interpreted? If it is, then not only is Aristotle not saying that universal ends are grasped through induction, he is not even talking about the way we grasp universal ends in this passage.

The response to this alternative interpretation is as follows. There are presumptive grounds for taking 1143a35-b5 to refer to an inductive inference to ends. If one can provide an interpretation of the passage that retains this reference *and* solves the problems raised above, then it will be preferable to the interpretation favored by my Humean critic. There is such an interpretation. It is confirmed, among other places, by what Aristotle says when he contrasts *nous* with *phronēsis*. By contrast, the interpretation favored by my Humean critic has problems of its own. Not only will it have to deal with the grounds for thinking that there is a reference to induction in the passage, it has no clear way of solving the second problem raised above. On balance it seems preferable to take 1143a35-b5 to be saying that general ends can be arrived at inductively through the exercise of *nous*.

In discussing induction elsewhere (e.g., *Posterior Analytics* 81a40, NE 1139b27-30), Aristotle says that the starting points for induction are provided by perception, and that induction proceeds from particulars to universals. These marks of induction are all present at 1143b3-5. What *nous* grasps it grasps through perception. What it grasps are starting points for an end. And the relation between what it grasps and ends is like that between particulars and universals. In the second place, immediately after 1143a35-b5 Aristotle says that *nous*, along with other practical faculties, comes at a certain stage of our lives. As a result we ought to pay attention to the undemonstrated sayings of experienced people, because experience has given them an eye to see aright (1143b6-14). Aristotle is saying here that *nous'* grasp of things comes through experience, and that what experience has provided those people to whose sayings we should pay attention is an implicit grasp of general principles.[15] But what comes from experience comes on the basis of induction. It is difficult to see how Aristotle could make these remarks if he hadn't just been talking about a grasp of ends that is also based on induction. If one puts this together with the marks of induction already present in 1143a35-b5, one has presumptive grounds for taking 1143a35-b5 to refer to an inductive grasp of universal ends through *nous*.

But how is one to solve the problems that have been raised for the passage? For instance, how is one to reconcile this reference to induction with what *nous* is said to grasp at 1143b2-3? Rather than translating '*tou eschatou kai endechomenou*' ("the ultimate and variable") as 'the last and variable fact' as Ross does, one should take it to refer to what is to be done in a particular situation. Aristotle does include things to be done in the class of variable *(endechomenou)* things (e.g., 1140a1-2), and he says that what is to be done is an ultimate (e.g., 1141b27-28, 1142a24-26, 1143a34-35) '*tēs heteras protaseōs*' should not be translated as 'the final minor premise'. Rather it should be given its literal meaning of 'the other proposition' and understood in terms of what it is contrasted with, the ultimate proposition in the other direction that *nous* grasps in its theoretical employment. So understood what *nous* grasps are propositions indicating what is to be done or what is good in a particular situation. These propositions are starting points for an inductive inference to universal ends. From propositions of the form 'This Ø is good' or 'This Ø is to be done' one can inductively infer universal principles of the form 'What is Ø is good' or 'What is Ø is to be done'.[16]

If one takes these ultimate propositions to have the form, 'This Ø is to be done' or 'This Ø is good', then one also has the basis for an answer to the second problem. In its theoretical employment *nous* provides an inductive grasp of universal principles. If what *nous* grasps are things of the form 'This Ø is to be done' or 'This Ø is good', then implicit in this grasp are universal principles of the form 'What is Ø is to be done' or 'What is Ø is good'. If the ability to grasp these ultimate propositions is acquired through experience, then one who acquires this ability has inductively acquired (at least an implicit) grasp of universal principles.[17] This is sufficiently close to what *nous* does in its theoretical employment to say that here too is the work of *nous*.[18]

This explanation of why *nous* is said to grasp these ultimate propositions receives some confirmation from what Aristotle says at 1142a24-31 when he contrasts *phronēsis* with *nous*. *Nous* is said to be concerned with the objects of scientific knowledge, whereas *phronēsis* is concerned with ultimate particulars grasped by perception, "not the perception of qualities peculiar to one sense but a perception akin to that by which we perceive that the particular figure before us is a triangle" (1142a27-29). This perception is already "*nous*-like," as I have described *nous* above. The perception of a particular figure as a triangle is the perception of a particular as an instance of a universal. The other side of the coin of perceiving a particular as an instance of a universal is perceiving the particular as having a certain universal instantiated in it.[19]

Thus, there is an interpretation of 1143a35-b5 that retains a reference to an inductive inference to universal ends and solves the problems that arise for the passage. On the other hand, the interpretation favored by my Humean critic has problems of his own. How is one to explain the presumptive grounds for thinking that a reference to induction is made in the passage, particularly Aristotle's going on to talk about those who have acquired an implicit grasp of general principles on the basis of experience? More important, how is one to explain Aristotle's description of this kind of perception as the work of *nous*? The mere perception of means doesn't seem to be enough to guarantee the presence of *nous*. On balance it seems preferable to interpret 1143a35-b5 as saying that reason in the form of *nous* apprehends universal ends on the basis of some form of induction.

What *nous* grasps are particular actions that are good or to be done. Its grasp of these is based on experience and hence on a kind of induction. Implicit in this grasp are universal ends that these actions promote. One sees the universal ends that one should be aiming at by seeing them in the actions that one recognizes one should perform. One sees them in these actions because, in recognizing that one should perform them, one recognizes that actions *like* them should be performed. Whether or not one can articulate the content of what one has grasped, one has inductively acquired a universal end. Thus, Aristotle does seem to be saying in 1143a35-b5 that universal ends are acquired through an inductive use of reason.

III. Apprehending versus Acquiring Ends

At this point, my Humean critic might grant virtually everything I have said and still maintain that I have not shown that Aristotle allows reason to play the role needed for practical reason to provide a basis for ethics. There is a distinction between *apprehending* and *acquiring* ends that up to this point has not been acknowledged. Once it is acknowledged, my critic might argue, one will see that much more has to be said before it can be maintained that Aristotle does allow ethics to be based on practical reason.

Apprehending an end is something that can be done solely on a speculative or theoretical level. A person can apprehend an end without really aiming at it in any of the actions that he performs. One is genuinely motivated to pursue an end only when one has *acquired* it. A useful parallel here is the distinction Aristotle draws between the speculative and practical employment of imagination at *De Anima* 433b28-32. A person can imagine something pleasant without being pleased, just as one can think of something terrifying without feeling fear. Imagination in its practical employment is the thought of something pleasant that makes a person pleased, something that in turn disposes one to pursue it. *Apprehension* of an end is like the speculative employment of imagination. *Acquisition* of an end, like the practical employment of imagination, carries with it a disposition to act. Since a person can be more or less disposed to pursue a given end, acquisition of an end will also be a matter of degree.

My critic might argue that on the basis of what has been said so far, all one has grounds for attributing to Aristotle is the view that induction and experience allow one to apprehend ends, not to acquire them. Induction and experience may provide a person with an opinion that certain things are good, but they do not insure that this opinion will carry with it any disposition to pursue those things. To the extent to which a person has such a disposition, it will be because that person has acquired it on the basis of habit and/or training, something that does not involve the use of induction. Unless induction and experience can be shown to go some way toward producing such a disposition, then even if one can apprehend general ends by means of induction, this will not constitute an exercise of *practical* reason.

The first response to this objection is that Aristotle himself draws a distinction much like that between apprehending and acquiring ends, but he does not restrict his talk about experience and induction to the analogue of apprehending ends.

In Ch. 10 of NE Bk. VI Aristotle distinguishes *sunesis* (understanding) from *phronēsis* (practical wisdom). *Sunesis* is like a purely intellectual or speculative grasp of moral ends, for it is primarily exercised when one passes judgment on the advice or moral pronouncements of someone else (1143a13-15). Aristotle distinguishes *sunesis* from *phronēsis* on the grounds that the latter issues commands, its end being what ought to be done, whereas the former only judges (1143a8-10). This distinction seems close to that between knowledge that is motivationally grounded and thus has an effect on what a person does, and knowledge that may function only on a speculative level. However, Aristotle does not restrict his talk about induction and experience to men who have *sunesis*. The particulars with which *nous* is concerned are ones that men who have *sunesis, gnōmē* (judgment), and *phronēsis* all deal with (1143a32-35). *Gnōmē* and *nous* are placed alongside *sunesis* as things that are acquired by experience (1143b6-7, 1143b9). And the practically wise man is included among those experienced men whose sayings should be listened to. If it is not clear that someone who has *gnōmē* is disposed to pursue the ends that he has grasped, it should be clear that someone who has *phronēsis* is so disposed. *Phronēsis* implies virtue (1144a35, 1144b16); indeed, it implies all the virtues (1145a2-3, 1152a9). The *phronimos* is said to be a man who will act (1140b4-6, 1146a5-9, 1142a7-9).

Aristotle, thus, wants to say more than that induction and experience are involved in forming opinions about what ends are to be pursued. He wants to say that they are involved in the disposition to pursue those ends as well.

But, my critic might respond, how can Aristotle say this? Why hasn't Aristotle just lumped together two separate states? A person may have a disposition to pursue certain sorts of things, and this disposition may be acquired by habituation and/or training. A person may also have a reflective knowledge of what should be pursued, and this may be arrived at by induction. These may (as in the case of the *phronimos*), coincide. A person may be disposed to pursue just what she knows she should pursue. But this coincidence is just that, a coincidence. There is as yet no reason for thinking that what led to the knowledge of what is to be pursued played any role in acquiring the disposition to pursue it. If it hasn't played such a role, then we have yet to see what entitles Aristotle to say that ethics is based on practical reason.

The point can be put in terms closer to the discussion of 1143a35ff. A person may through habit or training acquire a disposition to pursue certain ends. This disposition in turn may dispose him in particular situations to pick out certain actions as ones that are to be done. Experience with what he is disposed to pursue may provide him with whatever articulate grasp he has of those ends that he is disposed to pursue. Indeed, further reflection on what he has in fact picked out may provide him with a more articulate opinion of just what those ends are. But these ends will still be ends that he has already acquired. Any inductive inference that tells him what they are will have played no role in their acquisition. Although this may not be what Aristotle *wants* to say in 1143a35ff., it is all that he is *entitled* to say. Unless Aristotle can show that induction can and does play a role in acquiring certain ends, he will not be entitled to claim that practical reason provides a basis for ethics.

Two responses will be needed if one is to meet this last objection. The first is an account of an inductive inference that can play a role in acquiring a disposition to pursue certain ends. The second is an argument that it is just this kind of induction that Aristotle would have called attention to were he to have tried to respond to someone like my Humean critic. In the next section, I shall sketch a theory that I think meets the first of these two needs.[20] In succeeding sections, I shall try to provide an argument that meets the second of these two needs.

IV. A Sketch of a Theory

To see just what kind of induction it is that can contribute to the acquisition of general ends, it will be useful to look at what Aristotle would say is involved in determining what other living organisms are aiming at as an end. Take, for example, a tree. Aristotle would say, I think, that it is the nature of certain trees to grow straight and tall. How do we know this? By looking at various specimen trees and seeing how they grow. When trees have sufficient sunlight and room they do grow straight and tall. Even when one is faced with a tree that is crooked and gnarled, one can view the twists and turns of the trees as manifestations of the tree's attempt to grow straight and tall. They are, for example, attempts to reach toward the sun in spite of dense and shady surroundings. By examining specimen trees, one can discover what trees are aiming at. Even among those that don't achieve this end, the end is discernible in the unsuccessful attempts.

I think that it is an induction based on this sort of examination that Aristotle would say allows a person to acquire general ends. According to Aristotle, people aim at something by nature—the good. Not everyone consciously aims at this object. Some people only aim at the apparent good. Only the good person has the natural object of desire as the object of his conscious desires (1113a24-27, 1144a31-35). The good person, like the tall straight tree, is the best indication of what people aim at by nature. But I think Aristotle would maintain that even among those who do not consciously aim at what is good, a person with a discerning eye can see that their strivings after whatever ends they do have are just mistaken and unsuccessful attempts to secure the good.

What I have in mind is similar to what may go on when a person tries very hard over a long period of time to secure something, but when it is finally secured, the person still feels dissatisfied. In such a situation, one may conclude that what one was striving for, though it was something one wanted, was not what one *"really* wanted." One may then look back over his past actions for an indication of what one was really after. Looking back over one's life and the lives of others to see what oneself and others have really been aiming at is, I think, an example of the kind of induction that, according to Aristotle, is involved in the acquisition of ends. This kind of induction is the first step in what I shall call the reflective acquisition of general ends. The inference that one is by nature aiming at a certain end can give rise to a desire for that end and a desire to have one's other desires and dispositions conform to it. This desire can in turn lead a person to acquire desires and dispositions that do conform to it. Given a conception of what one should be aiming at (what one is "really aiming at"), a person can be led to engage in a process of self-habituation[21] or training (perhaps even seeking out the aid of others) to integrate the inferred end into one's psychological character. This integration may be more or less successful. But if it is successful, the person will have acquired general ends, and an inductive use of reason will have played a central role in it. It is not necessary to view this process as going on only when one goes through a marked change in desires and dispositions. The same sort of process may go on to reinforce actual desires or dispositions, or to introduce small corrections or refinements in them.

It is important to note that the inductive inference involved in this process is *not* the same thing as finding out those desires and dispositions at or close to the conscious level that explain one's actions. It is not the same thing as discovering ends that one has already acquired. It may be that having certain dispositions is necessary for having a correct grasp of what one is aiming at by nature, but this does not mean that one is prevented from inferring as an end anything other than what has already been integrated into her character. At most, it means that a person who has developed bad habits can acquire good habits only by a gradual process of becoming aware of what she ought to pursue. Given her bad habits she will at most be able to discern how to improve herself to some degree and to set about improving herself. Once she has improved she may be able to see the direction for further improvement. But in the process she will be acquiring new general ends.

Furthermore, it is not necessary to view this process as only going on at the reflective level. The same sort of thing can go on at an unreflective level. This would explain how people can come to believe at an unreflective level that certain sorts of things are good and how they develop various dispositions on the basis of experience.[22] Very roughly, what I think Aristotle would say goes on in such situations is that pleasure or pain, or perhaps the more general feelings of easiness or uneasiness, provide a person with cues as to how well his life and actions accord with what he by nature is aiming at.[23] The various dispositions and tacit beliefs about what is good that a person acquires from experience are attempts at accommodating his life to this natural aim. The directions that a person takes to find a life "he can feel comfortable with" represent unreflective analogues of conscious attempts to bring one's desires and dispositions in accord with a reflective inductive judgment about what one ought to be doing. That this is so would be seen by one with a discerning eye, in the same way that one can see that the twists and turns of a tree in dense and shady surroundings were all attempts at approximating the true end of the tree.

If one attributes to Aristotle this account of how ends can be acquired, then an inductive use of reason will be operative in more than the apprehension of ends; it can and will be an essential part of the acquisition of ends.

I think it should be clear that on the theory I have just sketched, practical reason does exist. I hope it is also at least plausible to say that the existence of practical reason satisfies the conditions necessary for it to provide an objective basis for ethics. According to this theory reason is a co-producer of motivation, for it is a co-producer of general ends. It does not produce general ends by itself, because habituation is also required. It does produce a desire for these ends and a desire to integrate these ends into one's character, but even here one might argue that reason does not by itself produce these desires. (For example, one might argue that human beings must also aim at something by nature.) Whether or not this is right, it is at least true that reason is a co-producer of motivation, and, as I argued in Chapter 1, this is sufficient for the existence of practical reason. Furthermore, on the theory I have sketched, the correct exercise of reason can lead a person to have certain ends, in particular, those ends that he is aiming at by nature. If it turns out that there is only one of these, then it looks as if the conditions set out in Chapter 1 for practical reason's providing an objective basis for ethics would also be satisfied. Even if more than one end exists, it seems plausible to say that man's nature will guarantee the harmony or order among ends needed for these conditions to be satisfied.

Thus, there is a way in which reason can play the role needed for ethics to be based on practical reason. If one could go on to argue that it is just such a theory that Aristotle would have accepted, then one would have the kind of answer needed to silence my Humean critic.

V. Objections

There are, however, a series of four objections that can be raised against attributing to Aristotle the theory sketched above, particularly if it is taken as a way of filling out what Aristotle says in 1143a35-b5. The first three are objections that my Humean critic would raise. The final objection is one that might be raised by someone much more sympathetic to the view that Aristotle's ethics rests on practical reason. In this final section I shall state all four objections and see what can be said in response to them. If I am right in what I say, we will not be finished with my Humean critic. However, we will have taken an important step in answering him.

The first objection is that the theory sketched above cannot be taken as a way of filling out what Aristotle says in 1143a35-b5 because it contains elements for which no textual basis exists. Even if one grants that in 1143a35-b5, Aristotle is talking about an inductive inference to general ends, nothing in the text can be construed as a reference to an inference to an end that one aims at by nature, or to a desire to integrate such an end into one's character. This is something that the above theory simply adds to the text. But it is precisely this addition that allows Aristotle to say that reason is involved in the acquisition of ends. On what basis can I attribute this addition to Aristotle?

There is a sense in which I have already conceded the premise of this objection. But I don't think that it has the force that my Humean critic would take it to have. What I argued in the first section of this chapter was that there are passages in which Aristotle says that reason plays a role in acquiring ends. The objection to this argument was that these passages need not be taken seriously, because Aristotle doesn't say *how* reason plays such a role. In Section II, I argued that there is a passage in which Aristotle says that universal ends are acquired by a kind of induction. It was objected here that Aristotle leaves no room for an inductive inference to play a role in the *acquisition* of ends. At most induction is involved in the *apprehension* of ends. The above sketch was given to show that Aristotle's psychology of action has room for an inductive inference to play a role in the acquisition of ends. No direct textual evidence exists for attributing such a view to Aristotle, but no *direct* textual evidence exists for the view my Humean critic attributes to Aristotle either.[24] What one has to do is see which view fits best with those passages that have some bearing on questions about the existence and scope of practical reason. Since a number of these passages have yet to be discussed, no final decision can be made on this matter at this stage of the argument. However, a few preliminary points can be made.

First, the passages I have discussed do require reason to play a role in the acquisition of ends. Second, the sketch I have attributed to Aristotle does allow reason to play such a role. Third, the view set out is one that Aristotle could have held. This last point is important, for if it is correct, then my Humean critic can no longer dismiss passages that commit Aristotle to basing ethics on practical reason on the grounds that Aristotle's psychology of action has no room for reason to play a role in the acquisition of ends. There is room. The passages that my Humean critic has dismissed must now be taken seriously. Although this is not the end of the argument with my Humean critic, it is an important beginning.

However, this brings us to the second objection that I want to consider in this section. And that is that it has yet to be shown that the theory sketched above is a view that Aristotle could have held. In particular, it is a mistake to think that anything like it lies behind 1143a35-b5. As it has been sketched, the theory describes an inductive inference from premises about what a person has done or what he wants, to a conclusion about what he "really wants" or what he is aiming at by nature. As 1143a35-b5 has been interpreted, it involves a grasp of general conclusion about what is to be done or what is good through a grasp of particular actions that are to be done or are good. The two inductions are simply different inductions. The first can not be an account of what is going on in the second.

However, the two inductions are not as different as they at first sight seem. We have already seen that Aristotle says that the object of desire is either the good or the apparent good. We have also seen that in his examples of practical syllogisms he takes the major premise to set out something as good, wanted, or needed. What a person wants is what he takes to be good. Thus, to the extent that a person tries to determine what he is "really aiming at" from looking at what he does want, to that extent he can be viewed as trying to determine a general account of what is good from particular premises indicating what he takes to be good. To the extent to which a person's actions are indications of what he wants and hence takes to be good, an attempt to find out what one is "really aiming at" by surveying one's past actions can also be viewed as an attempt to discover a general account of what is good by looking at particular premises that one accepts as saying what is good. Of course, the premises one accepts may not truly say what is good. What one takes to be good may not be good. But, I think, all this means is that one must take the kind of inference involved to be an instance of what Aristotle would call dialectic, rather than something with the form of simple enumerative induction.[25] That the inference in question turns out to be a form of dialectic would in fact be a welcome result. Part of the general thesis being argued for in this chapter is that universal practical principles are arrived at in much the same way that universal theoretical principles are arrived at. According to Aristotle, universal theoretical principles are arrived at through dialectic.

That the theory sketched above can provide a way of understanding the inductive inference involved in 1143a35ff can also be seen by looking at those whose undemonstrated sayings we ought to pay attention to. These people have acquired through experience a capacity to pick out the right thing to do on particular occasions. Since this capacity is not limited to just one occasion, it is in effect the implicit grasp of a general principle. But how is this capacity acquired through experience? In what way does experience of a wide variety of actions allow one to see that a particular action is to be done, or that actions like it are to be done? What kind of inductive inference is behind this "learning from experience?" One possible explanation is that what is going on is the unreflective analogue of what I have called the reflective acquisition of general ends. What experience gives these people is an implicit grasp of what they are aiming at by nature. Coming in contact with a wide variety of actions allows them to see that a life constituted by actions like this action is a life that they "can feel comfortable with." The theory I have sketched above, thus, does seem to provide one way of understanding the kind of induction involved in 1143a35ff.

The third objection that I want to consider is that the theory sketched above is not one that Aristotle could accept because it brings with it elements that are quite foreign to Aristotle. According to this theory, there is a kind of activity of reason that if one engages in correctly will lead one to acquire certain ends (the right ones), and that if one does not engage in correctly will lead one to acquire other ends (the wrong ones). That is, according to this theory, the desires and ends of a good person are rational in a way that the desires of a bad person are not. But, one might argue, this is not something that can be found in Aristotle.

Aristotle *may* admit that reason plays *some* role in the acquisition of ends. (Otherwise, how would he have a basis for saying that *boulēsis* is a desire in the rational part of the soul?) But the ends of both a good and a bad person are equally objects of *boulēsis*. According to the theory sketched above, Aristotle would be committed to the existence of two kinds of *boulēsis*, a rational kind and an irrational kind. But one finds no such distinction in Aristotle. There is only one kind of rationality that desires admit of, and any form of *boulēsis* is rational in this sense. Of course, *boulēsis* can have as its object either the good or the apparent good, but this distinction can't provide the basis for a distinction between a rational and an irrational form of *boulēsis*. In NE Bk. III Ch. 3 Aristotle says,

> If these consequences are unpleasing, are we to say that absolutely and in truth the good is the object of wish *(boulēsis)*, but for each person the apparent good; that that which is in truth an object of wish is an object of wish to the good man, while any chance thing may be so to the bad man, . . . For each state of character has its own ideas of the noble and the pleasant, and perhaps the good man differs from others most by seeing the truth in each class of things, being as it were the norm and measure of them. (1113a23-33)

Since the good person is the norm or standard for determining what the good is, the good *just is* what the good persom aims at. The desires of a good person, thus, are not based on anything like a correct discernment of the good. Being desired, by the good person, is what makes something good in the first place.

What is at issue here is extremely important. Unless one has a way of describing the desires or ends of a good person as rational in the way that those of a bad person are not, then even if Aristotle does admit the existence of practical reason, its scope won't be sufficient to provide a basis for ethics. As I argued in Chapter 1, if one can't say that the correct exercise of reason leads only to certain ends, then the existence of practical reason can't provide a basis for ethics. The final point made above also illustrates the importance of the existence and scope of practical reason for the *objectivity* of ethics, for if it is correct, then the objectivity of Aristotle's ethics is seriously threatened.[26] If each state of character carries with it its own conception of the good, and the good is what the good person takes to be good, then each state of character will have its own conception of who the good person is. In any dispute over whether a particular thing is good or not, it will be possible for both parties to provide the same sort of justification, each one arguing that his or her opponent is mistaken, because, not having the right state of character to start with, the opponent is in no position to assess correctly what the good is. Without some independent means of determining who the good person is or what the proper object of desire is, it is not clear what force the claim has that there is a correct conception of who the good person is and what the good is, and that thus there is a uniquely correct answer in such a dispute.

Since this objection is so important, I shall take some time to answer it. Even though passages have yet to be discussed that would provide the basis for an even more complete answer, I think that enough evidence exists in passages already discussed to see that the elements that this objection says are foreign to Aristotle are not foreign at all. The general points to be made are as follows. In the first place, Aristotle's account of the good relative to human beings in Bk. I as rational activity in accord with virtue has as a direct consequence that the desires of a good person are rational in the way that the desires of a bad person are not. Second, in both the passage from the *Metaphysics* discussed in Section I and in the passage quoted just above, Aristotle does recognize two forms of *boulēsis*, a proper form having the good as its object, and another having the apparent good as its object. Finally, the passage quoted just above should *not* be taken as saying that the good *just is* what the good person desires. It should be taken as saying that the desires of a good person rest on a correct discernment of the good.

In Bk. I Ch. 7 Aristotle says that the good person is one who engages in rational activity in accord with virtue. I take this to mean that the good person is one who engages in rational as opposed to irrational activity. It follows from this that the desires of a good person are rational in the way that the desires of a bad person are not.

One might argue that this way of taking Aristotle rests on a mistaken view about the virtue or virtues in accord with which the good person acts. If the virtue in question were just *phronēsis*, an excellence of the rational part of the soul, then perhaps what I have said would be correct. Rationality as opposed to irrationality does appear to be the excellence of the exercise of reason. But the virtues in question are virtues of the desiring part of the soul, virtues like courage, good temper, and magnificence. Since these are not virtues of the reasoning part of the soul, they do not require their possessors to be rational in a way that those who lack them are not. Of course, the good man does pursue his ends in accordance with *phronēsis*, but this means only that he adopts the right means to those ends that he has in virtue of having the relevant virtues. What gives him these ends (that is, what gives him these virtues) are either natural predispositions (natural virtue), or habit and training. Since neither of these require the exercise of reason, none of the relevant virtues require the excellence of reason where this is understood as rationality as opposed to irrationality.

However, the argument that Aristotle gives in Bk. I Ch. 7 *requires* that the virtues in question be excellence of rational activity, not the activity of some other part of the soul. Aristotle's claim about the good person is an instance of a schema according to which a good X is an X that engages in its characteristic activity *(ergon)* well.[27] Since what it is to be an X is to be capable of engaging in its characteristic activity, a good X is one that displays the excellence of its own characteristic activity. A good lyre-player is one who plays the lyre in accord with the virtue appropriate to lyre-playing, not the virtue appropriate to some other activity. It would be a nonsequitur to infer the goodness of a person from the fact that his or her rational activity accords with the excellence of some activity that did not essentially involve rational activity. Since the excellence of rational activity is rational as opposed to irrational activity, what Aristotle says in Bk. I Ch. 7 *should* be taken as saying that the good person is rational in a way that the bad person is not.

Even if the virtues in question are described as virtues of the desiring part of the soul, this does not mean that the good person does not display rational as opposed to irrational activity. As long as one cannot have these virtues without the excellence of rational activity, it is open to Aristotle to say that these virtues are rational in a way that their corresponding vices are not.[28] Nor will it do to say simply that *phronēsis* is concerned only with means. This presupposes that reason has nothing to do with ends, and if anything has been shown in this chapter, it is that there are passages in which Aristotle says that reason is concerned with ends. Aristotle is committed in at least one place to saying that the good person is rational in a way that the bad person is not.

In the second place the idea that two forms of *boulēsis* exist, one rational and the other irrational, is not all that foreign to Aristotle. In *Metaphysics* 1072a24-30, a passage discussed in Section I, Aristotle says,

> For the apparent good is the object of appetite, and the real good is the *primary* object of rational wish *(epithumēton men gar to phainomenon kalon, boulēton de prōton to on kalon)*. (1072a27-28, emphasis mine)

Here Aristotle seems to be distinguishing a proper form of *boulēsis*, one having the good as its object, from another form that has only the apparent good as its object. And at 1113a23-24, the beginning of the passage quoted in support of the objection we are considering, Aristotle says,

> are we to say that absolutely and in truth the good is the object of wish,
> . . . (Ross)

or

> perhaps we should say that what is wished for in the true and unqualified sense is the good, . . . (Rackham)[29]

Whichever translation one adopts, Aristotle again seems to be distinguishing two forms of *boulēsis*, a proper form having the good as its object, and another form having only the apparent good as its object.[30] Certainly a natural way of understanding this distinction is a distinction between a rational and an irrational form of *boulēsis*, the former being based on a correct discernment of the good.[31]

Finally, it is a mistake to dismiss this way of understanding the distinction on the grounds that the good *just is* what the good person aims at. What Aristotle says in 1113a23-33 is designed to avoid the unwelcome consequences of two views stated immediately prior to this passage. The second of these, "that there is no natural object of wish, but only what seems good to each man" (1113a21-22), forces one to give up the objectivity of judgments about the good. We have already seen that saying that the good *just is* what the good person desires also undermines the objectivity of judgments about the good. It would be more than ironic if the view put forward by Aristotle in its place falls prey to the same unwelcome consequence. More important, Aristotle says that "the good man judges each class of things *rightly,* and in each *the truth appears to him"* (1113a29-30), emphasis mine). He goes on to say,

> For each state of character has its own ideas of the noble and the pleasant, and perhaps the good man differs from others most by *seeing the truth in each class of things,* being as it were the norm and measure of them. (1113a30-33, emphasis mine)[32]

If the good person's desiring something made it good, there would be little point to Aristotle's saying that the truth appears to the good person, or that the good person sees the truth in each class of things. There would be no truth to be seen about what is good; the good person's desiring something would make it good. Rather than suggesting that the good *just is* what the good person desires, what Aristotle says suggests that the good person's desires do rest on a correct discernment of what the good is.

Thus, the elements involved in the theory sketched above are not foreign to Aristotle. They fit nicely with a number of passages that we have already discussed. The theory is one that Aristotle could have held.

The final objection I want to consider is one that might be raised by someone friendly to the view that Aristotle's ethics rests on practical reason. It is that the theory sketched in Section IV is unnecessary for Aristotle's ethics to be based on practical reason. According to this objection, Aristotle does say in 1143a35-b5 that *nous* allows one to see what it is that is to be done in a particular situation, and he does say that it is this kind of perception that leads one to acquire certain ends. But to see how this kind of perception allows one to acquire ends, one doesn't need to bring in any kind of special inductive inference of the sort I have sketched. All one needs is to recognize that according to Aristotle a determination of means is on some occasions a determination of an end. Besides means that instrumentally produce their ends, Aristotle recognizes means that are *constitutive* of their ends.[33] They spell out in a determinate fashion just what is involved in a previously indeterminate end. According to the objection under consideration, it is the perception of this sort of means that Aristotle is talking about in 1143a35-b5. But if this is right, then it looks as if one doesn't have to bring in the kind of elaborate induction I described in Section IV to explain reason's role in the acquisition of ends. To have a grasp of constitutive means is to have a grasp of the end that they constitute. The only "induction" that needs to be brought in is one that is involved in revising previously held ends in the light of newly discovered constitutive means. There is also a simple explanation of reason's role in the production of the desire for these newly determinate ends. If it is already acknowledged that practical reason is operative in the production of the desire for means to already given ends, then it will be this operation of practical reason that helps produce the desire for these newly determinate ends. In the case of constitutive means, a desire for the means is a desire for the end. The theory I have sketched, thus, seems unnecessary to explain how Aristotle's ethics can be based on practical reason.

Although we will be in a better position to assess the force of this objection when we have a more detailed discussion of the notion of constitutive means, it is important to take up this objection at this time. Not only is it an objection that might naturally be raised at this stage of the argument, unless one has a response to it, there seems little point to going on to ask whether there are any additional passages that support attributing to Aristotle the theory I have sketched. Instead one should go on to consider whether any additional passages support the view outlined in the above objection.

The first thing to be said in response to this objection is that even if the perception of what is referred to in 1143a35-b5 is the perception of constitutive means, one cannot so easily rid the passage of the kind of inductive inference I have been talking about. As I pointed out in the discussion of that passage, immediately after 1143a35-b5 Aristotle talks about those whose undemonstrated sayings we should pay attention to because experience has given them the capacity to see what to do on particular occasions. If what Aristotle is talking about in 1143a35-b5 is the perception of constitutive means, then what these people have is the capacity to pick out constitutive means. However, Aristotle says that these people have acquired this capacity on the basis of *experience*. Since what is acquired through experience is acquired on the basis of some form of induction, this capacity is acquired on the basis of some form of induction. This is not the kind of induction involved in revising previously held ends in the light of newly discovered constitutive means: it is an induction involved in the discovery of those means themselves. It is this kind of induction that needs to be explained and understood. The view advocated on the above objection doesn't seem capable of explaining it, because it doesn't acknowledge it. However, as I suggested in my reply to the second objection above, the theory I have sketched can be taken to explain this induction. Put in terms of constitutive means, experience with one's own actions and the actions of others provide a person with an implicit grasp of actions constitutive of a life one "can feel comfortable with." This is the unreflective analogue of an inference to actions constitutive of the ends one aims at by nature.

In the second place, unless some such inductive inference were at the basis of a person's grasp of constitutive means, there would be no grounds for thinking that this grasp is based on an exercise of *reason*, and hence no reason for thinking that the resultant desire for the determinate end is based on an exercise of practical reason. The mere perception that an action is to be done is compatible with both intuitionism and a moral sense theory, and both of these are compatible with the denial that ethics is based on practical reason. The perception that a particular action has a simple, unanalyzable property of rightness can be described as the perception of means constitutive of the end, "doing what is right." But if this is all there is to the discovery of constitutive means, it hardly seems to involve the exercise of *reason*. Even if a desire to do what is right were to result from the perception of such means, it would not be the result of the exercise of practical reason. The reason that a desire for instrumental means can be regarded as the result of the exercise of practical reason is that the discovery of instrumental means is based on an exercise of reason. It is essentially the discovery of a certain cause-effect relationship, and cause-effect relationships are discovered on the basis of induction. Unless a comparable exercise of reason is involved in the discovery of constitutive means (for example, the kind of inductive inference I have suggested), it looks as though the desire for the end that results from the discovery of constitutive means can't be taken to be the result of an exercise of practical reason. Thus, it does seem necessary to bring in something like the theory I have sketched if one is to argue that Aristotle's ethics is based on practical reason.

Let me briefly review the arguments of this chapter so that we can see exactly where we are in my argument against my Humean critic. I argued that in at least four different passages Aristotle says that reason plays a role in the acquisition of ends—NE 1139a21-26, NE 1142b31-34, *Metaphysics* 1072a24-30, and NE 1143a35-b5. I argued that in the last passage Aristotle says that universal ends are grasped by *nous* through an inductive inference, and that Aristotle maintains not only that this inference allows one to *apprehend* general ends, it also allows one to *acquire* them. Against the objection that Aristotle leaves no room for reason to play such a role, I sketched a theory according to which reason does play such a role. I argued that this is a theory that Aristotle could have accepted and that Aristotle's accepting this theory (or something like it), is essential to his having based his ethics on practical reason.

It does not follow from all of this that Aristotle did accept this theory. Whether he did or not can only be determined after the discussion of a number of other passages. But what does follow is that an important challenge of my Humean critic has been met. He argues that the passages in which Aristotle talks as if practical reason exists and provides a basis for ethics need not be taken seriously, because there is no room in Aristotle's psychology of action for reason to play the role in the acquisition of ends necessary for practical reason to provide a basis for ethics. However, if what I have argued in this chapter is correct, there is room in Aristotle's psychology of action for reason to play this role. The passages in which Aristotle talks as if practical reason exists and provides a basis for ethics must now be taken seriously. They do provide grounds for thinking that Aristotle's ethics is based on practical reason.

CHAPTER 4

The Pervasiveness
of Aristotle's Views
on Practical Reason

Up to now I have concentrated on the most direct textual evidence
there is for saying that Aristotle's ethics is based on practical reason.
Taken just by itself, however, it is not enough. To think that it is, my
Humean critic might argue, would be to take four passages, two of
which are ambiguous and the fourth of which is so controversial that
one should be reluctant to attach much weight to it, and simply in-
flate their importance. Besides, part of the view that I have attributed to Aristotle has been read into these passages. If one reads
these passages in light of the rest of the text, particularly those passages in which Aristotle seems to be restricting the role of reason to
the discovery of means, the most one gets is a tendency in Aristotle's
thought that gets outweighed in the total picture. Even if this over-
states the matter somewhat, one must take seriously the possibility
that Aristotle had more than one position on practical reason and its
relation to ethics, one that emerges from the passages I have discussed and one that comes out in the passages that my Humean critic
makes so much of. Unless something more can be said, one will not
have a strong case for saying that Aristotle's ethics is based on practical reason.

I shall devote this and the next chapter to seeing what more can be
said. In this chapter I shall argue that the picture I drew of the role
of reason in the acquisition of ends is not confined to the four passages discussed in Chapter 3. Using this picture as a basis, one can
understand a number of other passages as reflecting an acceptance
of the existence of practical reason as a basis for ethics. These are
passages that would be puzzling or arbitrary if Aristotle didn't accept

something like the view I have attributed to him, but that are quite intelligible if Aristotle did accept such a view. There is also a set of methodological remarks about ethics and politics that fits nicely with the view I have attributed to Aristotle. Read in light of passages already discussed, they too provide additional, indirect evidence for Aristotle's basing his ethics on practical reason.

In Chapter 5 I shall argue that the passages to which my Humean critic would appeal to show that Aristotle really shares Hume's views on practical reason do not show this at all. In fact, some of them fit the view I have attributed to Aristotle better than they do a Humean position on practical reason.

At the outset I should point out that the argument of Chapter 3 has already broadened the textual support for Aristotle's commitment to practical reason. My Humean critic recognizes passages other than the four discussed in Chapter 3 as ones in which Aristotle talks as if practical reason provides a basis for ethics. However, he dismisses them because he finds no room in Aristotle's psychology of action for reason to play the role necessary for ethics to be based on practical reason. However, if what I have argued in Chapter 3 is correct, there is room in Aristotle's psychology of action for practical reason to provide a basis for ethics. These passages, thus, can no longer be dismissed. They provide additional evidence that Aristotle accepted something like the view I have attributed to him. These passages include Aristotle's admission of desire in the rational part of the soul at *De Anima* 432b5-8, his claim that the good person is one who engages in rational activity in accord with virtue at NE 1098a12-18, and his talk about a rational part of the soul that urges people in the right direction at NE 1102b16-17.[1]

Besides these, however, three other sets of passages are puzzling and require an explanation on a Humean interpretation of Aristotle, but they become intelligible on the kind of view I have attributed to Aristotle. These provide further, indirect support for Aristotle's commitment to practical reason as a basis for ethics.

I. Practical Wisdom and Virtue

The first of these is a series of passages in which Aristotle draws an extremely close connection between practical wisdom *(phronēsis)* and virtue *(aretē)*. In NE Bk. II Aristotle defines virtue as

> a state of character concerned with choice lying in a mean, i.e. the mean relative to us, this being determined by a rational principle, and that principle by which the man of practical wisdom would determine it. (1106b35-1107a2)

In Bk. VI Aristotle says that virtue in the strict sense cannot exist without practical wisdom (1144b17, 1144b20-21). Thus, virtue is defined in terms of practical wisdom, and its existence implies the existence of practical wisdom. A similar connection seems to hold in the other direction. According to Aristotle, cleverness *(deinotēs)* is the ability to do whatever allows a person to achieve what he or she is aiming at. Practical wisdom involves cleverness (1144a24-28), but it involves more than cleverness (1144a28-29). What more is required is virtue (1144a29-30). A practically wise person has the right ends, and virtue provides a person with the right ends (1144a8, 1144a32-34). Thus, Aristotle's explanation of practical wisdom seems to involve an essential reference to virtue; and its existence implies the existence of virtue.[2] This mutual interdependence of practical wisdom and virtue is explicitly recognized at 1144b30-32 where Aristotle says,

> It is clear then from what has been said, that it is not possible to be good in the strict sense without practical wisdom, nor practically wise without moral virtue.

This interdependence between *phronēsis* and *aretē* raises at least two problems. The first is an apparent circularity in Aristotle's definition of virtue. The second is whether Aristotle's use of 'phronēsis' and 'aretē' rests on an arbitrary linguistic convention.

If virtue is defined in terms of a rule that a practically wise person would use, and a practically wise person is in turn described as one who not only has the ability to deliberate well about means but also as one who has the right ends, then Aristotle's definition of virtue seems to be circular. A person who has the right ends is just one has virtue. A serious consequence of this is that there appears to be no way to give any specific content to Aristotle's notion of virtue. In determining what dispositions constitute virtue, one will have to determine what rule would by employed to find the mean that virtue aims at. That is, one will have to determine what a practically wise person would do. But when one looks at a practically wise person, one is told that such a person would do what would enable him or her to achieve what a person with the right ends would be aiming at. These ends are just what one is looking for in trying to provide some specific content to Aristotle's notion of virtue. Of course, one can take Aristotle's discussion of particular virtues as a way of indicating what a virtuous person is disposed to choose, but, then, because of the apparent circularity noted above, one will have no way of connecting the discussion of these particular virtues with Aristotle's general account of virtue.

This problem is especially acute for one who takes a Humean

interpretation of Aristotle. On such an interpretation virtue has to be regarded as a state of the soul concerning the passions, something capable of moving a person to act. Practical wisdom must be taken as the ability to reason well about means, something that, since it involves just the exercise of reason, has nothing to do with motivation. If on this view one were to try to indicate just what dispositions relative to one's passions are involved in virtue by referring to practical wisdom, one simply will not be able to do it. There is nothing in the latter that provides any indication of what motivations a person will or should have. Any attempt to indicate just what dispositions a virtuous person has by appealing to practical wisdom will have to bring something like virtue in through the back door, and with it, circularity.

The second problem can be seen as arising in part from the first. If Aristotle cannot provide any content to the dispositions involved in virtue by appealing to practical wisdom without bringing in virtue through the back door, then it looks as if all there really is to the notion of practical wisdom is the capacity to deliberate well about means to ends, no matter what ends one has. That is, all that practical wisdom really amounts to is cleverness. Since a man can be clever without being virtuous, it seems that Aristotle's claim that virtue and practical wisdom are inseparable is either the result of a confusion that prevented him from seeing that practical wisdom and cleverness were not distinct, or the result of an arbitrary piece of linguistic legislation according to which Aristotle will refuse to apply the term 'phronēsis' to anyone who does not have the right ends. W. F. R. Hardie calls attention to this problem when he reports the following criticism that has been leveled at Aristotle.

> While Aristotle did not wish to identify, and believed that he could distinguish, practical wisdom and the intellectual capacity shown in the effective pursuit of a bad end, he does not succeed, especially when the question faces him in Book VI, 12 and 13, in distinguishing them. For he tells us that to have cleverness (deinotēs) is to be able to find the means to any proposed end (1144a24-26), and that it is the ethical virtue of the good man which determines his end, while his practical wisdom makes him do what leads to the end (1145a5-6). Here it seems that the effect of what Aristotle says is to identify practical wisdom with cleverness. His doctrine that ethical virtue and practical wisdom are inseparable (1144b30-32) can be reduced, it would seem, to the tautology that a man cannot be both clever and good unless he is good. (1980, p. 225)

Either Aristotle is confused and cannot tell that practical wisdom and cleverness are not really distinct, or the tautology that Aristotle's doctrine of the inseparability of virtue and practical wisdom reduces to is a result of his refusal to apply 'phronēsis' to someone who displays cleverness unless he also has virtue, and his refusal to apply 'aretē' to someone who has the right ends unless he is clever. Although Aristotle is not incapable of either confusion or linguistic legislation, such behavior does seem surprising coming from one who so often displays an acute ability to mark distinctions between the meanings of terms and note their basis in the nature of things. Again, this problem is especially acute for one who adopts a Humean interpretation of Aristotle.

However, if one attributes to Aristotle the view on practical reason that I have sketched, the two problems disappear, or at least are severely diminished. According to this view, practical wisdom involves more than the ability to deliberate well about means. It involves the capacity to see on the basis of induction just what it is that a person has by nature been aiming at. That is, practical wisdom gives a person a grasp of those ends that are part of virtue. Also, having developed dispositions largely in harmony with those ends enables a person to arrive at correct inductive conclusions about what one is by nature aiming at, thus, allowing one to introduce refinements into or reinforce those dispositions one has already established. Although more needs to be said about the exact connection between virtue and practical wisdom,[3] I think this is enough to show that on the theory I have attributed to Aristotle, practical wisdom and virtue are necessarily tied to one another and that, at least at the reflective level, the presence of one will imply the presence of the other. On this theory one would expect Aristotle to do just what one finds him doing, referring to one of these when he wants to explain the other and saying that the presence of one implies the presence of the other. Second, having seen what sort of induction is involved in the exercise of practical wisdom, one is in a position to break into the alleged circle of Aristotle's definition of virtue. To find out just what it is that a virtuous person is disposed to choose one must find out just what oneself and others are aiming at by nature. Admittedly, on the basis of what I have said so far, one is in no position to make many specific claims about what sorts of dispositions a virtuous person will have, but in theory at least the direction in which one must look to make such specific claims is clear enough.

Since the problems that surround Aristotle's claims about the inseparability of virtue and practical wisdom have a solution on the view about practical reason that I have attributed to Aristotle but do not have a solution on a Humean interpretation, I think these claims provide indirect evidence that Aristotle did hold a view like the one I have attributed to him.

II. Excellence in Deliberation

A similar problem arises in connection with Aristotle's discussion of *euboulia*—excellence in deliberation. Aristotle distinguishes *euboulia* from both cleverness *(deinotēs)* and practical wisdom *(phronēsis)*. But it is by no means clear how it can be distinct from both of these. In Bk. VI Ch. 9 Aristotle says that *euboulia* is a correctness of deliberation, but it is not every kind of correctness of deliberation (1142b17-18). *Euboulia* is a correctness of deliberation that arrives at a good end (1142b22-23).[4] Since *deinotēs* can be possessed by someone who has the wrong ends (1144a25-30), *euboulia* is not the same as *deinotēs*. What this means is that what allows people to determine the right means when they have the right ends is not the same as that which allows people to determine the right means when they do not have the right ends. On the other hand, *euboulia* is distinct from *phronēsis*. One of the tasks Aristotle has set himself in Bk. VI is to distinguish *phronēsis* from a number of other faculties or virtues similar to it (for example, *nous*, *gnōmē*, and *sunesis*). Ch. 9 is devoted to drawing the distinction between *phronēsis* and *euboulia*. But how can *euboulia* be distinct from both *deinotēs* and *phronēsis*? If one restricts *euboulia* to cleverness in the pursuit of right ends, it will be distinct from *deinotēs*, but then how does it differ from *phronēsis*? If one divorces *euboulia* from the pursuit of right ends it will be distinct from *phronēsis*, but then how does it differ from *deinotēs*?

These problems seem insurmountable on a Humean interpretation of Aristotle. On such an interpretation, what motivates a person is distinct and separable from the person's capacity to exercise reason. Since having the right ends is a matter of having certain motivations, it too is distinct and separable from the ability to exercise reason, including the ability to deliberate well about means. Indeed, the ability to deliberate well about means will be the same no matter what ends a person has. Of course, one can arbitrarily restrict this ability to those who have the right ends. This would allow one to distinguish *euboulia* from *deinotēs*. But then *euboulia* will be identical with *phronēsis*, for on a Humean interpretation *phronēsis* just is cleverness restricted to those who have the right ends. If one frees *euboulia* from this restriction, it then becomes identical with *deinotēs*. What is perhaps most puzzling, though, is how Aristotle could have thought that what allows people to determine the right means when they have the right ends is different from what allows people to determine the right means when they don't have the right ends. And yet, as I pointed out above, it is just this that Aristotle's distinction of *euboulia* from *deinotēs* implies.

However, the problems surrounding Aristotle's description of *euboulia* do have a solution on the kind of view I have attributed to Aristotle, although part of the solution rests on a consideration that will not be fully argued for until the next chapter. In the first place, it should be clear how Aristotle can distinguish *euboulia* from *phronēsis*. According to the view I have attributed to Aristotle, *phronēsis* involves more than the ability to deliberate well about means. It also involves the capacity to see on the basis of induction what ends a person should be aiming at. However, *euboulia's* sole concern *is* with means. It is a correctness of deliberation, and deliberation is of means. *Euboulia*, thus, is a *proper part* of *phronēsis*. Being a proper part, it is distinct from *phronēsis*. But how does it differ from *deinotēs*? In particular, why should what allows people to determine the right means when they have the right ends be different from what allows people to determine the right means when they don't have the right ends? Aristotle does say that deliberation provides one with the best and easiest means to a given end (NE 1112b16-17). Thus, what one takes to be the best among competing means will depend on what ends one has. But this is something that one who adopts a Humean interpretation can acknowledge. Two people who are equally adept at determining means will come up with different means if they have different ends, but they will still have the same ability to deliberate well about means.

Two things can be said to explain Aristotle's description of *euboulia* and mark it off from how *euboulia* looks on a Humean interpretation. First, on a Humean interpretation, what makes certain ends the right ends has nothing to do with the correct exercise of reason. If people have the right ends, their having them has nothing to do with their capacity for *rational* activity. Thus, whatever it is that allows one to determine the best among competing means, it will have to be a combination of two virtues, cleverness and moral virtue; and the latter will be a virtue of the nonrational part of the soul. However, on the view I have attributed to Aristotle, since a rational virtue is involved in the acquisition of the right ends, one can take that which allows one to determine the best among competing means to be a single virtue, a virtue of the rational part of the soul. This is just the picture that Aristotle seems to draw of *euboulia*.

More important, the kind of reasoning involved in the apprehension of the right ends need not be and is not entirely separate from the kind of reasoning that is involved in the determination of means. Although this will not be fully argued for until the next chapter, Aristotle's conception of means is such that on some occasions a determination of means is a determination of ends. The kinds of general ends a person acquires may, to a certain extent, be *indeterminate,* and the recognition of means can make them more determinate. For example, one may perceive a particular action (or a particular kind of action) as *constitutive* of a given end. ("Doing actions like this just is what it is to act in accord with that end.") The ability to determine this sort of means is not separable from the ability to apprehend the right ends, and hence will not be something found in someone who is merely clever. If one adds this conception of means to the view I have attributed to Aristotle, then one has a way of solving the problems surrounding *euboulia* that does not seem open to one who adopts a Humean interpretation of Aristotle.[5]

Thus, I think Aristotle's description of *euboulia* in Bk. VI Ch. 9 also provides indirect evidence that Aristotle held a view about practical reason like the one I have attributed to him.

III. Nature and the End of Action (NE 1114b16-25)

Another passage in which I think one can find Aristotle's position on practical reason at work is NE 1114b16-25.

> Whether, then, it is not by nature that the end appears to each man such as it does appear, but something also depends on him, or the end is natural but because the good man adopts the means voluntarily virtue is voluntary, vice also will be none the less voluntary; for in the case of the bad man there is equally present that which depends on himself in his actions if not his end. If, then, as is asserted, the virtues are voluntary (for we are ourselves somehow partly responsible for our states of character, and it is by being persons of a certain kind that we assume the end to be so and so), the vices will also be voluntary; for the same is true of them.

In this passage Aristotle is replying to someone who would try to excuse people for their wrongful acts on the grounds that they have no control over how the end appears to them, it being given by nature. Aristotle's reply is that whether the end is given by nature or not, vice will be as voluntary as virtue. And since virtue is voluntary (or at least Aristotle's opponent will grant that it is), a person cannot be excused from his vicious actions on the ground that the end of these actions was given to him by nature. In this reply Aristotle distinguishes two positions—(1) that the end that a man has is *not* due to nature but depends in part on the man himself (b16-17), and (2) that the end is given to man by nature, but the means he adopts to pursue it are voluntary (b18-20). His argument is that whether (1) or (2) is accepted, vice is as voluntary as virtue.

The main question that I am interested in is what position (1) amounts to. Just what is it that depends on the person and how does it contribute to the adoption of the end? Pamela Huby ([1967], p. 356) takes it to be a form of indeterminism or libertarianism, taking the passage as a whole to be a simple denial of determinism. W. F. R. Hardie correctly sees that the passage as a whole does not deny that the end is given to man by nature ([1968], pp. 276-77, [1980], pp. 178-80), but he also suggests that (1) is a form of libertarianism. He confesses, though, that Aristotle doesn't make the position he is discussing very clear.

> But, in the phrase translated, 'something comes also from the man himself', Aristotle perhaps draws back from closing with the conditional interpretation and suggests that choice is open in an unconditional sense, that a man is not merely the cause but the uncaused cause of his actions. But if this is what is in Aristotle's mind, he has not made his meaning explicit or clear. He leaves us with an enigmatic and not a precise statement of the alternatives which he distinguishes in this passage (1114b16-20).[6]

The problem is not just that Aristotle does not make the position very clear. If it is an indeterminist position that he has in mind, it seems to be the only mention of such a position in the whole of the ethics.[7] If one doesn't find any mention of indeterminism elsewhere in the ethics, then why should it arise here? Furthermore, it won't do to dismiss (1) as unimportant on the grounds that the point Aristotle wants to make in 1114b16-25 is one that holds whether or not (1) is true. It is clear that (1), or something like it, is what Aristotle himself wants to hold.[8] Aristotle treats (1) and (2) as if they were exhaustive alternatives, and elsewhere Aristotle rejects (2). The end that a good person has is determined at least in part by virtue, and virtue in the strict sense is not something one has by nature (NE Bk. II, Ch. 1, Bk. VI, Ch. 13). What ends people have are due at least in part to their states of characters, and these they have not by nature but by habit and training. Aristotle also seems to affirm something like (1) in his parenthetical remark at 1114b23-24 when he says, "for we are ourselves partly responsible for our states of character."[9] But, if we cannot dismiss (1), how are we to understand it? What is it that comes from the man himself, and how is it that it contributes to the end that he has? How can it be contrasted with nature and yet not amount to an uncaused cause?

The answers to these questions should be obvious by now. It is practical reason, playing the role that I have sketched, that comes from the man himself and contributes to the end. *Nous*, through its ability to make inferences about what a person really is aiming at, helps produce a desire for the end and a desire to integrate that end into the person's character. Practical mind in its deliberative capacity allows a person to determine means for integrating that end into his or her character and in part produces the desire for those means.

If these means are adopted, then the person will have acquired an end in part through the efforts of what lies within oneself, one's practical reason. Reason is something that can be contrasted with nature, and on the theory I have sketched there is no need to introduce any indeterministic element into the acquisition of ends. Reading the view on practical reason that I have attributed to Aristotle into 1114b16-25, thus, allows one to give a clear and intelligible account of (1). Without doing so, (1) and 1114b16-25 remain enigmatic and puzzling. Thus, I think 1114b16-25 also provides indirect evidence for the view about practical reason that I have attributed to Aristotle.

IV. Aristotle's Methodology in Ethics and Politics

The final set of passages I want to call attention to are some methodological remarks about ethics and politics that occur in Bks. I and X of the *Nicomachean Ethics*.

In Bk. I Ch. 3 Aristotle says that ethics and politics do not admit of the kind of precision or exactness *(akribēs)* that is possible in other sciences, because ethics and politics deal only with what is true for the most part (1094b12-28).[10] Aristotle also distinguishes between two objects of knowledge—what is known to us and what is knowable without qualification. He says that ethics must start with what is known to us (1095b1-4). Shortly afterward, he says that the fact is the starting point in ethics; one does not need the reason why the fact is so as well (1095b7-8). At 1098b2 Aristotle says that in ethics and politics the fact is the primary thing. It is a first principle or starting point *(archē)*. All of this indicates that Aristotle regards ethics and politics, or at least a major part of what Aristotle himself is doing in the ethics and politics, as an "inductive" inquiry rather than what goes on when one is operating within a demonstrative science.

Grant points out that the term *'akribeia'* carries with it more meanings than does the English term often used to translate it, 'exactness' ([1885], Vol. I, p. 452). Among other things, it means having the kind of completeness of statement and demonstrative foundation that one finds in mathematics. When Aristotle says that one is not to expect *akribeia* in ethics, he is at least saying that ethics is not a demonstrative science. This suggests that a large part of ethics, (or at least what Aristotle is engaged in when writing the ethics), involves an inductive inquiry.[11] This is confirmed by Aristotle's reason for not expecting *akribeia* in ethics and politics—that they can only discover what is true for the most part. Demonstrative science is concerned with what is universally and necessarily true *(Post. An.* 71b9ff).

That what goes on in ethics (or at least what Aristotle is engaged in when writing the ethics) involves an inductive inquiry is also confirmed by Aristotle's remarks that ethics does not start from the reasoned fact or from what is knowable without qualification. The latter are both marks of demonstrative sciences (*Post. An.* 71b8-12, 71b34-72a6, 79a2-4). When one starts from the fact but not the reasoned fact, and when one starts from what is known to us rather than what is knowable without qualification, one is starting from what is known by experience, especially what is known through sense experience (*Post. An.* 72a1-2, 79a3). But experience and sense experience are the starting points for induction (*Post. An.* 100a4-8, 100a15-b1, 100b4-5). Thus, to say that ethics starts from the fact but not the reasoned fact and from what is knowable to us, seems to be to say that general truths in ethics are to be arrived at inductively.[12]

That a fundamental part of ethics involves an inductive inquiry receives further confirmation from Aristotle's insistence that ethics can be studied profitably only by those who have had experience and the right kind of training (1095a2-4, 1095b4-6). Without this kind of experience or training one will not have or be able to get the *archai* of ethics. With this kind of experience one either has or can easily get them (1095b8). Now there is some ambiguity in Aristotle's use of 'archai' in these methodological remarks. It is not always clear whether he is talking about starting points for ethical inquiry, or whether he is talking about universal first principles. Either way, though, I think Aristotle is saying that general principles in ethics are arrived at inductively. Grant suggests that Aristotle exploits this ambiguity since, in a sense, universal first principles are already potentially in the dispositions or habits that one obtains from experience and training ([1885], Vol. I, p. 433). It is the latter, of course, that provide us with or enable us to obtain *archai*. However, even if Aristotle is only talking about starting points for ethics, what he says still provides grounds for thinking that general principles are arrived at inductively. What experience and training provide one with are particular judgments about what is good or what is to be done. These particular judgments are starting points only for an inductive inquiry, one that would have as its conclusion general ethical principles.

There is even a hint of the view that I have attributed to Aristotle in these last remarks. In ethics the end aimed at is action, not knowledge (1095a5-6). But inexperienced people tend to follow their passions (1095a4-5). Thus, even if they have knowledge they won't profit from it, because they won't act on it. This suggests that experience and training are needed not only to allow a person to see what ends he should be aiming at; they are also needed to integrate these ends into a person's character to insure that he will act on them.

The picture I draw from all of these methodological remarks is the following. What one starts with in ethics are particular facts about what is to be done in particular situations. These provide the basis for determining in general what is to be done. One will be in a position to pick out these facts only if one has had a good deal of experience and in the process has developed the right habits. These habits are already something like unreflective first principles. What the inquiry of ethics does is to bring to light, by a process of induction,[13] the universal principles that are or underlie these habits. The grasp of these principles will not profit a person unless she has the right sorts of habits, for unless these principles are integrated into her character she will not act on them. This is quite close to the theory on practical reason that I sketched in Chapter 3. Although there may be other ways of understanding these methodological remarks, given the evidence already cited for attributing this view to Aristotle, I think it is reasonable to take these methodological remarks to reflect just such a view.

Besides his methodological remarks, Aristotle's practice in Bk. I contains more than a hint of the procedure outlined just above. He begins by trying to extract from a number of opinions about what is good some account of what the good relative to human beings is.[14] Admittedly his first attempt (1097a15-b24) does not provide much content to the notion of the good, and his second attempt (1097b25-1098a19) appears to be a deduction from *a priori* premises about the nature of human beings. But Aristotle does say that his theory must harmonize with what has been said about the good (1099a9-11). And he goes on to point out that all the other candidates for the good — pleasure, wealth, honor, and virtue — are either necessary conditions, concomitants, or parts of the good as Aristotle has set it out (Chs. 8 and 9). That is, Aristotle does try to show that his own view has a kind of "inductive confirmation."

One way of explaining how what Aristotle has said would, if true, show that his view does harmonize with the data, is that, having shown that the other candidates for the good are closely connected to his own account of the good, Aristotle can now portray these other views as mistaken but not completely mistaken attempts to point to what is good. This in turn could be understood in either of two ways. First, these alternative views are mistaken attempts to indicate just what it is that people are really aiming at, based on the kind of experience that their proponents have had. The mistakes are understandable because the objects being claimed to be good are so closely connected with what is really good and because the kind of experiences that the people making the mistakes have had make the mistakes seem reasonable. Second, the alternative views reveal what people do consciously aim at. Once one sees how closely these ends are tied to what really is good, one can view them as misguided attempts to aim at what actually is good. In the same way that one with a discerning eye can see that a twisted and gnarled tree is by nature striving to be straight and tall, so the connection drawn between the ends people consciously aim at and what Aristotle says is good allows one to see that in striving for these ends people are by nature striving for what Aristotle says is good. Understood in either or both of these ways, Aristotle's attempt to show that his own view harmonizes with the data puts his own practice in line with what I have said is his account of the acquisition of general ends.[15] Again, there may be other ways of understanding how Aristotle's attempt to show that his own view harmonizes with the data does confirm his conception of the good, but given what has been argued so far, I think it is reasonable to maintain that what explains it is a view like the one I have attributed to Aristotle.

Finally, Aristotle's methodological remarks about political science in the *Nicomachean Ethics* also seem to reflect such a view. At the close of Bk. X Aristotle says,

First, then, if anything has been said well and in detail by earlier thinkers, let us try to review it; then in the light of the constitutions we have collected let us study what sorts of influences preserve and destroy states, and what sorts preserve or destroy the particular kinds of constitution, and to what causes it is due that some are well and others ill administered. When these have been studied we shall perhaps be more likely to see with a comprehensive view, which constitution is best, and how each must be ordered, and what laws and customs it must use, if it is to be at its best. (1181b16-23)[16]

(Aristotle prefaces these remarks by saying that these studies will only be useful to experienced people [1181b7-13]). This account of the methodology of political science is quite close to what I have said is involved in the acquisition of general principles in ethics. If I am right about the latter, then this is just what one would expect. According to Aristotle, ethics is subordinate to political science (1094a27-b12) and, thus, it should employ the same methodology. Again, some methodological remarks of Aristotle seem to reflect the view on practical reason that I have attributed to him.

To conclude, there is good reason for thinking that the view on practical reason that I have attributed to Aristotle (or something very much like it), is not confined to the four passages discussed in Chapter 3. It can be found right below the surface of a number of remarks throughout *De Anima* and *Nicomachean Ethics*. Aristotle's commitment to practical reason is more pervasive than one may have at first imagined.

The Apparent Support
for the Humean Position

Still, the most serious objection to the position I have been arguing for has yet to be considered. In some passages, Aristotle seems to reject practical reason as a basis for ethics and embrace a Humean position. Given these passages, even if I am right in most of what I have said so far, my Humean critic can argue that it simply represents a tendency in Aristotle's thought that gets outweighed in the total picture. Besides, one cannot yet dismiss the possibility that Aristotle had more than one position on practical reason, that at times what he says is incompatible with practical reason's providing a basis for ethics. In this chapter I shall consider the three sets of passages that seem to provide the strongest support for a Humean interpretation of Aristotle. I shall argue that none of them do support such an interpretation. In fact, some of them will be seen to fit the position I have been arguing for better than that of my Humean critic. With this I hope the last resistance to taking Aristotle's ethics to be based on practical reason will vanish.

I. Deliberation Is About Means

In NE Bk. III Ch. 3 Aristotle says,

> We deliberate not about ends but about means. For a doctor does not deliberate whether he shall heal, nor an orator whether he shall persuade, nor a statesman whether he shall produce law and order, nor does any one else deliberate about his end. They assume the end and consider how and by what means it is to be attained; and if it seems to be produced by several

means they consider by which it is most easily and best produced, while if
it is achieved by one only they consider how it will be achieved by this and
by what means *this* will be achieved, till they come to the first cause, which
in the order of discovery is last. (1112b11-20)

Later on he says, "For the end cannot be a subject of deliberation,
but only the means" (1112b34-35). Aristotle seems here to be
restricting the role of deliberation to a determination of means. As
a result, deliberation seems to have nothing to do with ends. If one
adds to this what Aristotle says about calculative imagination at *De
Anima* 431b7-9,[1] then the role that Aristotle allows reason to play
in desire and action seems to be restricted to the discovery of means
to already existing ends (deliberation), and identifying objects for
already existing desires (calculative imagination). This, however, is
precisely the role that Hume allows reason to play, and, as we have
seen in Chapter 1, according to Hume practical reason does not exist.
Even if Aristotle were to allow reason to play a role in the production of the desire for means, this still would not be sufficient for
practical reason to provide a basis for ethics.

I have already argued that there is some reason for thinking that
Aristotle's views on action on the basis of desire and calculative imagination do not coincide with those of Hume,[2] but we need not return to these arguments to show that what Aristotle says in NE Bk.
III Ch. 3 does not support a Humean interpretation of Aristotle.
Even if one takes Aristotle to be saying in Ch. 3 that deliberation has
nothing to do with ends, it does not follow that reason does not play
a role in the acquisition of ends. For this to follow, it would have to
be true that reason's *only* role in desire and action is in deliberation.
But nowhere in Bk. III Ch. 3 does Aristotle say that reason's role in
action is confined to deliberation. Deliberation occurs after one has
an end, and in Ch. 3 the end is simply taken as given. Nothing is said
about how one gets it. Furthermore, it isn't as if there are no candidates for reason's playing a role in the acquisition of ends. We have
seen that Aristotle says at 1143a35-b5 that *nous* plays such a role.
And there is also the dialectical apprehension of ends implied by
Aristotle's methodological remarks discussed in the last chapter.
Thus, even if one takes Aristotle to be saying in Ch. 3 that deliberation has nothing to do with ends, Ch. 3 itself is *neutral* as to the existence and scope of practical reason. It cannot by itself support a
Humean interpretation of Aristotle.

More important, there is good reason for *not* taking Aristotle to
be saying that deliberation has nothing to do with ends. Given Aristotle's conception of the means-end relationship, on some occasions
a determination of means *is* a determination of ends. If it is granted

that reason plays a role in the acquisition of the desire for means, then it would seem to follow that reason also plays a role in the acquisition of ends. Thus, a more complete account of what goes on in deliberation seems to support the kind of position I have been arguing for, not that of my Humean critic.

Up to now I have by and large neglected the differences between Aristotle's and Hume's conception of the means-end relationship.[3] It is now time to take a closer look at Aristotle's conception of the means-end relationship. When Aristotle says that deliberation is not about ends but about *"ta pros to telos,"* the term he uses expresses a vaguer, broader notion than does the term 'means'.[4] Certainly it is a broader notion than Hume's conception of means. According to Hume, the means-end relationship is the cause-effect relationship where the effect is an object of desire or passion (for example, [1964], p. 414). On this view means and ends are logically independent of one another. One cannot, for example, infer the existence of means from the existence of ends. However, on Aristotle's conception of means, means are not always logically independent of one another. On some occasions one can infer the existence of means from the existence of ends.

It has been standard practice since the time of Greenwood (1909) to distinguish two kinds of means in Aristotle's thought—*external* means and *internal* (or *constitutive*) means.[5] *External* means are causally instrumental in the production of their ends. As such they are logically independent of their ends. An example of external means occurs in *Metaphysics* 1032b6-10 where Aristotle talks about rubbing a person's body to produce warmth, which in turn produces a uniform state of the body. Rubbing a person's body is an external means to warmth. *Internal* means, however, are not causally instrumental in the production of their ends, and they are not logically independent of their ends. In a sense they "constitute" their ends. They specify "what it is" to act in accord with them. It is the case of internal means that a determination of means can be a determination of ends.

The existence of internal means is implied by Aristotle's distinction between production *(poiēsis)* and practice *(praxis)* (NE 1140b1-7).[6] Examples of the latter provide examples of internal means. Every activity has an end. The ends of production are separable from it, but those of practice are not. In a sense, practice is its own end. Rubbing a body to produce warmth is, again, an example of production. Good action *(eupraxia)* is an example of practice. It is something engaged in for its own sake and, thus, it is, in a sense, its own end. Where an activity is a case of production, means to its end will be external. Where an activity is a case of practice, there will be means to it that will be internal. For example, a particular good action will be a means to (it will "constitute") *eupraxia*. There are at least two ways in which internal means can be related to their ends. They can be *parts* of their ends, or they can be more *determinate instances* of an already given but (to some extent) indeterminate end. That Aristotle allows the means-end relationship to include the relationship of part to whole can be seen from at least two considerations. The first is his use of a geometrical construction as an illustration of deliberation at NE 1112b20-24. In a footnote to his translation of this passage Ross says that what Aristotle has in mind is a solution to a certain geometrical problem, the construction of a figure of a certain kind.

> We suppose the figure constructed, and then analyze it to see if there is some figure by constructing which we can construct the required figure, and so on till be come to a figure which our existing knowledge enables us to construct.

Suppose, for instance, that one is to construct a regular polygon, and one discovers that one can do so by constructing a seres of equilateral triangles, one already knowing how to construct them. Then, the various triangles constructed will be *parts* of the constructed polygon, and the constructions of each one of them will be *parts* of the construction of the polygon. If this is an illustration of what is going on when one discovers means to ends,[7] then means may be parts of their ends.

The second consideration that shows that means can be parts of their ends is the relation that exists between virtuous actions and *eudaimonia* (happiness). At NE 1105a26-34 Aristotle says,

> Again, the case of the arts and that of the virtues are not similar; for the products of the arts have their goodness in themselves, so that it is enough that they should have a certain character, but if the acts that are in accordance with the virtues have themselves a certain character it does not follow that they are done justly or temperately. The agent must also be in a certain condition when he does them; in the first place he must have knowledge, secondly he must choose the act, and choose them for their own sakes, and thirdly his actions must proceed from a firm and unchangeable character.

What is important is Aristotle's claim that when a person acts virtuously, he or she chooses virtuous actions for their own sake. In Bk. I of the *Nicomachean Ethics* Aristotle argues that *eudaimonia* (happiness) is the good relative to man, and he describes this good as, "that at which all things aim" (1094a2-3). Whether one takes this to mean that happiness is the one end for the sake of which people do what they do, or that happiness is only one of the things that people aim at for its own sake,[8] the virtuous person can and does consciously do what he or she does for the sake of *eudaimonia* when he or she acts virtuously. How is one to reconcile these two points? When virtuous actions are chosen for their own sake they seem to be ends in themselves. And yet if they are done for the sake of *eudaimonia*, they are means to *eudaimonia*. How can they be both means to *eudaimonia* and ends in themselves? The answer is that virtuous actions are *parts* of *eudaimonia*. *Eudaimonia* is not an end separate from or independent of the virtuous actions that are means to it. *Eudaimonia* is a life constituted by virtuous actions.[9] Given that this is so, virtuous actions can be chosen for themselves and for the sake of *eudaimonia*. In aiming at the parts of *eudaimonia* one is aiming at *eudaimonia*. On some occasions at least, the means-end relationship in Aristotle is the part-whole relationship.

The second way in which internal means can be related to their ends is as determinate instances of already given but (to some extent) indeterminate ends. This emerges most clearly from Aristotle's claim that ethics lacks precision or exactness *(akribeia)*.

> Our discussion will be adequate if it has as much clearness as the subject matter admits of, for precision is not to be sought for alike in all discussions, any more than in all the products of the crafts. Now fine and just actions, which political science investigates, admit of much variety and fluctuation of opinion, so that they may be thought to exist only by convention, and not by nature. And goods also give rise to a similar fluctuation because they bring harm to many people; for before now men have been undone by reason of their wealth, and others by reason of their courage. We must be content, then, in speaking of such objects and with such premises to indicate the truth roughly and in outline, and in speaking about things which are only for the most part true and with premises of the same kind to reach conclusions that are not better. (NE 1094b12-22)[10]

When Aristotle says that ethics lacks precision and that ethical principles are "only for the most part true," what does he mean? Is it that principles of the form 'What is Ø is good' or 'One must be Ø' only have most of their instances true? If so, what about such principles as 'Health is good,' 'One must be temperate,' or 'One must be just'? Are there occasions on which health isn't good, or when one needn't be temperate or just? These don't seem to be things that Aristotle would say. Indeed, the doctrine of the unity of virtues (NE 1144b30-1145a3) counts against the latter. But if this is not what Aristotle means, how are we to understand 'for the most part true'?

The answer is that principles like 'One must be temperate' are in an important respect vague or indeterminate. They have this vagueness or indeterminacy because the moral concepts contained in them are vague or indeterminate. It will not always be clear from an understanding of concepts such as temperance or justice whether a given action will be temperate or just. Temperance may always involve not drinking too much wine, but whether on a given occasion drinking a fourth glass of wine is intemperate may not be clear. It cannot be set out in advance how many glasses of wine it is temperate to drink, even though on many occasions it will be quite clear how many glasses is too much, and even though one may have a general principle setting down a number of glasses as too many that will be applicable in most situations. Where such unclarity exists, it will not be looking to a general principle that one will be able to determine what to do. Rather, it will be a matter of *perception*.

> But up to what point and to what extent a man must deviate before he becomes blameworthy it is not easy to determine by reasoning, any more than anything else that is perceived by the senses; such things depend on particular facts, and the decision rests with perception. (NE 1109b20-23)

However, this perception is not a bare perception of what is to be done unaided by anything else. It is based on *experience*. It is the kind of perception that those whose undemonstrated sayings we ought to pay attention to have acquired on the basis of experience (1143b11-14).[11]

John McDowell (1979) has provided a helpful way of understanding these matters.[12] According to McDowell, what lies behind Aristotle's remarks about the lack of precision in ethics is that ethical principles are in an important sense "uncodifiable." One may be able to give a rough general characterization of what it is to be just, according to which actions in certain unproblematic cases can be seen to be just or unjust. But for every such specification there will be other cases in which the justice of the actions cannot be seen from the specification. The best one can do for these problematic cases is to say that just actions are ones that *like* those in the unproblematic cases. Exactly how they are like them, though, one cannot say. Whether an action is like such actions is something that has to be dicovered by *perception*, but a perception based on *experience*.

McDowell likens the task of providing such content to ethical principles to what Wittgenstein discusses when he discusses how to specify the correct way of continuing a given series of numbers. If one says, for example, that the series is one that continues by increments of two because that is the way it has gone so far, there seems to be in principle no way of ruling out the possibility that instead it will change to increments of four when one reaches 1,000. The best general characterization one can give is to say that the rest of the series will be *like* what has gone on before. To understand exactly what this is one must learn from experience what our practice of counting such a series is. Similarly, one must learn from experience what our moral practice is.[13] This includes learning the content of ethical principles by learning what actions must be like to fall under them.

What is important for present purposes is that the perception of such actions is a perception of *means*. An action enjoined by a principle is a means to the end advocated by that principle. A survey of Aristotle's examples of practical syllogisms will show that a recognition of means can include the recognition that an activity is an instance of a more general kind. In the example involving dry foods at NE 1147a1-8, the minor premises allow the agent to recognize a certain piece of food as an instance of dry food and, thus, eating it as an instance of eating dry foods. Where an end has the kind of indeterminateness discussed above, the recognition of such instances will be the recognition of means that *constitute* that end. Thus, a second kind of internal means are means that make determinate an already given but indeterminate end.

For both kinds of internal means Aristotle's conception of means differs from Hume's. Not only are the part-whole and determinate-determinable relationships different from the cause-effect relationship, internal means are not independent of their ends in the way that causes are independent of their effects. For example, one can infer the existence of parts from the existence of a whole, in a way that one cannot infer the existence of a cause from the existence of an effect.[14] More important, though, in both cases of internal means, a determination of means is a determination of an end. Specifying what the parts of a given whole are is giving a more detailed specification of what that whole is, and discovering determinate instances of a given but indeterminate end is discovering more precisely what that end is. This by itself is not enough to show that Aristotle allowed reason to play a role in the acquisition of ends. However, I argued in Chapter 2 that according to Aristotle reason plays a role in the acquisition of the desire for means to already existing ends. Given this, on those occasions when a discovery of means is a discovery of internal means it looks as if reason would play a role in the acquisition of ends.

I want to make one final point before concluding this discussion of Aristotle's conception of means. That is that the foregoing account of how reason can play a role in the acquisition of ends is *not* a rival to the view on practical reason that I have argued for. Rather, it supplements the view I have argued for, and in turn needs to be supplemented by that view. Although part of what I shall say has been said earlier,[15] repeating it serves two purposes. It allows one to see more clearly how reason can play a role in the acquisition of ends through the grasp of constitutive means. It allows one to see the extent to which Aristotle's acknowledgment of constitutive means provides additional support for the position on practical reason that I have argued for.

At first sight it may seem that the recognition of constitutive means allows reason to play a role in the acquisition of ends without having to bring in any inductive inference of the sort that I sketched in Chapter 3. To have a grasp of constitutive means is to have a grasp of a new end, one that is more determinate than the one a person had before grasping those means. If it is already acknowledged that practical reason is operative in the acquisition of the desire for means to already given ends, then it will be this operation of reason that is involved in the acquisition of these newly determinate ends. There seems to be no need to bring in anything like the inductive inference that I sketched.

However, given the foregoing account of internal means, the kind of inductive inference I have argued for cannot so easily be got rid of. In the first place, one still needs an account of the acquisition of the indeterminate ends that are made more determinate by the grasp of constitutive means. If a person has temperance as a general end, how did he acquire it? Even if his conception of temperance is indeterminate, it will be determinate enough to rule out constant pursuit of bodily pleasure. How is it that the person comes to have as an end something that rules this out? One answer is that he has come to see that a life of constant indulgence of bodily desire is not something that he aims at by nature, that in fact a life in which he exercises some control over his bodily desires is what he "really wants."[16] In the second place, the account of internal means outlined above already involves something like the view I have argued for. The perception that a given action is an instance of some indeterminate moral end is not the bare perception of what is to be done unaided by anything else. It is a perception based on *experience*. What is learned from experience is learned on the basis of induction. Some account of the nature of the inductive inference involved in this "learning from experience" needs to be given. The kind of inductive inference I have argued for provides one such account. By experiencing a wide variety of actions one can come to see just what actions make up the kind of life that one is aiming at by nature (the kind of life that one "really wants").[17]

Indeed, unless some such inductive inference were at the basis of a person's grasp of constitutive means, there would be no reason for thinking that the resultant desire would be based on an exercise of practical reason. The mere perception that an action is to be done is compatible with both intuitionism and a moral sense of theory. But both of these are compatible with the denial that ethics is based on practical reason. The perception that a particular action has a simple, unanalyzable property of rightness can be regarded as the perception of means constitutive of the indeterminate end, "doing what is right." But if this is all there is to the discovery of constitutive means, it hardly seems to involve an exercise of reason. Even if a desire to do what is right (understood now as including this action) results from the perception of such means, it wouldn't be due to an exercise of reason. Its existence, thus, would provide no grounds for the existence of practical reason. It seems to be the mark of the exercise of reason that something *inferential* (or something inferential-like) has gone on. The reason that a desire for instrumental means can be regarded as the work of practical reason is that the discovery of instrumental means is the discovery of a cause-effect relationship and the discovery of a cause-effect relationship is made on the basis of induction. Unless there is a comparable exercise of reason involved in the discovery of constitutive means, it looks as if the desire for a newly determinate end won't be the work of practical reason. But if the ability to perceive constitutive means is based on the kind of inductive inference I have argued for, then the resultant desire will be the work of practical reason.

Not only can Aristotle's conception of internal means be easily fit within the theory I have attributed to him, unless something like that theory is part of Aristotle's conception of internal means, his acknowledgement of internal means will not provide grounds for saying that reason can play a role in the acquisition of ends.

Thus, a more complete account of what Aristotle thinks goes on when one deliberates about means not only doesn't support a Humean interpretation of Aristotle, it provides some grounds for something like the theory I have attributed to Aristotle. To the extent to which the grasp of internal means rests on experience, to that extent the acquisition of ends appears to be based on an inductive inference of the sort I have argued for.

II. Virtue Preserves First Principles

The second set of passages that seem to support a Humean interpretation of Aristotle are those in which Aristotle talks about that which preserves or destroys first practical principles. At NE 1151a15-19 he says,

> For virtue and vice respectively preserve and destroy the first principles, and in actions the final cause is the first principles, as the hypothesis are in mathematics; neither in that case is it argument that teaches the first

principles, nor is it so here—virtue either natural or produced by habituation is what teaches right opinion about the first principles.

Three aspects of this passage appear to tell against taking first principles to be acquired in the way I have suggested and in favor of a Humean account of the acquisition of first principles. First, Aristotle appears to be saying that virtue gives one first principles and vice prevents one from having any first principles at all. Second, Aristotle seems to be saying that first principles are not due to *any* form of argument. Third, Aristotle says that *natural* virtue can give a person the right first principles.

Let us begin with the first of these. On the view I have been arguing for, there is an exercise of reason that if one engages in correctly can lead one to have the right first principles and that if one engages in incorrectly can lead one to have the wrong first principles. Thus, on this view, at least some vicious people have the wrong first principles, acquired in part through a mis-exercise of reason. But if vicious people have no first principles, then it looks as if first principles cannot be due to any such exercise of reason. If they were, then there would be some vicious people who did have mistaken first principles. First principles, thus, must be due to a kind of nonrational habituation. Vicious people simply lack the kinds of habits that give people first principles.

However, I think it is a mistake to take 1151a15-19 to be saying virtue provides a person with first principles and vice prevents him from having any. Rather, I think Aristotle is saying that virtue preserves and vice destroys the *true* or *correct* first principles. Not only is this suggested by the end of 1151a15-19 where Aristotle says that virtue is what teaches right opinion about the first principle, it is clear from what he says elsewhere that Aristotle thinks that a vicious person can have first principles. Immediately prior to 1151a15-19 Aristotle contrasts the self-indulgent person with the incontinent one by saying that the former is convinced that one ought to pursue pleasures that are excessive (1151a11-13). This implies that some vicious people (self-indulgent people who have been corrupted by pleasure), do have first principles.[18] Aristotle's admission at 1142b18-20 that a bad person may deliberate also implies that a vicious person can have first principles. Finally, it would be hard to see how at 1144a35 Aristotle could speak of wickedness as *deceiving (diapseudesthai)* a person about first principles unless a wicked person had mistaken first principles.[19]

If one takes 1151a15-19 to be saying that virtue insures or preserves the correctness of first principles, then it is open to one to say that virtue is not entirely responsible for the first principles of a good person.[20] Not only does this allow room for reason to play a role in the acquisition of ends, it allows it to play just the role I have said that it plays. Virtue either allows one's inductively based judgments about what one ought to pursue to be correct, or it preserves these correct judgments by psychologically integrating them into a person's character, or both. There is even a sense in which the view I have attributed to Aristotle receives a slight bit of support from what Aristotle says in 1151a15-19, for that view explains why Aristotle would express his point by saying that virtue and vice preserve or destroy *the* first principles. According to this view, correct principles are those which people are "really" aiming at whether they realize it or not. Vice prevents people from seeing what these first principles are. Since these are the ultimate principles that people are aiming at, whether they realize it or not, they are *the* first principles.

The second feature of 1151a15-19 that seems to support a Humean interpretation of Aristoele is Aristotle's claim at 1151a17-18 that first principles are not taught by argument or a process of reasoning *(logos)*. A *fortiori* they are not acquired through the process of inductive reasoning that I have described. Instead, they must be due to a nonrational process of habituation or training.

However, I think that *'logos'* should not be understood as referring simply to any process of reasoning. Rather, it should be taken to refer to a specific kind of reasoning, deductive or syllogistic reasoning. Aristotle says that the situation is parallel to that in mathematics in which hypotheses *(hupotheseis)* are not taught by *logos*. Although some question exists as to whether *hupotheseis* should be taken to be assumptions of the existence of the primary objects of mathematics or to be axioms or postulates from which mathematic demonstrations proceed, it is clear, I think, that either way *hupotheseis* can be acquired through the exercise of reason. Indeed they would be acquired by *nous*. What Aristotle is saying is that they are not learned by demonstration or syllogistic proof, for all such demonstrations presuppose them. The parallel claim for first practical principles is that they are not acquired by anything like syllogistic reasoning, but are acquired by *nous* or something like *nous*. Not only does this parallel claim *not* support a Humean interpretation of Aristotle, it fits well with the position I have attributed to Aristotle.[21]

Finally, Aristotle says, "virtue either natural or produced by habituation is what teaches right opinion about the first principle" (1151a18-19). Whatever one says about virtue produced by habituation, natural virtue does not require the exercise of reason. So it looks as if Aristotle is saying that the ends involved in first principles are not acquired through the use of reason. Thus, his ethics cannot be based on practical reason.

However, this latter conclusion does not follow from what Aristotle says about natural virtue. If virtue produced by habituation allows one to acquire the same ends that natural virtue allows one to have, and if the proper exercise of reason is necessary for virtue produced by habituation (something I shall argue for in the next section), then this is all that one needs to claim that Aristotle's ethics are based on practical reason. If reason *can* play a substantial role in the acquisition of ends, then the ends that would be acquired if reason did play this role correctly are rational ends, whether or not someone who has these ends actually exercised reason in their acquisition. Furthermore, even if one were to look just at natural virtue, natural virtue only *in a sense* would provide one with the right ends. It does not fully and completely provide one with the right ends. To fully and completely acquire the right ends, one must have *phronēsis*. This means that the correct exercise of reason is involved in a full and complete acquisition of the right ends. (For an argument for this, again, see the next section.)

If all of this is correct, then there is nothing in 1151a15-19 that counts against Aristotle's having based ethics on practical reason, or against his having done it in the way I have suggested. If anything, what is said in 1151a15-19 counts in favor of the view I have attributed to Aristotle.

III. *Phronēsis* Provides One with the Right Means, *Aretē* with the Right Ends

The final set of passages, those that seem to provide the strongest grounds for a Humean interpretation of Aristotle, occurs in NE Bk. VI Chs. 12 and 13. At 1144a7-9 Aristotle says,

> Again, the work of man is achieved only in accordance with practical wisdom as well as with moral virtue; for virtue makes us aim at the right mark, and practical wisdom makes us take the right means.

Immediately afterwards he says,

> Now virtue makes the choice right, but the question of the things which should naturally be done to carry out our choice belongs not to virtue but to another faculty. (1144a21-23)

And at the end of Ch. 13 he says,

> the choice will not be right without practical wisdom any more than without virtue; for the one determines the end and the other makes us do things that lead to the end. (1145a4-6)

In these passages Aristotle seems to be saying that *phronēsis,* the virtue of reason in its practical employment, is *only* concerned with means (it provides one with the right means). Another faculty, *aretē*, determines the end (it provides one with the right end). And *aretē* in turn is something acquired by habit and training, not by the exercise of reason. In these passages Aristotle seems explicitly to be denying the view I have attributed to him and affirming a position almost identical with Hume's.

However, if one pays attention to the context of these remarks, two features show that these remarks do not support a Humean interpretation of Aristotle on practical reason. Not only are they compatible with the view I have attributed to Aristotle, they actually support it. The first feature is that the point of a large part of Bk. VI is to spell out in some detail what is involved in the two intellectual virtues, *sophia* (theoretical wisdom) and *phronēsis* (practical wisdom), and to do this by contrasting these virtues with other faculties or virtues like them. In Ch. 8, Aristotle contrasts both political wisdom *(politikē)* and *nous* with practical wisdom. In Ch. 9, he contrasts the excellence in deliberation included in practical wisdom with other kinds of correctness of thinking. In Ch. 10, practical wisdom and theoretical wisdom are contrasted with understanding *(sunesis)*, and in Ch. 11 these two are contrasted with judgment *(gnōmē)*. Chs. 12 and 13 return to the contrast between theoretical wisdom and practical wisdom and consider some questions about the usefulness and supremacy of practical wisdom and theoretical wisdom. The answers to these questions lead Aristotle to distinguish practical wisdom from virtue and to consider virtue once again. The passages quoted above occur in this contrast and reconsideration of virtue and practical wisdom. Once one sees how Aristotle draws contracts between theoretical and practical wisdom and other faculties or virtues elsewhere in Bk. VI, one will see how Aristotle can mark off practical wisdom from virtue by saying that the former gives one the right means whereas the latter provides one with the right ends, and *not* commit himself to the view that practical wisdom and virtue are confined to these tasks.

The second feature of the context of these remarks is that, at least in Ch. 13, Aristotle's discussion of virtue is an attempt to show just what is right and just what is wrong with Socrates' account of virtue. Once one sees what Aristotle takes the difference between his and Socrates' account to be, one will see that the above passages can be seen as ways of emphasizing this difference without implying that *phronēsis* is only concerned with means, *aretē* only with ends.

Let us begin with the first of these features. How is it in Bk. VI that Aristotle marks off *phronēsis* from other things like it? One way of showing that two faculties are distinct is by showing that one operates with or is concerned with objects that the other is not, or more generally, by showing that what is always true of one faculty is not always true of the other. Considerations such as these seem to be at the basis of Aristotle's distinction of *phronēsis* from *nous* in Ch. 8. *Nous* is concerned with objects, the first premises of theoretical knowledge, which *phronēsis* is not concerned with. Something is always true of *phronēsis*—it always deals with objects of perception —that is not always true of *nous*, for example, when it apprehends the first principles of theoretical knowledge. This shows that *phronēsis* and *nous* are distinct. But it does *not* imply that *nous* and *phronēsis* are never concerned with the same objects, or that one of these faculties can not be exercised when the other is. As was pointed out in Chapter 3, at 1143a35-b5 Aristotle says that *nous* is concerned with objects of perception, for in practical matters it grasps the starting points of universal first principles, and these are grasped by perception. If one can interpret Aristotle's remarks in Chs. 12 and 13 as marking off *phronēsis* from *aretē* in a similar way, then these remarks will also be compatible with the view that *phronēsis* is concerned with ends, *aretē* with means.

Initially it looks as if one could interpret these passages in this way. The key to understanding this is Aristotle's apparent recognition of natural virtue as a form of virtue.

> We must therefore consider virtue also once more; for virtue too is similarly related; as practical wisdom is to cleverness—not the same, but like it—so is natural virtue to virtue in the strict sense. For all men think that each type of character belongs to its possessors in some sense by nature; for from the very moment of birth we are just or fitted for self-control or brave or have the other moral qualities; but yet we seek something else as that which is good in the strict sense—we seek for the presence of such qualities in another way. For both children and brutes have the natural dispositions to these qualities, but without reason these are evidently hurtful. Only we seem to see this much, that while one may be led astray by them, as a strong body which moves without sight may stumble badly because of its lack of sight, still, if a man once acquires reason, that makes a difference in action; and his state, while still like what it was, will then be virtue in the strict sense. Therefore, as in the part of us that forms opinions, there are two types, cleverness and practical wisdom, so too in the moral part there are two types, natural virtue and virtue in the strict sense, and of these the latter involves practical wisdom. (1144b1-17)

Natural virtue provides one with dispositions for certain ends, the same ends that virtue in the strict sense provides. Natural virtue is unaided by reason (b8-14), and thus does not involve (among other things) the ability to pick out the right means. *Phronēsis* always involves the ability to pick out the right means. Thus, something is always true of *phronēsis* that is not always true of virtue. Objects that *phronēsis* is always concerned with (means) are not among the objects that *aretē* is concerned with in one of its forms, natural virtue. Thus, virtue and practical wisdom are distinct. But this does not entail that virtue in another of its forms, virtue in the strict sense, is not also concerned with means. In fact, Aristotle seems to say that it is.

> if a man once acquires reason it makes a difference in action; and his state, while like what it was (natural virtue), will then be virtue in the strict sense. Therefore, as in the part of us that forms opinions, there are two types, cleverness and practical wisdom, so too in the moral part there are two types, natural virtue and virtue in the strict sense, and of these the latter involves practical wisdom. (1144b12-17, parenthetical remark mine)

Since virtue in the strict sense involves[22] *phronēsis*, and since the reason for this is that natural virtue becomes virtue in the strict sense when one has acquired reason, it looks as if virtue in the strict sense is concerned with means.

Similarly, nothing prevents *phronēsis* from being concerned with the right ends. Aristotle suggests that it is by his refusal to describe cleverness as a form of practical wisdom in the same way that natural virtue is a form of virtue. Natural virtue is *similarly* related to virtue in the strict sense as cleverness is to practical wisdom; *"not the same but like it"* (b1-4, emphasis mine). There is no form of practical wisdom that is concerned only with means in the way that natural virtue is concerned only with ends. Cleverness is not a form of practical wisdom. (See, for example, 1144a28-29.) This strongly suggests that practical wisdom is concerned with both ends and means, for if it were not, there would be nothing to prevent one from calling cleverness a form of practical wisdom. Thus, if Aristotle's distinction of *phronēsis* from *aretē* in Chs. 12 and 13 parallels his distinction of *phronēsis* from *nous* in Ch. 8, then not only is what he says compatible with *phronēsis* and virtue in the strict sense being concerned with both means and ends, he seems to be saying that they are both concerned with means and ends.

There is, however, an objection to taking the distinction between *phronēsis* and *aretē* as parallel to the distinction between *phronēsis* and *nous* as I have set it out.[23] Doing so requires one to take both natural virtue and virtue in the strict sense as providing one with the right ends. But in Bk. III Ch. 8 Aristotle seems to deny that natural virtue provides one with the right ends. While discussing courage, he says,

> Passion also is sometimes reckoned as courage; those who act from passion, like wild beasts rushing at those who have wounded them, are thought to be brave, because brave men also are passionate; . . . brave men act for honour's sake, but passion aids them; while wild beasts act under the influence of pain; for they attack because they have been wounded or because

they are afraid, since if they are in a forest they do not come near one. Thus they are not brave because, driven by pain and passion, they rush on danger without foreseeing any of the perils, . . . the 'courage' that is due to passion seems to be the most natural, and to be courage if choice and motive is added.

Men, then, as well as beasts, suffer pain when they are angry, and are pleased when they exact their revenge; those who fight for these reasons, however, are pugnacious but not brave; for they do not act for honour's sake nor as the rule directs, but from strength of feeling; they have, however, something like courage. (1116b23-1117a9)

A person who fights from passion or anger seems to have a natural virtue in just the way that Aristotle talks about natural virtue in Bk. VI Ch. 13. He is disposed to act in the same way that brave men do (at least in some circumstances), and this form of behavior is said to be the "most natural" *(phusikōtatē)* (1117a4). His disposition is apt to lead him astray, for he will rush into danger without foreseeing any of the perils. His disposition is not courage (1116b31, 1117a7-8), but if something is added to it, it becomes courage, a virtue in the strict sense. If we look at what must be added, we see that it is something that provides him with the right end. The disposition becomes courage if, as Ross puts it, "choice and motive" are added. But what Ross translates as 'motive' is *'hou heneka'* ("that for the sake of which"), and this refers to something aimed at. Earlier Aristotle has said that brave people act for the sake of honor (1116b31), and two lines later, when explaining why people who act from passion are not brave, he says that they do not act for honor's sake (1117a8). What plays the role of *hou heneka* is honor, and thus *'hou heneka'* refers to the right end. Aristotle seems to be saying, then, that the natural virtue associated with courage does not provide one with the right end.

Initially this may seem to undercut the attempt to show that *phronēsis* is involved in the acquisition of the right ends, but a closer look will show that it does not. If natural virtue does not provide one with the right ends, then Aristotle is saying in Ch. 13 that *phronēsis* is involved in the acquisition of the right ends. What the passage in Bk. III tells us is that what is added to natural virtue to make it virtue in the strict sense provides one with the right ends. What Aristotle says in Bk. VI is that natural virtue becomes virtue in the strict sense once one has acquired *reason (nous)* (1144b12-14), and it is because of this that Aristotle goes on to say that virtue in the strict sense involves practical wisdom (1144b16-17). If a person who has natural virtue acquires the right ends when he or she acquires practical wisdom, it looks as if *phronēsis* is involved in the acquisition of the right ends.

But if natural virtue does not provide one with the right ends, how are we to understand the distinction between *phronēsis* and *aretē* in Chs. 12 and 13? Two ideas suggest themselves. The first is similar to the explanation given on the assumption that natural virtue does provide one with the right ends. Virtue always provides one with certain dispositions to act, dispositions which, when one has virtue in the strict sense, provide one with the right ends. It does not always provide one with the right means. *Phronēsis* does always provide one with the right means. Thus, *phronēsis* and virtue are distinct. Although this is a slightly awkward paraphrase of what Aristotle says, it has the virtue of explaining why Aristotle should bring into the discussion natural virtue, a notion he rarely mentions. The second is suggested by the role that reason plays in the acquisition of ends that I have attributed to Aristotle. Although reason can provide a person with a belief about what he is aiming at by nature and a desire to integrate this end into this character, this is not enough to acquire this end. Acquisition also requires proper habits and/or training. Although reason can provide one with a conception of the right end, virtue is necessary if one is actually to acquire the right end. Thus, one can say that it is *characteristic* of virtue to provide one with the right ends. Similarly one can say that it is *characteristic* of *phronēsis* to provide one with the right means. Although one cannot have the right means without having the right ends, the correct operation of at least part of the form of reason involved in *phronēsis* that deals with means (cleverness), will provide one with the right means relative to the ends that one does have.

Thus, either natural virtue provides one with the right ends and Aristotle's distinction between *phronēsis* and *aretē* parallels his distinction between *phronēsis* and *nous,* suggesting that *phronēsis* is concerned with ends, or natural virtue does not provide one with the right ends. But then what Aristotle says in Ch. 13 implies that *phronēsis* does play a role in the acquisition of ends. Either way Aristotle's remarks in Chs. 12 and 13 are not incompatible with the view I have attributed to Aristotle. In fact, they tend to support it.

But does natural virtue provide one with the right ends or doesn't it? The answer is not immediately obvious, for although Aristotle's discussion in Bk. III of those who act from passion suggests that natural virtue does not provide one with the right ends, we have seen in Section II that at NE 1151a15-19 Aristotle says that it does. What is one to say in the light of these apparently diverging views? Does natural virtue provide one with the right ends, or doesn't it? The answer, I think, is typically Aristotelian—in part it does and in part it doesn't, or, in a sense it does and in a sense it doesn't.[24] Natural virtue provides a person with dispositions to act that in a limited range of cases are the same as those of a person with virtue in the strict sense. Outside of these limited range of cases, for instance, in a new or noval situation, natural virtue either leaves a person unprepared to act, or disposed to act in the wrong way. (A person with a strong body but without sight may move easily in familiar surroundings, but in unfamiliar surroundings is apt to stumble.) Without reason to guide her, a person with only natural virtue may be led astray. In a sense (or in part) she has the right ends, but in a sense (or in part) she does not. To have the right ends fully, a person must have virtue in the strict sense, and this requires the correct exercise of reason. It requires *phronēsis*. If one accepts this answer, one can distinguish *phronēsis* from virtue by saying that virtue always at least in a sense or in part provides one with the right ends but it does not always provide one with the right means. *Phronēsis* always provides one with the right means. But *phronēsis* also plays a role in the acquisition of the right ends, for what is needed to acquire the right ends fully is the exercise of reason and this requires *phronēsis*.[25]

The second feature of Aristotle's remarks in Chs. 12 and 13 that shows that *phronēsis* is not restricted to providing the right means is their anti-Socratic tone. In Ch. 13 Aristotle says,

> This is why some say that all the virtues are forms of practical wisdom, and why Socrates was on the right track while in another he went astray; in thinking that all the virtues were forms of practical wisdom he was wrong, but in saying they implied practical wisdom he was right. (1144b17-21)

And again later,

> Socrates, then, thought the virtues were rules or rational principles (for he thought they were, all of them, forms of scientific knowledge) while we think they *involve* a rational principle. (1144b28-30)

As Aristotle would put the Socratic position, Socrates took moral virtue to be only a virtue of the intellectual part of the soul. Moral virtue does involve an intellectual virtue, but it involves more than this; it involves a virtue of the appetitive part of the soul. Without having developed certain traits of character, one won't be able to make a *correct* inference as to what the good is, and even if one could, without developing the right sorts of habits, one won't be able to acquire it. In short, one won't acquire the right ends without virtue. The Socratic view seems to assume that everyone's desires are all right from the beginning. Everyone does in fact desire the good. What is needed to attain the good is knowledge of its nature and the means to its acquisition. Aristotle is saying, however, that not everything is right with a person's desires from the beginning, and that without developing the right sorts of appetitive dispositions one will never know what the right ends are, let alone be in a position to secure them.

In marking off the differences between his own and Socrates' view, it would be only natural for Aristotle to emphasize the differences as he saw them. All practical wisdon, *as Socrates understood it,* could do, *when seen from Aristotle's point of view,* is insure one of the right means. Without virtue *as Aristotle understood it,* one would never acquire the right ends. Virtue, *as Aristotle understood it,* insures one of having the right ends. Thus, from Aristotle's point of view, the contrast between Socrates and himself can be put neatly if a bit oversimply by saying that practical wisdom provides one with the right means and virtue provides one with the right ends. So understood, nothing prevents one from saying that *phronēsis as Aristotle understood it* is also involved in providing one with the right ends.

There is one final reason for thinking Aristotle's remarks in Chs. 12 and 13 are compatible with the view I have attributed to him. In Chapter 4 Section I, I pointed out that Aristotle's remarks on the mutual dependence of practical wisdom and virtue would be based on a confusion or an arbitrary piece of linguistic legislation if he did not allow reason to play a role in the acquisition of ends. Chs. 12 and 13 is one of the places in which he notes this mutual dependence. If in these chapters he were also saying that virtue is only concerned with ends and *phronēsis* is only concerned with means, then he would be guilty of a confusion at the same time that he was pointing out its basis. He would be engaged in an arbitrary piece of linguistic legislation at the same time that he was pointing out its arbitrary basis. It seems preferable to interpret him in a way in which this does not turn out to be the case.

Thus, Aristotle's remarks in Chs. 12 and 13 do not provide evidence for a Humean interpretation of Aristotle on practical reason. Not only are they compatible with the view I have attributed to Aristotle, they actually seem to support it. Once this is acknowledged, I hope the final pockets of resistance to the view I have argued for will vanish.

CHAPTER 6

A Summary of the Argument

Since my argument for saying that the existence of practical reason provides an objective basis for Aristotle's ethics has been long and complicated, it will be useful if I summarize the argument and the view I have attributed to Aristotle, pointing out exactly how it allows practical reason to provide an objective basis for ethics.

I began by considering what must be true if practical reason is to exist. Although Hume seems to have thought that the existence of practical reason requires reason by itself to provide a motivation to act, I argued instead that a weaker condition will suffice, namely,

> (ii) in an appropriate sense of 'necessity' weaker than that of logical necessity, there are circumstances in which necessarily if a person's reason operates correctly he will have certain motivations, the motivations he would have not being necessitated by the circumstances themselves.

This condition will be satisfied if reason *co-produces* motivation along with desire, as well as if reason by itself produces motivation. I also pointed out that the mere existence of practical reason is not sufficient to provide an objective basis for ethics; other conditions must be satisfied as well. As plausible candidates for these conditions I suggested that (1) reason can play a role in the acquisition of ends, (2) the correct exercise of reason leads only to certain ends and not to incompatible ends, and (3) the correct exercise of reason can lead to a certain harmony or order among ends. I also suggested that if (4) the correct exercise of reason can lead to the acquisition of a single end, every other rational end being a means to or a part of it, then (1) through (3) will be satisfied.

The problem that surrounds Aristotle's views on practical reason is that although in a number of places what Aristotle says implies that practical reason exists and that its existence provides an objective basis for ethics, in other passages, where Aristotle is apparently indicating reason's role in motivation and action, the picture he gives *seems* to be identical with Hume's. According to Hume's view, practical reason does not exist. To argue that Aristotle did allow the existence of practical reason to provide an objective basis for ethics, I tried to answer a critic who argues that at heart Aristotle really does hold a Humean view on practical reason. Although Aristotle does sometimes talk as if practical reason exists, this talk can and should be discounted, for when it comes right down to it, Aristotle leaves no room for practical reason to operate. Furthermore, if it did operate, it would be confined to the production of desires for means to already existing ends. This would not be sufficient to provide an objective basis for ethics. I chose to respond to such a critic for two reasons. First, the position of the Humean critic approximates a bias that a number of readers bring with them to Aristotle's ethics, and this bias needs to be met head on. Second, if one can successfully answer such a critic, one will have the strongest argument possible for saying that Aristotle's ethics is based on practical reason.

To begin the argument, I set out Aristotle views on action as a result of appetite and action as a result of desire and deliberation. At first sight these views seem remarkably close to Hume's. However, when one looks at some of the details, discrepancies begin to appear. I argued that Aristotle's claim that mind is a source of movement and his criticism of a Humean-like division of the soul into a rational and an irrational part suggest that reason at least plays a role in the production of desires for means to already existing ends. I went on to consider whether there were any evidence for Aristotle's allowing reason to play a role in the acquisition of ends. I pointed out two passages, NE 1112b16-17 and *De Anima* 434a6-9, into which one could read the view that reason plays a role in the acquisition of ends, although the grounds for reading this view into them are hardly decisive. Even where Aristotle's and Hume's views appear to be the closest, there is some reason for thinking that they diverge.

None of what was said up to this point was decisive, and it certainly wouldn't be taken to be decisive by my Humean critic. Even if he granted everything I argued for so far, he could simply add the passages in question to those he claims can be discounted in the absence of any account of how reason can play a role in the production of motivation. To answer my Humean critic, one must find an account of how reason plays a role in the acquisition of ends. To do this, I turned to Aristotle's discussion of action on the basis of general ends. I argued that despite some ambiguities in them, in three passages (NE 1139a21-26, NE 1142b31-34, and *Metaphysics* 107a24-30) Aristotle says that reason plays a role in the apprehension of ends. But how does this happen? Unless one has a specific account of the role that reason plays in the apprehension of ends, my Humean critic will not have been answered. I turned to NE 1143a35-b5 and argued that despite a number of difficulties surrounding this passage, it should be understood as saying that reason in the form of *nous* apprehends general ends through a kind of induction.[1] Still, my critic could respond that *apprehending* ends through something like a theoretical use of reason is one thing, *acquiring* them in the sense that they provide one with a motivation to act is another. However, I argued that according to Aristotle the apprehension of ends by *nous* is part of their acquisition, and I sketched a specific account of the acquisition of ends where this turns out to be so.

My critic could still hold out, arguing that no reason exists yet to attribute this particular account to Aristotle. In the first place, no direct textual evidence exists for some details of the account. Second, the induction described is different from that talked about in 1143a35-b5. Finally, the account brings in something quite foreign to Aristotle—that the ends of a good man are rational in a way that the ends of a bad man are not. In response to these objections I conceded that no direct textual evidence exists for some details in the account of the acquisition of ends that I attributed to Aristotle, but I maintained that this is inevitable, since Aristotle did not undertake an explicit detailed discussion of the acquisition of general ends. There is no direct textual evidence for the position of my Humean critic either. What one has to do is to see which view fits the passages that are available. The argument to this point can be understood as maintaining that the account I sketched, or something very much like it, is required by passages already discussed. I also argued that the induction in the account sketched can be viewed as the same kind of induction talked about in 1143a35-b5. Finally, I argued that the position that the ends of a good person are rational in a way that the ends of a bad person are not is a position that Aristotle did hold. His description of the good man as one who engages in rational activity in accord with virtue commits him to such a position, and one can find in passages already discussed the distinction between the two kinds of *boulēsis* that such a position requires.

At this stage of the argument I feel I have met the main thrust of my Humean critic's argument, for I have provided an account of the role of reason in the production of motivation that he says is missing.

Admittedly the grounds for attributing the account to Aristotle are not as decisive as one would like. But some passages require such an account and it does seem to be an account that Aristotle could have held. It can no longer be argued that Aristotle left no room for reason to play a role in the acquisition of ends. My argument shows that there is room. Given that this is so, the passages my Humean critic has discounted can no longer be discounted. They also provide evidence that practical reason provides an objective basis for Aristotle's ethics.

However, my Humean critic is not finished. Isn't the textual evidence on which my argument rests too slim? Haven't I taken a few isolated passages and inflated their importance? If one balances these passages against the rest of the text, particularly against those passages in which Aristotle seems to be restricting the role of reason to the discovery of means, the result is at most a tendency that is outweighed in the total picture. Besides, one has to take seriously the possibility that Aristotle had more than one position on practical reason and its relation to ethics.

In response to this objection, I argued that the view I have attributed to Aristotle is not confined to a few isolated passages. A number of passages are puzzling on a Humean interpretation of Aristotle but become intelligible when the view I have attributed to Aristotle is read into them. These include passages in which Aristotle draws extremely close connections between virtue and practical wisdom, passages in which he distinguishes excellence in deliberation from cleverness (NE Bk. VI Ch. 9), and a passage in which he calls attention to that which contributes to a man's ends that depends on the man himself (NE 1114b16-25). The view also fits quite well with Aristotle's remarks on methodology in ethics and politics. Thus, in a number of passages, the account of practical reason that I have attributed to Aristotle, or something very much like it, can be found right below the surface.

Furthermore, the passages that seem to support a Humean view on practical reason can be seen on closer examination not to do so. Given that Aristotle operates with a conception of means that allows a determination of means to be a determination of ends, his claim in NE Bk. III Ch. 3 that deliberation is about means does not support a Humean interpretation of Aristotle. Instead, it provides an additional reason for thinking that reason can play a role in the acquisition of ends. Nor does the passage in which Aristotle says that virtue preserves first principles in ethics (NE 1151a15-19) show that he held a Humean view on practical reason. His claim that virtue preserves first principles should be understood as saying that virtue allows one to have the correct first principles, and this is compatible with the view I have attributed to Aristotle. The claim that first principles are not arrived at by reasoning should be understood as saying that first principles are not arrived at by deductive reasoning, something that suggests that they are arrived at by inductive reasoning. And the admission that natural virtue can provide one with first principles is not incompatible with the view that reason can play a role in the acquisition of ends.

Finally, the passages in which Aristotle says that practical wisdom provides one with the right means and virtue provides one with the right ends (NE Bk. VI Chs. 12 and 13), do not, when properly understood, commit Aristotle to the view that practical wisdom is only concerned with means and virtue is only concerned with ends. Given the way Aristotle distinguishes practical wisdom from other things like it, these passages can be read as saying that practical wisdom and virtue are distinct because virtue always (at least in part) provides one with the right ends but does not always provide one with the right means. Practical wisdom always provides one with the right means. *Natural virtue* provides one with the right ends in a limited number of cases, but it does not provide one with the right means. To have the right ends fully, one must have *virtue in the strict sense,* and this requires the correct exercise of reason (in particular, practical wisdom). Not only is this compatible with the practical wisdom's being concerned with ends, it implies that practical wisdom is concerned with ends. If one adds to this that part of the point of these passages is to mark off virtue as Aristotle understood it from what Aristotle took to be the Socratic view of virtue, one has further grounds for thinking that these passages do not confine the role of practical wisdom to a determination of the right means. The view I have attributed to Aristotle, thus, is not confined to a few isolated passages, and there is no evidence of another, Humean view on practical reason.

The argument, then, is that there is direct textual evidence that Aristotle admitted that practical reason exists and that its scope is sufficient to provide an objective basis for ethics. Direct textual evidence exists that Aristotle acknowledges the way in which reason operates when it allows one to acquire certain ends—it does so inductively. Although there is no direct textual evidence for the specific account of how an inductive inference can lead one to acquire general ends, an account can be supplied on Aristotle's behalf. What Aristotle says requires such an account, and a good deal of indirect evidence suggests that such an account can be found throughout Aristotle. The passages that seem to support a Humean view on practical reason, on closer examination do not really support such a view. In fact, they confirm the kind of view on practical reason that has been attributed to Aristotle. There seems sufficient evidence, then, to assert that the existence of practical reason does provide an objective basis for Aristotle's ethics.

Just what role does reason play in motivation and action on the view I have attributed to Aristotle? And how does it guarantee the existence of practical reason? How does it allow practical reason to provide an objective basis for Aristotle's ethics? And exactly how does it differ from Hume's view of the role that reason plays in motivation and action?

In the first place, reason plays a role in the acquistion of ends. By looking over one's past actions and the actions of others, reason in the form of *nous* can make an inductive inference to what one has been aiming at by nature. This inference (together, perhaps, with what a person has been aiming at by nature) produces a desire for that end. This desire, together with the recognition of the means for integrating the end into one's character, produces a desire for those means. If these desires lead through habituation and training to an integration of the end into one's character, then reason will have played an essential role in the acquisition of an end. Reason alone does not allow a person to acquire general ends. Without the right sort of habituation or training a person would not make a correct inference to what he is by nature aiming at. And without habituation or training, these ends would not be acquired in the sense of being integrated into a person's character. But these ends are not acquired by desire alone either. For there to be a desire for that end, there need not already be a conscious desire for what a person infers he is by nature aiming at. And without recognition of the means for integrating the end into her character, the desire for these means and the adoption of them wouldn't occur. Reason does not produce the end by itself, but without the inductive inference to an end and without the recognition of means for integrating that end into one's character (or their unreflective analogues), the end would never be acquired.[2]

Thus, there *are* certain circumstances in which it is causally necessary that if a person's reason operates correctly she will have certain motivations, the motivations she will have not being necessitated by the circumstances themselves. On the view I have attributed to Aristotle, practical reason, thus, does exist. Furthermore, the conditions needed for practical reason to provide an objective basis for ethics also seem to be satisfied. Reason can play a role in the acquisition of certain ends, and it is not implausible to assume that according to Aristotle man's nature will guarantee the consistency and harmony among the ends that one can acquire to allow practical reason to provide an objective basis for ethics. Perhaps more important, if the ends one would be led to acquire are all parts of *eudaimonia,* then the conditions necessary for practical reason to provide an objective basis for ethics would all be satisfied.

This picture of the role of reason in motivation and action differs sharply from Hume's. On Hume's view, reason only directs and guides already existing passions to their objects. For example, when reason indentifies some distant object as a dog, one is afraid of a dog only because one already has an aversion to dogs. The particular fear of the dog is produced by the already existing aversion, probably through some causal principle of association, and not through the exercise of reason. Similarly, if I stand in line to buy some tickets, my desire to stand in line is a result of an already existing desire for the tickets. Reason's recognition that standing in line is a means for acquiring the tickets only directs this already existing passion toward an appropriate object. The desire to stand in line is produced by the desire for the tickets, again through a causal principle of association. General desires or dispositions are produced by a kind of conditioning or habituation. They are caused, through some principle of association, by particular desires that one either has by nature, or has acquired in one of the two ways mentioned above. On this view, practical reason does not exist. It cannot, therefore, provide a basis for ethics. Even if Hume were to acknowledge the existence of practical reason in reason's guiding already existing desires to their approprate objects, his account of the acquisition of general desires would prevent practical reason from providing a basis for ethics.

Aristotle, thus, did not share Hume's views on practical reason. Unlike Hume's ethics, Aristotle's ethics is based on practical reason.

The Interest of Aristotle's Position on Practical Reason: Happiness and the Good Relative to Human Beings

If I am right in my argument that the existence of practical reason provides an objective basis for Aristotle's ethics, then one would expect that an understanding of his position on practical reason would illuminate a good deal of what he says throughout his ethics. This has already received some confirmation, for I have argued that a number of passages that appear puzzling when one adopts a Humean interpretation become intelligible when the position I have attributed to Aristotle is read into them. In this chapter I want to extend this discussion by showing how an understanding of Aristotle's position on practical reason allows one to solve some of the problems that arise in Aristotle's discussion of happiness and the good in NE Bk. I.[1]

In Bk. I Aristotle tries to provide a starting point for ethics by indicating just what the good relative to human beings *(to anthrōpinon agathon)* is. He argues that it is happiness *(eudaimonia),* and he tries to indicate in outline just what happiness is. His discussion falls into two parts, the first starting at the beginning of Bk. I, and the second starting at 1097b24. In the first part Aristotle takes the good relative to human beings to be in some sense *the* end of action, and he argues that, so considered, happiness is the good. Apparently he doesn't think he has established much, for he says, "Presumably, however, to say that happiness is the chief good seems a platitude, and a clearer account of what it is is still desired," (1094b22-24). This clearer account is given in the second part of Bk. I and arises from tying the good relative to human beings to the function or characteristic activity *(ergon)* of human beings.

I shall consider three problems that arise in connection with these two parts of Bk. I. First, in what sense is happiness *the* end of human action? Second, can the *ergon* of human beings provide a conception of human good that can serve as a starting point for ethics? Finally, can Aristotle's account of human good in terms of the *ergon* of human beings be regarded as a clearer account of the good relative to man begun in the first part of Bk. I? Aristotle's position on practical reason will play a prominent role in the solutions offered to each of these problems. One of the consequences of these solutions will be that some of Aristotle's arguments in Bk. I turn out to be much more plausible than some people have thought they are.

I. Happiness as the end of Action

Aristotle's concern in the first part of Bk. I is to find out what the good relative to human beings is, and, whatever else one says about it, the good relative to human beings is an *end (telos)*—something aimed at or sought. Almost at the outset Aristotle says, "the good has rightly been declared to be that at which all things aim" (1094a2-4). He goes on to say that if there is one thing for the sake of which we do the things we do, this will be the good he is looking for (1094a18-22). He notices that the good seems to be different for different actions and arts, and he asks what the good of each art is. His answer is that it is that for the sake of which everything else in the art is done (1097a15-19). He notices that some ends are chosen for their own sakes, and these he calls final ends. If one final end exists, then this is what he is looking for. If more than one exists, then "the most final" is what he is looking for (1097a24-30). At the beginning of Bk. I, then, Aristotle conceives of the good relative to human beings as an end.

Second, the good relative to human beings is in some sense *the* end of human action. Aristotle says that the good has *rightly* been declared to be that at which all things aim (1094a2-3). Furthermore, Aristotle is not concerned with just anything that might be called good relative to human beings; he is concerned with the *chief* or *supreme* good *(to ariston agathon)* (1094a22-27, 1097a26-31). Again, he says that if more than one final end exists, *the most final* end will be the good relative to human beings. The good relative to human beings then, is in some sense *the* end of human action.

Finally, it is clear that Aristotle is arguing that happiness *(eudaimonia)* is the good relative to human beings, and, thus, that happiness is in some sense *the* end of human action. In Ch. 4 Aristotle says that there is at least verbal agreement as to what the highest good achievable by action is, and that it is happiness. In Ch. 7 he says that the most final good is that which is always sought for its own sake and never for the sake of anything else. Happiness fits this criterion (1097a34-b7), as well as the other criterion Aristotle sets out for the chief good, self-sufficiency *(autarkes)* (1097b7-21). Aristotle concludes the first part of Bk. I by saying that happiness is the good relative to human beings. "Happiness, then, is something final and self-sufficient, and is *the* end of action" (1097a20-21, emphasis mine).

But in what sense is happiness the end of human action? Is Aristotle maintaining that whatever a person does he does with happiness as a conscious aim? Or is it possible not to aim consciously at happiness? If this is possible, then in what sense is happiness *the* end of action? Is it just the most final of all final ends? Is it something that people *should* aim at, because, for example, a good person would aim at it? Is it both of these? Or is there still some sense in which everyone does aim at happiness?[2] One of the reasons that answering these questions is important is that if Aristotle is saying that happiness is aimed at by everyone in all that they do, then it may look as if Aristotle's argument that happiness is the good rests on a simple inference from what people desire to what is good, an inference based on an implicit definition of 'good' as 'object of desire'. However, such an argument does not seem worth taking seriously because, among other things, the definition on which it rests rules out intrinsically bad desires.

It has often been thought that Aristotle does maintain that everyone consciously aims at happiness in all that they do, for it has often been thought that Aristotle *argues* that there is one thing at which all people consciously aim in all that they do when in Bk. I Ch. 2 he says,

> If, then, there is some end of the things we do, which we desire for its own sake (everything else being desired for the sake of this), and if we do not choose everything for the sake of something else (for at that rate the process would go on to infinity, so that our desire would be empty and vain), clearly this must be the good and the chief good. (1094a18-22)

As has been noted many times, if this is what he is arguing, then he is guilty of the fallacious inference from 'Everything desired is desired for the sake of something desired for its own sake' to 'There is something desired for its own sake, for the sake of which everything else is desired'.

However, I think that it is a mistake to take this passage as committing Aristotle to the view that all people consciously pursue one end in all that they do. In the first place, the passage does *not* assert that there is a single end for the sake of which everyone does what he or she does. Rather it says that *if* there is such an end, then it will be the chief good. Second, the passage need not be interpreted as making the fallacious inference from the premise that everything desired is desired for the sake of something desired for its own sake, to the conclusion that there is one thing for the sake of which everything is desired.[3] Finally, even if one can't acquit Aristotle of such a fallacy,[4] I think that one should still treat the passage as one part of a complex argument for the conclusion that happiness is the good, the other part of which is compatible with there being more than one end for the sake of which people do what they do. What Aristotle is then arguing in the first part of Bk. I is that if there is one end for the sake of which everything is done (and he may offer a fallacious argument for thinking that there is), then this is the chief good and the chief good turns out to be happiness. If there is more than one end for the sake of which things are done, then happiness still turns out to be the chief good. Either way, happiness is the good relative to human beings.[5] Since the second part of this argument is compatible with there being more than one end that people aim for in all that they do, the argument as a whole does not commit Aristotle to the existence of one end that people consciously pursue in all they do.

The second part of the argument occurs in Ch. 7 where Aristotle says that if more than one final end exists, the chief good will be the most final, and then goes on to argue that happiness is the most final end. A final end is something desired for its own sake, and, thus, the existence of more than one final end seems to be incompatible with there being one end for the sake of which everything is done. Aristotle does think that there is more than one final end, for in arguing that happiness is the most final end he says,

> but honor, pleasure, reason, and every virtue we choose indeed for themselves (for if nothing resulted from them we should still choose each of them also for the sake of happiness (1097b2-4)[6]

There is, however, a way of reconciling Aristotle's admission of more than one final end with happiness' being the one end for the sake of which everything is done. That is to take happiness as an *inclusive* end, in particular, as the sum total of things desirable for their own sake.[7] When a person does something for the sake of a final end other than happiness, he does it for the sake of something that is part of happiness. Thus, he also does it for the sake of happiness. Each person aims at what he takes happiness to be, his conception of happiness being constituted by what he aims at for its own sake. That is why, for example, Aristotle says in Ch. 4 that there is verbal agreement over what the highest good is. Everyone says that it is happiness, but different people identify happiness with different things. Each person aims at the sum total of things desirable in themselves, but each person gives a different account of what these things are.

However, this reconciliation will go through only if the content of this shared end is exhausted by something like "the sum total of things desirable in themselves." Aristotle's recognition that verbal agreement exists as to what the chief good is is also a recognition that there may be at most verbal agreements as to what the chief good is. That people give different accounts of happiness is as much evidence that people do *not* aim at a single end in all that they do, as their verbal agreement as to what the chief good is is evidence that they are all aiming at a single end. If one person identifies happiness with wealth and another does not, then even though each person may be aiming at something that she or he calls happiness, there is a clear sense in which each person is not aiming at the same thing. The only way to avoid this conclusion is to divorce happiness from any specific content that might be attached to it, treating its content as exhausted by something like "the sum total of things desirable for their own sake." But, then, not only does it not follow from the fact that a person does something for the sake of a final end that he or she does it for the sake of happiness, to say that everyone does what he or she does for the sake of this end is incompatible with what Aristotle says elsewhere. On the whole, it seems preferable *not* to take Aristotle's argument in the first part of Bk. I as an argument that one end exists for the sake of which all people do what they do.

When a person acts for the sake of something desired for its own sake, it doesn't follow that she also acts for the sake of happiness, even if her conception of happiness includes just what it is that she desires for its own sake. The person may act on impulse, without any thought about how what she does fits within some larger, inclusive end.

In the second place, if one is to operate with a plausible conception of happiness, happiness should not be understood as just "the sum total of things desirable for their own sake." There is no guarantee that everything that a person desires for its own sake will fit within a life that is possible for him to live. His final ends may conflict with one another. He will at least want a conception of happiness that allows him to resolve such conflicts. He may also attach different degrees of importance to his final ends, preferring that some be given greater attention in his life than others. In short, a plausible conception of happiness will have to be something like "*the best arrangement* of things desirable for their own sake." But then it is clear that a person who acts for the sake of some final end will not always do what he does for the sake of happiness. Not only are occasional impulsive actions possible, there may be people who don't act from any such complex plan of life. They "take things as they come," "living one day at a time." Even if a person often does act from a conception of such an ordered life, there is no guarantee that he will always be able to fit his actions within such a conception. His conception of this ordered life may not be determinate enough for him to see whether a given action fits with it, and even if it is determinate enough his action still may not fit with it. He may in fact act incontinently.[8]

Indeed, Aristotle seems to recognize that a person may fail to act from such a conception of an ordered life when in the *Eudemian Ethics* he says,

> Everyone who has the power to live according to his own choice should dwell on these points and set up for himself some object for the good life to aim at, whether honour or reputation or wealth or culture, by reference to which he will do all that he does, since not to have one's life organized in view of some end is a sign of great folly. (EE1214bff)[9]

What Aristotle says implies that there are some whose life is so organized that they do *not* aim at one thing in all that they do. Not only are there those whose lives exhibit folly because they are not so organized, unless it were possible for a life not to be ordered according to a single end, his injunction to people to so order their lives would have no point.

Aristotle's account of incontinence is also incompatible with there being a single end for the sake of which everything is done. (This should not be surprising, since, as we have seen, incontinence is incompatible with the existence of such an end.) The incontinent person is one who in some sense knows what is good but does not pursue it (1145b12-13). That person has the right first principles, but because of passion does not act on them (1151a20-26, 1152a20-24). Since the incontinent person knows what is good, but, when he or she is acting incontinently, does not pursue it, the incontinent person must pursue something other than the good when acting incontinently.[10] Again, it seems that Aristotle would acknowledge that people do not always do what they do for the sake of the same single end.

Finally, taking everyone always to be aiming at happiness by restricting the content of happiness to "the sum total of things good in themselves" or "the best arrangement of things desirable for their own sake" is at odds with the general task Aristotle sets for himself in Bk. I. Immediately following the Ch. 2 passage in which Aristotle has been thought to argue for a single end for the sake of which everything is done, Aristotle says,

> Will not the knowledge of it, then, have a great influence on life? Shall we
> not, like archers who have a mark to aim at, be more likely to hit upon
> what is right? If so, we must try, in outline at least, to determine what it is,
> and of which of the sciences or capacities it is the object. (109a22-27)

If what guarantees that happiness is the end pursued in everything
that is done is its lack of specific content, then how can it serve as a
mark, knowledge of which will have a great influence on life? If it is
to be such a mark, it must have some specific content. (This seems
borne out by Aristotle's dissatisfaction at 1097b22-24 with the
account of the good relative to human beings that he has given so far.
What he hasn't done is provide any real content to happiness.) But
once it is given some specific content, there will always be someone
who does not do what he or she does for the sake of this end.[11] Indeed, if all people *consciously* aimed at the good in all that they did,
there would seem to be no need for the kind of inquiry Aristotle
undertakes—indicating in outline what the good is. If people already
are consciously aiming at it, it looks as if they would already know,
at least in outline, what it is that they are aiming at.[12]

All in all it seems preferable to take Aristotle in the first part of
Bk. I to be offering a complex argument for happiness' being the
good, the second part of which is incompatible with there being one
end that people consciously aim at in all that they do. Happiness,
then, is not the end of human action in the sense that everyone
consciously aims at in all that he or she does.

But in what sense then is it *the* end of human action? Is it just that
it is the most final of all final ends? Is it that it is the end that everyone should aim at because, for example, the good person would aim
at it? Or is something more involved? At 1101b36-1102a3 Aristotle
says,

> to us it is clear from what has been said that happiness is among the things
> that are prized and perfect. It seems to be so also from the fact that it is a
> first principle; for it is for the sake of this that we do all that we do.

Unless 'we' here means 'those of us who have been brought up well
and can profit from the study of ethics', what Aristotle says implies
that there is a sense in which everyone aims at happiness. But given
what has been argued above, how can this be?

The position on practical reason that I have attributed to Aristotle
provides an answer to these questions. There is something that all
people aim at by nature, the good relative to man, even though not
all people consciously aim at it in all that they do. Some people only
consciously aim at the apparent good. However, just as one with a
discerning eye can see that a twisted and gnarled tree is in its twists
and turns striving to be straight and tall, so one with a discerning eye

can see that in a person's striving for whatever final ends that he does pursue, he is really striving after the good. If happiness is what people aim at by nature, then happiness can be something that everyone aims at without its being something that all people consciously aim at in all that they do. Second, the position I have attributed to Aristotle allows one to understand better how it is that happiness is something that people *should* aim at. On the view I have attributed to Aristotle what a person aims at by nature is what a person would consciously aim at if reason were operating correctly in that person. Since according to Aristotle a good person is one in whom reason does operate correctly with respect to practical matters, happiness will turn out to be an end that a good person would have, and in this sense it will be an end that people should aim at.

One important consequence of looking at Aristotle in this way is that it strengthens some of his arguments that happiness is the good relative to human beings. For example, on this way of understanding the good as the end of human action, one does not have to read Aristotle as making a simple, direct inference from what people desire to what is good. Nor does one have to take his arguments as resting on a definition of 'good' as 'object of desire', a definition that doesn't allow for intrinsically bad desires. On the view I have attributed to Aristotle, he is not arguing that happiness is the good simply because everyone desires it, or simply because it is the one thing desired for its own sake and not for the sake of anything else. Rather, he is saying that the relation between the actual desires of people and happiness provides an indication that happiness is what people are aiming at by nature. To put the point another way, that, for example, happiness is sought for its own sake and never for the sake of anything else is an indication that this is what a person would always aim at if his or her desires were rational. If there is any implicit definition of 'good' behind Aristotle's arguments it is that the good is what a person would desire if his or her desires were rational, or that the good is what a good person would desire, where the good person is one who possesses *phronēsis*, the virtue of reason in its practical employment.

Thus, not only does the view I have attributed to Aristotle provide a way of understanding how happiness is the end of human action, but taking Aristotle to be arguing on the basis of such a view strengthens some of his arguments in Bk. I.[13]

II. The Good as Fulfilling the *Ergon* of Human Beings Well

As I have already indicated, Aristotle does not think that he has established much when he concludes in the middle of Ch. 7 that happiness is the good. He says that a clearer account of what it is is needed.

> This might perhaps be given, if we could first ascertain the function (*ergon*) of man. For just as for a flute-player, a sculptor, or any artist, and, in general, for all things that have a function or activity, the good and the 'well' is thought to reside in the function, so would it seem to be for man, if he has a function. (1097b24-29)

The term 'function' is a slightly misleading translation of *'ergon'*, being tied as it is to artifacts that are specifically designed for certain ends, or to persons insofar as they adopt certain well-defined roles. So understood, it may look as if human beings don't have an *ergon*. However, *'ergon'* has a much broader use than does 'function', and it might be better to translate it as 'characteristic activity' rather than as 'function' (as Kenny [1965-66] suggests, p. 96). As I understand Aristotle's use of *'ergon'*, a thing has an *ergon* if to *be* that thing is to be capable of a certain characteristic activity. A knife has an *ergon*, since to be a knife is to be capable of cutting. Similarly, a shoemaker has an *ergon*, since to be a shoemaker is to be capable of making shoes. A human being also has an *ergon* according to Aristotle, since to be a human being is to be capable of rational activity. It is this activity that is characteristic of human beings, marking them off from other living things (1097b33-34).

Aristotle concludes from rational activity's being the *ergon* of human beings that human good is rational activity in accord with virtue.

> Now if the function of man is an activity of soul which follows or implies a rational principle, and if we say 'a so-and-so' and 'a good so-and-so' have a function which is the same in kind, e.g. a lyre-player and a good lyre-player, and so without qualification in all cases, eminence in respect of goodness being added to the name of the function (for the function of a lyre-player is to play the lyre and that of a good lyre-player is to do so well): if this is the case . . . human good turns out to be activity of the soul in accordance with virtue, and if there are more than one virtue, in accordance with the best and most complete. (1098a7-18)

What lies behind Aristotle's conclusion is a certain general connection that holds between 'good' and *'ergon'*. If to be an X is to be capable of engaging in a certain activity, then a good X will be one that engages in that characteristic activity *well*. Since the virtue of a thing is that which enables it to be a good thing of its kind, a good X will be one that engages in its *ergon* in accord with virtue. If rational activity is the *ergon* of human beings then a good human being will be one who engages in rational activity in accord with virtue. Thus, Aristotle concludes that the good relative to human beings, happiness, is rational activity in accord with virtue.

At least two criticisms can be raised against this account of happiness as the good relative to human beings. Both of them can be found in Siegler (1967). The first is that Aristotle has not successfully connected man's *ergon* with a notion of good that can serve as a starting point for ethics. But providing such a starting point is just what Aristotle's discussion of happiness in Bk. I is supposed to do. Second, although the argument based on man's *ergon* may set out one notion of good associated with man, it is not the notion that Aristotle was talking about in the first part of Bk. I. It cannot, therefore, be a clearer account of what Aristotle was discussing there. I shall take up the first of these criticisms in this section, and I shall argue that the position on practical reason that I have attributed to Aristotle provides a defense against it. I shall take up the second criticism in the next section.

That Aristotle's position on practical reason provides him with a defense against the first criticism can be seen once the criticism is set out in some detail. The first thing to be said in raising this criticism is that there is no *general* connection between a thing's *ergon* and anything like moral goodness. A good X will be an X that fulfills its *ergon* well, but terms for a large number of things can replace the variable 'X' in this formula, including 'knife', 'typewriter', 'blackjack', 'carpenter', 'shoemaker', 'thief', and 'man'. A good shoemaker need not be morally praiseworthy. Almost certainly a good thief will not be morally praiseworthy. A good blackjack is likely not to be used for moral purposes. As Siegler puts it, "A harpist *qua* harpist is praised for performing his function well. There is nothing morally praiseworthy about that." ([1967], p. 42)

One might object that since Aristotle draws no distinction setween the moral and nonmoral, this lack of connection between *ergon* and moral goodness is beside the point. Nevertheless, the general point can still be made. Whatever the notion of good is that Aristotle is trying to base on the *ergon* of human beings it must be something that can provide a basis for ethics. It must have some connection with the kind of life a person should lead, or with the kind of person who is a fit subject of praise and whom others should pattern their lives after. *In general* no connection can be made between a thing's *ergon* and any such notion of good. If any relevance for ethics inheres in the notion of a good X, it will have to arise in connection with certain values of the variable 'X', e.g., human being.

This may come as no surprise, for ethics does not seem to be concerned with what is good relative to any chance role that a person might play. It is concerned with what it is to be good *qua man*. Although a good harpist may not be someone whose life can be a guide to the life one ought to lead, the life of one who is good *qua man* can be such a guide. However, Siegler says,

> But man *qua* man can be praised on two separate (though perhaps related) ac-
> counts. He can be praised for performing his function well. That is by no
> means moral praise. And he can be praised for performing his function well
> for morally praiseworthy ends or aims. And as I have suggested, it may be
> a necessary condition for moral praise that a man be able to reason well
> about his aims, but that is not sufficient. He must have the right aims. And
> having the right aim is unfortunately not any more peculiar to human
> beings than having the wrong aims. ([1967], p. 42)

Whether what it is to be good *qua* man can provide a starting point
for ethics depends on just what man's *ergon* is. Of course, man's
ergon is rational activity, but how are we to understand 'rational
activity'? Siegler takes it to be that which is involved in acting from
reasons. And he says that there are two senses of 'acting from reasons', a neutral sense and a nonneutral sense. The neutral sense does
not presuppose any particular ends that a person might have. The
nonneutral sense presupposes that a person has the right ends. According to Siegler, it is the neutral sense of 'acting from reasons'
that is peculiar to human beings and makes up their *ergon*.

> For what is peculiar to human beings, we agreed, is acting on reasons or for
> the sake of reasons, but not in the sense of having the right reasons, or the
> right ends in view. Although it does seem to be peculiarly human to help a
> lady because she is in need, an action for the sake of a reason, it is, unfor-
> tunately, no less peculiarly human to shoot a lady because she is a bore, an
> action for the sake of a reason. Acting for the sake of reasons is perhaps
> peculiar to human beings, but it is no more or less peculiar to human be-
> ings to act with the right reasons or for the right ends than it is to act for
> unjustifiable reasons or for the wrong ends. ([1967], p. 38)

Given this picture of what the *ergon* of human beings is, it doesn't
follow that the life of a man who fulfills his *ergon* well is a life worth
emulating.

> since it is the peculiar function or ability of man to act on reasons, it would
> follow that a man who was skilled or had a high standard in that particular
> function is a man highly skilled in reasoning; he is a man who deliberates
> carefully, plans with precision, and organizes his activities so that he can
> achieve his aims, whatever they may be. But of course, from this it does not
> follow that a man who performs in accordance with the function of man
> (reasoning) is *eo ipso* a morally praiseworthy man. Acting on reasons or hav-
> ing reasons for one's actions may be a necessary condition for moral worth
> and being a *skillful* reasoner may be a necessary condition for moral worth.
> But neither of these conditions is sufficient for moral worth since a clever
> bank robber has reasons carefully designed for his aims. ([1967], p. 40)

There is also a sense in which one who acts from reasons well does
lead a life worth emulating. This is the nonneutral sense of 'acting

from reasons', in which one who acts from reasons well has deliberated carefully and efficiently about the right ends. But this sense of 'acting from reasons' is not what is characteristic of human beings. Confining the *ergon* of human beings to the kind of rational activity that is characteristic of them, the *ergon* of human beings does not provide a conception of goodness that can serve as the starting point for ethics.

Having set the criticism out in this much detail, it should be obvious how Aristotle's position on practical reason provides a defense against it. The criticism rests on a conception of rational activity that is limited to deliberation about means to already existing ends. Given that it is only this deliberative ability that is peculiar to human beings, the only notion of goodness derivable from the *ergon* of human beings will be cleverness, and Aristotle would be the first to admit that cleverness by itself cannot provide an adequate starting point for ethics. However, on the view I have attributed to Aristotle, reason plays a role in the acquisition of ends as well as in deliberation about means. If *this* kind of rational activity has been engaged in well, a person will have the right ends as well as having deliberated carefully and efficiently about means. A person who deliberates well about the right ends does seem to be one whose life can be a guide to the life one ought to lead. If Aristotle's position on practical reason is taken into account when one spells out the kind of rational activity involved in the *ergon* of human beings, it looks as if the *ergon* of human beings would provide a conception of goodness that could provide a starting point for ethics.

It is important to distinguish the account of rational activity that I have said is included in the *ergon* of human beings from Siegler's non-neutral sense of 'acting from reasons'. According to Siegler, if one takes the *ergon* of human beings to involve reasoning with regard to the *right* ends, then reasoning well will be morally praiseworthy. But acting from reasons in this sense will not be peculiar to human beings and cannot serve as their *ergon*. I have said that the rational activity involved in the *ergon* of human beings includes something that allows a person to acquire ends. But I have *not* said that if one engages in this kind of rational activity one will necessarily have the right ends. This kind of rational activity can go on when one acquires any sort of end, right or wrong. Since acquiring ends through reason and reasoning about how to secure them is as peculiar to human beings as is simply reasoning about how to secure one's ends, this kind of rational activity *can* serve as the *ergon* of human beings. But since engaging in this kind of reasoning *well* allows one to have the right ends, fulfilling the *ergon* of human beings well in this sense of reasoning does seem to provide one with a conception of something like moral goodness.

There is another important difference between Aristotle's argument from the *ergon* of human beings when it is interpreted as involving Siegler's nonneutral sense of rational activity and when it is interpreted in the way I have suggested. Taking the rational activity involved in the *ergon* of human beings to be reasoning with regard to the right ends, the argument appears to be trivial and uninformative, if not circular. (See Siegler for example, [1967], p. 38.) If one takes the *ergon* of human beings to be reasoning with regard to the right ends, moral goodness, or something very much like it will have been built into the *ergon* of human beings, for having the right ends is close to, if not identical with, being morally praiseworthy. It will not be surprising or very interesting, if it turns out that fulfilling the *ergon* of human beings well is morally praiseworthy. If having the right ends is close to if not identical with moral praiseworthiness, then one who is interested in knowing just what it is to be praiseworthy will not have been told much when one is told that it is fulfilling the *ergon* of human beings well. Part of what such a person wants to know is just what the conditions are under which a person has the right ends. Nothing will have been said about what these conditions are, if the *ergon* of human beings is understood in Siegler's nonneutral sense of rational activity.

No such charge of triviality can be leveled at the argument on the interpretation I have suggested. On this interpretation, the *ergon* of human beings includes reasoning about ends as well as deliberation about means, but it does not imply that when one is reasoning about ends, one is reasoning about the right ends. As a result, the conclusion that fulfilling the *ergon* of human beings is morally praiseworthy is not already contained in the premise that the *ergon* of human beings is rational activity. Furthermore, it *can* be informative to one who is interested in just what praiseworthiness is to be told that fulfilling the *ergon* of human beings well is praiseworthy. Of course, one is not told much about what the right ends are by being told that they are the ends one will have when one reasons toward an end well; but if one is armed with an account of just what goes on in such reasoning, one will be in a position to at least begin to see what ends one will acquire when this reasoning is engaged in well. It was just such an account that was sketched in Chapter 3 Section IV.

Again, if one looks at one of Aristotle's arguments in Bk. I with his position on practical reason in mind, the arguments turn out to be ones that deserve to be taken more seriously than one might at first have thought.

III. The Good for Human Beings and the Good Human Being: Their Connection

I now want to turn to the second criticism mentioned in the last section—that Aristotle's attempt to base an account of the good on the *ergon* of human beings cannot be a clearer account of the notion of the good discussed in the first part of Bk. I. Again, I think Aristotle's position on practical reason provides him with a defense against this criticism.

In the first part of Bk. I, the good relative to human beings is thought of as something to be desired, sought, or aimed at. It is an *end* of human action, and this end is said to be happiness (*eudaimonia*). A person has acquired *eudaimonia* when, among other things, he or she is "well off." In this sense, the good relative to human beings includes what is of benefit to human beings; it can be thought of as involving what is "good *for* human beings." In the second part of Bk. I the notion of the good relative to human beings seems to be a quite different one. The kind of goodness associated with a thing's *ergon* is what makes a thing a good thing. Applied to human beings, it is that which makes a person a *good human being*, something that makes him or her a fitting subject of praise. But the notion of goodness involved in what is *good for human beings* is not the same notion involved in what it is to be a *good human being*. Not only are the notions distinct, there is as yet no reason for thinking that when a person has acquired one, he or she has acquired the other.

In the first place, there is no *general* guarantee that when an X acquires that which makes it a *good X* it has also acquired what is *good for an X*. In fact, there are some cases in which one can talk about a good X but it seems to make no sense to talk about what is good for an X. Nor is it obvious that one can move from what makes an X a good X to what is good for an X in the special case of human beings. Fulfilling the *ergon* of human beings well may make a person morally praiseworthy, but is moral praiseworthiness good *for* a person? Will a person have benefitted simply by becoming a praiseworthy person? It is not at all obvious that one will. Until Aristotle says something to show that one will, it looks as if he would not be entitled to claim that his discussion of the good relative to human beings in the second part of Bk. I provides a clearer account of the notion of the good discussed in the first part of Bk. I.[14]

The point can be put more generally. However else one understands *eudaimonia*, it is clear that in the first part of Bk. I, it is an object of desire or interested activity, an *end* of action. Furthermore, it is a *final* end, something sought for its own sake. Unless Aristotle can show that a life in which one fulfills one *ergon* well is something to be sought and sought for its own sake, then he is not entitled to say that the account of the good relative to human beings developed in the second part of Bk. I is an elucidation of the account discussed in the first part. As much as one would like to say that the life of a good person should be sought for its own sake, it is not at all obvious that this is so. Is, for example, the life of a praiseworthy person something to be aimed at for its own sake, or is it something to be sought only for the benefits it has for others?[15] Unless Aristotle has an answer to questions like this, he is not entitled to say that he has given an elucidation of the notion of the good relative to human beings with which he began Bk. I. The most one can say is that he ends up giving a different starting point for ethics from the one he started with.

One might be tempted to grant that Aristotle brings in a new notion of good at 1097b24, for one might think that at this point Aristotle *is* making a fresh start in his discussion of the good relative to human beings. When he says that happiness' being the good is a "platitude" or "truism" *(homologoumenon)*, what he is saying is that it is an empty tautology. Trying to find the good relative to human beings by looking at the ends of action simply has not turned up anything that can serve as a starting point for ethics. What is needed is a fresh start, and the *ergon* of human beings provides the basis for such a fresh start.

As tempting as this defense may be, it is mistaken. Evidence exists that Aristotle did take his account of good based on the *ergon* of human beings to be an elucidation of the notion of good discussed in the first part of Bk. I. In Ch. 8, Aristotle argues that his account of human good based on the *ergon* of human beings fits with what has been said about the good.

> The characteristics that are looked for in happiness seem also, all of them, to belong to what we have defined happiness as being. For some identify happiness with virtue, some with practical wisdom, others with a kind of philosophic wisdom, others with these, or one of these, accompanied by pleasure or not without pleasure; while others include also external prosperity. Now some of these views have been held by many men of old, others by a few eminent persons; and it is not probable that either of these should be entirely mistaken, but rather that they should be right in at least some respect or even in most respects. (1098b22-29)

Prominent among these views are ones which Aristotle set out in the first part of Bk. I as candidates for the end of human action—pleasure, wealth, honor, virtue, and the contemplative life. All of these (except for the contemplative life) are discussed in Ch. 8 and are argued to be necessary conditions or concomitants of a life of rational activity in accord with virtue.[16] Given that Aristotle is arguing that his own conception of happiness based on the *ergon* of human beings fits with what has been said about happiness taken as the end of human action, I think it is clear that he takes his own conception of happiness to be the correct account of happiness considered as the end of human action. His own view is supposed to capture the whole truth that these views capture only in part. He does think that he is elucidating the notion of good that he discussed in the first part of Bk. I.

But if this is so, isn't he just mistaken? The two notions of good are different notions. Unless Aristotle can show that a life of rational activity in accord with virtue is the end of human action in the way that happiness is thought to be the end of human action, he will have illegitimately changed the subject when he says that human good is fulfilling the *ergon* of human beings well. But can he show this? In what sense does or should anyone aim at rational activity in accord with virtue and aim at it for its own sake?[17]

There is a general connection that seems to hold between desire and a good X that at first sight one might think can be exploited to answer the above questions. If a thing of a certain sort X has an *ergon* (if to be an X is to be capable of engaging in a certain characteristic activity), then it seems to be true if it is an X that one wants, one will want a good X, one that engages in that characteristic activity well. If to be a knife is to be something that can cut, then if it is a knife that one wants, it looks as if one would want not only something that cuts, but something that cuts well. Similarly, if being a shoemaker is what one wants, then it looks as if one would want to be a good shoemaker. Applying this to the case of human beings, if one wants to be a human being, then one will want to be a good human being, that is, one who engages in rational activity in accord with virtue. If Aristotle could show that people do or should want to be human beings, then it looks as if he could argue that people do or should want to be good human beings, thus connecting his two accounts of the good relative to human beings.

Initially it may seem that Aristotle can use the special relationship that holds between any particular human being and what it is to be a human being, to argue that any person must want to be a human being. According to Aristotle, being human is the *essence* of any particular human being. A human being cannot cease to be human and still be. Since this is so, it may appear that one cannot want not to be a human being. Such a desire would seem to amount to wanting to be and yet not be human, something that is impossible. Since one cannot want not to be a human being, it may appear that one must want to be a human being. And if this is so, then it looks as if one must also want to be a good human being.

A little reflection will reveal, however, that this won't work. In the first place, one can want not to be a human being even if it is one's essence to be human. Such a desire is or involves the desire not to be, and people can want not to be. Second, it doesn't follow from the fact that one can't want not to be a human being that one must want to be a human being. If wanting not to be a human being is beyond the possibility of desire, then wanting to be a human being would also seem to be beyond the possibility of desire. The general connection between desire and a good X does not guarantee a motive for being a good human being, thus it can't be used to connect Aristotle's two discussions of the good relative to human beings.[18] How then can the two discussions be connected?

What is needed to connect these two discussions depends on just what Aristotle is saying in the first part of Bk. I when he says that happiness is the end of human action. If he is saying that happiness is something that all people consciously aim at in all that they do, then to connect the two discussions it looks as if Aristotle will have to show that all people consciously aim at rational activity in accord with virtue in all that they do. This seems to be a difficult if not impossible task. However, I argued in Section I of this chapter that Aristotle takes happiness to be the end of human action only in the sense that happiness is what people aim at by nature. It is what people would aim at if their desires were all rational. If this is correct, then Aristotle's task is a more manageable one. What he has to show is that rational activity in accord with virtue is what people would aim at if their desires were rational.

At the outset it may seem trivially true that what a person aims at by nature is rational activity in accord with virtue. Indeed, it seems to be a tautology that rational activity in accord with virtue would be the object of rational desire. Given the position on practical reason that I have attributed to Aristotle, what reason apprehends and allows one to acquire as an end is just what a person aims at by nature. These ends, whatever they are, are the objects of rational as opposed to irrational desire. A life of rational activity in accord with virtue, then, will be a life lived with these ends as one's conscious ends together with the ability to secure them. That is, a life of rational activity in accord with virtue would be one in which one pursued and secured, to the extent that one was capable of securing, those ends which one aims at by nature. Surely, one might think, this sort of life *is* what one aims at by nature. How could rational desire *not* have the good performance of rational activity as its object?

As tempting as this line of argument may be, it is not enough to secure the connection between the two accounts of human good that Aristotle needs. All that follows from it is that if one lives a life of rational activity in accord with virtue, one will aim at and secure, to the extent possible, what one aims at by nature. But it doesn't follow from this argument that rational activity in accord with virtue is *in itself* something that one aims at by nature. Since it is something that allows one to secure what one aims at by nature, it would be rational to desire it as a means to those ends, but the good relative to human beings is supposed to be a final good, something sought for its own sake. In particular, if there were other means for securing one's natural aims, for example, a combination of natural virtue and a good fortune, one might argue that such a combination would be preferable to rational activity in accord with virtue, if only because it requires less discipline and training and thus would be less troublesome. What needs to be seen is not that rational activity in accord with virtue allows one to secure what one aims at by nature. Rational activity in accord with virtue must itself be something one aims at by nature.

There are, I think, a number of things Aristotle could say to support the claim that rational activity in accord with virtue is itself something one aims at by nature. First, he could point out that means are sometimes inseparable from their ends. He could argue that rational activity in accord with virtue is inseparable from the ends one has by nature. Second, he could argue that there is no other way of securing what one aims at by nature. Natural virtue cannot itself guarantee that one will always act in accord with one's natural ends, nor can one rely on good fortune to occur. As Aristotle says of natural virtues, "one may be led astray by them, as a strong body which moves without sight may stumble badly because of its lack of sight" (NE 1144b11-13). Only virtue in the strict sense will guarantee action in accord with one's natural aims, and this requires *phronēsis,* the virtue of practical reason. Finally, Aristotle could argue that what one aims at by nature are not just ends that might be achieved in any old way. Part of what one aims at is a certain kind of control over one's life, *self*-control. What one wants is that one's ends be achieved by oneself.[19] This kind of self-control is possible only through rational activity. If pressed to justify this, Aristotle could fall back on what I think all of the previous replies would lead to eventually, looking at the actions of oneself and others to see just what people really are aiming at. What people really want is a life in which the guidance of their actions by reason plays a central role. *If* this is so, then Aristotle is entitled to say that the life of a good human being is something that people aim at by nature. It is something which one would desire for its own sake if one's desires were rational. To the extent that securing what one aims at by nature makes one "well off," it is also something that will be good *for* human beings. Read in the light of his position on practical reason, Aristotle's account of human good based on the *ergon* of human beings can be taken as a further elucidation of the good relative to human beings that he discussed in the first part of Bk. I.[20]

Thus, an understanding of Aristotle's position on practical reason not only provides a better understanding of Aristotle's arguments in Bk. I, it also shows that they deserve more serious attention than they otherwise might be thought to deserve.

Does Aristotle's Position on Practical Reason Provide an Adequate Basis for Ethics?

Aristotle's position on practical reason is of interest not only for the illumination of parts of his ethics, but also for its bearing on contemporary issues in ethics. Although there are a number of topics on which Aristotle's position has some bearing,[1] its primary interest, I think, is the contribution it makes to the problem outlined in the Introduction. There is an apparent tension between two sides of morality—its "practical" side and its objectivity. This tension would disappear if ethics had a basis in practical reason. In the Introduction I suggested that one will make little progress in trying to discover whether practical reason can provide a basis for ethics if one simply tackles this question in general. What are needed are specific examples of views according to which practical reason exists and its existence seems to provide a basis for ethics. The view I have attributed to Aristotle is an example of such a view, and as such, it seems to deserve to be taken seriously and explored further. In this chapter, I shall consider some obvious objections that might be raised against it and see what might be said in its defense. Even though I am inclined to think that one of these objections does show that Aristotle's position *by itself* cannot provide an adequate basis for ethics, I do not think that this robs Aristotle's position of its interest. I shall argue that even if this objection holds, any adequate attempt to base ethics on practical reason will have to include something like Aristotle's position as a part of it. Although all of the issues raised in the chapter cannot be discussed here in the detail they deserve, I hope that what I say is sufficient to show that the position I have attributed to Aristotle deserves to be taken seriously.

I. Initial Objections

At least three objections might initially be raised against Aristotle's position, as I have set it out. First, it is too indeterminate for one to know whether or not it should be taken seriously. Second, it rests on a teleological conception of nature that has rightfully been discarded. Finally, basing ethics on it constitutes a form of naturalism that can easily be seen to be mistaken.

As I have set out Aristotle's position, there is as yet no indication of any particular end that people are supposed to aim at by nature. One might argue that unless one knows what these ends are supposed to be, not only will one be unable to say whether people do aim at these ends by nature, one will be unable to say whether people aim at anything by nature. If one can't even say that there are things that people aim at by nature, then one is not in a position to take Aristotle's position seriously. I admit that not enough has been said about Aristotle's position to determine what ends people are supposed to aim at by nature; and I admit that until this is done it will be open to question whether there are any ends that people aim at by nature. But, I think, to dismiss Aristotle's position has a bearing on the problem mentioned above is enough reason to try to fill in the details of the position to see whether it does hold or not. Besides, if the details of the ethical theory that rests on it turn out to be anything like Aristotle's own position, this would be enough to show that the position merits attention.

Still, one might argue, some features of Aristotle's position show that it needn't be taken seriously. For example, it rests on a teleological conception of nature that is no longer reasonable to accept. One might think that people by nature aim at something if one thinks that every living organism has some purpose or end that is its nature to pursue. But if anything has been learned in the history of science, it is that there are no such ends. Trees don't grow straight and tall to achieve some end, and the twists and turns of a gnarled tree are not properly viewed as attempts to achieve the end of a tree. The twists and turns of a tree can be perfectly well understood in terms of the way plants react to sunlight without bringing in some end that it is trying to achieve. If one rejects this teleological picture of nature, it looks as if one would have to reject the whole basis of Aristotle's position on practical reason.

It is true that as I have sketched Aristotle's position it does rest on such a teleographical picture of nature, but it is not necessary for a position like Aristotle's to rest on such a teleogical view.[2] All that is needed is that there be something that people aim at by nature in the sense that this be something that everyone "really wants," such that a large part of people's lives can be understood as an attempt to understand just what it is and to acquire it. It is possible for this to be true of an organism like man, whose life can be and is determined by the way he brings reason to bear on what he does and wants, without its being true of every other living organism. Of course, there is no guarantee that something exists that everyone "really wants," in terms of which one can understand a large number of people's actions. But there should be no guarantee. If the view I have attributed to Aristotle makes a substantive claim about human beings' having a natural end, then it should be a claim that could turn out to be false. The most natural way to find out whether it is true or false is to try to make the kind of inductive inference in Aristotle's position. Look at one's own life and the lives of others to see whether there isn't something that oneself and everyone else "really wants." (Or, perhaps, look at what psychologists have said about the existence of basic needs or wants in terms of which human action can be understood and explained.) If this procedure does turn up some common ends in terms of which one can explain a large number of actions of human beings, then it looks as if people would aim at something by nature. If it does not turn up such ends, then it looks as if Aristotle's position would not hold. Either way, though, one will not have to assume a teleological picture of nature.[3]

However, if one separates Aristotle's position on practical reason from his teleological view of nature, one is faced with another problem.[4] On Aristotle's view of nature, each species has its own end, so that if one is trying to find the natural end of a given organism, one already has a limit on the relevant sample that one will look at. One will confine one's attention to members of the same species. However, if only some organisms can be said to have natural ends, how does one determine the relevant sample over which to perform the inductive inference? It will make a difference which sample one looks at. If one draws the sample wide enough to include animals other than human beings, it may turn out either that there are no ends that all such animals pursue, or, if there are, they are things like very simple or basic pleasures. A life dedicated to the pursuit of these sorts of ends is a far cry from the life controlled by reason suggested at the end of the last chapter. Unless one has a nonarbitrary way of limiting the sample on which the induction is to be performed, it looks as if one won't have sufficient grounds for the claim that ends exist that people aim at by nature, let alone the kinds of ends that might be thought to provide a suitable basis for ethics.

This problem is not insurmountable. If, as I have suggested, what makes it plausible to talk about a natural end in the case of human beings is their capacity to bring reason to bear on what one does and wants, then one can use the presence of this capacity as a non-arbitrary way of limiting the sample on which the induction is to be performed. Or, one might argue that it only makes sense to talk about a natural end if the organism in question is capable of being aware of its pursuit of that end. One could, thus, use the capacity for self-consciousness of what one is aiming at as a way of limiting the relevant sample. Either one of these provides a possible solution to the problem just raised.

One might object that the use of these criteria for limiting the relevant sample will be circular. At least in the case of the first one, applying it assumes that people's desires, wants, and actions are under the control of reason in the way they would be if practical reasons were to exist. But it is the existence of practical reason that is at issue. However, this apparent circularity is only apparent. One needn't assume the very capacity involved in the exercise of practical reason to provide a nonarbitrary way of limiting the relevant sample. It is arguable that an organism has the capacity to bring reason to bear on its actions and desires that makes it possible to talk about a natural end only if it is capable of deliberation about means to ends. This capacity can be used to mark off the sample for induction in a nonarbitrary way. It does not imply the existence of practical reason in the relevant respect.[5] Furthermore, even if one did assume the existence of that capacity involved in practical reason and then restricted the sample to those organisms that seem to display that capacity, the argument in support of the Aristotelian question would still not beg the question at issue. It would beg the question if this assumption guaranteed Aristotle's position on practical reason as a conclusion of the argument. But there is no such guarantee. The only role the assumption plays is to limit the relevant sample for induction. Given such a limitation, there is still no guarantee that on the basis of such an induction one will discover any common ends in terms of which people's actions can be explained. As a result, I think that there is no serious problem in limiting the relevant sample for the kind of induction that might be used to see whether Aristotle's position holds or not.

Finally, one might object that Aristotle's position constitutes a form of naturalism which long ago was rightfully discarded—that what is good is analyzable in terms of what human beings aim at by nature. Such a form of naturalism is unacceptable, among other reasons, because it rules out the possibility of the natural aims of human beings not being good. It does make sense to ask whether what human beings aim at by nature is good. And if one can aim at something else, (and one can on Aristotle's position on practical reason), it makes sense to ask whether one *should* aim at something else. Since the kind of naturalism that Aristotle's position embodies rules out these possibilities, it, and along with it Aristotle's position, deserve to be discarded.

However, Aristotle's position on practical reason is *not* committed to such a form of naturalism. Although it is true on this view that what people aim at by nature is good, the truth of this does not rest on an analysis of goodness in terms of people's natural aims. As I suggested in the last chapter, if Aristotle is committed to any analysis of goodness, it is to one in terms of something's being an object of rational as opposed to irrational desires, or to one in terms of what a good person would want, where a good person is understood as one who exhibits the virtue of reason in its practical employment. Not only does a position resting on these analyses allow questions like 'Are the natural ends of human beings good?' and 'Should one aim at something else?' to arise, it explains why one should give certain answers to them. The natural ends of human beings are good because these are what one would aim at if one's desires were rational. One should not aim at something else, for if one did, one's desires would be irrational. If Aristotle's position on practical reason does embody a form of naturalism, it seems to be a form of naturalism that deserves to be taken seriously.[6]

II. The Incompleteness of Aristotle's Position

A more serious objection, however, can be raised against the attempt to base ethics on Aristotle's position on practical reason: it leaves out something essential to any adequate ethics, a way of limiting the pursuit of a person's own ends when they come in conflict with those of others. Although I am inclined to think that this objection does hold, I do not think that this eliminates the interest of Aristotle's position. I think that any attempt at limiting interpersonal conflict based on the existence of practical reason will have to rely on something that does the same job as Aristotle's position. That is, Aristotle's position, or something very much like it, will have to be a *part* of any adequate attempt to base ethics on practical reason.

There are at least two ways of raising the above objection. The first is that any adequate basis for ethics must be objective in a stronger sense than the one I have been using so far in this book. Whatever else ethics is concerned with, a proper part of it is the resolution of conflicts that arise between different people. If the pursuit of one person's ends is incompatible with a second person's pursuit of his ends, an adequate ethics will have a way of determining which if either of them is entitled to pursue his or her ends. For example, a theory of *justice* will be part of any adequate ethics, and a large part of justice is concerned with adjudicating just such disputes. An adequate ethics, thus, must provide principles which, if they do not eliminate interpersonal conflicts, at least limit them to a tolerable level. Ethics must be objective in the sense that it provides principles that *everyone* can act on. The kind of ethics based on Aristotle's position on practical reason, however, seems not to be objective in this sense. According to Aristotle's position, a person ought to act so as to fulfill one's natural ends. However, if these ends can conflict with one another (if, for example, the resources for securing them are scarce), then not everyone will be able to fulfill his or her natural ends. People's pursuit of their natural ends will produce rather than limit interpersonal conflicts. The principle that everyone ought to pursue natural ends is, thus, not one that everyone can act on. It looks as if an ethics based on Aristotle's position on practical reason will not be objective in the relevant sense.

The second way of raising the objection is to maintain that any adequate ethics must require a minimal form of altruism. Whether or not an adequate ethics will require a considerable effort on the part of people to promote the interests of others, it will at least demand that on occasion people curtail the pursuit of their own ends to avoid interfering with other people's pursuit of their ends. However, an ethics based on Aristotle's position on practical reason seems to have no basis for such a curtailment of people's pursuit of their ends. If people's natural ends can conflict with one another, then it seems that people will be justified in pursuing their own natural ends even if doing so would prevent others from pursuing their ends. If this is right, then an ethics based on Aristotle's position on practical reason will not require the minimum form of altruism that must be part of any adequate ethics.

A complete discussion of these objections would require at least one of two elements—a detailed articulation of the ends that people do aim at by nature to see whether the pursuit of them would in fact lead to interpersonal conflicts, and/or a detailed investigation of the particular virtues that Aristotle takes to constitute *eudaimonia* to see whether acting in accord with them would produce interpersonal conflicts. I have time for neither of these tasks. However, a brief glance at Aristotle's discussion of the virtues suggests some reason for thinking that the objections do hold. There are two places in Aristotle's ethics where it would be natural to look to see if it does provide the kind of limitation on the pursuit of one's ends discussed above, Aristotle's discussion of justice and his discussion of friendship. On the face of it, neither of them provide much help in answering the above objections.

Aristotle distinguishes two forms of justice,[7] a narrower one in which justice and injustice have to do with honor, money, or safety (NE 1130b1-3), and a broader one which amounts to the whole of virtue insofar as it involves other people (NE 1129b25-26, 1130b17-20). The narrower sense seems to be too narrow to provide the curtailment of a person's pursuit of his or her ends in all of the contexts where such curtailment is needed, and the broader sense throws the issue back to a consideration of all the other virtues. Initially, though, it looks as if the pursuit of a life of these virtues would lead to interpersonal conflicts. For example, in NE Bk. I Ch. 8 Aristotle says that external goods are necessary for a life of virtue. If these external goods and the resources for obtaining them are scarce (as they seem to be), then it looks as if people's pursuit of a life of virtue would lead to interpersonal conflicts.

If one turns to Aristotle's discussion of friendship,[8] one finds that Aristotle's ethics does provide for a limited kind of altruism. Aristotle argues that friendship will be part of a virtuous man's life (NE Bk. IX, Ch. 9), and friendship does carry with it a curtailment of a person's pursuit of his or her own ends in the face of other people's pursuit of their ends. One regards a friend as a second self (1166a29-31), taking his or her ends or interests as one's own. One will, thus, be willing to curtail the pursuit of one's own ends when they conflict with the ends of a friend, at least as much as one will be willing to curtail the pursuit of some of one's ends when they conflict with other of one's ends. The problem is that this form of altruism is too limited. Friendship is by its nature selective (NE 1158a10-12). One will not and cannot be friends with everyone. In fact, the good person will have as friends only good people (1158b3-35). (See also 1156b7-8, 19-21, 1165b22-30.) But the desired curtailment of people's pursuit of their own ends seems to extend to situations other than ones involving their friends. If so, Aristotle's ethics does not provide for the minimal kind of altruism required by an adequate ethics.

Let us suppose the worst. Let us suppose that the above objections do hold. Does this eliminate the interest of Aristotle's position on practical reason? I think not. I think that any attempt to base ethics on practical reason that does provide for the desired curtailment of a person's pursuit of his or her own ends will have to have as part of it something that does the same job as Aristotle's position on practical reason. I will not argue here for this thesis in general, but I shall try to make it plausible by arguing for a more specific version of the thesis in the case of three views that can be regarded as among the most plausible attempts to provide a basis for the curtailment of people's pursuit of their ends on principles of practical rationality — Kant's attempt to base morality on the categorical imperative, Thomas Nagel's attempt to argue for altruism as a requirement of practical rationality, and John Rawls's two principles of justice. The form of the argument will be the same in each case. The principles put forward are all *formal* principles in the sense that they require something else to provide their *matter* for them to be applied. What is needed for their matter is supplied by Aristotle's position on practical reason. Thus, Aristotle's position on practical reason, or something else that does the same job, will have to be part of any one of these attempts to base the curtailment of people's pursuit of their own ends on principles of practical rationality.

Let us begin with Kant's attempt to base morality on the categorical imperative. The first thing to note is that this is an attempt to base morality on the existence of practical reason. According to Kant (1964), a central feature of morality is that it holds necessarily. It is unconditionally binding on all rational beings (389).[9] People cannot opt out of morality or claim that it doesn't apply to them because of the kind of people they are. Morality applies to them whether they like it or not. This feature is enough for Kant to say that morality has its source in reason. Necessity is the mark of the *a priori*, and the *a priori* is the province of reason (389). Furthermore, morality as Kant conceives of it rests on *practical* reason. Kant accounts for the necessary applicability of morality by saying that morality rests on categorical imperatives. An imperative is the formula of a command of reason, something that expresses an objective principle of action and is addressed to one who does not always act on objective principles (413). An objective principle is a principle that a person would act on if one's will were determined by reason (412-413). That is, an imperative indicates what a person would do if one were to act rationally. A categorical imperative is an imperative that applies independently of any particular desires or ends that a person might happen to have (416). Thus, a categorical imperative shows what it would be rational to do independently of any particular desires or ends that a person might happen to have. That this conception of rational action rests on the existence of *practical* reason can be seen from what Kant takes to be involved in the possibility of imperatives — that any rational being would be motivated to act on them (417, 447, 454). Thus, Kant's attempt to base morality on categorical imperatives is an attempt to base ethics on practical reason.

The second thing to note is that the categorical imperative seems designed to provide just the kind of curtailment of people's pursuit of their own ends that is needed for an adequate ethics. This can be seen in either one of two ways. It has already been suggested that if ethics is to provide the desired kind of curtailment, moral principles must be principles that everyone can act on. According to Kant, any categorical imperative is equivalent to an imperative that commands people to act only on maxims that they can will to be a universal law (420-421). This appears to be just a restatement of the foregoing requirement. To pursue matters a bit further, a maxim can fail to be one that can be willed to be a universal law if either it cannot be *conceived* to be a universal law, or if willing it to be a universal law leads to the will's *being in contradiction with itself* (424). The first of these again appears to be a restatement of the requirement that moral principles be principles that everyone can act on. And whatever exactly is involved in the second of these, it seems to represent the kind of conflict that an adequate ethics is supposed to eliminate. A second way of seeing how the categorical imperative might provide the desired kind of curtailment stems from the suggestion that an adequate ethics must require a minimal form of altruism. Kant thinks that the categorical imperative does demand a limited form of altruism. One ought sometimes to come to the aid of others even if it is not in one's interest to do so, because a maxim of nonbenevolence cannot be willed to be a universal law without one's will being in contradiction with itself (423).

The categorical imperative, thus, is one way in which one might try to base the desired curtailment of people's pursuit of their own ends on principles of practical rationality.

What remains to be seen is in what sense the categorical imperative is a *formal* principle requiring something like Aristotle's position on practical reason to provide it with its matter. To do this we need a closer look at what is involved in a will's being in contradiction with itself.[10] This can be obtained by looking more carefully at Kant's attempted derivation of a duty of limited benevolence noted above.[11]

I shall assume that when a person's will is in contradiction with itself, the person is committed under certain circumstances to willing incompatible states of affairs. That is, I shall assume that a contradiction of the will can be expressed by the schema, 'I will that if C then P and −P'. I shall also assume that the relevant maxim of nonbenevolence is 'Never help another unless it is in your interest to do so.' The question is why willing the universalization of this maxim should lead to a contradiction of the will.

If I will the universalization of the maxim of nonbenevolence I am committed to

1) I will that no one help another unless it is in his interest to do so.

From this it follows that

2) I will that if I am in need and it is in no one's interest to help me, then no one help me.

However, according to Kant,

a will which decided in this way would be in conflict with itself, since many a situation might arise in which the man needed love and sympathy from others, and in which, by such a law of nature sprung from his own will, he would rob himself of all hope of the help he wants for himself. (423)

That is,

3) If I am in need, I will want help.

From this it seems to follow that

4) I will that if I am in need and it is in no one's interest to help me, then someone help me.

From (2) and (4) it follows that

5) I will that if I am in need and it is in no one's interest to help me, then someone help me and no one help me.

This expresses a contradiction of the will.

At least two things need to be understood to grasp what is behind this derivation. What is the basis for (3)? And how does (4) follow from it? At first sight it may seem that (3) holds as a contingent matter of psychological fact, and that (4) follows from it because willing is understood in terms of wanting. However, not only does this prevent the categorical imperative from providing the curtailment of people's pursuit of their own ends in cases where such curtailment is needed, it is also incompatible with Kant's whole enterprise of basing morality on categorical imperatives.

If it is only a contingent psychological fact that a person would want help if she were in need, then it is possible for there to be someone who as a matter of fact wouldn't want such help. For example, a "self-reliance fanatic" might prefer not to be helped if she were in need. It looks as if such a person wouldn't will that someone help her if she were in need, and, as a result, the above derivation wouldn't go through for her. She, it would seem would not have a limited duty of benevolence. But if the categorical imperative is to provide an adequate curtailment of people's pursuit of their own ends, it should provide for this curtailment even in the case of a "self-reliance fanatic." More important, this understanding of the above derivation makes it incompatible with Kant's attempt to base morality on categorical imperatives. It makes a contradiction of the will depend on what particular ends a person happens to have. But the whole enterprise of basing morality on categorical imperatives was to explain how moral requirements hold independently of any particular ends that a person might happen to have.

The way around these difficulties is to recognize that willing does not amount to wanting, and to recognize that (3) does not rest on a contingent psychological fact about what particular people want. Kant identifies the will with *practical reason* (412), not desire. His other example of a derivation of a contradiction of the will provides a basis for understanding just what is required for a claim about what a person wills. In arguing that one cannot will a maxim of neglect of one's talents to be a universal law Kant says,

> For as a rational being he necessarily wills that all his powers should be developed, since they serve him, and are given him, for all sorts of possible ends. (423)

One wills that his talents be developed because necessarily as a rational being he wants them developed. (As a rational being he wants them developed because they are useful as means for whatever ends he might happen to have. Necessarily a rational being wants to adopt means to his ends [417] .) What is necessary for a claim about what a person wills, then, is a premise about what one must want insofar as one is rational. A contradiction of the will arises when what a person wills is incompatible with what one must want insofar as one is rational.

(3), then, must be taken as a claim about what anyone would want insofar as one is rational. As long as Kant has a way of arguing for this, he can claim that even a "self-reliance fanatic" has a limited duty of benevolence.[12] He too ought sometimes to curtail the pursuit of his ends. As long as such a fanatic is a rational being, he will want help if he is in need. It makes no difference if as a matter of contingent fact his overall preference would be that he not be helped. Such contingent preferences are irrelevant to what can be willed. This way of understanding a contradiction of the will keeps Kant's derivation of the duty of benevolence in line with his overall enterprise of basing morality on categorical imperatives. Even though on this interpretation moral requirements depend on certain ends, they do not depend on particular ends that people *happen* to have. They depend only on ends that people *necessarily* have insofar as they are rational. As a result the requirements of morality turn out to be inescapable.

On the interpretation I have been arguing for, the categorical imperative curtails the pursuit of a person's ends by saying that it is irrational to pursue a given end if the universalization of the maxim on which it would be pursued is incompatible with what anyone would want insofar as one is rational.[13] So understood, the categorical imperative is a *formal* principle, requiring something else to provide it with its *matter*. Unless there are some ends that it would be rational for anyone to pursue, the categorical imperative can not be applied. Kant says that such ends exist (for example, freedom, happiness, and perfection), but nowhere does he provide any arguments for their existence.[14] However, it is just such arguments that Aristotle's position on practical reason promises to provide. If Kant's categorical imperative is any indication of what is needed for practical reason to provide an adequate basis for ethics, then it looks as if Aristotle's position on practical reason, or something like it, will have to be part of any such basis.

A similar conclusion can be drawn in connection with Thomas Nagel's attempt to base a limited form of altruism on a principle of practical reason ([1970], Chs. IX-XII). We have seen that one way of putting the criticism raised against Aristotle is that an adequate ethics must require at least a minimal form of altruism. If the kind of altruism that Nagel argues for can be based on a principle of practical reason, it looks as if it will provide what Aristotle's position lacks. However, the principle Nagel puts forward as the basis for altruism is a *formal* principle, requiring something else to provide it with its matter in order for it to be applied. Again, Aristotle's position on practical reason is one place to look to find such matter.

According to Nagel, altruism can be based on the principle that whatever a person has a *subjective reason* to promote, he has an *objective reason* to promote ([1970], p. 96). A *subjective reason* is a reason that involves an essential reference to the agent for whom it is a reason ([1970], p. 90). For example, if a person has a reason to promote her interest because it is *her* interest that is being promoted, then the reason is a subjective reason. The reason—that the act is in *her* interest—makes an essential reference to the agent. An *objective reason* contains no such reference to the agent ([1970], p. 90). For example, if a person has a reason to promote her interest because in promoting it she would be promoting *someone's* interest, then the reason is an objective one. The reason—that what she does would promote *someone's* interest—makes no reference to the agent.[15]

It is a feature of subjective reasons that if a person has a subjective reason for promoting a given state of affairs, it does not follow that anyone else has a reason to promote that same state of affairs ([1970], p. 92). Suppose that I have a reason to promote my interest because it is *my* interest that is being promoted. Even though reasons are universal ([1970], p. 90), all that follows is that everyone else has a reason to promote his or her interest. It does not follow that they have a reason to promote *my* interest. However, it is a feature of objective reasons that if a person has an objective reason for promoting a given state of affairs, then everyone else has a reason to promote that same state of affairs ([1970], p. 92). Suppose that I have a reason to promote my interest because promoting it is a case of promoting *someone's* interest. Then it follows from the universality of reasons that everyone else has a reason to do what will promote someone's interest, including my own. Whatever one person has an objective reason to promote, everyone has a reason to promote.

Given this feature of objective reasons, one can see why Nagel's principle might be thought to provide a basis for altruism. Virtually everyone will grant that people have subjective reasons to promote their own interest. But if whatever a person has subjective reason to promote he or she has objective reason to promote, then everyone will have an objective reason to promote his or her own interest. Since whatever one person has an objective reason to promote everyone has a reason to promote, it follows that everyone has a reason to promote the interest of everyone else. The latter seems to be just what altruism maintains.

It is clear that Nagel takes his principle to be a principle of practical reason. Our capacity to acknowledge objective reasons is not due to our having a general sympathy with others or to any other special desire ([1970], pp. 80-81). It is the result of our being able to adopt an "impersonal" conception of ourselves, according to which we view ourselves merely as one person among others, all of whom are equally real ([1970], pp. 99-100). The application of this impersonal view to our practical lives carries with it the admission of objective reasons. Whatever aspect of our lives can be viewed impersonally can be expressed impersonally ([1970], pp. 102-3). A reason that can be expressed impersonally is a reason that can be expressed independently of any reference to the agent for whom it is a reason ([1970], pp. 119-20). That is, it is an objective reason. Thus, the capacity to view ourselves impersonally carries with it the capacity to acknowledge that what we have subjective reason for promoting, we have objective reason for promoting. Since the capacity to view ourselves impersonally is a rational capacity, the principle that we acknowledge objective reasons for what we have subjective reasons for doing is a rational principle. Since the impersonal recognition of reasons carries with it a *motivational content* ([1970], pp. 110-13),[16] this principle is a principle of practical reason.

If altruism really can be based on Nagel's principle, then it looks as if one will have a basis in practical reason for what Aristotle's position lacks, a way of reducing interpersonal conflicts. However, Nagel's principle by itself is not enough to reduce interpersonal conflicts. It is a *formal* principle ([1970], p. 81, p. 123). It only provides derivative (objective) reasons for doing what one has primary (subjective) reasons for doing. Without a general theory of value to provide an account of what people have primary reasons to do, Nagel's principle cannot be used to show that one has a reason to do anything.[17] For a complete defense of altruism Nagel must show that people really do have (subjective) reasons for promoting their own interest. Nagel cannot rely on the fact (if it is a fact) that people want to promote their own interest, for the mere existence of a want is not sufficient to provide a reason for promoting the object of that want ([1970], pp. 43-44). Nor will it do to argue that everyone will grant that people have reasons to promote their own interest, for not everyone will grant this. Nagel himself points out that a religious eccentric who admitted as reasons only things dictated by a certain deity could admit the existence of objective reasons and still deny that he had any reason to promote anyone's interest in any familiar sense of this term ([1970], p. 125).

Indeed, if altruism itself, and not just the principle on which it is based, is to be a requirement of practical rationality, then the failure to acknowledge that one has a reason to promote one's own interest will itself have to be criticizable on the grounds of irrationality. Nagel himself seems to recognize this, for he suggests that a religious eccentric of the sort described above would be dissociated from his natural desires and the demands of his body ([1970], p. 126). Dissociation appears to be a mark of irrationality.

What this means is that for Nagel to complete the task of showing that altruism is a requirement of practical reason, he will have to have in his general theory of value a theory that indicates which ends it would be rational to pursue and irrational not to pursue. However, it is precisely this kind of theory that Aristotle's position on practical reason promises to provide. If Nagel's attempt to base altruism on a principle of practical reason is any indication of what is needed for practical reason to provide an adequate basis for ethics, then Aristotle's position on practical reason, or something like it, will have to be part of any such basis.

The same conclusion can be drawn if one takes John Rawls's (1971) principles of justice to provide a way of basing the curtailment of people's pursuit of their own ends on principles of practical reason.

According to Rawls, the principles of justice are those principles that would be chosen by certain people in an "original position" faced with a certain choice ([1971], pp. 11-12). The choice is to adopt principles governing the basic institutions of society that will in turn govern the parties' behavior after they leave the choice situation. The principles are to be general, universal in application, public, capable of adjudicating disputes that arise when people press completing claims, and final ([1971], pp. 131-35). The parties in the choice situation are free, rational, disinterested in the interests of others, and yet interested in pursuing their own ends ([1971], pp. 13-14). Their choice is made from behind a "veil of ignorance." The parties do not know their own place in society, their particular assets or liabilities, their own particular psychological make-up, their own conception of the good, or the particular economic, political, or cultural level of their society ([1971], p. 137).

At least three assumptions underlie this way of looking at principles of justice. They also explain the elements contained in the choice situation. First, justice is taken primarily to be a virtue of social institutions. Thus, the principles chosen are ones that govern the basic institutions of a society. Second, justice is thought of as morality's response to situations in which people press competing claims against one another. The parties in the choice situation are taken to be interested in pursuing their own ends, so that they will be the kind of people who will press competing claims against one another. The conditions of generality, publicity, etc. are designed to build in the features of a moral response to the adjudication of such disputes. Finally, justice is taken to be a form of fairness, where what is fair is taken to be what everyone would agree to from an initial position of equality. The "veil of ignorance" is designed to insure that the situation of choice is one of initial equality. Given these assumptions, one can understand why Rawls would think that the principles that emerge from such a choice situation are principles of justice.

The principles that Rawls says will emerge from such a choice situation are the following.

> First, each person is to have an equal right to the most extensive total system of equal basic liberties compatible with a similar system of liberty for all.
> Second, social and economic inequalities are to be arranged so that they are both
>> (a) to the greatest benefit of the least advantaged, and
>> (b) attached to offices and positions open to all under conditions of fair equality of opportunity.

The first principle is prior to the second in that liberty can only be restricted for the sake of liberty. The second part of the second principle is prior to the first part of the second principle ([1971], pp. 302-3).

Initially, it may seem odd to take Rawls's principles of justice as supplying what Aristotle's position on practical reason seems to lack. There is, after all, more to determining when people ought to curtail the pursuit of their ends than determining which principles ought to govern the basic institutions of society. And there is as yet no indication as to why these principles might be thought to be principles of practical reason. However, principles that govern the basic institutions of society will be at least part of what is needed to determine when people ought to curtail the pursuit of their own ends. And Rawls's attempt to assimilate what he does to Kant's attempt to base morality on practical reason ([1971], pp. 252-57) does suggest that he regards these principles as principles of practical reason. Rawls even says that those who act from these principles act as though their nature as free and equal rational beings were decisive in determining their actions ([1971], pp. 252-53). This seems quite close to saying that these principles are principles of practical rationality.[18]

However, even if one takes these principles as supplying part of what is needed to provide a basis in practical reason for the curtailment of people's pursuit of their own ends, why think that something like Aristotle's position on practical reason will be needed to supplement them? The answer is that Rawls's principles of justice are also *formal* principles in the sense that I have been using this term. They are essentially principles for distributing certain goods. One needs an account of what the goods are that need to be distributed before one will get any specific principles of justice. For example, it is only because basic liberties are among what Rawls calls "primary goods" that the first principle requires a certain distribution of basic liberties. Primary goods turn out to be goods that any rational being would want ([1971], pp. 395-99).

Still, one might think that what this shows is that a position like Aristotle's does *not* have to be brought in. At least in *A Theory of Justice,* primary goods seem to be just those things that would be useful as means no matter what particular ends a person might happen to have ([1971], p. 93). Here is a conception of what it would be rational to want, but it doesn't rest on anything like Aristotle's position on practical reason. However, in a more recent work Rawls makes it clear that primary goods are *not* simply means that would be useful no matter what particular ends a person might happen to have ([1980], pp. 525-27). They are goods that would be useful for a certain kind of person, one who among other things has a highest-order interest in forming, revising, and rationally pursuing a conception of the good. If Rawls's principles of justice are to provide *unconditional* principles of practical rationality (that is, principles about what would be rational independent of particular ends that people happen to have), then one will need an argument to show that having this as a highest-order interest is itself something that is rational. Again, Aristotle's position on practical reason promises to provide the kind of argument needed to see whether it is rational.

If Kant's, Nagel's, and Rawls's views are at all representative of attempts to base principles curtailing the pursuit of a person's ends on practical reason, then such attempts need not be viewed as rivals or competitors to Aristotle's position, for such attempts presuppose something like Aristotle's position. Aristotle's position and these attempts can be regarded as complementary positions, each one providing something that the other needs. The reason for this is that any plausible rational principle capable of providing the desired restriction on people's pursuit of their own ends would seem to be a formal principle, requiring a theory of rational ends to provide it with at least part of its matter. If this is right, then even if by itself Aristotle's position on practical reason cannot provide an adequate basis for ethics, it will still be of considerable philosophical interest. It will provide part of what any such basis needs.[19]

III. Objectivity Once More

There is one other potential problem that deserves to be mentioned. And that is a problem that threatens to prevent Aristotle's position on practical reason from providing an *objective* basis for ethics. What raises this problem is the claim that one must already to some extent have the right habits and dispositions to be able to make a correct inference about what one is aiming at by nature. If this claim is so strong that it implies that one cannot infer what the good relative to humanity is without already having a virtuous character, then it is doubtful that ethical judgments will turn out to be objective.

As I have been using the term 'objective' in most of this book, ethical judgments are objective just in case for any two people if one were to affirm a particular judgment about what is good and the other were to deny it, then one of them must be mistaken. However, if each state of character carries with it its own conception of what the good is, then each state of character will carry with it its own conception of who the good person is and hence of what habits and dispositions one must have to make a correct inference about what it is that one aims at by nature. In any dispute over whether something is to be done, it will be possible for both parties to provide the same sort of justification for their different views, each one arguing that one's opponent is mistaken, because, not having the right state of character to begin with, one is in no position to assess corectly what the good is. Without some independent means of determining who the good person is or what the proper object of desire is, it is not clear what force there is to the claim that there is a correct conception of who the good person is or what the good is, and therefore that one of the parties in the dispute is mistaken.[20]

Although this is a potential problem for Aristotle's position, it need not be an actual problem. As I have sketched Aristotle's position, it is possible to take to be good something that one does not aim at in one's conscious desires and dispositions. Thus, it is possible to take to be a good person someone who does not share one's own character traits. As long as this is possible, it will be possible to say that there is a correct conception of who the good person is. It is that conception that one would reach by a succession of inductive inferences, each one resting on the previous conception's having been integrated into one's character. Of course, there is no guarantee that there will be such a correct conception of who the good person is. People might reach different conceptions by such a succession of inferences. But as I said in Section I of this chapter, there should be no such guarantee. If Aristotle's position on practical reason makes a substantive claim about there being a correct conception of who the good person is, then this should be a claim that could turn out to be false. It will turn out to be false, if actual application of the kind of inductive inference mentioned in the position yields no common conception of who the good person is. But as long as this claim has not turned out to be false, one can still maintain that Aristotle's position on practical reason provides an objective basis for ethics. What is important to remember, though, is that there is an aspect of Aristotle's position that when pushed to its limit will prevent Aristotle's position from providing an objective basis for ethics.

Aristotle's position on practical reason has, I think, more than historical interest. It is plausible enough in its own right to be taken seriously. And even if by itself it cannot provide an adequate basis for ethics, it provides part of what is needed for an adequate basis of ethics on practical reason.

Part Two
Aristotle and Weakness of the Will

CHAPTER 9

The Traditional Interpretation: Some Problems and Preliminaries

I suggested in the Introduction that one criterion of adequacy for any attempt to base ethics on practical reason is that it admit the existence of genuine cases of weakness of the will. Traditionally Aristotle has been interpreted as denying the existence of genuine cases of weakness of the will. If this interpretation is correct, then what led Aristotle to this denial? Was it his position on practical reason? If so, then another objection should be added to those raised in Chapter 8. On the other hand, if Aristotle's position on practical reason didn't commit him to denying genuine cases of weakness of the will, then what did? Or could the traditional interpretation of Aristotle on weakness of the will be mistaken? If Aristotle's position on practical reason didn't commit him to denying genuine cases of weakness of the will, could it have provided him with a way to acknowledge their existence? Not only does an investigation of Aristotle's position on weakness of the will promise to shed light on the adequacy of Aristotle's position on practical reason, his position on practical reason may shed light on just what Aristotle's position on weakness of the will is.

Aristotle's explanation of weakness of the will is also worth investigating in its own right. Although at first sight Aristotle seems to deny genuine cases of weakness of the will, some passages appear to be incompatible with such a denial. Can these passages be reconciled with the way Aristotle has traditionally been interpreted? Does an inconsistency run through his discussion of weakness of the will? Or did Aristotle provide a different explanation of weakness of the will from the one that has traditionally been attributed to him?

In this second part of this book I shall try to argue that the traditional interpretation is mistaken and that Aristotle did allow genuine cases of weakness of the will. Aristotle's position on practical reason will play an important part in this argument. However, in this chapter I shall be content to set out the traditional interpretation of Aristotle, indicate what some of the problems are that arise for it, and point to some preliminary matters that need to be kept in mind in any attempt to discuss these problems.

I. The Traditional Interpretation

Aristotle's main discussion of weakness of the will *(akrasia)* occurs in NE Bk. VII, and his most detailed explanation of what goes on in incontinence or weakness of the will is found in Ch. 3. It consists in a series of four remarks. The first three seem to set out ways in which it can easily be understood how action contrary to a person's knowledge can occur. The fourth combines elements from the previous three into an explanation of *akrasia*. At first sight, what Aristotle says seems to run as follows.

First (1146b30-34), Aristotle distinguishes two senses of 'know', one in which a person is exercising knowledges that he possesses, and the other in which he is not exercising that knowledge. Aristotle remarks that it would be strange for a person to act contrary to knowledge that he is actually exercising, but it would not be strange if the knowledge were not being exercised.

Second (1146b35-1147a10), Aristotle distinguishes two kinds of premise that can occur in a practical syllogism, a universal premise indicating what is good or what is to be done, and more particular premises relating the universal premise to the situation at hand. He gives as an example of a universal premise, 'Dry food is good for any man.' Included among the particular premises related to this universal premise are, 'Such and such is dry food' and 'This is such and such'. What Aristotle is calling attention to are two kinds of knowledge that are involved in knowing what to do on a particular occasion—knowledge of a general principle that might be brought to bear on a particular situation, and knowledge needed to bring that principle to bear on that particular situation. Aristotle suggests that an incontinent person either lacks or is not exercising knowledge of the most particular of these premises (in his example, 'This is such and such'). He says that to fail to act on one's knowledge while failing to have or exercise knowledge of such a premise would not be strange, but that failure to act while one knows and is exercising both kinds of premise would be extraordinary.

Third (1147a10-24), Aristotle points to a subclass of cases in which people have but do not exercise knowledge. He describes these as cases in which people in a sense do and in a sense do not have knowledge. His examples include those who are mad, asleep, or drunk. He says that this is the condition of people under the influence of their passions. He says that an incontinent person is in a similar condition.

Finally (1147a24-1147b19), Aristotle combines elements from these three passages into an explanation of *akrasia*. An incontinent person knows how to behave in the situation that faces him in the sense that he knows the general principle that applies to his situation. He fails to act on this principle because appetite prevents him from having or exercising knowledge that he is in a situation to which his general principle applies. This same appetite causes him to act as he does.

To use Aristotle's example, when a person knows that certain things ought not to be tasted, but also has the opinions that everything sweet is pleasant and that what is in front of her is sweet, and when appetite is present, appetite may prevent her from recognizing that the sweet thing in front of her is one of the things that ought not to be tasted. Seeing it only as something sweet, the person is led by her appetite to taste it, contrary to her general knowledge that it ought not to be tasted.

What seems to emerge from these passages is that weakness of the will is possible only because incontinent people do not have full and complete knowledge of how they ought to behave in the situation that faces them. Although in a sense they know that they ought not to act as they do (they have knowledge of the general principle that applies to their situation), it is in part because of a lack of knowledge that they act as they do. They do not have or are not exercising knowledge about the particular situation that they are in. As a result, they fail to recognize that the particular action they perform is one that they ought not to perform. Aristotle, thus, seems to share the Socratic view that action contrary to full and complete knowledge is impossible. He even seems to admit this when he says, "the position that Socrates sought to establish actually seems to result" (1147b15-16).[1]

Although these four sets of passages will have to be discussed in more detail, I think the above does capture in outline what at first sight Aristotle seems to be saying about weakness of the will. It also comprises the core of the interpretation that commentators traditionally have given Aristotle's explanation of *akrasia*.[2] The question I want to raise is whether such an interpretation is correct.

II. Some Problems for the Traditional Interpretation

A. A Minor Worry and its Solution

There is a passage that when first noticed often raises a question about the adequacy of the above interpretation of Aristotle's explanation of *akrasia*. And that is Aristotle's criticism of the Socratic position on *akrasia*, that it is contrary to the "observed facts" *(phainomena)* (1145b28). The observed facts that the Socratic position seems most at odds with are the facts that people do actually act contrary to full and complete knowledge of how they ought to behave. But if this is Aristotle's criticism of Socrates, how could he come up with an explanation of *akrasia* that is open to the same objection? Could he have been so blind that he failed to notice that his own position is contrary to the same observed facts?

This worry does not post a serious problem for the traditional interpretation.[3] It arises from a failure to understand what Aristotle is referring to when he says that the Socratic position is contrary to the *phainomena*. This failure is in part due to the translation of *'phainomena'* as 'observed facts'. Aristotle does sometimes use *'phainomena'* to refer to observed fact, but on other occasions he uses it to call attention to something else. For example, when in Bk. I Ch. 8 Aristotle tries to show that his own view of *eudaimonia* fits the *phainomena,* what he shows is the extent to which it fits "what has been said" *(legomena)* about *eudaimonia*.[4] This includes both what common people have said, who identify *eudaimonia* with pleasure or external goods, and what the wise have said, some of whom identify *eudaimonia* with virtue. It is this latter use of *'phainomena'* that occurs in NE Bk. VII. Right at the outset (Ch. 1) Aristotle sets out what has been said *(legomena)* about *akrasia*. These include (1) that *akrasia* is said to be blameworthy; (2) that the incontinent person is said to act from passion knowing that what he or she does is bad; and (3) that the incontinent person has been both assimilated to and distinguished from the self-indulgent person. A little reflection will show that the Socratic view is at odds with these *phainomena* in a way that Aristotle's view as outlined above is not.

According to the Socratic view,[5] anyone who acts badly does so involuntarily or out of ignorance. Since either of these conditions provides a person with an excuse, an incontinent person will not be blameworthy. Second, since on the Socratic view, no one knowingly does what is wrong, the so-called incontinent person cannot really be said to know that what he or she does is bad. Although in a sense such a person acts from passion, a better explanation would be that the person has miscalculated what is truly good and acts on the basis of this miscalculation.[6] Finally, since on the Socratic view, all wrong action is either involuntary or due to ignorance, there will be no way of distinguishing an incontinent person from a self-indulgent person. Although this would allow Socrates to explain why the incontinent person and self-indulgent person have been assimilated, it leaves him no basis for explaining why they have been distinguished. Socrates' position, thus, does seem to be at odds with these three *phainomena*.[7]

Aristotle's position as outlined above, however, can be seen to fit these *phainomena* in a way that the Socratic position does not. Initially, one might think that Aristotle cannot maintain that *akrasia* is blameworthy. According to the above outline, the *akratēs* is ignorant of at least some of the particular circumstances surrounding his action; according to Aristotle, this kind of ignorance excuses (1110b34-35). However, Aristotle also distinguishes acting *by reason of* ignorance *(di'agnoian)* from acting *in* ignorance *(agnoounta)* (1110b24-25). One of his examples of someone who acts in ignorance is someone who acts while drunk (1110b25). Aristotle says that people who act in ignorance can be blamed if they are responsible for their ignorance, and he cites in support of this the fact that penalties are doubled if a person acts wrongly while drunk (1113b30-34). Since the *akratēs* is in a state like drunkenness (1147a17-18), he too acts *in* ignorance. Thus, he too can be blameworthy.[8]

Second, according to the above outline, there is a sense in which the incontinent man knows that what he does is bad. He knows the general principle that applies to his situation. It is also true that he acts from passion. Passion not only prevents him from recognizing that the action that he does falls under his general principle, but that same passion moves him to act as he does.

Finally, one can understand why the incontinent person has been both assimilated to and distinguished from the self-indulgent person. Both the incontinent person and the self-indulgent person pursue the same object, pleasure (1148a13-15). Thus, one can understand why they might be assimilated. However, the incontinent person has general knowledge of how he ought to behave; the self-indulgent person does not. The self-indulgent person pursues bodily pleasure through deliberate choice; the incontinent person does not (1148a16-17). The incontinent person is likely to repent; the self-indulgent person is not (1150b29-30). Thus, one can understand why they might be distinguished.

Given what Aristotle has in mind when he says that Socrates' position is contrary to the *phainomena*, Aristotle's position is not open to the same criticism that he raises against Socrates. If all one had to go on were this criticism, one would not have serious grounds for doubting the adequacy of the traditional interpretation.

B. Three Apparently Incompatible Passages

However, more serious problems arise for the traditional interpretation. At least three other passages in the *Nicomachean Ethics* appear to be incompatible with that interpretation.

In Bk. VII Ch. 7 Aristotle says,

> Of incontinence one kind is impetuosity, another weakness. For some men after deliberating fail, owing to their emotion, to stand by the conclusions of their deliberation, others because they have not deliberated are led by their emotions. (1150b19-22)

What is worrisome here is that Aristotle seems to recognize a kind of *akrasia*, weakness, not countenanced by the traditional interpretation. According to the traditional interpretation, the *akratēs* does not complete his deliberation, because he does not have or is not exercising one of the elements needed to complete it. To use Aristotle's example, the person who eats something sweet, contrary to her knowledge that certain things ought not to be tasted, does not know that the sweet thing in front of her ought not to be tasted, because she does not have or is not exercising the knowledge that the thing in front of her is of the kind that ought not to be tasted. She does not draw the conclusion that it ought not to be tasted, because she does not have or is not exercising all of the materials needed to draw it. However, in 1150b19-22 Aristotle seems to say that a weak *akratēs* does draw such a conclusion, for he says that a weak *akratēs* fails to stand by the conclusions of her deliberation.[9]

The admission of weak *akrasia* is especially serious if, as many have thought, Aristotle maintained that the conclusion of a practical syllogism is an action. If the practical syllogism sets out the results of deliberation and the conclusion of a practical syllogism is an action, then weak *akrasia* is impossible. The weak *akratēs* is one who draws the conclusion of his or her deliberation but yet fails to act on it. Nevertheless, Aristotle's admission of weak *akrasia* raises a worry for the traditional interpretation even if the conclusion of a practical syllogism is not taken to be an action.[10] What is troubling is that Aristotle says that the weak *akratēs* draws the conclusions of his deliberation. Whether this conclusion is an action, an intention, a resolution, a decision, or something else, what needs to be explained is how an incontinent person can draw this conclusion if such a person does not have or is not exercising all of the premises needed to draw it.

The second passage that raises a worry for the traditional interpretation follows shortly after the one just noted. At the beginning of Ch. 8 Aristotle says,

Vice is unconscious of itself, incontinence is not. (1150b37)

On one reading of this passage, what Aristotle is saying is that an incontinent person can know that he or she is incontinent at the time of incontinent action. If an incontinent person can know this, then he or she can have and exercise all of the premises needed to know that the particular action that he or she performs is wrong, including the final minor premise. But, according to the traditional interpretation, it is knowledge of this premise that an incontinent person lacks or fails to exercise. How, then, can one know that one is acting incontinently?

Of course, at least two other readings exist according to which this passage doesn't raise this problem. On one Aristotle is only saying that incontinent people can recognize their incontinence after the fact. On the other Aristotle is saying that incontinent people can recognize that they are the sort of people who from time to time act incontinently. Neither of these requires the incontinent person to be able to have and exercise knowledge of the final minor premise. However, what makes the initial reading I suggested plausible is that immediately afterward Aristotle says,

> (of incontinent men themselves, those who become temporarily beside themselves are better than those who have the rational principle but do not abide by it, since the latter are defeated by a weaker passion, and do not act without previous deliberation like the others) (1151a1-3)

That is, the passage occurs in a context in which Aristotle recognizes the existence of weak *akrasia*. We have just seen that the weak *akratēs* does seem to have and exercise all of the knowledge needed to know what he does is wrong. It is just this knowledge that would allow such an *akratēs* to know that he is acting incontinently.[11]

The third passage that raises a problem for the traditional interpretation occurs in NE Bk. I Ch. 13, where Aristotle says,

> There seems to be also another element in the soul — one that in a sense, however, shares in a rational principle. For we praise the rational part of the continent man and of the incontinent, and the part of their soul that has such a principle, since it urges them aright and towards the best objects; but there is found in them also another element naturally opposed to the rational principle which fights against and resists that principle. (1102b13-19)

What Aristotle seems to be saying here is that in both continence (*enkrateia*) and incontinence the agent can be beset by a genuine conflict of motives. In continence it is the motive aligned with the rational principle that wins out, whereas in *akrasia* this motive is defeated. But in both cases a genuine conflict can occur. The problem that this raises is that on the traditional interpretation there can be no genuine conflict of motives in *akrasia*. Incontinent people are not moved to act in accord with their general knowledge of how to act, because they don't recognize that the situation at hand falls under that knowledge. There is only one operant motive at the time that they act, and that is the appetite on which they in fact act.

Thus, we seem to find Aristotle saying three things that are incompatible with the traditional interpretation—(1) that there is a kind of incontinence in which people reach conclusions about what their behavior should be in the situations that face them and yet they fail to abide by those conclusions, (2) that people who act incontinently can know that they are acting incontinently at the time that they act, and (3) that there can be a genuine conflict of motives in incontinence. In all three cases the problem is essentially the same. What Aristotle says seems to imply that the incontinent person can have and exercise all of the premises needed to apply his or her general knowledge to the case at hand. But it is precisely this that the traditional interpretation denies. What is one to say in the light of this? Can these apparently incompatible passages be reconciled with the traditional interpretation? Was Aristotle inconsistent? Or did Aristotle provide a different explanation of *akrasia* from the one attributed to him by the traditional interpretation, one that allows the incontinent person to know that the particular action that he or she does is wrong?

C. Practical Reason and Weakness of the Will: Another Problem

There is one additional problem for the traditional interpretation that I want to call attention to at this time. It arises in connection with the position on practical reason that was argued for in the first part of this book.

Initially, Aristotle's admission of the existence of practical reason may seem to support the traditional interpretation. As I pointed out in the Introduction, if practical reason exists and its scope is broad enough to include moral judgments, then there is a sense in which weakness of the will will be puzzling. It will always stand in need of an explanation. Since people will always be motivated to act as they know they ought to act, action contrary to that knowledge will require an explanation. Furthermore, if one has some reason for thinking that this motive will always be strong, then something like the traditional interpretation will appear as a natural and attractive way of explaining how people can be said to know what they ought to do and yet not do it.

If one takes a cursory look at the position argued for in Part One, it looks as if the motive that a person has when he or she knows in a particular situation what ought to be done will be a relatively strong one. According to this position, two of the areas in which reason contributes to motivation are the determination of the best among competing means, and the determination of the best among competing ends. A person who knows in a particular situation what ought to be done will have not only a motive to do the action provided by the recognition that it is a means to some end that the person has, it looks as if such a person would have an additional motive provided by the recognition that the end to which the action is a means is the best among competing ends. Since any motive to act contrary to this knowledge won't have this additional motivation, it may seem that in comparison it won't be as strong. If one did draw this conclusion, then it would be natural to try to explain cases of weakness of the will along the lines of the traditional interpretation. Initially, Aristotle's position on practical reason may seem to support the traditional interpretation.

However, if one pursues the matter further, Aristotle's position on practical reason not only doesn't support the traditional interpretation, it suggests a quite different picture of *akrasia*. According to the way I have set out Aristotle's position on practical reason, a person acquires general ends in part through an inductive inference to what it is that one has been aiming at by nature. What is important here is that except for the virtuous person and perhaps also the truly vicious person, one can and will infer as an end something that is not fully integrated into his or her character. Although people may not be able to make an inference to an end unless their desires and dispositions are already to *some* extent in accord with that end, it will still be true that what people infer may not be fully integrated into their characters. Typically, it will take further habituation or training before this end will be fully acquired.

What this means is that Aristotle's position on practical reason allows him to rank on a continuum those who have a correct idea of the good, depending on just how well this end has been integrated into their character. At the top of the continuum will be the *phronimos,* who has the natural ends of human beings fully integrated into his character. They are so fully integrated that in a situation when he ought to be pursuing these ends, not even conflicting desires arise.[12] That they are so fully integrated explains in part why Aristotle says that it would be absurd to say that a practically wise man would act contrary to his knowledge.

Is it *practical wisdom* whose resistance is mastered? That is the strongest of all states. But this is absurd; the same man will be at once practically wise and incontinent, but *no one* would say that it is part of a practically wise man to do willingly the basest acts. Besides, it has been shown before that the man of practical wisdom is one who will *act* (for he is a man concerned with individual facts) and who has the other virtues. (1146a4-9)

The *phronimos* not only has the good fully integrated into his character, he also has the ability to deliberate well about means to this end, including the ability to recognize situations that fall under this end. He won't fail to act on his general knowledge either through lack of motivation or through failure to recognize that he is in a position to act on his knowledge.

On this explanation of what Aristotle says, it is not just a verbal matter that the *phronimos* will act on his knowledge. The state to which Aristotle attaches the term *'phronēsis'* involves practical reason in its most successful and perfect form, when practical reason has played the role it is supposed to play in helping people to acquire and act on the ends that they ought to have. As such, it can be regarded as an ideal form of *practical knowledge,* knowledge whose function it is to (help) produce action. It is an ideal against which other forms of practical knowledge can be measured. Understanding *phronēsis* in this way, it would be quite natural to say that a person does not have *full* and *complete* practical knowledge unless he has *phronēsis.* But it should be remembered that having full and complete knowledge in this sense is not restricted to having and exercising all of the premises needed to know on a particular occasion what one ought to do. It also involves being sufficiently motivated to do what one recognizes one ought to do. The argument of Part One explains why some such motivation should be regarded as part of anything that deserves to be called *practical* knowledge.

Next on the continuum will be one who has to a large extent integrated the natural ends of human beings into her character, but who has not fully integrated them into her character. Unlike the *phronimos,* she has not integrated these ends fully enough to prevent conflicting desires from arising. But she has integrated them fully enough that when conflicting desires do arise, she will act on her natural ends rather than on the conflicting desires. Such a person would naturally be called continent. So understood, continence will often involve a genuine state of conflicting motives.

At the bottom of the continuum will be one who has neither integrated the natural ends of human beings well enough to prevent conflicting motives from arising nor to insure that he will act on them rather than on those conflicting desires. His natural ends are partially integrated into his character, because otherwise he would not have a proper conception of the good. Thus, he will have some desire to act as he ought. But it will not always be strong enough to insure action. Such a person would naturally be called incontinent.[13]

It is important to see what forms of *akrasia* this position on practical reason leaves open. Even though according to this position an *akratēs* may not have full and complete knowledge of how he ought to behave, he can still recognize that the situation he is in is one to which his general knowledge applies. He can know that the particular action he engages in is wrong. Furthermore, he can act from a genuine state of conflict. If he does recognize that his situation is one to which his general knowledge applies, he will have a motive to act on it. But since this knowledge is not sufficiently integrated into his character, he can at the same time have a motive to do something else, one that is strong enough to generate action. In short, Aristotle's position on practical reason leaves open just those kinds of *akrasia* whose possibility the traditional interpretation denies, and whose possibility Aristotle seems to acknowledge in the three passages cited above.

I am not saying here that Aristotle's position on practical reason is *incompatible* with the traditional interpretation. There would be nothing inconsistent in Aristotle's closing off a possibility that his position on practical reason leaves open. He might have had independent reasons for thinking that it isn't a genuine possibility. What I am saying, though, is that given Aristotle's position on practical reason one would expect him to provide an explanation of *akrasia* that allows the *akratēs* to know that his situation is one to which his general knowledge applies. If, when he gives his detailed explanation of *akrasia*, Aristotle doesn't allow for this possibility, one would at least want an explanation of why he does not. Barring such an explanation, one may wonder whether an interpretation that closes off such a possibility can be correct.[14]

III. The Seriousness of These Problems

One might wonder whether the problems I have raised are sufficiently worrisome to take seriously the possibility of reinterpreting Aristotle's explanation of *akrasia*. After all, if the inconsistencies are there, they won't be the first to have been found in Aristotle. And failure to recognize a possibility allowed by what one has said elsewhere is hardly a sign of incompetence. If one adds to this the questions that arise over the state of the texts,[15] it may seem even less surprising that the sorts of problems I have outlined arise. If what we have are a set of lecture notes written over different periods of time with revisions and amendations added at later times, or if what we have are students' notes of Aristotle's lectures collected and edited at a later time, then it would be natural for inconsistencies to arise or possibilities to be neglected. A person's views change over time, along with his recollection of what his earlier views leave open. One need only look at students' lecture notes, or at old notes of someone's past lectures, to see how easy it is for inconsistencies to arise or for possibilities to be neglected.

However, one need not hold that great minds are incapable of inconsistency or of lapses of memory to take the above problems seriously and to entertain the possibility that Aristotle might be offering a different explanation of *akrasia*. All one needs is a fairly weak principle of charity, according to which one should make certain that one has interpreted a person correctly, before attributing to him either inconsistencies or the failure to recognize a possibility left open by what he has said elsewhere. Besides, it isn't as if the problems arise in connection with some minor details of Aristotle's explanation of *akrasia*. They arise over the central question of whether the *akratēs* can recognize that what he does is wrong.

The difficulties might not be so formidable if the only inconsistencies that arose were between Bks. I and VII. Not only is there the possibility that Bks. I and VII were written at different times, Aristotle's discussion in Bk. I is based on a psychology that he admits is only as precise as the occasion demands. Bk. VII with its technical apparatus of the practical syllogism might be thought to be based on a more detailed psychology. It wouldn't be surprising if what is said on the basis of a psychology that doesn't pretend to be accurate were to turn out to be inconsistent with something based on a more detailed psychology. However, Chs. 3, 7, and 8 of Bk. VII appear to be parts of a unitary, sustained discussion.[16] If Aristotle did write all of these parts of Bk. VII, it is difficult to see how he could have failed to notice the apparent inconsistencies noted above. Their existence has in part led one author to deny Aristotle's authorship of Ch. 3 (Cook Wilson [1912]), and it has provided part of the basis for another author's reinterpretation of Aristotle's explanation of *akrasia* (Kenny [1966], [1979]). Nor do I think I have exaggerated the importance of Aristotle's failure to leave open a possibility provided for by his position on practical reason. If Aristotle's position on practical reason is as central to his ethics as I have said it is, one would expect it to influence his discussion of *akrasia*. If it doesn't, one would like to know why.

Certainly a more careful look at what Aristotle says is warranted before concluding either that he was inconsistent or that he simply neglected a possibility left open by his position on practical reason.

IV. Variations of the Traditional Interpretation

As I said at the beginning of this chapter, I shall be arguing for an alternative to the traditional interpretation, one that allows the *akratēs* to recognize that the particular action that he does is wrong. But for any such interpretation to be acceptable, it must be preferable to any of the forms of the traditional interpretation. There are three main forms that the traditional interpretation has taken. Setting them out will clarify what it is that I will have to argue against and it will begin to familiarize us with the details of Aristotle's explanation of *akrasia*. It is against these details that ultimately any interpretation will have to be tested.

The three main versions of the traditional interpretation differ in just what they take to be involved in the ignorance that, according to them, prevents the *akratēs* from acting as he ought to act. I think one can best see why the traditional interpretation has taken these forms by starting with a claim that is often associated with the traditional interpretation, that the conclusion of the practical syllogism is an action.

The primary evidence for this claim comes from *De Motu Animalium* and NE Bk. VII Ch. 3.[17] At *De Motu* 701a8-15 Aristotle says,

> What happens seems parallel to the case of thinking and inferring about the immovable objects of science. There the end is the truth seen (for, when one conceives the two premises, one at once conceives and comprehends the conclusion), but here the two premises result in a conclusion which is an action—for example, one conceives that every man ought to walk, one is a man oneself; straightway one walks.

And at NE 1147a26-32 Aristotle says,

> The one opinion is universal, the other is concerned with the particular facts, and here we come to something within the sphere of perception; when a single opinion results from the two, the soul must in one type of case affirm the conclusion, while in the case of opinions concerned with production it must immediately act (e.g. if 'everything sweet ought to be tasted' and 'this is sweet', in the sense of being one of the particular sweet things, the man who can act and is not prevented must at the same time act accordingly).

What seems to be a consequence of this claim is that if one has knowledge of both premises of a practical syllogism, one will act on it unless one is in some way unable to do so. If one applies this consequence to Aristotle's explanation of *akrasia*, a certain problem arises. One's answer to it determines which of the three forms of the traditional interpretation one will take.

At 1147a32ff Aristotle seems to refer to two competing syllogisms, one that the *akratēs* fails to act on (the syllogism of reason), and the other that he does act on (the syllogism of desire).[18] Aristotle seems quite clear about what is contained in the syllogism of desire. Its major premise is 'Everything sweet is pleasant', and its minor premise is 'This is sweet'. Its conclusion is the eating of the sweet thing. However, Aristotle is not at all clear about what is contained in the syllogism of reason. He only says that there is a universal opinion forbidding tasting. He doesn't say what its minor premise or premises are. The problem that arises is that if knowledge of both the major and minor premises of a practical syllogism is sufficient for acting on it, then it looks as if the final minor premise of the syllogism of desire cannot be the same as the final minor premise of the syllogism of reason. The *akratēs* possesses knowledge of the universal premise of the syllogism of reason. If he were also to possess knowledge of its minor premise, then it looks as if he would act on it. Since he doesn't act on it, it looks as if he doesn't have knowledge of its minor premise. He does, however, have knowledge of the minor premise of the syllogism of desire, for this is a syllogism that he does act on. Hence, it looks as if the minor premise of the syllogism of desire could not be the same as the minor premise of the syllogism of reason.

The first form of the traditional interpretation accepts this apparent consequence. According to this view, the syllogism of reason would be something like 'One ought to avoid fattening foods. Candy is a fattening food. This is candy. So I avoid this.' Or, to borrow an example from Professor Anscombe, it might involve knowledge that a culinary worker might possess, for example, 'One must not taste things in the kitchen. This is something in the kitchen. So I avoid tasting this.' On this version of the traditional interpretation, passion prevents the person from perceiving the piece of food in front of him as candy or as something in the kitchen. It is perceived only as something sweet. Since appetite for sweet things is present, the person tastes it.[19]

One problem with this version of the traditional interpretation is that in some circumstances it is difficult to see how a person could have knowledge of one minor premise without having knowledge of the other. One could perhaps forget that one was at work and nibble on some of the sweets being used to prepare dessert. But how could one recognize a piece of candy as something sweet without also recognizing it as a piece of candy? The first version of the traditional interpretation commits Aristotle to saying that the *akratēs* fails to recognize features of his situation that in some cases seem too obvious to miss.

The second version of the traditional interpretation avoids this by maintaining that possession of the major and minor premises of a practical syllogism is not sufficient to insure drawing the conclusion. The premises also have to be *combined*. What goes wrong in at least some cases of *akrasia* is that passion prevents the *akratēs* from making this combination. At 1147a7-8 Aristotle says that a person may fail to possess *or exercise* knowledge of a minor premise. One who holds this second version of the traditional interpretation will say that it is when the knowledge of the minor premise is possessed but not exercised that failure to combine the premises occurs. As Joachim points out ([1951], pp. 226-29), this failure is similar to one that occurs in theoretical reasoning (e.g., *Prior Analytics* 66b18-67b26). An instance of a general principle is recognized as having features that make the principle applicable, but the features are not recognized *as* ones that make the principle applicable. Thus, the *akratēs* can know that he ought to avoid fattening foods, know that sweet foods are fattening, and know that this is sweet. But passion prevents him from recognizing that the sweetness of the food in front of him makes it something that he should avoid. He recognizes it only as something that makes the food pleasant, and that is why he eats it.[20]

The third version of the traditional interpretation is like the first in that it maintains that the minor premises of the two syllogisms cannot be the same. But it avoids having to say that the *akratēs* lacks obvious perceptual knowledge by saying that the minor premise of the syllogism of reason is *evaluative* in a way that the minor premise of the syllogism of desire is not. It takes very seriously the existence of "internal means" discussed in Chapter 5, particularly those that make more determinate an already existing but indeterminate end. On this version, the major premise of the syllogism of reason will be something like, 'One must not eat an excessive number of sweets,' and the minor premise will be 'Eating this would be eating an excessive number of sweets'. According to this version, the *akratēs* can know that what is in front of him is sweet, fattening, or whatever. What he doesn't recognize is that tasting the food in front of him is excessive and therefore harmful. His failure is not a failure to perceive certain *facts*. It is a failure of that kind of *moral perception* that allows a person to see what to do on a particular occasion.[21]

On each of these three versions of the traditional interpretation there is a different account of the kind of failure of knowledge that occurs in *akrasia*. On one it is a failure to recognize certain facts. On another it is a failure to recognize the relevance of certain facts. On the third it is a failure of moral perception to recognize the case at hand as one that falls under a given moral principle. Nevertheless, on all three versions *akrasia* occurs because the *akratēs* fails to recognize that his general knowledge applies to the situation at hand. That is why they are all versions of the traditional interpretation. And that is also why the problems I have raised in this chapter arise for all three versions.

The importance of having these three versions on hand is that if one is to argue for an alternative to the traditional interpretation, it will have to be an alternative that is preferable to each of these three versions of the traditional interpretation.

V. A Methodological Problem

One final problem deserves to be mentioned, and that is one that arises no matter what kind of interpretation of Aristotle on *akrasia* one is arguing for. It is how one is to argue for a particular interpretation without begging the question against alternative interpretations. The problem can be illustrated by reference to NE 1150b19-22, the passage in which Aristotle acknowledges the existence of weak *akrasia*.

There is one way of making 1150b19-22 consistent with the traditional interpretation, and that is to read into it a time-lag between the time the weak *akratēs* draws the conclusions of his deliberations and the time that he fails to abide by them. When he draws them, he acts on them. When he fails to abide by them he no longer draws them. One might admit that this is not the most natural reading of the passage, particularly when the passage is taken by itself. But, one might argue, the passage cannot be taken just by itself. It is part of a longer discussion of *akrasia*. One might argue that when it is read in connection with this longer discussion (particularly what Aristotle has said in Ch. 3), reading in the time-lag is preferable to not reading it in. However, to one who is pointing to 1150b19-22 to cast doubt on the adequacy of the traditional interpretation, this argument seems to beg the question. It presupposes that something like the traditional interpretation is the correct account of what Aristotle says in Ch. 3. To such a person, it is precisely this which is at issue. On the other hand, simply to insist that 1150b19-22 is incompatible with the traditional interpretation and, therefore, that it provides evidence against the traditional interpretation, seems to beg the question against one who wants to argue that a time-lag should be read into the passage because of the context in which it occurs.

The difficulty one is faced with here and throughout Aristotle's discussion of *akrasia* is trying to find passages whose interpretations are not themselves in dispute to determine how to interpret a passage whose interpretation is in dispute. Unless there is something that can be established independently of any particular interpretation of the details of Aristotle's explanation of *akrasia*, to which one can appeal to interpret disputed passages in Aristotle's explanation of *akrasia*, it is going to be difficult to give an argument for any interpretation of Aristotle's explanation of *akrasia* that doesn't leave itself open to charges of question-begging.

In what follows, whether I am setting out considerations in favor of the traditional interpretation or arguing for an alternative interpretation, I shall try to present the matter in such a way that it minimizes charges of question-begging.

CHAPTER 10

An Argument for
the Traditional Interpretation

Although ultimately I want to argue for an alternative to the traditional interpretation, I first want to set out what I take to be the strongest argument that can be given for the traditional interpretation.[1] I do this for two reasons. If the argument I go on to give is stronger than this argument, then I will have given the strongest grounds possible for such an alternative interpretation. Second, in setting out the argument, a number of suggestions that have been made that might be thought to support an alternative interpretation will be examined. We shall see that, as they stand, they are not sufficient to support such an alternative. The net result will be that one will have a clearer picture of just what needs to be done if one is to argue that Aristotle did allow the *akratēs* to know that the particular action that he does is wrong.

To avoid charges of question begging, the argument will try to provide grounds independent of Aristotle's explanation of *akrasia* that he is committed to an explanation of *akrasia* along the lines of the traditional interpretation. It will then use these grounds as part of a non-question begging way of dealing with disputed passages within Aristotle's explanation of *akrasia*. To be more specific, the argument begins by arguing that there are grounds independent of Aristotle's explanation of *akrasia* for attributing to Aristotle a thesis about knowledge and action that commits Aristotle to the traditional interpretation. It then argues that what Aristotle says before giving his detailed explanation of *akrasia* reflects the acceptance of this thesis and paves the way for an explanation along the lines of the traditional interpretation. Given these considerations, one is in a position to see just how well the traditional interpretation does fit the details of Aristotle's explanation of *akrasia*. What he says appears to be what the traditional interpretation says he says. Where it is possible to interpret him as saying something else, one has non-question begging grounds for not interpreting him in that way. Finally, the problems I raised in the previous chapter all have a solution.

I. A Thesis About Knowledge and Action

There is a thesis about knowledge and action that can be attributed to Aristotle on grounds independent of his explanation of *akrasia*. Put in terms of the practical syllogism, it is that anyone who possesses and combines the premises of a practical syllogism will act on it if he or she is able to do so. If accepted, this thesis would commit Aristotle to the traditional interpretation. The *akratēs* possesses the universal premise of the syllogism of reason (1147a32, 1151a20-26). If he were to possess all of the minor premises and combine them with the universal premise, then, given the above thesis, he would act in accord with that syllogism. Since the *akratēs* does not act in accord with the syllogism of reason, he must fail to possess or combine one of its minor premises. It is just this sort of failure that, according to the traditional interpretation, is at the center of Aristotle's explanation of *akrasia*.

Looked at apart from Aristotle's explanation of *akrasia*, there are two bases for attributing the above thesis to Aristotle. The first is Aristotle's claim in *De Motu Animalium* that the conclusion of the practical syllogism is an action. This claim supports the above thesis about knowledge and action in that the thesis follows from this claim and the assumption that one who possesses and combines the premises of a practical syllogism draws its conclusion. If a person who possesses and combines the premises of a practical syllogism draws its conclusion, and if the conclusion is an action, then one who possesses and combines the premises of a practical syllogism will act on it (unless one is unable to act).

The second basis is the claim argued for in Chapter 2 Section III, that the practical syllogism is a model for explaining actions, taken in the sense that the practical syllogism contains all of the elements needed to explain a given action. Suppose that the practical syllogism were a model for explaining actions in this sense and yet knowledge and combination of the premises of a practical syllogism were not sufficient for action in accord with it. That is, suppose that an agent possessed and combined the premises of a practical syllogism but did not act in accord with it, doing something else instead. Since the practical syllogism is a model for explaining actions, there would then be another syllogism explaining the action that he did perform. But then there would have to be something not contained in either of the two syllogisms to explain why the agent acted on one syllogism rather than the other. This would mean, however, that the practical syllogism is not a model for explaining actions, at least not in the sense that it contains all of the elements needed to explain a given action. Thus, if the practical syllogism is a model in this latter sense, then knowledge and combination of the premises of a practical syllogism will be sufficient for action. The argument in Chapter 2 for taking the practical syllogism to be a model for explaining actions was the strong parallel that exists between Aristotle's explanation of action from desire and the elements of the practical syllogism. This parallel in turn rested mainly on passages from *De Anima, De Motu Animalium,* and NE Bk. III. Thus, it rests on considerations independent of Aristotle's explanation of *akrasia.*

I shall concentrate on the first of these two bases. I shall consider the evidence in *De Motu Animalium* for taking the conclusion of the practical syllogism to be an action, and for saying that a person who combines the premises of a practical syllogism will act on it if he or she is able. I shall then defend these claims from objections that might be brought against them.

At *De Motu* 701a8-13 Aristotle contrasts theoretical and practical reasoning on the grounds that in the former case when one grasps the two premises one will conceive and grasp the conclusion, whereas in the latter case the conclusion is an action.

> What happens seems parallel to the case of thinking and inferring about the immovable objects of science. There the end is the truth seen (for, when one conceives the two premises, one at once conceives and comprehends the conclusion, but here the two premises result in a conclusion which is an action).

There follow examples in which the conclusion is given as an action,

> for example, one conceives that every man ought to walk, one is a man oneself; straightway one walks. (701a13-15)

In connection with an example involving a coat Aristotle says,

> And the conclusion I must make a coat is an action. (701a20)

In summary of two of his examples he says that one acts provided nothing prevents or compels (701a15-16). Not only does Aristotle seem to be saying that the conclusion of a practical syllogism is an action, his summary of his two examples seems itself to be a statement of the thesis that is supposed to follow from the conclusion's being an action.

At least two objections, however, can be made against taking the conclusion of a practical syllogism to be an action. The first rests on some general features of the practical syllogism. The second rests on evidence taken from *De Motu Animalium.* I shall argue that neither of them is sufficient to show that the conclusion of a practical syllogism is not an action.

The first objection is that it just doesn't make sense to say that the conclusion of a practical syllogism is an action. Given that this is so, Aristotle's talk about the conclusion of a practical syllogism being an action will have to be understood in some other way. Besides being a model for explaining actions, the practical syllogism is part of a theory of practical *inference,* a theory in which something like *validity* plays a central role. Thus, the relation between premises and conclusion is a *logical* relation. But logical relations only hold between entities that are proposition-like. They don't hold between things like propositions and actions. If one is to make any sense of a practical syllogism, its conclusion will have to be proposition-like. It may be something that has an intimate connection with an action (for example, it expresses a decision to act), but it cannot be an action.

However, this is not enough to show that the conclusion of a practical syllogism cannot be an action. If there is something proposition-like that is intimately tied to an action that is the conclusion of a practical syllogism, then the logical relation that stands between premises and conclusion can be understood as holding between the premises and the action when a similar set of relations holds between the premises and the proposition-like entity that is intimately tied to the action. In the second place, quite apart from this, there are at least two other ways in which Aristotle could have taken an action to be the conclusion of a practical syllogism.

In the case of theoretical reasoning we can and do talk about a person's *beliefs* (the person's *believing* something) being conclusions of certain inferences. Believings are not the sorts of thing that are proposition-like. In this respect they resemble actions more than they do propositions. Of course, *we* would be inclined to say that this talk is to be understood in terms of talk about propositions believed. But there is no guarantee that Aristotle would have been inclined to say the same thing, particularly if Aristotle did not always keep firmly in mind the distinction between believing and what is believed.[2] There are at least two ways that Aristotle might have viewed relations like validity that would have allowed him to take the conclusion of a practical syllogism to be an action.

It is quite common for Aristotle to say that the standard of excellence in any area is the person who possesses the virtue appropriate to that area. In light of this, Aristotle could say that a practical syllogism was valid just in case a practically wise person who accepted its premises would perform the action that was its conclusion. Putting the matter this way would provide Aristotle with a common account of validity for both theoretical and practical syllogisms, for he could say that a theoretical syllogism was valid just in case were a theoretically wise person to accept its premises he or she would accept its conclusion. Even though in the case of theoretical syllogisms there is another account of validity (one that in part explains why a theoretically wise person would accept the conclusion of a valid syllogism whose premises he or she accepted), putting the matter in this way points to a connection between the two kinds of syllogism that would explain why a term like 'validity' can be applied to both of them.

A second possibility comes from Anthony Kenny ([1979], p. 114).[3] According to Kenny, one can regard a valid theoretical syllogism as one in which the truth of the premises is "communicated to" ("causes") the truth of its conclusion. Similarly, a valid practical syllogism is one in which the goodness of its major premise is "communicated" to the action that makes up its conclusion. Either one of these suggestions explains how Aristotle could have taken the conclusion of a practical syllogism to be an action.

The second objection against taking the conclusion of a practical syllogism to be an action comes from *De Motu Animalium* itself. The objection comes from Kenny ([1979], pp. 142-43, [1966], p. 182). Kenny points out that at 701a15-16 Aristotle says that one who conceives of the premises of a practical syllogism acts *provided nothing prevents or compels.* But prevention or compulsion need not mean that a person's reasoning has been inconclusive. Thus, it looks as if a person can draw the conclusion of a practical syllogism and yet not act on it. (The person can be prevented from acting on it.) According to Kenny, in such a case the conclusion of a practical syllogism is a *decision.* Kenny thinks that Aristotle also recognizes a decision as a conclusion of a practical syllogism in what is almost the next example.

> I need a covering, a coat is a covering: I need a coat. What I need I ought to make, I need a coat: I make a coat. And the conclusion *I must make a coat* is an action. And the action goes back to the beginning or first step. If there is to be a coat, one must first have B, and if B then A, so one gets A to begin with. (701a18-22, emphasis mine)

According to Kenny, the words 'I must make a coat' express a conclusion, a conclusion that is a decision. The reason it is a decision is that action has been postponed. As the rest of the passage shows, further steps must be taken before making a coat can begin.[4]

I do not think that this objection shows that the conclusion of a practical syllogism is not an action. Let us begin with the example involving the coat.[5] The proposition-like form of the conclusion 'I must make a coat' can be explained by its being an *intermediate* conclusion in the syllogism in which it occurs. Further deliberation is required before one will be able to draw the final conclusion. As Aristotle says, one must first have B, and if B, then A. (For example, to make a coat one must cut material to the right size, and to do this one needs both material and a cutting tool.) Until one realizes this, one will not be in a position to act. Once one realizes it, however, one acts. As Aristotle says, "One gets A to begin with." *This* is the conclusion of the full syllogism, and this is an action. This is confirmed by what Aristotle says immediately afterward, "Now that the action is the conclusion is clear" (701a23). It would not be clear if Aristotle had just said that the conclusion was a decision.[6, 7]

Let us now turn to the case of one who has been compelled or prevented from acting. This too does not show that the conclusion of a practical syllogism is not an action. Suppose that reasoning in such a case is not inconclusive. Something results from this reasoning, a deliberate desire. There will also be something proposition-like that expresses this desire. But why say that this is the conclusion of a practical syllogism? It might be argued that saying that it is the conclusion is so much like saying that the conclusion of a practical syllogism is *not* an action, that merely to assume that it is the conclusion would beg the question at issue. Of course, simply claiming that it is not the conclusion would also beg the question. But if one turns to the rest of the passage to see which of these claims has some support, the number of occasions on which Aristotle seems to say that the conclusion of a practical syllogism is an action seems to tell against taking what results from reasoning in a case of compulsion to be the conclusion of a practical syllogism. Rather, one should say that in a case like this the person has been prevented from drawing the conclusion, even if he has combined all of the premises.

What is more important, though, is that even if this is wrong, it does not follow that Aristotle did not hold the thesis about knowledge and action that we are concerned with. That thesis says that a person who combines the premises of a practical syllogism will act on it *if he or she is able.* If the only cases in which people combine the premises of a practical syllogism but don't act on them are ones in which the people are physically unable to act, then even if the conclusion of a practical syllogism is not an action, Aristotle did hold the thesis in question.

It might be objected that when Aristotle says that a person who combines the premises of a practical syllogism will act provided nothing prevents or compels (*kōluē ē anagkazē*), he does have in mind more than those who suffer from physical inability. If the category of those prevented (*kōluē*) didn't include, for example, those who are prevented from acting by a conflicting internal desire, then Aristotle's use of the verb *'kōluō'* would be redundant.[8] (*'Anagkazē'* does seem to refer to something like external compulsion.) However, not only is there the possibility that redundancy in this passage can be explained,[9] there are general reasons for not construing *'kōluē'* so broadly that a conflicting desire can prevent a person from acting. If this were true, then any time a person acts intentionally, he will have been prevented from acting otherwise. This doesn't seem to be something that Aristotle would want to say. Furthermore, Aristotle's claim that one who possesses the premises of a practical syllogism will act on them unless prevented or compelled would run the danger of collapsing into the trivial claim that a person will act on the premises of a practical syllogism unless he or she does something else.[10] If faced with the choice between redundancy and triviality, it looks as if one should restrict the category of those who are prevented or compelled to those who suffer from something like physical inability. So restricted, what Aristotle says at 701a15-16 not only doesn't undermine his acceptance of the thesis about knowledge and action in question, it actually constitutes a statement of that thesis.

Thus, even if Aristotle is not saying in *De Motu* 701a8ff that the conclusion of a practical syllogism is an action, he is at least saying that someone who combines the premises of a practical syllogism will act on it unless he or she is unable to act. If one adds to this the other basis mentioned, then it looks as if grounds independent of Aristotle's explanation of *akrasia* exist for attributing to him a thesis that commits him to the traditional interpretation. Of course, this does not decide the matter of whether Aristotle accepted this thesis. There is also evidence that can be drawn from Aristotle's explanation of *akrasia* itself. But it is enough to provide the beginning of a non-question begging argument that Aristotle's explanation of *akrasia* should be interpreted along the lines of the traditional interpretation.

II. Aristotle's General Approach to *Akrasia*

To have strong, non-question begging grounds for interpreting disputed passages in Aristotle's explanation of *akrasia,* one needs more than independent evidence that Aristotle accepted a thesis about knowledge and action that committed him to the traditional interpretation. One also needs reasons for thinking that this thesis is at work in Aristotle's explanation of *akrasia,* reasons that do not themselves rest on the controversial details of Aristotle's explanation of *akrasia.* The argument for the traditional interpretation continues by maintaining that these reasons can be found in the general approach

Aristotle takes to *akrasia* in NE VII prior to his detailed explanation of *akrasia* at 1147a24ff.

At least three things in this part of Bk. VII suggest that the above thesis is at work in Aristotle's discussion of *akrasia*. The first is the fact that *akrasia* gets all the attention when it looks as if the subject of discussion is both *akrasia* and *enkrateia*. The second is the way in which Aristotle poses the main question that he thinks needs to be answered in connection with *akrasia*. The third are the three sets of passages that immediately precede his detailed explanation of *akrasia*.

Although at the beginning of Bk. VII it looks as if both *akrasia* and *enkrateia* are to be the subjects of discussion, it turns out that only *akrasia* receives any detailed attention. This suggests that *akrasia* is in need of explanation in a way in which *enkrateia* is not. This in turn can be explained by the above thesis about knowledge and action. The *enkratēs* is one who possesses and combines the premises of the syllogism on which he ought to act. Given the above thesis, he should act on it. Since this is what he does, there is as yet nothing about his action that requires explanation. However, one of the *phainomena* surrounding *akrasia* is that the *akratēs* is said to know that what he does is wrong (1145b12-13). If this knowledge consists in the possession and combination of the premises of the syllogism on which he ought to act, then, given the above thesis, he won't act incontinently. In what sense then can he be said to know that what he does is wrong? Since the above thesis explains why Aristotle would focus his attention on *akrasia*, there is at least some reason for thinking that this thesis is operative in his discussion of *akrasia*.

That this thesis is operative receives additional support from the main question that Aristotle raises in his discussion of *akrasia*. It is just the question that arises given the above thesis about knowledge and action. As Hardie points out ([1980], pp. 266-67), the question that begins Ch. 2 should not be translated as 'In what sense can a man who has right understanding behave incontinently?', implying that the *akratēs* does have a correct conception of what he ought to do. Rather it should be translated as 'In what sense does a person who behaves incontinently have right understanding?',[11] implying that the sense in which the *akratēs* has a correct conception of what he ought to do is what is at issue. This is confirmed by the fact that immediately after raising this question, Aristotle points to difficulties in taking the *akratēs'* state to involve any one of the three forms of understanding *(hupolēpsis)* that he typically acknowledges— *epistēmē* (knowledge), *phronēsis* (practical wisdom), and *doxa* (opinion) (1145b21-1146a9). It is further confirmed by Aristotle's summary of the question he is raising at the beginning of Ch. 3, "We must consider first, then, whether incontinent people act knowingly or not, and in what sense knowingly" (1146b8-9). Since the above thesis about knowledge and action explains why Aristotle would raise this question, we again have reason for thinking that this thesis is operative in his discussion of *akrasia*.

Finally, the three sets of passages that immediately precede Aristotle's detailed explanation of *akrasia* all seem to reflect this thesis at work. In 1146b30-34 Aristotle distinguishes two senses of 'know', one in which people are not exercising knowledge that they possess and the other in which they are exercising it. Aristotle says that it would be strange *(deinos)* for a man to act contrary to knowledge that he is actually exercising. Two things in this passage seem to reflect the above thesis about knowledge and action. The first is the remark that it would be strange for someone to act contrary to knowledge that is being exercised. A person who possesses and combines the premises of a practical syllogism does appear to be one who is exercising knowledge. According to the above thesis, it would be strange for such a person to act contrary to this knowledge. The second is the distinction itself between knowledge possessed and exercised and knowledge possessed but not exercised. Traditionally, commentators have taken this distinction to be a distinction between actual knowledge (knowledge that a person is actually conscious of), and potential knowledge (knowledge that at the time a person is not conscious of).[12] Since Aristotle goes on to take *akrasia* to be a case in which a person has but does not exercise knowledge (1147a10ff), it looks as if Aristotle is saying that at the time that he acts the *akratēs* cannot be consciously aware that what he does is wrong. This is just what one would expect him to say given the above thesis about knowledge and action.

In 1146b35-1147a10 Aristotle discusses knowledge of what to do in terms of the practical syllogism. He distinguishes two kinds of premise in a practical syllogism, universal and particular, and says that it is possible to possess the universal premise without possessing or exercising all of the particular premises. He says that it would be astonishing *(thaumastos)* if one were to fail to act when one possessed and exercised knowledge of both kinds of premise, but it would not be astonishing if one did not have or did not exercise one of the particular premises. Again, this is just what Aristotle would say on the above thesis about knowledge and action.

Indeed, the mere presence of these two passages suggests that Aristotle approached his detailed explanation of *akrasia* with the above thesis in mind. Given this thesis, it would be tempting to say that the *akratēs* does *not* know that what he does is wrong. However, this is essentially the Socratic view, and Aristotle has said that this view is contrary to the *phainomena* (1147a27-28). How then can the *akratēs* be said to know that what he does is wrong? One would have an answer if there were cases in which it was perfectly intelligible for a person to have knowledge and not act on it, and *akrasia* could be seen to fall under these cases. 1146b30-34 and 1146b35-1147a10 provide cases in which it is perfectly intelligible for a person to have knowledge and not act on it. What Aristotle is calling attention to in these two passages is just what one would expect him to call attention to if he were operating with the above thesis about knowledge and action. All that is needed to confirm this is Aristotle's arguing that *akrasia* does fall under one or both of these two cases.

That is precisely what happens in 1147a10-24, the last of the three passages that precede Aristotle's detailed explanation of *akrasia*. Aristotle calls attention to people who in a sense do and in a sense do not have knowledge. His examples include those who are mad, asleep, or drunk. He says that a person under the influence of passion is in a state like this; and he says that an *akratēs* is in a similar state (1147a14-18). These sort of people do seem to fall under the kinds of cases mentioned in the two previous passages. Those who in a sense do and in a sense do not possess knowledge are specifically said to be a subclass of those who possess but do not exercise knowledge (1147a11-13). Those who have knowledge in the way that someone drunk or asleep has knowledge don't seem to have or exercise all of the premises needed to support that knowledge. Having said this much, Aristotle has not yet fully explained the sense in which the *akratēs* knows that what he does is wrong. This will come at 1147a24ff. But he has said enough to confirm that it is the above thesis that is operative in his discussion of *akrasia*.

Not only is there evidence independent of Aristotle's discussion of *akrasia* that Aristotle accepted a thesis that commits him to explaining *akrasia* along the lines of the traditional interpretation, there is evidence that this thesis is at work in his discussion of *akrasia*.

III. The Details of Aristotle's Explanation of *Akrasia*

We are now in a position to look at the details of Aristotle's explanation of *akrasia* at 1147a24-1147b9. Given what has been argued, one would expect Aristotle to explain *akrasia* along the lines of the traditional interpretation. Read in light of these expectations, that is just what Aristotle seems to do. What he says seems to be just what the traditional interpretation takes him to say. On those few occasions where he might be thought to say something else, one has non-question begging grounds for arguing that he isn't saying something else.

The argument in this section falls into four stages. First, the details of Aristotle's explanation of *akrasia* are set out as they are understood under the traditional interpretation. This will show how easy it is to read them along the lines of the traditional interpretation. Second, a series of objections are raised against reading the details in this way. These objections suggest an alternative to the traditional interpretation. The interpretation is essentially one argued for by Anthony Kenny. Third, it is argued that none of these objections hold. When one looks more carefully at what these objections are based on, it seems preferable to read the details of Aristotle's explanation of *akrasia* along the lines of the traditional interpretation rather than along the lines of the alternative interpretation. The conclusions drawn in Sections I and II will play an important role in this part of the argument. Finally, a passage is noted that provides a major stumbling block not only for the alternative just discussed, but also for any other alternative to the traditional interpretation. Thus, a careful look at the details of Aristotle's explanation of *akrasia* seems to provide strong support for the traditional interpretation.

A. The Details According to the Traditional Interpretation

Right at the beginning Aristotle seems to reaffirm the thesis about knowledge and action argued for in Sections I and II.

> Again, we may also view the case as follows with reference to the facts of human nature. The one opinion is universal, the other is concerned with particular facts, and here we come to something within the sphere of perception; when a single opinion results from the two, the soul must in one type of case (*entha*) affirm the conclusion, while in the case of opinions concerned with production (*poiētikais*) it must immediately act (e.g. if 'everything sweet ought to be tasted', and 'this is sweet', in the sense of being one of the particular sweet things, the man who can act and is not prevented (*dunamenon kai mē kōluomenon*) must at the same time act accordingly. (1147a24-32)

Aristotle seems to be saying here both that the conclusion of a practical syllogism is an action, and that one who possesses and combines the premises of a practical syllogism will act on it if he is able to act on it. The introduction of this thesis seems explicitly meant to pave the way for an explanation of *akrasia* along the lines of the traditional interpretation.

What follows fits this expectation quite well. Aristotle sets out a particular instance of *akrasia* in which the agent knows that certain things ought not to be tasted, but also knows that everything sweet is pleasant and that the piece of food in front of him is sweet (1147a32-33). What this means is that there are two syllogisms relevant to the case at hand. One (the syllogism of reason) has as a major premise something that forbids tasting objects of the sort in front of the agent. The other (the syllogism of desire) has as its major premise 'Everything sweet is pleasant' with 'This is sweet' as its minor premise. Even though one thing (the universal premise of the syllogism of reason that forbids tasting) tells him to avoid the object *(hē men oun legei pheugein touto)* (1147a34), appetite is present (1147a34). This appetite leads the *akratēs* to taste the sweet thing (1147a34-36). The minor premise of the syllogism of desire, 'This is sweet', is active (1147a33-34), because the *akratēs* acts on that syllogism. He does not act on the syllogism of reason, because the minor premise of that syllogism is either not possessed or possessed only in the sense in which a drunken person has knowledge.

> The last premise *(hē teleutaia protasis)* both being an opinion about a perceptible object, and being what determines our actions, this a man either has not when he is in the state of passion, or has it in the sense in which knowledge did not mean knowing but only talking, as a drunken man may mutter the verses of Empedocles. (1147b9-12)

That is, appetite for sweet things has prevented the *akratēs* from possessing or exercising the minor premise of the syllogism of reason. This leaves just this appetite to move him to act as he does.

Having said this, Aristotle is in a position to answer the question raised at the beginning of Ch. 2, "In what sense does an *akratēs* have a correct conception of what he ought to do?". The *akratēs* does not have knowledge of what he ought to do in the sense in which one who possesses and combines the premises of the syllogism of reason knows what he ought to do. In a sense he possesses knowledge of what he ought to do and in a sense he does not. He possesses (and may exercise[13]) knowledge of the universal premise of the syllogism on which he ought to act. But he either does not have or does not exercise knowledge of its final minor premise. His possession of that particular knowledge (if in fact he does possess it) is like the knowledge of one who is mad, asleep, or drunk. People in that condition don't know what they are talking about. It is passion that has got them into this condition. Thus, it is passion that prevents the *akratēs* from recognizing that the action that he eventually performs is one that he ought not to perform. In the absence of this recognition, this same passion moves him to act as he does, contrary to what he "knows" he ought to do.

Aristotle, thus, has incorporated the elements of the three passages preceding his most detailed explanation of *akrasia,* allowing him to explain in what sense the *akratēs* does know that what he does is wrong. The explanation is just what one would expect given the arguments of Sections I and II.

B. *Objections to the Traditional Interpretation*

There are, however, a series of objections that can be raised against this way of understanding the details of Aristotle's explanation of *akrasia*. Each one of them is also an objection to the thesis about knowledge and action argued for in Sections I and II, and to the claim that the conclusion of a practical syllogism is an action.[14] Thus, they will provide an opportunity to revise the conclusions drawn in those sections.

The first objection is that at 1147a24-32 Aristotle is not affirming the thesis about knowledge and action argued for in Sections I and II. He is also not saying that the conclusion of a practical syllogism is an action. The second objection is that there are not two syllogisms in Aristotle's explanation of *akrasia;* there is only one. Once one recognizes this, one will see that what Aristotle goes on to say commits him to saying that the *akratēs* does draw the conclusion of the syllogism on which he ought to act. The third objection is that Aristotle refers to this conclusion at 1147a34 *(hē men oun legei pheugein touto).* The final objection is that *'hē teleutaia protasis'* at 1147b9 also refers to this conclusion.[15]

According to the first objection, 1147a24-32 does not say either that the conclusion of a practical syllogism is an action or that a person who possesses and combines the premises of a practical syllogism will act on it if he is able to. Traditionally the passage has been interpreted as drawing a contrast between theoretical and practical reasoning. But the text does not specifically mention theoretical reasoning. Rather, Aristotle refers to two kinds of premise, a universal premise and a premise concerned with particulars that are grasped by perception (1147a26-27). He is concerned with situations in which a single opinion results from these two kinds of premise (1147a27). He draws a contrast between the soul's affirming a conclusion *entha,* and between cases involving *poiētikais,* where the soul is said immediately to act (1147a27-28).[16] Traditionally *'entha'* has been translated as 'in one type of case' and *'poiētikais'* has been taken to contrast with *'theōrētikais'.* Understood in this way, the contrast becomes a contrast between cases of theoretical reasoning, where affirmation of a conclusion results from combination of the premises, and between cases of practical reasoning, where action results from such a combination. However, Kenny argues that a reference to theoretical reasoning is out of place here. One of the kinds of premise that Aristotle is talking about involves particulars, and, according to Aristotle, theoretical reasoning does not involve reference to particulars ([1966], p. 177). Rather *'entha'* should be translated as 'immediately', and *'poiētikais'* should be taken to mark the familiar contrast between *poiēsis* (production) and *praxis* (practice).[17] So understood, the contrast becomes a contrast between what happens in all cases of combining practical premises (a conclusion is immediately drawn), and between what happens in some practical cases, straightforward cases of technical reasoning where there is no conflicting desire to prevent action (action immediately occurs). These latter cases in turn provide an implicit contrast with cases that Aristotle is going to go on to talk about, cases of ethical reasoning where a conflicting desire is present (cases of *akrasia*) ([1979], p. 157).

Kenny also argues that when Aristotle says of someone who has combined the premises of a practical syllogism that the person must act if able and not prevented *(dunamenon kai mē kōluomenon)* (1147a30-31), it is a mistake to take *'kōluomenon'* to refer only to external compulsion. He argues that it probably means 'being prevented by a conflicting internal factor'. Otherwise *'mē kōluomenon'* only repeats what is said by *'dunamenon'.* Also, the verb *'kōluō'* will have to be taken to refer to different factors at line 31 *(kōluomenon)* and at line 32 *(kōluousa).* In the latter Aristotle talks about a universal opinion (an internal factor) that forbids tasting ([1966], p. 177).[18] If *'kōluomenon'* does refer to an internal factor, then not only will it be possible for a person to combine the premises of a practical syllogism without acting on it, Aristotle will have left open the possibility that the *akratēs* can draw the conclusion on which he ought to act.[19]

The second objection is based on an argument that there is only one syllogism in Aristotle's explanation of *akrasia*. Traditionally Aristotle has been taken to refer to two syllogisms, one having a major premise forbidding tasting, the other having 'Everything sweet is pleasant' as its major premise. Kenny argues, however, that *'hē men katholou'* at line 32 should be taken as *'the* universal premise', implying that there is only one syllogism under discussion. He thinks that the reason people have not taken it in this way is that they have an oversimplified view of the practical syllogism, and because they have taken 'everything' *('pan')* in 'Everything sweet is pleasant' *('pan gluku hēdu')* as signaling another universal premise ([1966], p. 179).

The oversimplified view is that the practical syllogism consists of two premises of the form 'What is Ø ought to be done' and 'This is Ø'. However, at 1146b35ff Aristotle says that there is nothing to prevent people from acting against their knowledge if they exercise only the universal premise and not the particular. If exercising the universal premise means applying it to a more particular case, then in order for the universal but not the particular premise to be exercised, a practical syllogism will have to have a composite minor premise, one of whose elements is exercised in connection with the universal premise, and the other of which is not exercised at all. This is borne out by Aristotle's example, 'Dry food is good for any man. Such and such is dry food. I am a man. This is such and such.' 'Dry food is good for any man' can be exercised together with 'Such and such food is good for any man'. But the minor premise 'This is such and such' may still not be exercised at all.

Once one recognizes this, one can easily see how to treat 1147a32ff as involving only one syllogism. 'Everything sweet is pleasant' and 'This is sweet' are parts of a composite minor premise. One tends to think that 'Everything sweet is pleasant' is another universal premise because of the occurrence of 'everything' in it. But as Aristotle's example involving dry food shows, a premise need not be singular to be a particular or minor premise. It need only be more particular than the major premise. The major premise of this one syllogism turns out to be one that prohibits tasting things insofar as they are pleasant. Since the *akratēs* shares the principles of a temperate man (1148a4-10, 1151a11-15, 1152a4-7), his major premises will be concerned with avoiding excessive pleasure. Since the case in question is one involving taste, it will be a premise that prohibits tasting insofar as tasting is pleasant. Taken with its composite minor premise, this major premise yields the conclusion 'Don't taste this' ([1979], p. 159).

Kenny thinks that this way of understanding 1147a32ff is made "almost certain" by 1149a32-b2 where Aristotle says,

> For argument or imagination informs us that we have been insulted or slighted, and anger, reasoning as it were that something like this must be fought against, boils up straightway; while appetite, if argument or perception merely says that an object is pleasant, springs to the enjoyment of it. Therefore, anger obeys argument in a sense, but appetite does not.

Kenny takes this passage to say that appetite does not reason at all, and, thus, that there is no such thing as a syllogism of desire ([1966, p. 180).[20]

Given the one syllogism that Kenny says occurs in Aristotle's explanation of *akrasia,* one is in a position to see why what Aristotle goes on to say would commit him to saying that the *akratēs* draws the conclusion on which he ought to act. At 1147a33-34 Aristotle says that the final minor premise of this syllogism, 'This is sweet', is active *(touti de gluku [hautē de energei]).* Its activity can only consist in its being applied to the case at hand. That is, the conclusion 'Don't taste this' must be drawn ([1966], p. 182).[21]

The third objection arises from what is said almost immediately after 'This is sweet' is said to be active. At 1147a34 Aristotle says,

"One thing says to avoid this *(hē men oun legei pheugein touto)"*
(my translation). Taken just by itself, this seems to refer to the conclusion of the syllogism on which the *akratēs* ought to act. The final
minor premise of the syllogism on which the *akratēs* ought to act
does not say to avoid anything, and its major premise does not refer
to the particular object at hand, at least not by the demonstrative
'this' *('touto')* ([1966], p. 182). This confirms and is confirmed by
the previous objection. If Aristotle has just acknowledged the activity of a premise whose activity would consist in the drawing of a conclusion, then one would expect him to acknowledge that this conclusion has been drawn. That is just what he does on the above reading
of 1147a34.[22]

The fourth and final objection rests largely on one or both of the
last two objections. Although initially *'hē teleutaia protasis'* at 1147b9
might be more naturally translated as 'the last premise', *'protasis'*
does have as a general sense 'proposition'. If there is only one syllogism in Aristotle's explanation of *akrasia* and if its final minor
premise has just been said to be active, then it looks as if *hē teleutaia
protasis* cannot be this final minor premise. *'Hē teleutaia protasis'*
is said either not to be possessed or not exercised (1147b9-13). It
can only be "the last proposition" of that syllogism, that is, the conclusion ([1966], p. 183).[23] This is made even more plausible if Aristotle has just referred to such a conclusion at 1147a34. *'Hē teleutaia
protasis'* simply picks up this reference again.

Given these four objections, one is in a position to put together an
alternative to the traditional interpretation according to which the
problems I have raised in Chapter 10 also seem not to arise.[24] First
(1147a24-32), Aristotle paves the way for his explanation of *akrasia*
by calling attention to the possibility of drawing the conclusion of
a practical syllogism without acting on it. He then goes on to explain
akrasia in terms of a case where the *akratēs* does draw the conclusion
of the syllogism on which he ought to act.[25] The *akratēs* knows that
he ought not to taste things insofar as they are pleasant, and he also
holds the opinions that everything sweet is pleasant and that this is
sweet. This in turn means that tasting the object falls under the
prohibition of the major premise. It also means that tasting it is an
object of *epithumia* (appetite), *epithumia* being understood as a
desire for what is pleasant. It is this desire that the *akratēs* eventually
acts on. It is because this desire results from the foregoing piece of
reasoning that Aristotle says that *akrasia* is the result of both reasoning *(logos)* and opinion *(doxa)* (1147b1). The *akratēs'* action is not
due to any failure to possess or exercise the minor premise of the
syllogism on which he ought to act, for there is only one minor
premise in Aristotle's explanation of *akrasia* and this premise is active.

The *akratēs* knows that the action he engages in is wrong, because he draws the conclusion on which he ought to act. There is also a conflict between reason and desire in *akrasia,* for desire prompts the *akratēs* to act contrary to what reason tells him to do.

> Yet both Aristotle's general doctrine of conflict and Socrates' doctrine of knowledge emerge unscathed. There is a genuine conflict because *epithumia* fights against a conclusion reached by reasoning. Yet knowledge is not dragged about like a slave, because the conclusion which *epithumia* overcomes is neither general (since it concerns *this*) nor epistemonic (since it contains the practical imperative). . . . If all this is correct, it is wrong either to blame or praise Aristotle for failing to consider the case of a man acting in a way which he fully knows at the time to be wrong. For he considers just such a case when he discusses the case in which the conclusion of the practical syllogism is drawn. (Kenny [1966] , pp. 183-84)

What this means is that this alternative interpretation has the added attraction of not having to deal with the problems raised for the traditional interpretation in Chapter 9.

C. Replies to the Objections

As they stand, however, these objections do not hold. And despite appearances to the contrary, the interpretation summarized above does not avoid the problems raised. Given the present state of the argument, it cannot be taken to be preferable to the traditional interpretation.

Let us begin with the first objection. In the first place 1147a24-32 should be read as saying that the conclusion of a practical syllogism is an action.

If the arguments in Section I are at all persuasive and Aristotle is saying in *De Motu* 701a8ff that the conclusion of a practical syllogism is an action, then I think one will have to admit that here too he is saying the same thing. The passages are too close to one another to take them to be saying something different. In *De Motu* Aristotle first distinguishes between two kinds of reasoning, theoretical and practical. In the former when a person comprehends the two premises he conceives and comprehends the conclusion (701a11-12). In the latter the conclusion is said to be an action (701a13-14). There follow examples in which the conclusion is given as an action. Aristotle says in summary of two of them that one acts provided nothing prevents or compels *(kōluē ē anagkazē)* (701a16-17). All of these elements appear to be present in 1147a24-32. First, there is a distinction between two kinds of cases in which there is reasoning. The first is said to be one in which the combination of the two kinds of premises results in a conclusion. The second is said to concern *poiētikais.*

An example is given, and it is said that when the two premises are combined one must immediately act. The passages are so much alike that it is hard to deny that Aristotle is saying the same thing in both passages.

Of course, no explicit reference is made to theoretical reasoning in 1147a24-32, and Kenny would argue that such a reference is out of place given that one of the two kinds of premises talked about is said to be concerned with particulars discovered by perception. Furthermore, 'poiēsis' is often contrasted with 'praxis'. If one also gives 'entha' its common meaning of 'immediately', the contrast drawn becomes one between all cases of practical reasoning where a conclusion is drawn and certain cases of technical reasoning where action immediately follows.

However, in Aristotle's discussion of error in the *Prior Analytics* (66b18-67b26), there is a geometrical example involving reference to particulars that, if one is classifying examples along the theoretical-practical distinction, can only be classified as a case of theoretical reasoning. Thus, on a fairly broad construal of theoretical reasoning, theoretical reasoning can involve reference to particulars. And although it is true that 'poiēsis' is often contrasted with 'praxis', 'poiētikais' is also used in contrast with 'theōrētikais'. The most important instance is *De Motu* 701a23, the passage that appears to be the exact parallel of 1147a24-32. Although 'entha' does have as a common meaning 'immediately', it also has as a common meaning 'in the one case'. Reading 'poiētikais' and 'entha' in the latter two ways, the contrast is between theoretical and practical reasoning. Given the parallel that seems to exist between *De Motu* 701a8ff and 1147a24-32, it seems preferable to read the contrast in this way.[26]

What is more, taken in the way the traditional interpretation takes it, 1147a24-32 seems to fit what follows better than it does on Kenny's interpretation. On the traditional interpretation what is said is that in contrast to theoretical reasoning, when a person possesses and combines the premises of a practical syllogism, action occurs. Since in *akrasia* the appropriate action does not occur, something must have gone wrong in the possession and/or combination of the premises. What follows explains just what has gone wrong. On Kenny's interpretation Aristotle's explanation of *akrasia* is introduced more awkwardly. The contrast drawn with the case Aristotle will go on to discuss is only drawn implicitly, and the contrast that is drawn explicitly is drawn imperfectly. The latter contrast is a contrast between all cases of practical reasoning and *some* cases of technical reasoning (straightforward ones in which there is no conflicting desire). But it is not clear that this latter qualification is in the text.[27] This qualification has to be understood if the contrast between the case Aristotle will discuss is to be drawn even implicitly. On balance, it seems preferable to take the contrast in 1147a24-32 to be the one that the traditional interpretation says is drawn. So understood, one half of it says that the conclusion of a practical syllogism is an action.

In the second place, Aristotle's qualification at 1147a30-31 that a person who combines the premises of a practial syllogism will act on it if able and not prevented should not be taken as allowing a person to be prevented from acting by a conflicting internal desire. Rather, it should be taken to refer to a more restricted class of limiting factors, ones involving something like external compulsion. Even though taking it in this way makes Aristotle's use of '*kōluomenon*' at line 31 redundant, we saw in Section I that there are general reasons for accepting this redundancy. Taking '*kōluomenon*' to refer to a conflicting internal desire would commit Aristotle to saying that any time a person acts intentionally she will have been prevented from acting otherwise. It also threatens to collapse Aristotle's qualification that a person who combines the premises of a practical syllogism will act on it if able and not prevented into the trivial claim that a person will act on a practical syllogism unless she does something else.[28] Redundancy seems preferable to triviality. Nor is the fact that Aristotle uses '*kōluō*' at line 32 to refer to an internal state sufficient to rebut these general considerations. '*Kōluō*' can be used to mean either 'to prevent' or 'to prohibit'. At line 31 it is used in the former sense; at line 32 it is used in the latter. The fact that when it is used in the latter sense it can refer to an internal factor does not mean that it can refer to an internal factor when it is used in the former sense. Without further argument to rebut the general considerations raised above, it seems preferable to restrict Aristotle's qualification at 1147a31-32 to cases like external compulsion.

Finally, even if one takes '*kōluomenon*' to refer to a conflicting internal desire, it is still possible to maintain that the conclusion of a practical syllogism is an action. Aristotle's qualification that a person who combines the premises of a practical syllogism will act on it if she is able and not prevented provides a counterexample to this claim only if one who combines the premises of a practical syllogism draws its conclusion. However, as we saw in Section I, a proponent of the traditional interpretation can argue that this latter claim is so close to what is at issue that merely to assume that it is true begs the question. But if one looks at what Aristotle has to say elsewhere about the conclusion of a practical syllogism (esp. *De Motu* 701a8ff), his repeated insistence that it is an action provides grounds for thinking that the mere combination of the premises of a practical syllogism will not always be sufficient for the drawing of its conclusion.[29]

Thus, it seems preferable to take 1147a24-32 to reaffirm both the claim that the conclusion of a practical syllogism is an action and the thesis about knowledge and action that this claim seems to support.

Let us now turn to the second objection. It was based on an argument that there is only one syllogism in Aristotle's explanation of *akrasia*. However, not only is this argument insufficient to show that there is only one syllogism in Aristotle's explanation of *akrasia*, even if it were, it would not be enough to show that the *akratēs* can draw the conclusion on which he ought to act.

In the first place, contrary to what Kenny suggests, there is reason for thinking that the major premise of the syllogism on which the *akratēs* ought to act is something other than 'Taste nothing in so far as it is pleasant'. If one looks at what the likely candidates for it are, one will see that there is reason for taking 'Everything sweet is pleasant' and 'This is sweet' to be parts of a second syllogism.

If one looks at all of Aristotle's examples of practical syllogisms,[30] virtually every one of them seems to be a medical example, with a major premise setting out something that is conducive to health.[31] The only possible exceptions appear to be the example under question and the one that immediately precedes it, 'Everything sweet ought to be tasted' and 'This is sweet' (1147a29-30).[32] If one takes the predominance of medical examples seriously, taking the immediately preceding example also to be a medical example, then it is likely that Aristotle's example in his explanation of *akrasia* is a medical example as well. It will then have as a major premise something like 'One ought to avoid fattening goods', rather than 'Taste nothing insofar as it is pleasant'. Its minor premise will then be something like 'Candy is fattening' and 'This is candy'. But then 'Everything sweet is pleasant' and 'This is sweet' will have to be parts of a second syllogism.[33]

If the example is taken to be a nonmedical example, there is still some reason for thinking that 'Everything sweet is pleasant' and 'This is sweet' will be parts of a second syllogism. If, for example, the immediately preceding example is a "culinary" one, then this suggests that Aristotle's example in his explanation of *akrasia* is also a "culinary" one. It then will have something like 'Taste nothing in the kitchen' as its major premise. 'Everything sweet is pleasant' and 'This is sweet' will then be parts of another syllogism.

Finally, even if the immediately preceding example is an ethical example, and even if its major premise is a principle that a temperate man would have, it is more likely that this premise is 'Don't taste an excessive number of sweets' rather than 'Taste nothing insofar as it is pleasant'. Again, this suggests that 'Everything sweet is pleasant' and 'This is sweet' are parts of a second syllogism.[34]

What is more, the considerations that Kenny thinks have led people to say that there are two syllogisms in Aristotle's explanation of *akrasia* do not, when abandoned, force one to admit that there is only one syllogism. One can admit that a practical syllogism can have the form, 'What is Ø is good for any person. What is Ø is Ʊ. I am a person. This is Ʊ', and still maintain that there are two syllogisms in Aristotle's explanation of *akrasia*. The above example involving fattening foods can easily be put into this form. One can also recognize that not every premise with 'everything' in it will be a major premise and still maintain that 'Everything sweet is pleasant' is part of a second syllogism, particularly if one has grounds for thinking that the major premise of the syllogism of reason is not 'Taste nothing insofar as it is pleasant.'[35]

Nor does the passage that Kenny thinks makes the claim that there is only one syllogism in Aristotle's explanation of *akrasia* "almost certain" show that there is no such thing as a syllogism of desire. What Aristotle says at 1149a32-b2 is

> For argument or imagination informs us that we have been insulted or slighted, and anger, reasoning as it were that something like this must be fought against, boils up straightway; while appetite, if argument or perception merely says that an object is pleasant, springs to the enjoyment of it. Therefore anger obeys argument in a sense, but appetite does not.

According to Kenny, Aristotle is saying that appetite does not reason, and this in turn implies that there is no syllogism of appetite. But this is not the point of the passage. Anger obeys argument in the sense that argument or imagination tells us that we have been insulted and that *anything like this must be fought against*. This is reasoning *to* a (relatively) general principle, something that can function as a major premise. A practical syllogism involves reasoning *from* a major premise, setting out means for acting on a general principle. The distinction drawn in 1149a32-b2 has nothing to do with the practical syllogism. Rather, it distinguishes those forms of desire, *boulēsis* and *thumos*, the apprehension of whose ends involves the use of mind *(nous)* or the calculative faculty *(logistikon)*, from that form of desire, *epithumia*, which does not involve such a use of mind.[36, 37]

Thus, no strong reason has been given for thinking that there is only one syllogism in Aristotle's explanation of *akrasia*. If anything, there is reason for thinking that there are two syllogisms in this explanation. The burden of proof seems to be on anyone who would deny this.

What is more important, the existence of only one syllogism in Aristotle's explanation of *akrasia* does not show that the *akratēs* draws the conclusion on which he ought to act. The existence of only one syllogism is compatible with two of the three forms that the traditional interpretation has taken. In the first place, even if Aristotle's explanation contains only the one syllogism that Kenny suggests it contains, having 'Taste nothing insofar as it is pleasant' as its major premise, this syllogism is more complicated than Kenny lets on. As Kenny himself notes ([1966], p. 181), what follows from the complex minor premise 'Everything sweet is pleasant and this is sweet' is 'This is pleasant'. This together with the major premise yields the conclusion, 'Don't taste this'. But then it looks as if 'This is pleasant' is the final minor premise of the syllogism on which the *akratēs* ought to act. Thus, even if 'This is sweet' is active, this does not mean that the final minor premise of this syllogism is active. At most the activity of 'This is sweet' implies that 'This is pleasant' is *possessed.* However, someone who holds the second form of the traditional interpretation can admit that the final minor premise of the syllogism on which the *akratēs* ought to act is possessed. What he denies is that it is *exercised* in combination with its major premise. If it isn't exercised in this way, then the conclusion of the syllogism in question won't be drawn. That is, even if there is just the one syllogism that Kenny says there is, it doesn't follow from what Aristotle goes on to say that its conclusion is drawn.

In the second place, one could admit that there is only one syllogism in Aristotle's explanation of *akrasia*, but argue that its major premise is 'Don't taste an excessive number of pleasant things' rather than 'Taste nothing insofar as it is pleasant'. 'Everything sweet is pleasant' and 'This is sweet' are parts of a composite minor premise, but the activity of 'This is sweet' implies only that the intermediate conclusion 'This is pleasant' is drawn. This shows that the object in question *may* fall under the prohibition of the major premise. But to know that it *does* fall under this prohibition, one will have to perceive that tasting it would be pursuing pleasure to excess. That is, the final minor premise of this syllogism is 'Tasting this would be tasting an excessive number of pleasant things'. Someone who held the third form of the traditional interpretation could argue that the *akratēs* does not possess this premise because passion has obscured his moral perception.

Thus, not only is there reason to think that there are two syllogisms in Aristotle's explanation of *akrasia*, but even if there is only one, it does not follow from this and the activity of 'This is sweet' that the conclusion of this syllogism is drawn.[38] The second objection fails to show that the *akratēs* can draw the conclusion on which he ought to act.

Once this is recognized one is in a better position to deal with the third and fourth objections. Two reasons were offered for taking,

'One thing says to avoid this *(hē men oun legei pheugein touto)'* at 1147a34 to refer to the conclusion on which the *akratēs* ought to act. First, Aristotle has just said that the final minor premise of the syllogism of reason is active, and its activity could only involve drawing the conclusion. Second, taken by itself 1147a34 is most naturally understood as referring to this conclusion. *'Pheugein touto'* ('Avoid this') is both particular (it contains the demonstrative *'touto'*) and prescriptive. Neither the major nor final minor premise of the syllogism of reason exhibit both of these features. However, we have just seen that there are reasons for thinking that Aristotle has not said that the final minor premise of the syllogism of reason is active, or, that if he has, that its activity does not imply that the conclusion of the syllogism of reason is drawn. As a result the third objection must rest entirely on the naturalness of taking 1147a34 by itself to refer to this conclusion.

However, a proponent of the traditional interpretation can admit that, taken by itself, 1147a34 is most naturally understood as referring to the conclusion of the syllogism of reason. He will argue, however, that it cannot be taken just by itself. 1147a34 occurs in the context of Aristotle's explanation of *akrasia*, and it must be understood within that context. 1147a34 *can* be understood as referring to the major premise of the syllogism of reason, a premise that tells the *akratēs* to avoid the object in front of him because it tells him to avoid every member of a class of which the object in front of him is a member. Read in context, it *should* be so understood. The argument that has been presented so far shows that independent reasons exist for thinking that Aristotle's explanation of *akrasia* is along the lines of the traditional interpretation. As yet there are no other good reasons for thinking that the details of Aristotle's explanation do not follow these lines. Read in this context, 1147a34 is best understood as referring to the major premise of the syllogism of reason.[39]

There are even stronger reasons for not taking *'hē teleutaia protasis'* at 1147b9 to refer to the conclusion of the syllogism of reason. In contrast to 1147a34, *'hē teleutaia protasis'* is initially more naturally translated as 'the last premise'. Although *'protasis'* can have the general sense of 'proposition', in a context such as Aristotle's explanation of *akrasia*, where a good deal of syllogistic vocabulary has been used, it is more naturally understood as 'premise'. Aristotle has already used a more technical term at 1147a27 to refer to a conclusion *('sumperanthen')*, and had he wanted to refer to a conclusion at 1147b9 he would have used it or some other term that clearly designates a conclusion. The only positive reasons for taking *'hē tlelutaia protasis'* to refer to a conclusion are that Aristotle has just referred to such a conclusion at 1147a34, and that he has said that the final premise of the syllogism of reason is active whereas '*hē teleutaia protasis*' is said to be either not possessed or not exercised (1147b11-12). But we have just seen that there are reasons for not taking 1147a34 to refer to such a conclusion, and we have seen that the activity of 'This is sweet' does not imply that the final minor premise of the syllogism of reason is active. Robbed of this kind of support, it looks as if one should take '*hē teleutaia protasis*' in the more natural way as referring to the final minor premise of the syllogism of reason.

Thus, none of the four objections raised against the traditional interpretation seem to hold. The traditional interpretation still seems to provide the best account of the details of Aristotle's explanation of *akrasia*.

D. The Greatest Stumbling Block for Anyone Denying the Traditional Interpretation

If all of the above were not enough, an even greater difficulty seems to face anyone trying to support an interpretation according to which the *akratēs* can recognize what he ought to do in the situation that faces him. I think that such a person will have to take '*hē teleutaia protasis*' to refer, not to the final minor premise of the syllogism of reason, but to something that expresses this recognition.[40] Suppose he were able to answer the objections raised above against taking '*hē teleutaia protasis*' in this way. What Aristotle goes on to say is,

> *hē teleutaia protasis* both being an opinion about a perceptible object, and being what determines our actions, this a man either has not when he is in a state of passion, or has it in the sense in which having knowledge did not mean knowing but only talking, as a drunken man may mutter the verses of Empedocles. (1147a9-13)

Aristotle's reference to the drunk muttering the verses of Empedocles is a clear reference back to 1147a10-24, where Aristotle discusses cases in which a person in a sense does and in a sense does not have knowledge, cases that include those who are mad, asleep, or drunk. These seem to be people who do *not* understand or believe what they are saying at the time they are saying it. Thus, even if '*hē teleutaia protasis*' does refer to something that could express the *akratēs*' recognition of what he ought to do in the situation that faces him, it looks as if the *akratēs* can not understand what this is. To grant this last point is to grant the essential part of the traditional interpretation.

What this means is that unless there is some other way of explaining what Aristotle is saying in 1147b9-13, whether he likes it or not, a proponent of the interpretation posed in Part B above will be forced to acknowledge that the *akratēs* does not recognize what he ought to do in the situation that faces him. Even if he draws the conclusion that would express this recognition, he does not understand what this conclusion says. Not only does this prevent this interpretation from being a genuine alternative to the traditional interpretation, it means that most of the problems raised for the traditional interpretation in Chapter 9 arise for this interpretation as well.

If '*hē teleutaia protasis*' refers to the conclusion on which the *akratēs* ought to act, but the *akratēs* possesses it only in the sense in which a drunk muttering the verses of Empedocles knows what he is talking about, it is hard to see in what sense the *akratēs* really does draw the conclusion of his deliberations. He may utter the words that express this conclusion, but as Aristotle says, "the fact that men use the language that follows from knowledge proves nothing" (1147a18-19). What this means is that Aristotle's distinction between weak and impetuous *akrasia* remains puzzling. If these words aren't understood, then the conclusion won't be drawn in any sense that allows the *akratēs* to know that he is acting incontinently at the time that he acts. Furthermore, if the *akratēs* doesn't understand what he is saying when he says how he ought to act, it is hard to see how he can be *motivated* to act as he ought to act. Although there may be a conflict between what he *says* and how he is motivated to act, there will be no genuine conflict of motives in *akrasia*. But it is just such a conflict that Aristotle seems to acknowledge at NE 1102b14-18. He says there that there is a rational part of the soul of the *akratēs* that "urges" (*parakalei*) the *akratēs* in the right direction, against which another part of the soul "fights against and resists" (*machetai kai antiteinei*). The verb '*parakaleō*' suggests more than *saying* how one ought to act. It suggests that the person is "excited" (that is, motivated) to act. And '*machetai kai antiteinei*' certainly suggests the kind of conflict that exists between conflicting motives.[41] Finally, to the extent to which the *akratēs* can't recognize or be motivated to do what he ought to do in the situation that faces him, to that extent Aristotle has closed off a possibility left open by his position on practical reason. Again, this would seem to require an explanation.

Unless one has another way of understanding 1147b9-13, the same problems raised in Chapter 9 for the traditional interpretation arise for the alternative interpretation posed at the end of Part B. A consequence of this result is that these problems cannot be used as additional support for this interpretation.[42] Furthermore, this is not something that is peculiar to this interpretation. Unless one has another way of understanding 1147b9-13, it looks as if *any* alternative to the traditional interpretation will be faced with the same problem. That is why I have described 1147b9-13 as the greatest stumbling block for anyone who wants to argue for an alternative to the traditional interpretation.[43]

IV. Solutions to the Problems Raised for the Traditional Interpretation

This brings us to the final stage of the argument for the traditional interpretation—solutions to the problems raised in Chapter 9.

Let us begin with Aristotle's admission that *akrasia* is conscious of itself (1150b36). The first thing to note is that the text does not specifically say that *akrasia* is conscious of itself at the time that *akrasia* occurs. It is compatible with what is said that the *akrasia* is aware of his *akrasia* only after the fact (or that the *akratēs* is only aware that he is the sort of person who from time to time acts incontinently). Second, there are grounds for reading one or both of these claims into the passage. The passage appears to apply to both the weak and the impetuous *akratēs*, but the latter cannot be aware of his *akrasia* at the time that he acts. He does not even deliberate, let alone draw the conclusions of his deliberations. At most he can be aware of his *akrasia* after the fact. Furthermore, reading one or both of these claims into 1150b36 makes this passage consistent with the details of Aristotle's explanation of *akrasia*. We have already seen that there are grounds for thinking that this explanation does not allow the *akratēs* to know at the time that he acts that what he does is wrong. These same grounds can now be used to support a similar reading of 1150b36. Since an important part of these grounds were independent of the details of Aristotle's explanation of *akrasia*, relying on them at this point will not be question-begging.

Once this is admitted, it is easy to argue for a similar interpretation of 1150b19-22, the passage in which Aristotle distinguishes weak from impetuous *akrasia*. Again, the text does not specifically say that the weak *akratēs* fails to abide by the conclusions of his deliberations at the time that he draws them. If one reads in a time-lag between the time the weak *akratēs* draws the conclusions of his deliberations and the time that he fails to abide by them, the passage becomes compatible with the traditional interpretation. So understood, the weak *akratēs* is like a man at a party who for a time refuses a third drink because he knows he shouldn't overindulge. Finally, however, appetite gets the best of him, and he says, "One more won't hurt." At this time he no longer realizes that taking the third drink would be overindulging. Given his appetite for drink, he accepts it. When the weak *akratēs* draws the conclusions of his deliberations he abides by them. When he no longer abides by them, he no longer draws them. One might admit that this is not the most natural way of reading this passage when it is taken just by itself, but one can argue that it cannot be taken just by itself. When it is taken as part of a more general discussion in which the *akratēs* is said not to know that what he does is wrong at the time that he does it, it then becomes preferable to read in the time-lag. Since the argument for reading Aristotle's explanation of *akrasia* as denying that the *akratēs* can know that what he does is wrong did not beg the question in favor of the traditional interpretation, the present argument for reading a time-lag into 1150b19-22 also does not beg the question.[44]

If one should resist this argument, arguing that reading a time-lag into 1150b19-22 is just too unnatural or too *ad hoc,* a proponent of the traditional interpretation can even grant this. He will argue, though, that too much evidence has been presented for the traditional interpretation for 1150b19-22 to be able to tip the scales against it. 1150b19-22 will then be inconsistent with Aristotle's explanation of *akrasia,* but this inconsistency can be explained as just another instance of a familiar pattern that Aristotle follows when discussing philosophical issues. In dealing with a philosophical issue, Aristotle often treats only a favored case, thinking, without taking the time to check, that the same account will provide a basis for accounts of the other cases as well.[45] The same account does not always serve as a basis for handling the other cases. 1150b19-22 is simply another instance when this turns out to be so. In Ch. 3 Aristotle provides an explanation that is appropriate only to impetuous *akrasia.* He then assumes that this explanation will serve as a basis for handling weak *akrasia* as well. In this he was mistaken. But that he was mistaken didn't mean that he didn't make the assumption, or that his explanation of *akrasia* wasn't what the traditional interpretation says that it is.

Let us now turn to NE 1102b13-19. I argued in Section III Part D that this passage should be taken as saying that there can be a genuine conflict of motives in *akrasia.* This is incompatible with the traditional interpretation. However, there are a number of things that can be used to argue that this incompatibility provides no grounds for giving up the traditional interpretation. None of them excludes any of the others.

First, unlike 1150b19-22 and 1150b36, 1102b13-19 is detached from Aristotle's explanation of *akrasia.* Not only is it possible that 1102b13-19 was written at a different time than NE VII, it is possible that Aristotle wrote each of the two passages without having the other in mind. If this were so, it would not be surprising if 1102b13-19 turned out to be inconsistent with Aristotle's explanation of *akrasia.*

Second, 1102b13-19 is part of a discussion in which Aristotle admits that he is not speaking precisely. He says that the student of politics must know something about psychology, but his knowledge need have only the precision that the subject of politics requires (1102a16-25). He says that what is contained in the "exoteric discussions" will be adequate for the purposes at hand (1102a26-28). Without trying to settle what the "exoteric discussions" are, Aristotle does not seem to be committing himself in any strong way to the details that follow. He says that there is a rational and an irrational element in the soul, but he says that it is still open whether these elements are parts of the soul in the way something divisable has parts (1102a28-30). One might argue that given this context it won't be surprising if what Aristotle says is at odds with his explanation of *akrasia*. Aristotle's explanation of *akrasia* contains the technical device of the practical syllogism. This suggests that he is speaking precisely. If what a person says when he is not speaking precisely is at odds with what he says when he is speaking precisely, it is clear which of the passages should be given the greater weight.

Third, as already noted, Aristotle often proceeds by examining a favored case, thinking that he has provided a basis for an account of all other cases. One might argue that Aristotle's explanation of *akrasia* is another instance of this tendency. Aristotle supplies an explanation of *akrasia* that fits cases in which no conflict of motives exists, and thinks, without taking the time to check, that essentially the same account will handle cases in which there are conflicts of motives. In this he was wrong. But his being wrong doesn't count against his giving the explanation of *akrasia* that he did give.

Fourth, there is something in Aristotle's explanation of *akrasia* itself that is very close to a denial that a genuine conflict of motives can occur in *akrasia*. Aristotle says of *hē teleutaia protasis* that if it is possessed, it is possessed only in the sense in which a drunk muttering the verses of Empedocles knows what he is talking about. Even if *hē teleutaia protasis* is the conclusion of the syllogism of reason, it looks as if Aristotle is saying that the *akratēs* does not possess this conclusion in any sense in which he would be motivated to act in accord with it. If he is not so motivated, then there cannot be the kind of conflict of motives mentioned in 1102b13-19.

To this one might add what Aristotle goes on to say at 1147b13-17,

And because the last term is not universal nor equally an object of scientific knowledge with the universal term, the position that Socrates sought to establish actually seems to result; for it is not in the presence of what is thought to be knowledge proper that the affection of incontinence arises (nor is it this that is dragged about as a result of the state of passion), but in that of perceptual knowledge.

The Socratic position that Aristotle is referring to is that knowledge cannot be dragged about like a slave. (See, for example, NE 1145b22-24.) Knowledge proper is not dragged about like a slave because *akrasia* does not occur in the presence of knowledge proper. What *akrasia* occurs in the presence of and what is dragged about is perceptual knowledge, knowledge of the final minor premise of the syllogism of reason. Passion overcomes or obscures this knowledge, but the universal knowledge embodied in the major premise is left untouched. But if the *akratēs* were moved by rational desire to act in accord with the syllogism of reason, then it looks as if knowledge proper would be dragged about like a slave.

One might argue that even here it would not be dragged about like a slave, for what is overcome is particular knowledge of how to behave. Aristotle maintains that knowledge proper is universal. However, this reply seems too easy. If universal knowledge is applied to the case at hand and the *akratēs* acts contrary to it, then there is a sense in which the *akratēs* acts "in the presence of" universal knowledge. It is "present" to the extent that it is applied.[46] If Aristotle denies that knowledge proper is dragged about like a slave in *akrasia*, then it looks as if he is denying the existence of a genuine conflict of motives in *akrasia*.

Finally, there is the simple point that on balance 1102b13-19 is outweighed by all the other evidence.

Let us now turn to the problem raised by Aristotle's position on practical reason. Assuming that Aristotle did hold something like the position attributed to him in Part One, why should he close off a possibility that this position leaves open? The most plausible answer, I think, is that it is Aristotle's use of the practical syllogism as a model for explaining actions that closes off this possibility. When one tries to explain every action solely in terms of a universal premise about an end that is to be pursued together with more particular premises about means to this end, there is no longer any room for a people to have a major premise that they are not sufficiently motivated to act on. What Aristotle is left with is an overly rational picture of human action, one that rules out the kind of irrationality in which people's actions fail to accord with their acknowledged principles. However, this fact could easily have been overlooked by Aristotle, for his explanation of action in terms of the practical syllogism leaves open two other kinds of irrational action—the pursuit of ends based on mistaken beliefs or faulty inferences, and the pursuit of means inappropriate to one's ends.[47]

The proponent of the traditional interpretation, thus, has a way of dealing with each of the problems I raised. If one puts this together with what has been argued in the previous sections, one obtains a formidable argument for the traditional interpretation.

V. A Summary of the Argument

Since the argument of this chapter has been long and complicated, it will be useful to have a summary of its main points. The argument was designed to show that there are grounds independent of Aristotle's explanation of *akrasia* for thinking that he is committed to an explanation along the lines of the traditional interpretation. These grounds can then be used to provide a non-question begging way of dealing with disputed passages within his detailed explanation of *akrasia*, allowing one to argue that this explanation is along the lines of the traditional interpretation. Finally, all of the problems raised for the traditional interpretation have a solution. In short, strong grounds exist for accepting the traditional interpretation and no good grounds for rejecting it.

The argument began by pointing out that there are grounds independent of Aristotle's explanation of *akrasia* for attributing to him a certain thesis about knowledge and action. The thesis is that those who possess and combine the premises of a practical syllogism will act on it if they are able to. There were two bases for attributing this thesis to Aristotle. The first was Aristotle's use of the practical syllogism as a model for explaining actions. This use can be seen from the parallel that exists between the practical syllogism and Aristotle's explanation of action on the basis of desire. This parallel emerges in *De Anima, De Motu Animalium,* and in Bk. III of the *Nicomachean Ethics.* The second basis came from *De Motu* 701a8ff where, among other things, Aristotle seems to say that the conclusion of a practical syllogism is an action. Not only does the thesis in question seem to follow from this claim about the conclusion, Aristotle seems to affirm this thesis when he says of someone who has combined the premises of a practical syllogism that one will act if nothing compels or prevents one.

Of course, there are objections to reading *De Motu* 701a8ff in this way. For example, it has been argued that when Aristotle says that 'I must make a coat' is a conclusion, he is identifying the conclusion of a practical syllogism with something other than an action. And it can be argued that when Aristotle says that a person who combines the premises of a practical syllogism will act if nothing compels or prevents him, the notion of prevention is broad enough to include being prevented by a conflicting internal desire. However, 'I must make a coat' is an intermediate conclusion of a syllogism whose final conclusion is an action. And there are strong general reasons for not construing the notion of prevention so broadly that it allows a conflicting internal desire to prevent a person from acting. So understood, Aristotle would be committed to saying that whenever a person acts intentionally he will be prevented from doing anything else. So understood, Aristotle's claim that a person who combined the premises of a practical syllogism will act if neither compelled nor prevented would also be threatened with triviality.

The argument continued by noting that evidence exists that this same thesis is at work in Aristotle's general approach to his explanation of *akrasia*. Attributing this thesis to Aristotle explains why it is that *akrasia* gets all the attention in this discussion, when at the outset the subject appears to be both *akrasia* and *enkrateia*. It also explains the main question that Aristotle raises in this discussion of *akrasia*, 'In what sense does the *akratēs* have knowledge of what he ought to do?'. The thesis seems also to be at work in the three passages that immediately preceded Aristotle's detailed explanation of *akrasia*. Each one of them articulates a sense of knowledge that one would attribute to an *akratēs* if one held the above thesis about knowledge and action. All of this provides grounds for expecting Aristotle's detailed explanation of *akrasia* to be along the lines of the traditional interpretation.

These expectations are confirmed when one looks at those details. Aristotle begins by reaffirming the above thesis about knowledge and action. He then provides a particular example of *akrasia* in which the final minor premise of the syllogism of reason is either not possessed or not exercised. Passion prevents the possession or exercise of this premise. This leaves just the syllogism of desire to be acted on. Thus, the *akratēs*' knowledge of what he ought to do is confined to the knowledge that comes from having the right general principles. It does not include knowledge that would result from applying these principles to the situation at hand.

Again, there are objections that have been raised against this way of interpreting these details. It has been argued that at the beginning of this explanation Aristotle does not affirm the above thesis about knowledge and action. He doesn't say that the conclusion of a practical syllogism is an action. And he does allow a person to be prevented from acting by a conflicting internal desire. Furthermore, once one recognizes that Aristotle's explanation of *akrasia* contains only one syllogism and not two, one will see that the activity of its final minor premise, 'This is sweet', implies that the conclusion on which the *akratēs* ought to act has been drawn. Third, when Aristotle says at 1147a34, 'One thing says to avoid this', he is talking about just this conclusion. Finally, the same conclusion is referred to by '*hē teleutaia protasis*' at 1147b9.

Again, however, there are replies to all of these objections. The parallel that exists between the opening lines of Aristotle's explanation of *akrasia* and *De Motu* 701a8ff provides grounds for thinking that Aristotle is reaffirming the thesis about knowledge and action. And the general reasons provided in connection with the *De Motu* passage for not taking the notion of prevention to allow a person to be prevented from acting by a conflicting internal desire apply to the NE passage as well. In the second place, not only are there grounds for thinking that there are two syllogisms in Aristotle's explanation of *akrasia*, even if there were only one, the activity of 'This is sweet' wouldn't imply that its conclusion was drawn. Third, even though, 'One thing says to avoid this' might be most naturally taken to refer to the conclusion of the syllogism of reason if it were taken just by itself, it cannot be taken just by itself. It is part of a more general discussion of *akrasia*. Given what has been argued so far, there are strong, non-question begging rounds for taking this discussion to follow the lines of the traditional interpretation. Thus, 'One thing says to avoid this' should be taken to refer to the major premise of the syllogism of reason, not its conclusion. A similar line of reasoning confirms what there are initial reasons for, anyway, that '*hē teleutaia protasis*' refers to the final minor premise of the syllogism of reason.

If this weren't enough, what Aristotle goes on to say about *hē teleutaia protasis* provides the greatest stumbing block for anyone who wants to reject the traditional interpretation. Even if *hē teleutaia protasis* is the conclusion on which the *akratēs* ought to act, what Aristotle says seems to deny that the *akratēs* can possess this conclusion in any way that would allow him to understand or believe what it says. This seems to all but clinch the case for the traditional interpretation.

Finally, all of the problems raised for the traditional interpretation seem to have solutions. Both Aristotle's recognition that *akrasia* can be conscious of itself, and his distinction between weak and impetuous *akrasia*, have interpretations that are compatible with the traditional interpretation. Although Aristotle's admission of a genuine conflict of motives in *akrasia* cannot be made compatible with the traditional interpretation, there are reasons for not taking this admission to cast doubt on the traditional interpretation. There is even an explanation of why Aristotle closed off a possibility left open by his position on practical reason. It was his use of the practical syllogism as a model for explaining actions that led him to close off this possibility.

This does seem to clinch the case for the traditional interpretation. Not only are there strong grounds for accepting the traditional interpretation, there are no good grounds for rejecting it. The argument for the traditional interpretation does seem to be a formidable one.

CHAPTER 11

An Argument for
an Alternative Interpretation

Despite the formidable appearance of the argument just given, I think it is possible to give a stronger argument for an alternative interpretation. The alternative is nominally like the traditional interpretation, for it too maintains that according to Aristotle a person cannot act contrary to full and complete knowledge of how one ought to behave. However, it differs radically from the traditional interpretation at the point at which it locates failure to have full and complete knowledge. It takes seriously the view that Aristotle acknowledged a specifically *practical* form of knowledge, a view supported by the position on practical reason argued for in the first part of this book. According to this view, people may lack full and complete practical knowledge because their knowledge isn't sufficiently *practical,* that is, because it hasn't been sufficiently integrated into their characters to insure they will act on it. Unlike the traditional interpretation, it maintains that failure to have full and complete practical knowledge need not involve the failure to entertain, understand, or believe something proposition-like. Since it need not, people can fail to have full and complete knowledge of what they ought to do and still recognize what they ought to do in the situation that faces them. According to the interpretation I shall be arguing for, it is just such a possibility that Aristotle acknowledges in his explanation of *akrasia.*

The form of the argument for this interpretation is borrowed from the argument given in the last chapter. First it is argued that there are grounds independent of Aristotle's explanation of *akrasia* for thinking that Aristotle does allow the *akratēs* to know what he ought to do in the situation that faces him. Second, it is argued that the grounds offered in the last chapter for attributing to Aristotle a thesis that commits him to the traditional interpretation do not support such an attribution. In fact, there are grounds for thinking that Aristotle did *not* accept such a thesis. Third, Aristotle's general approach to *akrasia* fits the alternative interpretation as well as it does the traditional interpretation. This approach, therefore, cannot be used to provide grounds for believing that Aristotle's explanation of *akrasia* will be along the lines of the traditional interpretation. Armed with all of this, one is in a position to see that the details of Aristotle's explanation of *akrasia* do indeed fit this alternative interpretation, including even the passage in which Aristotle says that what particular knowledge the *akratēs* has, he has in the sense in which a drunken man muttering the verses of Empedocles knows what he is talking about. Finally, that the problems raised in Chapter 9 for the traditional interpretation do not arise for this interpretation provides additional support for it.

I. Conflicts of Motive and *Akrasia*

When the matter is considered independently of Aristotle's explanation of *akrasia*, there are two main reasons for thinking that Aristotle allows an *akratēs* to know what he ought to do in the situation that faces him—the position on practical reason argued for in Part One of this book, and Aristotle's admission that a genuine conflict of motives can occur in *akrasia*. I have already spent enough time on the first of these, so I shall concentrate here on the second. It is worth noting, though, that these two reasons are not independent of one another. To the extent that Aristotle did adopt the position on practical reason argued for in Part One, he should have acknowledged that a genuine conflict of motives can occur in *akrasia*. Where it is possible to interpret him as acknowledging such a conflict, his position on practical reason provides grounds for doing so. And to the extent that Aristotle acknowledges a genuine conflict of motives in *akrasia*, to that extent one has grounds for attributing to him a position on practical reason that makes such a conflict possible. Thus, there is a sense in which these two reasons mutually support one another. Nevertheless, what I shall concentrate on here is evidence that Aristotle acknowledged that a genuine conflict of motives can occur in *akrasia*. If he did, then he also acknowledged that an *akratēs* can know what he ought to do in the situation that faces him. An *akratēs* won't be motivated by reason to do the action that he ought to do unless he recognizes what it is.

I have already argued that Aristotle acknowledges the existence of a genuine conflict of motives in *akrasia* at NE 1102b13-19.[1] Two other sets of passages in Aristotle's ethics can be added to this one as support for the same conclusion.

In Bk. II Ch. 8 of the *Eudemian Ethics* Aristotle is discussing the nature of the voluntary and the involuntary. In the course of this discussion, he considers *akrasia* and *enkrateia*, because both of them have been thought to involve compulsion. Although ultimately Aristotle denies that *enkrateia* and *akrasia* do involve compulsion, in pointing out why they have been thought to involve compulsion, it becomes clear that he thinks that both of them can involve a genuine conflict of motives.

> So the compulsory act seems always painful, and no one acts from force and yet with pleasure. Hence there arises much dispute about the continent and incontinent, for each of them acts with two tendencies mutually opposed, so that (as the expression goes) the continent forcibly drags himself from the pleasant appetites (for he feels pain in dragging himself against the resistance of desire) while the incontinent forcibly drags himself contrary to his reason. (EE 1224a30-36)

> For it is only when something *external* moves a thing, or brings it to rest against its own internal tendency, that we say this happens by force. But in the continent and incontinent it is a present *internal* tendency that leads them, for they have both tendencies. . . . Further, there is both pleasure and pain in both; for the continent feels pain now in acting against his appetite, but has the pleasure of hope, i.e. that he will be presently benefitted, or even the pleasure of being actually at present benefitted because he is in health; while the incontinent is pleased at getting through his incontinence what he desires, but has a pain of expectation, thinking that he is doing ill. (EE 1224b5-21), slight variation of the Oxford translation)

Aristotle says here that both the *enkratēs* and the *akratēs* "drag themselves" *(aphelkei)* against the "resistance" *(antiteinousan)* of an opposing desire. Both of them have two opposing tendencies (1224b10). These two tendencies are present at the time because the *akratēs* and *enkratēs* feel both pleasure and pain as they act. In fact, their feeling pain as they act would be sufficient for both tendencies to be present at the same time, for the reason they feel pain is that they act contrary to a present desire. Thus, both *akrasia* and *enkrateia* involve a genuine conflict of motives.[2]

The second set of passages occurs in NE, IX, 4, where, talking about certain inferior people, Aristotle says,

> they are at variance with themselves *(diapherontai)*, and have appetites for some things and rational desires for others. This is true, for instance, of incontinent people; for they choose, instead of the things they themselves think are good, things that are pleasant but hurtful; while others again, through cowardice and laziness, shrink from doing what they think best for themselves. (1166b7-11)

Therefore also such men do not rejoice or grieve with themselves; for their soul is rent by fraction (*stasiazei*), and one element in it by reason of its wickedness grieves when it abstains from certain acts, while the other part is pleased, and one draws them this way and the other part, as if they were pulling them in pieces (*diaspōnta*). If a man cannot at the same time be pained and pleased, at all events after a short time he is pained *because* he was pleased, and he could have wished that these things had not been pleasant to him; for bad men are laden with repentance.

Therefore the bad man does not seem to be amicably disposed even to himself, because there is nothing in him to love. (1166b18-26)

The language in these passages strongly suggests that a genuine conflict of motives can occur in *akrasia*. The *akratēs* is said to be *diapherontai* ("rent by faction," "carried in different ways," "torn asunder"). His soul is described as *stasiazei*, ("divided into factions," "torn by strife"), the elements of it *diaspōnta* ("tearing it apart," "pulling it into pieces"). This sort of language strongly suggests that the two opposing elements in the soul are both operative at the same time.[3] If this is right, then these passages also acknowledge the existence of a genuine conflict of motives in *akrasia*.[4]

However, the proponent of the traditional interpretation had a way of dismissing NE 1102b13-19 and he might think that the same considerations can be used to dismiss these two sets of passages. NE 1102b13-19 occurs in a context in which Aristotle says he is not speaking precisely about matters of psycology. If what Aristotle says in such a context conflicts with a passage in which the technical device of the practical syllogism indicates that he is speaking precisely, then it is clear which passage should be given the greater weight. If one turns to the above two sets of passages, one might argue that they too occur in contexts in which Aristotle is not speaking precisely about matters of psychology. For example, the *Eudemian Ethics* passages are based on the same division of the soul which in NE Bk. I Aristotle says is sufficient for the purposes at hand.[5] And even though one cannot find exactly the same grounds for discounting the NE IX passages, one might argue that when one compares them with Aristotle's explanation of *akrasia*, the conspicuous presence of the technical device of the practical syllogism in the latter and the absence of anything like it in the former provides grounds for thinking that Aristotle is speaking more precisely in the latter than he is in the former. If this is right, then the above two sets of passages cannot bear much weight in an argument for an alternative to the practical interpretation.

If a proponent of the traditional interpretation were to argue in this way, I think he would be grasping at straws. Nevertheless, it must be admitted that the argument being put forward in this section would be stronger if one had a way of responding to such an argument.

Fortunately, there is a way. If ever Aristotle does speak precisely about matters of psychology, he does so in *De Anima*. But in some passages in *De Anima* Aristotle also acknowledges the existence of conflicts of motives in *akrasia*. Interestingly enough, one of them is immediately followed by a reference to the practical syllogism. These passages show that Aristotle's acknowledgement of a genuine conflict of motives in *akrasia* must be taken seriously. They also provide further evidence that Aristotle did make such an acknowledgement.

At *De Anima* 433b5-10 Aristotle says,

> Since appetites run counter to one another *(enantiai)*, which happens when a principle of reason and a desire are contrary *(enantiai)* and is possible only in beings with a sense of time (for while mind bids us hold back because of what is future, desire is influenced by what is just at hand: a pleasant object which is just at hand presents itself as both pleasant and good, without condition in either case *(kai haplōs hēdu kai agathon haplōs)*, because of want of foresight into what is farther away in time)

This passage seems most naturally read as acknowledging the existence of a genuine conflict of motives. Such a conflict occurs when a principle of reason and an appetite *(epithumia)* are opposed to one another *(enantiai)*. Appetite moves a person one way on the basis of considerations about what is just at hand, while reason, taking into account considerations about the future, moves the person in the opposite way.[6]

It is perhaps less clear that *akrasia* is included in the kind of conflict acknowledged in the passage. There is no specific mention of *akrasia*. And although the passage seems to acknowledge the possibility of a person's acting on *epithumia* rather than reason, one might argue that this possibility cannot be both a case of *akrasia* and a genuine case of conflict. The possibility described is one in which *epithumia* is *un*influenced by considerations about the future. One might think that this rules out the presence of reason, for if reason were present, *epithumia* would be *influenced* by considerations about the future.[7] If this is right, then the possibility mentioned cannot be a case of *akrasia* in which a conflict of motives occurs. At most it will be a case of impetuous *akrasia*, where there is no conflict, because reason is not present. Of course, the possibility still exists that a genuine conflict occurs when appetite *is* influenced by considerations about the future. (Appetite will no longer present the object as pleasantest and best, but it will still present it as pleasant. This would be enough to move a person to act.) But, one might argue, such a conflict can occur only in *enkrateia*. Aristotle has been interpreted as restricting genuine conflicts of motives to enkrateia (for example, Santas [1969]),[8] and one might take this as grounds for reading a similar restriction into this passage.

I think it would be a mistake to treat this passage in this way. As I have already noted (n. 6 above), *epithumia*'s being uninfluenced by considerations about the future is *not* incompatible with the presence of reason. Thus, a genuine conflict of motives can occur when *epithumia* is uninfluenced by considerations about the future. Furthermore, given the present context of argument, there is no good reason to restrict cases of conflict to cases of *enkrateia*. The interpretation of Aristotle that involves such a restriction (Santas [1969]) seems to rest solely on an interpretation of Aristotle's explanation of *akrasia*. Considered apart from that explanation, there is no good reason for reading such a restriction into the passage. Considering the context of the present argument, the passage seems best understood as allowing genuine conflict to occur in *akrasia*.[9] Still, it will be of some importance if a proponent of the traditional interpretation admits that the passage allows that a genuine conflict of motives can occur in *enkrateia*.[10]

There is another passage in *De Anima* in which Aristotle seems to acknowledge the existence of a genuine conflict of motives in *akrasia*. At 432b26-433a3 Aristotle says,

> Further, neither can the calculative faculty or what is called 'mind' be the cause of such movement; for mind as speculative never thinks what is practicable, it never says anything about an object to be avoided or pursued, while this movement is always in something which is avoiding or pursuing an object. But, not even when it is aware of such an object does it at once enjoin pursuit or avoidance of it; e.g. the mind often thinks of something terrifying or pleasant without enjoining the emotion of fear. It is the heart that is moved (or in the case of a pleasant object, some other part). Further, even when the mind does command and thought bids us pursue or avoid something, sometimes no movement is produced; we act in accordance with desire as in the case of moral weakness.

Aristotle admits here that mind can be aware of an object without a person's being moved to pursue it (b29-a1). He describes this as a situation in which mind does not enjoin, command, or urge *(keleuei)* pursuit or avoidance (b30). Aristotle then considers situations in which mind does command or order *(epitattontos)*, situations in which thought does bid or order *(legousēs)* pursuit or avoidance. He says that sometimes, as in the case of *akrasia*, a person acts from desire instead (a1-3). Given that the cases in which a person is *not* moved to act have been described as ones in which mind does *not* command pursuit, it is reasonable to take cases in which mind *does* command pursuit to be ones in which a person *is* moved to act. If in such a case a person acts from desire instead, he will have acted in the face of a conflicting motive. Since Aristotle says that cases of *akrasia* are included in such cases, it looks as if he is again saying that a genuine conflict of motives can occur in *akrasia*.[11]

Finally, there is a cryptic passage which when deciphered, I think, will eliminate the last resistance to saying that a genuine conflict of motives can occur in *akrasia*. Translated literally it says,

> Sometimes (appetite) overpowers (rational desire) and moves (whatever is moved). At other times the latter (overpowers) the former (and moves) (whatever is moved). Just as a sphere (overpowers) (a sphere) (and moves) (whatever is moved), (so) an appetite (overpowers) an appetite (and moves) (whatever is moved). (This occurs) when *akrasia* occurs. But by nature the higher (is) always more fit to rule and moves (whatever is moved). So that now motion (can be seen as involving) three motions. (434a12-15, my translation, parenthetical remarks added to the text to make literal sense.)

Since the difficulties surrounding this passage are considerable, I have devoted a separate appendix to its interpretation.[12] Here I shall simply summarize the main results of that discussion.

Three things are important to note about this passage. First, two cases are talked about in which rational desire and appetite are said to be at odds with one another. Second, these cases are the cases of *enkrateia* and *akrasia*. Finally, the same thing is said about both of them. Taken as a description of *enkrateia*, what is said is best understood as asserting the existence of a genuine conflict of motives. Since the same thing is said about *akrasia* that is said about *enkrateia*, the passage also says that a genuine conflict of motives can occur in *akrasia*.

What is perhaps just as important, immediately following this passage Aristotle makes an explicit reference to the practical syllogism (434a16-21).

Thus, when Aristotle is speaking precisely about psychological matters, he still acknowledges the existence of a genuine conflict of motives in *akrasia*. He even acknowledges such a conflict when he is using the technical device of the practical syllogism. Aristotle's admission of a genuine conflict of motives in *akrasia*, thus, cannot be dismissed; it must be taken seriously. Once it is taken seriously, one has grounds independent of Aristotle's explanation of *akrasia* for saying that the *akratēs* can recognize what he ought to do in the situation that faces him.

II. The Thesis about Knowledge and Action Reconsidered

However, to point out that Aristotle's acknowledgement of a genuine conflict of motives in *akrasia* commits him to saying that an *akratēs* can recognize what he ought to do is not enough to support the interpretation I am arguing for. There is still the evidence set out in Chapter 10 that Aristotle accepted a thesis that commits him to denying that the *akratēs* can have such knowledge. Unless one can argue that Aristotle did not accept such a thesis, the most one can conclude is that there are two conflicting strands in Aristotle, one that commits him to the traditional interpretation, and one that commits him to the kind of interpretation I am arguing for. One will not be in a position to argue that his explanation of *akrasia* should be read in the light of one of these rather than the other.

In this section I shall argue that the evidence put forward in Chapter 10 is insufficient to show that Aristotle accepted the thesis in question. In fact, considered independently of Aristotle's explanation of *akrasia*, there are grounds for thinking that Aristotle did *not* accept this thesis. If this is right, then we are left only with presumptive grounds for the kind of interpretation I am arguing for.

The thesis in question is that a person who recognizes what one ought to do in a particular situation will do it if he or she is able to do it. Put in terms of the practical syllogism, it is the thesis that a person who possesses and combines the premises of a practical syllogism will act on that syllogism if he or she is able to act on it. Two main reasons were offered for attributing this thesis to Aristotle — that the conclusion of a practical syllogism is an action, and that the practical syllogism is a model for explaining actions in the sense that it contains all of the elements needed to explain a given action. I shall begin with the first of these.

The first thing to be said is that the claim that the conclusion of a practical syllogism is an action is *irrelevant* to whether Aristotle accepted the thesis in question. This claim seems to be relevant because the thesis follows from it together with the additional premise that a person who combines the premises of a practicall syllogism draws its conclusion. However, an objection to this claim arises that can be met only by abandoning the additional premise. Either way the claim loses its capacity to support the thesis in question.

When Aristotle says that people who possess and combine the premises of a practical syllogism will act on it if they are able and nothing prevents them (*De Motu* 701a16-17, NE 1147a31-32), he is at least acknowledging that people can combine the premises of a practical syllogism but be prevented from acting on it by external compulsion. Such people, however, can still recognize what the syllogism tells them to do in the situations that faces them. Nothing in external compulsion prevents them from having this recognition.[13] Now people in such situations either draw the conclusion of the syllogism on which they are prevented from acting, or they do not. If they do, then the conclusion of a practical syllogism is not an action, and the claim that it is an action can not be used to support the thesis in question. On the other hand, one might argue that the frequency with which Aristotle says that the conclusion of the practical syllogism is an action makes it preferable to say that what people have been prevented from doing in such a situation is drawing the conclusion.[14] This allows one to retain the claim that the conclusion of a practical syllogism is an action, but then the additional premise needed to support the thesis in question no longer turns out to be true. Combination of the premises of a practical syllogism will no longer be sufficient for drawing its conclusion. Either way, the claim that the conclusion of a practical syllogism is an action cannot be used to support the thesis in question. The truth of this claim turns out to be irrelevant to whether Aristotle held the thesis in question.

What is relevant are the conditions under which people can combine the premises of a practical syllogism, recognize what it tells them to do, and be prevented from doing it. If these conditions are restricted to cases like external compulsion, then Aristotle did in fact hold the thesis in question. If, however, the conditions can include more than this (if, for example, a person can be prevented from acting by a conflicting desire), then not only did Aristotle not accept the thesis in question, it will be open for him to say that an *akratēs* can recognize what he ought to do in the situation that faces him.

In what follows, I shall assume that the conclusion of a practical syllogism *is* an action. I do this for two reasons. First, I take seriously the arguments given in Chapter 10 in support of this claim. Second, with one exception,[15] making this assumption makes it harder rather than easier to argue for an alternative to the traditional interpretation. I shall also assume that what always results from the possession and combination of the premises of a practical syllogism is something that expresses the agent's deliberate desire to act as the syllogism tells one to act. In the case of a syllogism of reason, this will express the agent's *prohairesis*. The real question, then, is what the conditions are under which a person can be prevented from acting on such a deliberate desire.

There are two reasons for thinking that these conditions include more than just external compulsion. The first involves Aristotle's use of the verb, '*kōluō*'. We saw in Chapter 10 that one of the things that makes it possible to think that these conditions involve more than external compulsion is the use of this verb in the statements that a person who combines the premises of a practical syllogism will act if able and not prevented.[16] If the use of this verb is not redundant, then it seems to allow for conditions other than external compulsion to prevent a person from acting in accord with a practical syllogism.[17] However, we also saw in Chapter 10 that there are general reasons for *not* taking Aristotle's use of '*kōluō*' so broadly that a person can be prevented from acting by a conflicting desire. Taken in this way, Aristotle seems committed to saying that every time a person acts intentionally he has been prevented from doing something else. This does not seem to be something that Aristotle would want to say. Furthermore, Aristotle's claim that a person who combines the premises of a syllogism will act on it if he is able and not prevented is threatened with triviality. Redundancy seems preferable to either of these.[18]

However, I think that a closer look at Aristotle's use of 'kōluō' will show that these general considerations can be overcome. In the first place, Aristotle's use of 'kōluō' in other contexts extends far beyond cases of external compulsion.

At *Physics* 255b6-11 Aristotle applies it to conditions that might prevent natural objects from exercising certain capacities. At *Politics* 1309a17-19 he uses it to talk about preventing wealthy people from undertaking expensive and useful public services.[19]

In the second place, there is a passage that suggests an account of what is involved in a person's being prevented by a conflicting desire that avoids both of the general objections raised above. (It also allows an *akratēs* to be someone who is prevented from acting by a conflicting desire.) In *Metaphysics* Bk. V Aristotle defines compulsion *(bia)*. He says that it is

> that which hinders and prevents *(kōlutikon)* contrary to impulse or choice *(prohairesis)*. For the compulsory is called necessary (whence it is painful, as Evenus says: 'For every necessary thing is ever irksome'), . . . and necessity is held to be something that cannot be persuaded—and rightly, for it is contrary to the movement which accords with choice *(prohairesin)* and reasoning. (1015a26-33, slight variation of Ross's translation)

Aristotle's use of 'kōluō' in this passage applies to more than cases of external compulsion. The compulsory is defined as a special case of what prevents, (what prevents contrary to impulse or choice). What prevents, then, includes more than what compels. Furthermore, Aristotle mentions three criteria of the compulsory—that it is contrary to choice, that it is unpleasant, and that it cannot be persuaded. *Akrasia* satisfies *two* of these criteria. It is contrary to choice (NE 1151a6); and it is pleasant, both because the *akratēs* feels repentance afterwards (1150b30), and because, as I have argued, the *akratēs* can act from a genuine conflict of motives. However, the *akratēs* is susceptible to persuasion (1151a11-15).

What this means is that there is a notion of prevention (one that meets the first two but not the third of these three criteria) that is broader than external compulsion, yet falls short of implying that any time a person acts from desire he or she has been prevented from acting otherwise. Furthermore, reading this notion of prevention into

Aristotle's claim that a person who combines the premises of a practical syllogism will act on it if he or she is not prevented, does *not* turn it into something trivial.[20] In addition, the notion seems to fit many of Aristotle's other uses of '*kōluō*'[21]. As I have already noted, it clearly fits the case of *akrasia*.

If one adds all of these facts about Aristotle's use of '*kōluō*' to the fact that Aristotle's use of it at *De Motu* 701a16-17 and NE 1147a31-32 would be redundant if it didn't allow for more than external compulsion, then I think one has some reason for reading a broader notion of prevention into these two passages. So understood, however, they affirm something other than the thesis about knowledge and action in question.

The second reason for thinking that Aristotle did not accept this thesis comes from a consideration of *enkrateia*. Whether or not one accepts all of the arguments of Section I, I think one will at least have to admit that a genuine conflict of motives can occur in *enkratia*. If it can't occur in *enkrateia*, then it is not clear where it can occur. What this means is that in a case of *enkrateia* there can be two practical syllogisms whose premises the *enkratēs* possesses and combines, a syllogism of reason and a syllogism of desire.[22] Since the *enkratēs* acts only on the syllogism of reason, there is a syllogism (the syllogism of desire), whose premises he possesses and combines but does not act on. This provides another counterexample to the thesis about knowledge and action.

If one adds this to what has already been said, including the arguments of Section I, then I think one has fairly strong grounds for saying that when the matter is considered independently of Aristotle's explanation of *akrasia*, Aristotle did not accept the thesis about knowledge and action attributed to him in Chapter 10.

At this point a proponent of the traditional interpretation might turn to the second basis offered in Chapter 10 for thinking that Aristotle accepted the thesis in question. He might claim that this provides grounds for discounting the argument just given. If the practical syllogism is a model for explaining actions in the sense that it contains all of the elements needed to explain a given action, then, one might argue, people cannot possess and combine the premises of two syllogisms at the same time. If they did, there would have to be something not contained in either syllogism to explain why they acted on one of them rather than the other. But then the practical syllogism would not contain all of the elements needed to explain a given action. Given this argument, one might think that at least when Aristotle was applying the practical syllogism as a model for explaining action, he would not allow a person to act from a genuine conflict of motives. At least in this context, he did accept the thesis about knowledge and action in question. (Of course, it is in just this context that Aristotle's explanation of *akrasia* occurs.)

A number of things can be said in reply to this argument even if, for the time being, one ignores the arguments of Section I. In the first place, when it was argued in Chapter 2 that the practical syllogism was a model for explaining actions, it was far from clear that the argument supported this claim in the sense in which the above argument requires, i.e., that the practical syllogism contains *all* of the elements needed to explain a given action. In the second place, this latter claim is false. Its falsity can be shown by cases of external compulsion. Given that a person can possess and combine the premises of a practical syllogism and yet be prevented by external compulsion from acting on it, then there are elements needed to explain action not contained in the practical syllogism—in particular, the presence or absence of external compulsion.[23] Finally, even if one restricts this claim, maintaining that except for considerations of the agent's ability the practical syllogism contains all of the elements needed to explain a given action, the above argument, that action from a genuine conflict of motives is impossible, is not valid. As long as the two syllogisms are different, there is no reason why what is contained in one or both of them can't explain why the agent acts on one rather than the other.

This latter point, however, may suggest a final way in which the proponent of the traditional interpretation might try to rescue something like the thesis in question. He might acknowledge a good deal of what I have just said, including that Aristotle did not hold the thesis attributed to him in Chapter 10 because it does not allow for action from a genuine conflict of motives. Nevertheless, he might argue, the practical syllogism's being a model for explaining actions still rules out *akrasia* as a case in which a person possesses and combines the premises of the syllogism of reason. There is a difference in content between the syllogism of reason and the syllogism of desire. The syllogism of reason portrays action in accord with it as the best means for securing the best among competing ends. The syllogism of desire only portrays action in accord with it as (a) (the best) means for securing something wanted. This difference is enough to explain why when both syllogisms are present the agent will act on the syllogism of reason. For example, the recognition that an action is the best means to the best among competing ends provides an extra motivation that is not present in the syllogism of desire. Hence a case in which an agent possesses and combines the premises of syllogism of reason but acts from the syllogism of desire instead will still turn out to be impossible.

According to this latter argument, the practical syllogism's being a model for explaining action does not support the thesis attributed to Aristotle in Chapter 10. Rather it supports a *revised* thesis according to which a person who possesses and combines the premises of a *syllogism of reason* will act on it if he or she is able to do so. But this revised thesis can function in an argument for the traditional interpretation in the same way that the thesis in Chapter 10 functioned in the argument set out there. Indeed, Santas's interpretation is an example of an interpretation according to which Aristotle did accept this revised thesis.[24]

There are three things that can be said against this final attempt to rescue a version of the thesis about knowledge and action. The first is that the arguments given about the conditions under which a person can be prevented from acting cast as much doubt on this revised thesis as they do on the original thesis. Second, if one considers the matter independently of Aristotle's explanation of *akrasia,* there are grounds for thinking that the difference in content between a syllogism of reason and a syllogism of desire will not explain why if both syllogisms are present the agent will act on the syllogism of reason. The point here is the same point that was made in Chapter 9 Section II Part C. Initially, Aristotle's admission of the existence of practical reason might lead one to think that there will always be an additional motive attached to the syllogism of reason that will make a person act on it rather than the syllogism of desire. But a closer look at Aristotle's position on practical reason shows that this is not so. A person's general ends may be partially or fully integrated into his or her character. If they are only partially integrated, then the motivation to act in accord with them will not always be sufficient to insure action in the face of a conflicting desire. The arguments in Section I of this chapter only reinforce this conclusion.[25]

Finally, on the interpretation I am arguing for, there is a way of explaining how an *akratēs* can act from a genuine state of conflict without having to refer to anything outside the syllogisms of reason and desire. Given that Aristotle's position on practical reason allows him to talk about a genuinely practical form of knowledge, one can regard the strength of the motivation associated with a syllogism to be determined by the way in which its major premise and conclusion are possessed. A major premise will be *fully* known (possessed) only if the end mentioned in it has been sufficiently integrated into a person's character to insure action on it. The degree to which the major premise is known will in turn determine the degree to which a conclusion based on it (if possessed) will be known. If the degree to which a premise and conclusion are known is one of the elements of a practical syllogism, then a syllogism of reason can contain the basis for an explanation of why the agent acts on a syllogism of desire rather than on it. If the way in which a premise is known is *not* one of the elements of a practical syllogism, then it is simply false that apart from considerations about the agent's ability the practical syllogism contains all of the elements needed to explain an action. Even on the traditional interpretation, the failure to possess or exercise one of the elements of the syllogism of reason (its final minor premise) is part of the explanation of the action of an *akratēs*. Either way, then, the claim that, apart from considerations of ability, the practical syllogism contains all of the elements needed to explain action cannot be used to support attributing the revised thesis to Aristotle.

Considered independently of Aristotle's explanation of *akrasia,* there is no reason to attribute to Aristotle any thesis about knowledge and action that commits him to the traditional interpretation. Indeed, given Aristotle's position on practical reason, the arguments of Section I, and the additional arguments provided in this section, there is strong, independent evidence for thinking that Aristotle did allow an *akratēs* to recognize what he ought to do in the situation that faces him.

III. Aristotle's General Approach to *Akrasia*

One final hurdle has to be faced before this independent evidence can be used to interpret Aristotle's detailed explanation of *akrasia*. In Chapter 10 Section II it was argued that Aristotle's general approach to his explanation of *akrasia* shows the thesis about knowledge and action at work, paving the way for an explanation along the lines of the traditional interpretation. If this is correct, then despite the arguments of Section I and II, one still has evidence for thinking that Aristotle's explanation of *akrasia* will be along the lines of the traditional interpretation. Since this evidence comes from a place where *akrasia* is the specific topic of discussion, it might be thought that it will outweigh whatever independent evidence there is to the contrary.

Three features of Aristotle's general approach were mentioned in Chapter 10—that it is *akrasia* that gets all the attention; that Aristotle's primary question is 'In what sense does a man who behaves incontinently have right understanding?'; and the three passages that immediately precede his detailed explanation of *akrasia*. In what follows I shall argue that, with one proviso, these three features fit the alternative interpretation I am arguing for as well as they do the traditional interpretation. As a result, they do *not* provide additional evidence that Aristotle's explanation of *akrasia* will be along the lines of the traditional interpretation.

Let us begin with the first of these three features. The first thing to be said is that there is a way of explaining why *akrasia* receives all of the attention that is independent of whether Aristotle thought that *akrasia* was puzzling in a way that *enkrateia* was not. *Akrasia* was a topic of current philosophical discussion, and in VII, 2 Aristotle lists some of the problems that arose in the discussion of it. Perhaps the most important of these was Socrates' denial of *akrasia*. However, the Socratic position did not include a corresponding denial of *enkrateia*. At least part of the reason for Aristotle's concentration on *akrasia* was that he inherited the topic from his predecessors. Second and more important, even if his focus on *akrasia* does show that Aristotle took it to be puzzling in a way in which he did not think *enkrateia* was puzzling, this can be explained without attributing to Aristotle any version of the thesis about knowledge and action. On the interpretation I am arguing for, Aristotle operates with a peculiarly practical form of knowledge, one understood through its ideal form, *phronēsis*. His conception of this paradigm is that action contrary to it is impossible (NE 1146a5-8). Since the *akratēs* fails to act in accord with his knowledge, his knowledge can not be that of the paradigm. In what sense then does he have knowledge? No similar question arises in the case of *enkrateia*.[26] Since this first feature can be explained as well on my alternative interpretation as it can on the traditional interpretation, it cannot provide any evidence for thinking that Aristotle's explanation of *akrasia* will be along the lines of the traditional interpretation.

Since the question that arises on my alternative interpretation is just the question that Aristotle takes to be the main question in his discussion of *akrasia*, the second feature mentioned in Chapter 10 also doesn't provide any grounds for favoring the traditional interpretation over my alternative interpretation. This leaves us with just the three passages that immediately precede Aristotle's detailed explanation of *akrasia*. I shall argue that, with one proviso, they too fit my alternative interpretation as well as they do the traditional interpretation.

There were two features of three passages that seemed to support the traditional interpretation—the fact that they occur in Aristotle's discussion of *akrasia*, and what is said in them. All three passages call attention to knowledge that is less than full and complete. This suggests that there is something that the *akratēs* doesn't know about what he ought to do. Furthermore, in 1146b24-35 Aristotle draws a distinction between knowledge possessed and exercised and knowledge possessed but not exercised. Traditionally, this has been interpreted as a distinction between actual and potential knowledge (knowledge that is occurrent and knowledge that is only dispositional).

This in turn suggests that the *akratēs'* knowledge of what he ought to do is only dispositional. By calling attention to the possibility of a person's failing to have or exercise the final minor premise of a practical syllogism, 1147a1-10 suggests the same thing. Finally, 1147a10-24 says that the *akratēs'* knowledge is like that of one who is mad, asleep, or drunk. These sort of people don't seem to believe or understand what they are talking about. Again, this suggests that the *akratēs* really doesn't know what he ought to do in the situation that faces him.

That these three passages occur in Aristotle's discussion of *akrasia* can be explained on my alternative interpretation in the same way that it was explained on the traditional interpretation. On the interpretation I am arguing for, the *akratēs* also does not have full and complete knowledge of what he ought to do. Since this is so, it would be natural for Aristotle to look to cases where a person has less than full and complete knolwedge to explain in just what sense the *akratēs* does know what he ought to do. This is just what he does in these three passages. 1146b24-35 and 1147a1-10 both set out situations in which a person does not have full or complete knowledge and yet action contrary to the person's knowledge is intelligible. If *akrasia* can be seen to fall under one or both of these situations, then one would at least have the beginning of an account of the way in which an *akratēs* can know what he ought to do. 1147a1-10 clearly leads to an explanation of impetuous *akrasia*. Since the kind of case to which the *akratēs* is specifically likened in 1147a10-24 falls under the kind of knowledge distinguished in 1146b24-35,[27] *akrasia* can be seen to fall under the situations mentioned in this passage as well. Thus, the occurrence of these passages can be given the same explanation on my alternative interpretation as was given by the traditional interpretation.

But what about their content? How can this be made to fit with my proposed interpretation? Let us begin with 1146b24-35. There are at least two reasons for thinking that the distinction drawn there should *not* be understood as the distinction between occurrent knowledge and knowledge that is only dispositional. In 1147a1-10 Aristotle mentions the possibility of having but not exercising the final minor premise of a practical syllogism. This in turn implies a distinction between having and not exercising such a premise, and not having it at all. But what could this distinction amount to if having and not exercising knowledge involves only dispositional knowledge? The knowledge in question is a particular piece of perceptual knowledge (for example, 'This is bread', where bread is one kind of dry food). Anyone who has perceptual capacities at all would seem to have this knowledge dispositionally. To mark off someone who has it but is not exercising it from someone who does not have it, it looks as if one would have to bring in some occurrent knowledge about the object.[28] Second, the kind of knowledge discussed in 1147a10-24 is specifically said to be a subclass of knowledge possessed but not exercised.[29] Any account of this latter sort of knowledge will have to fit the cases mentioned in 1147a10-24. These cases, however, form a broad spectrum, ranging from those who are mad or asleep, to the beginners of science (1147a21-23). Although someone who is asleep may have the relevant knowledge only dispositionally, I shall argue in Section IV of this chapter that in the case of the beginners of science the knowledge in question can include occurrent knowledge.[30] *If* this is right, then not only could what is said in 1146b24-35 be made to fit my proposed interpretation, so could what is said in 1147a10-24. Finally, as I have already mentioned, 1147a1-10 can be regarded as providing a basis for an explanation of impetuous *akrasia*. Since on the interpretation I am arguing, Aristotle makes an explicit reference to both weak and impetuous *akrasia* in his explanation of incontinence,[31] the occurrence of a passage that provides a basis for explaining impetuous *akrasia* will not be unexpected.[32]

Thus, provided the range of cases in 1147a10-24 can be seen to be broad enough to include those who do believe and understand what they are talking about, the three passages that immediately precede Aristotle's detailed explanation of *akrasia* would fit the interpretation I am arguing for as well as they do the traditional interpretation. If this proviso can be met, Aristotle's general approach to *akrasia* would provide no additional evidence that Aristotle's explanation of *akrasia* would be along the lines of the traditional interpretation.

IV. The Details of Aristotle's Explanation of *Akrasia*

The final test of any interpretation is how well it fits the details of Aristotle's explanation of *akrasia*, and it is time that we turned to them. However, when we approach them now, we are in a different position than we were in Chapter 10. Given the arguments of Sections I-III, one has independent grounds for reading disputed passages in such a way that they allow the *akratēs* to recognize what he ought to do in the situation that faces him. Put in psychological terms, the arguments of Sections I-III generate a set of expectations according to which Aristotle *will* allow the *akratēs* to recognize what he ought to do in the situation that faces him. Read in the light of these expectations, that is just what Aristotle's explanation of *akrasia* turns out to do.

Aristotle begins (1147a24-32) by noting that in contrast to

theoretical reasoning, one who possesses and combines the premises of a practical syllogism will act on it if he is able and not prevented. Since the *akratēs* does not act on his knowledge, and since one cannot say that he was unable to act on it,[33] the *akratēs* must either have failed to possess or combine the premises of the syllogism of reason, or he has combined them but has been prevented from acting on the result of this combination. If the latter occurs, then the *akratēs* will have acted from a genuine conflict of motives. This is exactly what Aristotle goes on to say.[34]

> When, then, the universal opinion is present in us forbidding us to taste, and there is also the opinion that 'everything sweet is pleasant' and that 'this is sweet' (now this is the opinion that is active), *and when appetite happens to be present in us, one thing says to avoid this object, but appetite leads us toward it* (for it can move each of our bodily parts). (1147a32-35, slight variation of the Oxford translation, emphasis mine)

The presence of a universal opinion forbidding tasting along with the opinions that everything sweet is pleasant and this is sweet, provides the potential for a conflict of motives. But for a genuine conflict to occur, appetite must be present. Without it, recognition that the object in front of him is of the forbidden kind would simply move the agent not to taste. Aristotle says, though, that appetite *is* present *(tuchē d' epithumia enousa)* (1147a34). He then specifically mentions the conflict. One thing says to avoid the object *(hē men oun legei pheugein touto)* (1147a34-35). What says to avoid the object is what results from the combination of the premises of the syllogism of reason—something that expresses the agent's recognition of what he ought to do in the situation that faces him.[35] '*Pheugein touto*' tells us what the content of this is: 'Avoid this object.' This is the most natural way to take 1147a34-35, if only for the occurrence of the demonstrative 'this' (*'touto'*). The arguments of Sections I-III also provide independent grounds for taking it in this way. Thus, 1147a34-35 provides one of the elements in a genuine conflict of motives, something that moves the *akratēs* to avoid tasting the object. Aristotle then immediately supplies the other element. Appetite moves the *akratēs* to taste *(hē d' epithumia agei)* (1147a35). Here, then, seems to be a clear statement of the kind of conflict than can occur in *akrasia*.

Two other passages in Aristotle's explanation of *akrasia* can also be taken to refer to a genuine conflict of motives. At 1147b3-5 Aristotle says,

> It also follows that this is why the lower animals are not incontinent, viz. because they have no universal judgment but only imagination and memory of particulars.

Aristotle is referring here to what marks off humans from animals, their ability to act from rational desire *(boulēsis)*. He refers to it in terms of the capacity to act from universal judgments. In *De Anima* he refers to it as something that comes with a sense of time (433b5ff) and with the capacity for calculative imagination (432b26ff). In these latter two passages the difference between humans and animals is explicitly linked with the possibility of conflicts of motives. And at both 432b26ff and 434a12-15 Aristotle says that *akrasia* provides one of the occasions on which such a conflict occurs.[36] In light of this it is not unreasonable to think that this is also what underlies Aristotle's remark at 1147b3-5. The reason why animals are not incontinent is that, unlike humans, they do not act from a genuine conflict of motives.

The third passage in which there is a reference to a conflict of motives is Aristotle's explanation at 1147b12-19 of why the Socratic position seems to result. I shall discuss this passage shortly.

In each of these passages, then, there is a reference, explicit or implicit, to the *akratēs'* recognition of what he ought to do in the situation that faces him. Thus, when it comes to his detailed explanation of *akrasia*, Aristotle does allow the *akratēs* to know what he ought to do in the situation that faces him.

There is one additional passage in which I think Aristotle refers to this recognition, and that is in his use of *'hē teleutaia protasis'* in 1147b9-12. It has been objected against other attempts at taking *'hē teleutaia protasis'* to refer to that which expresses the *akratēs'* recognition of what he ought to do, that in a context that makes use of the technical apparatus of the practical syllogism, *'protasis'* is much more naturally translated as 'premise' than as 'conclusion'. For instance, Aristotle has already used the more technical term *'sumperanthen'* to refer to the conclusion of a practical syllogism at 1147a27, and had he wanted to refer to it again, he would have used it or some other term that clearly designates a conclusion. We are now in a position to answer these objections.

In the first place, what expresses the *akratēs'* recognition of what he ought to do is *not* the conclusion of the syllogism of reason. I have already acknowledged that the conclusion of a practical syllogism is an *action,* and the *akratēs* does not act on the syllogism of reason. What expresses the *akratēs'* recognition is something proposition-like that results from the combination of the premises of the syllogism of reason.[37] Since this is *the last proposition* that occurs in such a syllogism, the use of *'hē teleutaia protasis'* (literally, "the last proposition") to refer to it is a natural one.[38] If one adds to this the independent reasons that exist for thinking that Aristotle does allow the *akratēs* to recognize what he ought to do, along with the earlier reference at 1147a34-35 to such a recognition, then it becomes even more natural to take '*hē teleutaia protasis*' to refer to something that expresses this recognition. Finally, taking it in this way allows Aristotle to recognize, in his detailed explanation of *akrasia,* the two forms of *akrasia* that he explicitly distinguishes later, impetuousness and weakness. At 1147a10-11, Aristotle says that the *akratēs* either fails to possess or fails to exercise *hē teleutaia protasis.* The impetuous *akratēs* will be one who fails to possess it. The weak *akratēs* will be one who possesses it, but fails to exercise it. All in all, then, there seem to be reasons for taking '*hē teleutaia protasis*' at 1147b9 to be another place where Aristotle refers to the *akratēs'* recognition of what he ought to do.[39]

However, this just brings us to the major stumbling block for this or any other alternative to the traditional interpretation, what Aristotle goes on to say at 1147b9-12.

> *hē teleutaia protasis* both being an opinion about a perceptible object, and being what determines our actions, this a man either has not when he is in the state of passion or has it in the sense in which having knowledge did not mean knowing but only talking, as a drunken man may mutter the verses of Empedocles.

The reference to the drunk muttering the verses of Empedocles is clearly a reference back to 1147a10-24, where Aristotle talks about those who in a sense do and in a sense do not have knowledge. His examples of such people include those who are mad, asleep, or drunk. These do not seem to understand or believe what they are talking about at the time that they say it. Thus, even if *hē teleutaia protasis* does express what the *akratēs* ought to do in the situation that faces him, it looks as if the *akratēs* really wouldn't recognize what this is. And if he doesn't recognize what this is, how can he be motivated to do it? If *this* is the kind of knowledge that the *akratēs* has, then in spite of what I have argued, it looks like passages like 1147a34-35 *shouldn't* be taken as mentioning a genuine conflict of motives.

Let us look more closely at 1147a10-24. One of the first things to be noted is that it includes a mixed bag of examples. They range from those who are mad, asleep, drunk, to actors reciting lines on a stage, and to those who have just begun to learn a science. The *akratēs* is said to be in a state similar to these (1147a17-18), but since there seem to be such great differences between the examples cited, it is not clear what this amounts to other than the *akratēs'* not acting on his knowledge.

The second thing to note is that if one were to classify Aristotle's examples according to the theoretical-practical distinction, they would all fall on the theoretical side of the line. The utterances specifically mentioned by Aristotle are the demonstrations or phrases of a science, and the verses of Empedocles. The former certainly aren't practical, and the latter wouldn't ordinarily be cited as an example of practical knowledge.[40] What this means is that if one is to find out what kind of practical knowledge Aristotle is talking about, one will have to look at the practical *analogue* of theoretical cases. What occurs in such an analogue will not be exactly the same as what occurs in the theoretical case. It will only be its analogue.

If one now looks at the practical analogue of the example of the beginners of science, I think one will see that the range of cases Aristotle is talking about is sufficiently wide to include cases in which people do recognize what they ought to do in a particular situation but their knowledge has not been sufficiently integrated into their characters to insure that they will act on it. The key to understanding this example is the remark that those who have just begun to learn a science may string together its phrases but they do not know it, "for it has to become part of themselves, and that takes time" (1147a22). Aristotle says something about what it is about sciences that requires time to acquire them in NE Bk. VI.

> What has been said is confirmed by the fact that while young men become geometricians and mathematicians and wise in matters like these, it is thought that a young man of practical wisdom cannot be found. The cause is that such wisdom is concerned not only with universals but with particulars, which become familiar from experience, but a young man has no experience, for it is length of time that gives experience; indeed one might ask this question too, why a boy may become a mathematician, but not a philosopher or a physicist. Is it because the objects of mathematics exist by abstraction, while the first principles of these other subjects come from experience, and because young men have no conviction about the latter, but merely use the proper language, while the essence of mathematical objects is plain enough to them? (1142a12-20)

Part of what Aristotle is saying here is that it takes time to become a philosopher or a physicist because experience is needed to provide the basis for the first principles of these disciplines. By contrast mathematics is a discipline whose subject matter is so abstract that one can intuit its first principles without much experience at all. But I think Aristotle is also saying that experience is necessary to acquaint a person with the various particulars to which the universal principles of the science apply. A person who believes scientific truths with *conviction (pistouousin)* not only can provide the reasons why these truths hold by reference to their first principles, but also can easily recognize instances to which they apply and will in fact apply them. The question is, what is the practical analogue of this?

The answer, I think, is that time and experience are needed to provide people with habits or dispositions that not only allow them to acquire general principles, but also insure that they will act on them. In NE Bk. I Aristotle says,

> Hence any one who is to listen intelligently to lectures about what is noble and just and, generally, about the subjects of political science must have been brought up in good habits. For the fact is the starting point, and if this is sufficiently plain to him, he will not at the start need the reason as well; and the man who has been well brought up has or can easily get the starting points. (1095b4-8)

> Hence a young man is not a proper hearer of lectures on political science; for he is inexperienced in the actions that occur in life, but its discussions start from these and are about these; and, further, since he tends to follow his passions, his study will be vain and unprofitable, because the end aimed at is not knowledge but action. And it makes no difference whether he is young in years or youthful in character; the defect does not depend on time, but on his living, and pursuing each successive object as passion directs. For to such persons, as to the incontinent, knowledge brings not profit; but to those who desire and act in accordance with a rational principle knowledge about such matters will be of great benefit. (1095a2-11)

Experience is needed to provide people with the right sort of habits or dispositions, which give them or from which they can obtain the proper first principles. Experience also allows people to see cases to which their principles apply.[41] But most important for our purposes, these same habits make the knowledge that they acquire profitable, for they allow people to achieve the end of the study of politics, *action* (1095a4-6). Where the end of a discipline is action, applying one's principles amounts to acting, not just recognizing instances of them. At 1095a8-9 the inexperienced person who lacks the proper habits is specifically likened to the *akratēs*. They are both described, not as people who don't have knowledge of what to do, but as people who, although they have knowledge, won't profit from it. Since the end of political science is action, not profiting from one's knowledge means not acting in accord with it.

If this is right, then the practical analogue of the beginners of science are those who may know what they ought to do, those who may even recognize instances in which they ought to apply this knowledge, but those in whom this knowledge has not been sufficiently integrated to insure that they will act on it. They lack knowledge in the sense that their practical principles have not yet become "a part of themselves." Talk about a lack of knowledge in this sense will be plausible if, as I have argued, Aristotle operates with a genuinely *practical* form of knowledge. Failure to have full and complete practical knowledge can be due to the knowledge's not being sufficiently practical, as well as to the failure to entertain or believe something proposition-like.

This way of taking the case of the beginners of science is made even more plausible once one realizes that other cases that Aristotle talks about in 1147a10-24 admit of degrees. A drunk uttering the phrases of a science may be too drunk to understand what he is saying, but he may also be only drunk enough that he doesn't grasp all of what he is saying at the time that he is saying it. Although able to supply some of the foundations for what he says, and able to apply what he says to some cases (including a simple case at hand), he may not be in enough possession of his faculties to supply a complete explanation, or to recognize its application to more difficult or complex cases. (Similarly, a person can be "half asleep," understanding and believing part of what he says.) The practical analogue of these sorts of cases would also seem to include those who recognize what they ought to do on a particular occasion but are not strongly enough motivated to do it. If this is right, then 1147a10-24 contains a range of cases, one that is broad enough to include both impetuous *akrasia,* where the agent doesn't recognize what it is that he ought to do, and weak *akrasia,* where the agent does recognize what he ought to do.[42]

If one reads a reference to this range of case into 1147b9-12, then what Aristotle says in that passage ceases to be incompatible with the interpretation I am arguing for.[43] The *akratēs* can have knowledge of what he ought to do in the sense in which a drunk muttering the verses of Empedocles knows what he is talking about and still recognize what he ought to do in the situation that faces him.

That this is how one should take 1147b9-12 is confirmed by what Aristotle says immediately afterwards, in the third passage that I said can be read as containing a reference to a genuine conflict of motives in *akrasia.*

> And because the last term *(ton eschaton horon)* is not universal nor equally an object of scientific knowledge with the universal term, the position that Socrates sought to establish actually seems to result; for it is in the presence of what is thought to be knowledge proper that the affection of incontinence arises *(ou gar tēs kuriōs epistēmēs einai dokousēs parousēs ginetai to pathos)* (nor is it this that is 'dragged about' by passion [*oud' hautē perielketai dia to pathos*]), but in that of perceptual knowledge. (1147b12-17, slight variation of Ross's translation)

Aristotle not only denies here that *akrasia* arises in the presence of knowledge proper and that knowledge proper is dragged about in *akrasia,* he implies that *akrasia* does occur in the presence of perceptual knowledge and that it is perceptual knowledge that is dragged about by passion. On the traditional interpretation it is difficult to see how this could be so. Whatever this perceptual knowledge is, it is expressed by the last term *(ton eschaton horon)*; and it is clear that *'ton eschaton horon'* refers to the same thing as does *'hē teleutaia protasis'* on line 9. However, if the *akratēs* possesses *hē teleutaia protasis* only in the sense in which a drunk muttering the verses of Empedocles knows what he is talking about, and one takes this as saying that the *akratēs* doesn't understand or believe what he is saying, then it is hard to see how it is in the presence of this sort of knowledge that *akrasia* occurs.[44] For the same reason it is difficult to see how this knowledge could be dragged about by passion in *akrasia*. However, if one takes this perceptual knowledge to be the *akratēs'* recognition of what he ought to do in the situation that faces him, and if one reads 1147b9-12 in the way I have suggested, then *akrasia* does occur in the presence of such knowledge and this knowledge is dragged about by passion. That is, what Aristotle says in 1147b12-17 confirms the reading I have given of 1147b9-12. Taking 1147b12-17 in the say I have just suggested also turns it into another passage in which Aristotle says that the *akratēs* acts from a genuine conflict of motives.[45]

Thus, the major stumbling block to the alternative to the traditional interpretation that I have suggested can be overcome. The details of Aristotle's explanation of *akrasia* do fit the interpretation I am arguing for.

There is one last point to be made before the body of the argument for this interpretation is completed. That the problems raised in Chapter 9 for the traditional interpretation do not arise on my alternative interpretation provides additional support for it. Not only does it turn out on my interpretation that Aristotle's explanation of *akrasia* is compatible with his later distinction between weak and impetuous *akrasia*, he actually acknowledges both of these forms of *akrasia* in his explanation of *akrasia* (at 1147b9-12). Since on my interpretation the *akratēs* can recognize what he ought to do in the situation that faces him, he can also be aware of his incontinence at the time that he acts incontinently. And, of course, Aristotle's explanation of *akrasia* is compatible with his admission of a genuine conflict of motives in *akrasia*. It explicitly mentions such a conflict. Nor is there any need to explain why Aristotle closed off a possibility left open by his position on practical reason. On my interpretation he did no such thing.

If one adds this to everything else that has been said, then I think one gets quite a strong argument for an alternative to the traditional interpretation.[46]

V. Two Final Objections

Two final objections however, might be raised against my interpretation. The first is that my interpretation is incompatible with what Aristotle says about *akrasia*'s being a temporary, abnormal condition. The second is that on my interpretation Aristotle's explanation of *akrasia* turns out to be no explanation at all. If these objections are correct, then perhaps the argument I have given is not as strong as I have said it is.

At 1147b6-9 Aristotle says,

> The explanation of how the ignorance is dissolved and the incontinent man regains his knowledge, is the same as in the case of the man drunk or asleep and is not particular to this condition; we must go to the students of natural science for it.

And at 1150b33-35 he says,

> for wickedness is like a disease such as dropsy or consumption, while incontinence is like epilepsy;

According to Aristotle, *akrasia* involves a bodily condition brought about by passion, one that is similar to the condition of sleep or drunkenness. It is also a condition that disappears after the *akratēs* has acted incontinently. In this respect it is like epilepsy, whose seizures occur intermittently, rather than like consumption or dropsy, whose coughing or swelling occur continuously. Furthermore, the disappearance of this condition is to be explained by natural scientists *(phusiologoi).* One might argue, however, that on my interpretation *akrasia* is a continuous condition. If the *akratēs'* knowledge of how he ought to behave is not fully integrated into his character, then this is something that is so continuously. It does not disappear after the *akratēs* acts incontinently. And if it ever does disappear, its disappearance doesn't seem to be something that would be explained by *phusiologoi.* My interpretation seems to take *akrasia* to be the wrong kind of condition—a continuous one rather than an intermittent one. The traditional interpretation, however, is not open to any such objection.

The first thing to be said in reply to this objection is that in spite of the passages quoted above, Aristotle does take *akrasia* to be a condition that a person has continuously. At 1152a28-29 Aristotle distinguishes excitable incontinent people from those who are incontinent through habituation, and from those whose incontinence is innate. The incontinence of at least the latter two sort of people certainly seems to be a condition that is present continuously. Furthermore, what Aristotle compares *akrasia* to is epilepsy, not epileptic seizures. An epileptic has epilepsy continuously; it is his seizures that are intermittent. The problem for my interpretation is not that it takes *akrasia* to be a condition that is present continuously. The problem is explaining why the *akratēs* acts from this condition only intermittently, and explaining why, when he acts on it, it involves a bodily state whose disappearance is to be explained by *phusiologoi*. These problems, however, I think can be solved.

According to the position on practical reason that I have attributed to Aristotle, a person can acquire the right first principles only if he is already to some extent disposed to act on them. Since the *akratēs* does have the right first principles, he can be expected to act on them, even in the face of (some) conflicting desires. It is only when these conflicting desires are fairly strong that he will act contrary to his knowledge.[47] Furthermore, it is plausible to regard these strong, conflicting desires as arising only intermittently, and as desires whose presence and absence will ultimately be explained by *phusiologoi*.[48] According to Aristotle, *akrasia* without qualification occurs in connection with desires like hunger and thirst, desires that are associated with certain bodily states (1147b23-35). These bodily desires tend to increase the longer they go unsatisfied, and to decrease or disappear once they have been satisfied. Thus, desires of this sort will be strong enough to make a person act incontinently only intermittently, and they will normally disappear once they have been satisfied. Insofar as their waxing and waning is due to some bodily condition, their presence or absence will ultimately be explained by *phusiologoi*. Thus, the interpretation I have argued for does fit Aristotle's remarks about the intermittency of incontent action.

The second objection is that my interpretation cannot be correct because it reduces Aristotle's explanation of *akrasia* to an uninteresting triviality. According to my interpretation, the *akratēs* acts incontinently because his knowledge is not sufficiently integrated into his character. But to say this is to say no more than that the *akratēs* doesn't act on his knowledge because he doesn't want to strongly enough. This, however, could be said of any action. It is utterly trivial, and its triviality turns Aristotle's explanation of *akrasia* into no explanation at all. An interpretation that turns a discussion whose point is to explain how and why an incontinent man acts incontinently into no explanation at all does not seem to be an interpretation that deserves to be taken all that seriously.

A number of things can be said in reply to this objection. The first is that the main point of Aristotle's discussion of *akrasia* is *not* to provide an explanation of incontinent action. As I pointed out in

Chapter 10 Section II, Aristotle's main concern is with the sense in which the *akratēs* knows what it is that he ought to do. It is not with why he does it. If I am right in maintaining that knowledge that has not been fully integrated into a person's character is a kind of knowledge that falls short of full and complete practical knowledge, then on my interpretation one has an answer to Aristotle's main concern, and one has it whether or not one also has a nontrivial explanation of incontinent action.

In the second place, it is *not* trivial to say on a particular occasion that an *akratēs* acted incontinently because his knowledge was not fully integrated into his character. How trivial this claim is depends on how strong a motivation to act goes along with the presence of this kind of knowledge. If what I have said in response to the first objection above is correct, then a fairly strong motivation to act does go along with this kind of knowledge. Thus, to assert on a given occasion that an *akratēs* failed to act because his knowledge was of this sort is to imply that he acted as he did only because of the existence of a strong, conflicting desire. This is not something that could be said of just any action, and to say it is not to say something trivial.

Finally, it was never intended on my interpretation that one take the failure of an *akratēs'* knowledge to be fully integrated into his character to be a *complete* explanation of his incontinent action. To say of a person that he has this kind of knowledge is to say that he is liable not to act on it in the face of a strong conflicting motive. It is not to say how or why such a strong conflicting motive arises, nor is it to say how or why this liability itself arose. A complete explanation of a particular incontinent action would have to include an explanation of both of these. My answer to the first objection above contains a suggestion as to how the existence of a strong conflicting desire might be explained, and what Aristotle says at 1152a28-29 suggests that there will be at least two kinds of explanation needed for the *akratēs'* liability not to act in accord with his knowledge. However, my primary concern in this book has not been to provide what Aristotle would have taken to be a complete explanation of incontinent action. It has not been to provide a complete explanation of everything that Aristotle has said about *akrasia*. Rather, it has been to determine whether Aristotle allowed an *akratēs* to recognize what he ought to do in the particular situation that faces him. If on the basis of what I have said one does not have a complete explanation of incontinent action, then all this shows is that more needs to be said than I have said. It doesn't show that what I have said isn't right.

The interpretation I have argued for, thus, does deserve to be taken seriously. The evidence that can be marshaled in support of it is considerable.

VI. A Summary

Since the argument for the interpretation I have been supporting has been long and complicated, it will be useful if I summarize briefly both the interpretation and the argument I have given for it.

The main question in Bk. VII is in what sense the *akratēs* knows that what he does is wrong. One of the reasons that this question arises is that on Aristotle's conception of full and complete practical knowledge—*phronēsis*—action contrary to it is impossible. The *akratēs*, thus, can't have full and complete practical knowledge of what he ought to do. In what sense, then, does he know what he ought to do?

Aristotle begins by setting out two situations in which a person lacks full and complete knowledge, situations in which failure to act on it is intelligible. The first is a case in which a person possesses but is not exercising knowledge (1146b24-35). The second is one in which a person has knowledge of a universal principle that applies to a particular situation but fails to have or exercise knowledge about the particular situation itself (1147a1-10). If *akrasia* can be seen to fit under one or both of these cases, then one would have at least a beginning of an account of just what kind of knowledge the *akratēs* has.

Aristotle indicates that this can be done. He points to a subset of cases in which a person has but is not exercising knowledge (1147a10-24). If one looks carefully at the practical analogues of these cases, one discovers that they range from situations in which people don't recognize that they are in a position to act on their knowledge (cases that exemplify the pattern of 1147a1-10 [cases of impetuous *akrasia*]), to situations in which people can realize that they are in a position to act on their knowledge, but their knowledge is not sufficiently integrated into their characters to insure action on it (cases of weak *akrasia*).

Finally, Aristotle spells out his answer more completely. He reminds one of the strong connection that holds between practical knowledge and action (1147a26-32). A person who recognizes that she is in a position to act on her knowledge will act on it unless she is prevented from doing so. One of the things that can prevent a person from acting on her knowledge is a strong conflicting desire. If this is what happens in *akrasia,* then Aristotle must go on to indicate that the *akratēs* is in a genuine state of conflict. This he does. He considers a case in which a man has a universal premise forbidding the tasting of certain things (1147a32), and the opinions that everything sweet is pleasant and that what is in front of him is sweet

(1147a33). If this is all there were to it, there would be no conflict of motives and no akratic action. But appetite is present (1147a34). This means that the agent is in a state of conflict. One thing (his knowledge of what to do in the particular situation) tells him not to taste what is in front of him (1147a34-35), but appetite leads him to taste it (1147a35). It is the latter on which he acts. The existence of such conflicts in *akrasia* is also the reason why animals are not incontinent. They lack the capacity to make the kinds of judgments that make genuine conflicts of motives possible (1147b4-6).

In general, if one considers that which expresses what the *akratēs* ought to do in the situation that faces him *(hē teleutaia protasis)*, the *akratēs* either does not have it (a case of impetuous *akrasia*), or he has it only in the sense in which a drunk reciting the verses of Empedocles knows what he is talking about. The latter is a reference back to the practical analogues of the cases mentioned in 1147a10-24, and these include cases where the agent knows what she ought to do but her knowledge is not sufficiently integrated into her character to insure that she will do it. These latter turn out to be cases of weak *akrasia*. In a sense, then, the Socratic position does seem to result (1147b12-17), for knowledge proper is not present and dragged about in *akrasia*. Perceptual knowledge is present and dragged about, but this perceptual knowledge is not knowledge proper. Not only is knowledge proper universal and not particular, knowledge proper in practical matters is fully integrated into a person's character, and an *akratēs* does not have this kind of knowledge.

Aristotle, thus, has indicated the senses in which an *akratēs* can know that what he does is wrong. In doing so, he acknowledges that an *akratēs* can know what he ought to do in the situation that faces him. His knowledge of general principles is sufficiently integrated into his character to insure that he will often act on them, but it is not sufficiently integrated to prevent either conflicting desires from arising, or to prevent action on strong conflicting desires should they arise. In this way his knowledge differs from both that of the *enkratēs* and the *phronimos*.

In arguing for this interpretation I first argued that evidence exists independent of Aristotle's particular discussion of *akrasia* that he allowed the *akratēs* to recognize what he ought to do in the situation that faces him. Not only does Aristotle's position on practical reason allow for this, but his admission that the *akratēs* acts from a genuine conflict of motives implies the same thing. Aristotle acknowledges such a conflict of motives in both the *Eudemian Ethics* (Bk. II) and in the *Nicomachean Ethics* (Bks. I and IX). These passages cannot be discounted on the grounds that Aristotle is not there speaking precisely about matters of psychology. In *De Anima*, where Aristotle is speaking precisely about matters of psychology, he also acknowledges the existence of a genuine conflict of motives in *akrasia.*

I then argued that this evidence cannot be offset by Aristotle's acceptance of the thesis that a person who possesses and combines the premises of a practical syllogism will act on it if he is able to do so. The main issue here is what the conditions are under which a person can be prevented *(kōluomenon)* from acting on a practical syllogism. I argued that a closer look at Aristotle's use of the verb *'kōluō'* shows that a person can be prevented from acting by a conflicting desire. And I argued that reading this notion into what Aristotle says does not trivialize his claim that a person will act on a syllogism whose premise he has combined if he is not compelled or prevented. That Aristotle did not accept the thesis in question is also confirmed by the case of *enkrateia.* Nor will it do to defend Aristotle's acceptance of this thesis on the grounds that a practical syllogism contains all of the elements needed to explain a given action. I argued that either it is false that the practical syllogism contains all of the elements needed to explain a given action, or that what is contained in a practical syllogism *can* explain why a person who is prevented from acting on a given syllogism by a conflicting desire acts as he does. Considered independently of Aristotle's explanation of *akrasia,* there are grounds only for thinking that Aristotle did allow the *akratēs* to know what he ought to do in the situation that faces him.

I then argued that Aristotle's general approach to his discussion of *akrasia* cannot provide any additional evidence that the *akratēs* cannot recognize what he ought to do in the situation that faces him. Given that Aristotle operates with a genuinely practical form of knowledge, one can explain both why *akrasia* gets all the attention in this discussion, and why Aristotle's main concern is with the sense in which the *akratēs* knows what he ought to do, without having to say that the *akratēs* lacks some particular knowledge about the situation that faces him. Since the *akratēs* cannot have full and complete practical knowledge of what he ought to do, one can also understand why Aristotle would begin his explanation of *akrasia* by examining cases in which people have less than full and complete knowledge. Provided that the range of the practical analogues of the kinds of cases mentioned is broad enough to include those who recognize that they are in a position to act on their knowledge, Aristotle's approach to his discussion of *akrasia* is as compatible with an interpretation that allows the *akratēs* such a recognition as it is with an interpretation that does not.

One can now approach the details of Aristotle's explanation of *akrasia* from a new perspective. Where there are passages whose interpretation is controversial, one now has independent, non-question begging grounds for interpreting them as allowing the *akratēs* to recognize what it is that he ought to do in the situation that faces him. For example, taken by itself 1147a34-35 is quite naturally taken to refer to something that expresses the *akratēs'* knowledge of what to do in his particular situation. We now have additional independent grounds for so taking it. So taken, it is part of an explicit reference to a genuine conflict of motives in *akrasia*, just what one would expect on the interpretation being argued for. (Aristotle also makes implicit reference to such a conflict in his explanation of why animals cannot be incontinent, and in his explanation of why the Socratic position seems to result.) Even what seems to be the greatest stumbling block for this interpretation can be overcome. Even if the conclusion of a practical syllgism is an action, *'hē teleutaia protasis'* can still refer to that which expresses the *akratēs'* knowledge of what he ought to do, for the latter is "the last *proposition*" that results from possession and combination of the premises of the syllogism of reason. That the *akratēs* possesses this knowledge only in the sense in which a drunk reciting the verses of Empedocles knows what he is talking about also doesn't show that the *akratēs* doesn't understand or believe what he says. Included among those who have this sort of knowledge are the beginners of science, and the reason they have this kind of knowledge is that their knowledge has yet to become a part of themselves. The practical analogue of such people are those whose knowledge has not been sufficiently integrated into their character to insure that they will act on it. Thus, the knowledge expressed by *'hē teleutaia protasis'* is a knowledge that the *akratēs* can actually have. This is confirmed by what Aristotle says in his explanation of why the Socratic position seems to result. It too implies that the knowledge expressed by *'hē teleutaia protasis'* is present in *akrasia.*

If one adds to all of this that the problems initially raised for the traditional interpretation do not arise on my interpretation, then I think one has quite a strong argument for an interpretation according to which Aristotle does allow an *akratēs* to recognize what he ought to do in the situation that faces him. The reader, of course, will decide for himself whether it is stronger than the argument already given for the traditional interpretation. But I, for one, am inclined to think that it is.

Concluding Remarks

The argument of the two parts of this book have, to a large extent, been given independently of one another. Nevertheless, they are quite closely connected. In these final remarks I want to give a general picture of just what this connection is. I then want to indicate what the conclusions are that I think can be drawn from the arguments of both parts of this book, and to point to some of the work that remains to be done.

Although the positions argued for in Parts One and Two of this book do not imply one another, they are still mutually supportive. The position on practical reason attributed to Aristotle in Part One provides for the possibility of just those cases of weakness of the will argued for in Part Two. According to that position, the exercise of practical reason can provide one with a motivation to act on an end that one has inferred one ought to act on, but it does not guarantee that this end will be sufficiently integrated into one's character that one will always act on it. Thus, the kind of cases of weakness of the will argued for in Part Two are genuine possibilities. This is not enough to *commit* Aristotle to the existence of such cases, since other considerations might lead him to close off this possibility. But in the absence of any such further considerations, one would expect Aristotle to acknowledge their existence. Indeed, a large part of the argument of Part Two amounts to the claim that no such further considerations exist. For example, it is argued that Aristotle's use of the practical syllogism as a model for explaining actions does not close off this possibility. The position argued for in Part One, then, is one of the general premises on which the arguments of Part Two rest.

219

Nevertheless, it is still possible to accept the arguments of Part Two without having to attribute to Aristotle the position on practical reason argued for in Part One. For example, it is argued that Aristotle's admission of the existence of genuine conflict of motives in *akrasia* committed him to allowing the *akratēs* to know what he ought to do at the time that he acts, and it is certainly possible to take Aristotle to admit this without attributing to him the position on practical reason argued for in Part One. One of the consequences of this possibility, though, is that the arguments in Part Two can be used in a non-question begging way to support the position argued for in Part One. To the extent to which Aristotle did allow for the possibility of cases in which the *akratēs* can know what he ought to do at the time that he acts, Aristotle ought to have maintained a position on the connection between reason and motivation that allows for the existence of such cases. Since the position on practical reason argued for in Part One does just that, everything else being equal, one has grounds for attributing it to Aristotle.

Thus, the arguments of the two parts of this book mutually support one another without it being the case that if one rejects the conclusion of one of them one must also reject the conclusion of the other. Still, granting even this, what is one to make of the arguments of the book taken as a whole?

This book has had both a philosophical and a historical purpose. The philosophical purpose has been to set out a particular alternative according to which practical reason provides an objective basis for ethics, an alternative that deserves to be taken seriously. The historical purpose has been to argue that Aristotle's ethics is based on practical reason, and that Aristotle did allow genuine cases of weakness of the will. Although the alternative set out is not entirely complete, I think that the philosophical purpose has to a large extent been achieved. It is less clear that the historical purpose has been achieved, but even here I think significant progress has been made.

The prospect of basing ethics on practical reason is attractive, if only because it allows one to reconcile two apparently incompatible aspects of moral judgments—their "practical" side and their objectivity. As I suggested in the Introduction, I do not think that one will be able to answer the general question of whether ethics can be based on practical reason unless one has on hand some specific alternatives according to which practical reason does exist, and its existence provides an objective basis for ethics. Whether Aristotle held the view or not, the position attributed to him in Part One is just such an alternative. It provides conditions under which practical reason would exist and conditions under which its existence would provide an objective basis for ethics. Although it does not indicate which particular ends would be rational for anyone to have, it does outline a kind of reasoning that if engaged in correctly would lead a person to acquire certain ends. In this way it provides for the possibility of finding out just what ends, if any, are rational for anyone to have. Furthermore, the view does deserve to be taken seriously. If anything like the content of Aristotle's ethics emerges from it, then it presents a way of life that deserves to be taken seriously. Although it may not be able to deal adequately with all occasions on which one ought to curtail the pursuit of one's own ends when they come in conflict with the ends of others, as I argued in Chapter 8, it looks as if something like the view attributed to Aristotle will have to be part of any view that does attempt to deal with all such occasions on the basis of principles of practical reason. Finally, whether or not the position on weakness of the will argued for in Part Two is one that Aristotle accepted or not, it is compatible with the position on practical reason argued for in Part One. Thus, this latter position satisfies at least the criterion that it acknowledges genuine cases of weakness of the will.

Of course, a good deal of work must be done before one can make anything like a final decision on whether the view in question can provide even part of an adequate basis for morality. The most obvious task is to indicate more clearly just what ends turn out to be rational ends according to this view. This would involve being more specific about the kind of inductive reasoning involved in the view, using it to see what ends people are supposed to have if they are to be fully rational. The second task is to determine whether the kind of ethics that would emerge from this view would be sufficient to minimize interpersonal conflicts. This would include determining to what extent man has a social nature, which, if properly developed, would lead to feelings of sympathy and friendship that would reduce interpersonal conflicts. Finally, one would want to look more carefully at the position on weakness of the will argued for in Chapter 11. Not only must more be said before one will have a complete account of weakness of the will; there are questions of adequacy that arise with respect to the part of it that we do have. For example, is weakness of the will always atypical in the way that this view suggests? In spite of all this, I think that the positions on practical reason and weakness of the will attributed to Aristotle provide an important starting point for articulating a view that both bases ethics on practical reason and deserves to be taken seriously. If this is right, then a large part of the philosophical purpose of this book has been achieved.

It is perhaps, less clear that the historical purpose of the book has been achieved. Any reader will have doubts about some parts of the arguments of this book. But even waiving such doubts, some questions arise that lead one to wonder whether one can say with any confidence that Aristotle held either of the two positions that have been attributed to him. Beginning with the arguments about Aristotle's position on practical reason, the main question that arises is the extent to which these arguments rely on indirect textual evidence. Nowhere does Aristotle give anything like an explicit treatment of the existence of practical reason. Nowhere does he provide anything like an explicit discussion of the relation between reason and the ends of action. Even the passage that I have taken to be Aristotle's most explicit statement on the acquisition of universal ends, NE 1143a35-b5, contains no reference to many of the details of the position attributed to him. These details have all been read into the text on the grounds that they are required by what Aristotle has said in this and other passages. But, one might argue, even if this is true, it is not enough to show that Aristotle did have a position on practical reason, let alone the one I have attributed to him. Without more direct textual evidence to rely on, the most one is entitled to say is that the position I have attributed to him is one that he would have held had his attention been directed to this topic, or that it is one that he was groping toward at the time that he wrote the *Eudemian* and *Nicomachean Ethics*. There simply isn't enough evidence to conclude that it is a view that he actually held.

It must be conceded that one would be in a much better position to say just what Aristotle's position on practical reason and its relation with ethics was if he had provided an explicit treatment of these topics. But his failure to do so doesn't mean that he didn't have a position on these issues, or that it wasn't what I have said it was. His relative silence would be understandable if he felt that there was no need for an explicit treatment. *We* feel that an argument is needed because we have read philosophers like Hume who have denied the existence of practical reason. Thus, *we* take seriously the possibility that ethics can't be based on practical reason. But if none of Aristotle's contemporaries or immediate predecessors maintained a Humean position, Aristotle would have felt no similar need. Instead, he would have done just what we find him doing, making occasional remarks about practical reason when they are relevant to a particular point he is making, or when they are needed to mark off his own view from other views that are similar to his. Admittedly, not a great deal is known about Aristotle's contemporaries or immediate predecessors outside of Socrates and Plato, but there is no strong indication that any of them held a Humean position on practical reason.[1] Not even Aristotle's criticism of the division of the soul into a rational and an irrational part at *De Anima* 433b5ff seems directed specifically at someone who held a Humean position. If there was no one to force Aristotle into an explicit discussion of the existence of practical reason, then I don't think it is at all unreasonable to attribute to Aristotle a specific position on practical reason on the basis of the kind of indirect evidence that I have relied on.

However, if one resists this last conclusion, and maintains, for example, that the most I am entitled to is that the position I have attributed to Aristotle is one that he was groping toward, this will not bother me a great deal. This is still a conclusion that will be of considerable historical interest. One way we have of understanding what a person says, is understanding what he is trying to say when he says it. If the position I have attributed to Aristotle is one that he was working toward, then we have an important vehicle for understanding just what it was that he was saying when he wrote the ethics.

Still, even if one grants me the stronger conclusion, there is work to be done. As I have already indicated, more needs to be said about the kind of inductive inference involved in the acquisition of universal ends. Without a clearer account of what is involved in it, one won't be able to see why Aristotle thought that certain ends were rational ends. Without the latter, one won't, for example, be able to connect Aristotle's more general discussion of the good life to his more specific discussions of particular virtues. The natural direction in which to look to see what more might be involved in such an inference, is to those occasions on which Aristotle himself makes specific inferences about what specific things aim at by nature. Two places naturally suggest themselves—his biological works and his politics. Of these two, the politics seems more promising, for there one has the avowed intention of examining the structure and constitution of actual states to find out what the make-up of a good state is. If Aristotle actually carries out this intention, then one will have some actual examples of how Aristotle thinks such inferences can be made. Seeing how such inferences are made in these cases would give one a clearer indication of how similar inferences would be made in ethics.

Turning now to Aristotle's position on weakness of the will, the main question that needs to be answered is whether the argument presented in Chapter 11 is indeed stronger than the one presented in Chapter 10. However, even if one grants that it is, more work needs to be done before one will have anything approaching a complete interpretation of Aristotle on weakness of the will. As I suggested at the end of Chapter 11, one needs a more complete explanation of how people become incontinent,[2] as well as a more complete explanation of the waxing and waning of the conflicting desires that incontinent people act on. One would also like to see if similar explanations can be given for cases that are not cases of incontinence in the strict sense.[3] More important, one needs an investigation of the extent to which Aristotle would allow incontinent action to be *intentional*. If all one said about weakness of the will were what I have said, then whether a person acted incontinently or not would boil down to the relative strengths of the desires that were present at the time of action. But this is compatible with a person's *finding* himself acting incontinently, in the way that one can find oneself scratching one's nose from a nervous habit. If this were to turn out to be true, the person would not be acting incontinently intentionally. However, when Aristotle says that the *akratēs* does what he does willingly (1152a15-17), it looks as if he is saying that the *akratēs* does what he does intentionally. How does this fit with what I have said about Aristotle on *akrasia*? Any answer to this question will depend on an investigation of the extent to which Aristotle would say that the *akratēs* acts *hekousion* (voluntarily or intentionally). Although I am fairly confident that what I have said will fit the results of such an investigation, it is not an investigation I have undertaken.[4] A similar investigation will also have to be undertaken to determine whether Aristotle's position on weakness of the will can provide an adequate basis for an acknowledgement of genuine cases of weakness of the will. Genuine cases of weakness of the will do seem to be ones in which the agent does what he does intentionally.

In spite of this incompleteness, I think that the arguments of the second part of this book do provide an important beginning for understanding Aristotle's views on weakness of the will. If one can decide which of the two arguments offered in Part Two is the stronger, one will be well on his way to understanding just what Aristotle's views on weakness of the will were.

Appendixes

Appendix I NE1143a35-b5

A crucial part of the argument of the first part of this book is the thesis that according to Aristotle universal ends are acquired through induction. A major part of the support for this thesis comes from the interpretation I have offered of NE 1143a35-b5. However, one might argue, this passage is too controversial to bear the weight I have put on it. Unless one has a satisfactory way of dealing with at least the major difficulties that arise in interpreting this passage, any argument that rests on it can not be all that strong. In this appendix, I try to show that the major difficulties that surround this passage can be dealt with, and, thus, that the passage can bear the weight I have placed on it.

Although I shall argue for a slightly different translation, Ross's translation is sufficient to bring out the two main difficulties that surround this passage.

And intuitive reason (*nous*) is concerned with ultimates in both directions, for both the first terms and the last are objects of intuitive reason and not of argument, and the intuitive reason which is presupposed by demonstrations (*apodeixeis*) grasps the unchangeable and first terms, while the intuitive reason involved in practical reasoning (*tais praktikais*) grasps the last and variable fact, i.e. the minor premise (*tou eschatou kai endechomenou kai tēs heteras protaseōs*). For these variable facts are the starting points for the apprehension of the end (*archai gar tou hou heneka hautai*), since the universals are reached from particulars (*ek tōn kath' hekesta gar ta katholou*); of these therefore we must have perception, and this perception is intuitive reason (*nous*).

227

The first difficulty arises in trying to understand just what contrast Aristotle is drawing in the passage. One side of it seems fairly clear. It is the work of *nous* in apprehending first principles for theoretical syllogisms.[1] The other side is said to be the work of *nous* as it is involved in what is practical *(tais praktikais)* (1143b2). But what is this? On the face of it it looks as if it is the work of *nous* in an inductive inference to a universal end. *Nous* is said to grasp the starting points for an end (b3-4), and the relationship between these starting points and the end is likened to the way in which universals depend on particulars (b4-5). This certainly suggests that what *nous* grasps are premises for an inductive inference to a universal end. However, at b2-3 Aristotle says that *nous* grasps "the last and variable" *(tou eschatou kai endechomenou)*. Ross takes this to be the particular fact that is the end point in deliberation, that which is expressed by the final minor premise of a practical syllogism. This seems borne out by the next phrase, *'tēs heteras protaseōs'*, which Ross translates as 'the minor premise'. However, if what Aristotle is talking about is *nous'* grasp of premises for an inductive form of reasoning *to* universal ends, why would he say that what *nous* grasps are premises in a deductive form of reasoning *from* universal ends?[2] One might try to minimize this problem by saying that the premises of a practical syllogism can on another occasion serve as premises for an inductive form of practical reasoning. However, if what *nous* grasps are final minor premises of a practical syllogism, Aristotle will not have provided all the materials needed for an inductive inference to a universal end. The final minor premise is of the form 'This is ∅'. Without an additional premise of the form 'This is good' or 'This is to be done', one will never get a universal conclusion of the form 'What is ∅ is good' or 'What is ∅ is to be done'.[3]

Thus, it is not clear just what contrast Aristotle is drawing in this passage. In particular, it is not clear whether Aristotle is referring to an inductive inference to universal ends.

The second major problem arises in trying to understand why in 1143a35-b5 Aristotle would say that *nous* is involved in practical matters. What *nous* is said to grasp in *tais praktikais* are particulars, for what *nous* grasps it grasps through perception (1143b5), and perception is of particulars. However, three chapters earlier (1142a24-31) Aristotle contrasted *nous* with *phronēsis* on the grounds that the latter deals with particulars that are grasped through perception, whereas *nous* grasps what is universal and first in scientific knowledge. Why should Aristotle apparently reverse his position now and admit that *nous* is involved in the perception of particulars of the sort that *phronēsis* is involved with?[4]

These problems and others have led commentators to suggest a wide variety of accounts of what is going on in 1143a35-b5, including a contrast between two kinds of practical reasoning, a contrast between two applications of theoretical reasoning, and the denial that there is any reference to an inductive inference to ends in 1143a35-b5.[5] The last-mentioned presents the greatest challenge to my interpretation, so I shall concentrate on that.

What can be said on behalf of such an interpretation?[6] When Aristotle says that *nous'* grasp of the starting points *(archai)* for an end are like the way in which universals depend on particulars *(ek tōn kath' hekasta gar katholou)*, he doesn't mention any specific dependency relation. Rather than taking it to refer to the way the apprehension of universals depend on apprehending particulars, one can take it to refer to the way securing universal ends depends on pursuing particular means. For example, obtaining a covering is achieved only by getting a particular kind of covering, a cloak, and this is achieved by adopting particular means, for instance, making it from these pieces of material. Particular means are starting points *(archai)* for obtaining what one is aiming at, a universal end. Read in this way, the passage presents no problem in reconciling what Aristotle says *nous* grasps at 1143b2-3 with the way in which universals depend on particulars. What *nous* grasps, particular means, are just what universal ends depend on. Read in this way, 1143a35-b5 does not make any surprisingly new claim about how one arrives at universal practical principles through an inductive use of reason. It isn't even talking about the way in which universal ends are grasped. It only makes the familiar claim that perception is required to recognize that means are at hand for achieving one's ends. Why isn't this the way that 1143a35-b5 should be interpreted?[7]

The general response I shall give is as follows. There are presumptive grounds for taking 1143a35-b5 to refer to an inductive inference to ends. Thus, if an interpretation can be found that preserves this reference and solves the problems raised above, it will be preferable to this alternative interpretation. There is such an interpretation. It is confirmed by what Aristotle says immediately after 1143a35-b5, by what he says when he contrasts *nous* with *phronēsis* at 1142a24-31, by what he says in NE Bk. I when he says that ethics lacks precision and is concerned with what is true for the most part, and by the way it solves a minor puzzle that surrounds 1143a35-b5. By contrast, the alternative interpretation not only has to deal with the presumptive grounds for thinking that there is a reference to induction in 1143a35-b5, but it has no clear way of solving the second difficulty raised above. On balance, it seems preferable to take 1143a35-b5 in the way I have suggested.

Two considerations, when taken together, provide presumptive

grounds for thinking that 1143a35-b5 refers to an inductive inference to ends. The first has already been mentioned. In discussing
induction elsewhere (for instance, *Posterior Analytics*, 81a40-b9, NE
1139b27-30), Aristotle says that perception provides the starting
points for induction, and that induction proceeds from particulars to
universals. These marks of induction are all present in 1143a35-b5.
What *nous* grasps it grasps through perception (b5). What it grasps
are starting points for an end *(archai gar tou hou heneka hautai)*
(b3-4). And the relation between what it grasps and these ends is
like that between particulars and universals *(ek tōn kath' hekasta gar
ta katholou)* (b4-5). Of course, given the alternative interpretation
set out above, this cannot be decisive, but it does suggest that Aristotle is talking about an inductive inference to universal ends. In the
second place, immediately after 1143a35-b5, Aristotle says,

> This is why these states are thought to be natural endowments — why, while
> no one is thought to be a philosopher by nature, people are thought to
> have by nature judgment, understanding, and intuitive reason. This is
> shown by the fact that we think our powers correspond to our time of
> life, and that a particular age brings with it intuitive reason and judgment;
> . . . Therefore, we ought to attend to the undemonstrated sayings and
> opinions of experienced and older people or of people of practical wisdom
> not less than to demonstrations; for because experience has given them an
> eye they see aright. (1143b5-14)

Although Aristotle says that judgment, understanding, and *nous* are
thought to come by nature, he is saying that *nous'* grasp of things
comes through experience.[8] He is also saying that experience has
provided those whose undemonstrated sayings we should pay attention to, an implicit grasp of general principles. Experience has provided them with the capacity to pick out the right thing to do in
specific circumstances, and this capacity is an implicit grasp of a
general principle.[9] Since what comes from experience comes on the
basis of induction, these people have an inductively based (implicit)
grasp of general principles.[10] It is difficult to see how Aristotle could
go on to talk about such a grasp of general principles, if he had not
just been talking about an inductive grasp of universal ends. If one
puts this together with the marks of induction already noted in
1143a35-b5, one gets presumptive grounds for taking the passage to
refer to an inductive grasp of universal ends.

If an interpretation can be found that preserves this reference and
solves the problems that surround the passage, then it looks as if it
would be preferable to the alternative interpretation set out above.
But where is one to find such an interpretation and how are the
problems to be solved?

The key to finding such an interpretation is 'tou eschatou kai endechomenou kai tēs heteras protaseōs' at 1143b2-3. Although Ross takes 'tou eschatou kai endechomenou' ("the last [or ultimate] and variable") to refer to the last and variable fact, I think rather it should be taken to refer to an action that is to be done. Aristotle includes things to be done (ta prakta) in the class of variable (endechomenou) things (e.g., 1140a1-2), and he also says that what is to be done is an ultimate (eschaton).

> Prudence is not the same as Scientific knowledge: for as has been said, it apprehends ultimate particular things, since the thing to be done is an ultimate particular thing. (1142a24-26, Rackham's translation, emphasis mine.)[11]

More important, immediately prior to 1143a35-b5 Aristotle says that things to be done are ultimates (1143a34-35). Aristotle also allows a judgment about what is to be done to be a matter of perception, for at 1113a1-2 he says that whether a loaf of bread is baked as it should be is a matter of perception. The same point is suggested by his remarks at 1109b21-24 and 1126b3-5, where he says that how much a person may deviate from the mean before one is blameworthy is a matter of perception. 'Tou eschatou kai endechomenou' then, should be taken to refer to a premise or proposition indicating what is to be done in a specific situation.[12]

Accordingly, 'tēs heteras protaseōs' should not be translated as 'the minor premise'. Rather it should be given its literal meaning of 'the other premise' or 'the other proposition'.[13] What it refers to should be understood in terms of what it is being contrasted with as "other." The most natural point of contrast is with what nous grasps in its theoretical employment, the ultimate proposition in the other direction. So understood, 'tēs heteras protaseōs' refers to the same thing as does 'tou eschatou . . .', a proposition indicating that a particular action is to be done.[14]

Aristotle is not referring at 1143b2-3 to the minor premise of a practical syllogism. He is referring to a proposition indicating that a particular action is to be done, something that if it occurred in a practical syllogism would be more like the conclusion than the minor premise.[15]

How does this allow one to solve the problems surrounding 1143a35-b5? The first thing to note is that it removes the apparent incompatibility between what nous is said to grasp at 1143b2-3 and the reference to an inductive inference to universal ends that I have argued exists at 1143b3-5. If what nous is said to grasp at 1143b2-3 are particular propositions of the form 'This ∅ is to be done' or 'This ∅ is good', then what nous grasps does provide the starting points for an inductive inference to a universal end. One can infer universal principles of the form 'What is Ø is to be done' or 'What is Ø is good', from premises of the form 'This Ø is to be done' or 'This Ø is good'.[16] Furthermore, one can understand why the grasp of these propositions is said to be the work of *nous*, since it is the work of *nous* in its theoretical employment to provide an inductive grasp of universal first principles.[17]

However, more than this must be said if these answers are to be fully satsifactory. Why should one admit that what *nous* grasps are propositions of the form, 'This Ø is to be done' rather than propositions of the form 'This is to be done'? Nothing has been said to support the former over the latter, and, if the latter were so, it looks as if *nous* would *not* provide all the starting points for an inductive inference to a universal practical principle. Furthermore, pointing to the fact that these propositions do provide starting points for a universal practical principle isn't sufficient to explain why they are said to be grasped by *nous*. In its theoretical employment *nous* grasps the *conclusion* of an inductive inference to a universal principle. What are grasped here are *premises* for such an inference. Indeed, if simply apprehending particular truths that can serve as premises for an inductive inference were enough to guarantee the operation of *nous*, then *nous* would be operative whenever perception occurs. But Aristotle does not want to say that *nous* is operative whenever perception occurs. Why should Aristotle say that *nous* is at work in the perception of practical particulars, when he would not say that it is operative on other occasions when particulars are perceived?

The answers to all these questions are closely related to one another. The reason why *nous* is said to grasp particulars in practical matters is that implicit in the grasp of these particulars is the grasp of a general principle. People do not just grasp the bare fact that an action is to be done. They grasp it on the basis of some feature relevant to its being done. Implicit in this grasp is the general principle that actions with this relevant feature are to be done. That is, what a person grasps is 'This Ø is to be done (because it is Ø)'. Implicit in the latter is the general principle, 'What is Ø is to be done'. This kind of implicit grasp of a general principle is not part of every case of perception of a particular.[18]

That Aristotle is saying that a general principle is implicit in what *nous* grasps comes out more clearly in the case of those whose undemonstrated sayings we ought to pay attention to (1143b6-14). As I have already argued, these people do not just grasp that a particular action is to be done in a particular situation. Since their grasp is due to experience, it is a grasp that actions like this in situations like this are to be done. But this is just the implicit grasp of a general principle. Since their grasp that the particular action is to be done is itself based on experience, it is the result of an (implicit) inductive inference. What is grasped is not just that the action is to be done, but that actions like it are to be done.

That a general principle is implicit in the perception of what is to be done is also confirmed by what Aristotle says in Bk. VI Ch. 8 where he contrasts *phronēsis* with *nous*.

> That practical wisdom is not scientific knowledge is evident; for it is, as it has been said, concerned with the ultimate, since the thing to be done is of this nature. It is opposed, then, to intuitive reason; for intuitive reason is of the limiting premises, for which no reason can be given, while practical wisdom is concerned with the ultimate, which is the object not of scientific knowledge but of perception—not the perception of qualities peculiar to one sense but a perception akin to that by which in mathematics we perceive (the) (an) ultimate to be a triangle. (1142a24-29, slight variation of Ross's translation)

The relevant point here is that the perception in question is already "*nous*-like," in the way I have just characterized *nous* in its practical employment.

There are two ways of taking the example in this passage. The first takes it to be a case where one perceives a particular mathematical figure to be a triangle. On this way of taking it, the perception in question is like one in which a particular is perceived as an instance of a universal. The other side of the coin of perceiving a particular to be an instance of a universal is perceiving the particular as having a certain universal instantiated in it. The second way is to take it to refer to the perception that a certain triangle is the last mathematical figure into which a given geometrical figure can be divided, and hence the first step in the construction of that figure. This is a perception of a *part* of the figure to be constructed; indeed it is the perception of the first of a series of parts the construction of which will constitute the construction of the figure itself. Taking these parts to be analogous to constitutive means, the example suggests that implicit in the perception of what is to be done is the grasp of a universal end of which it is a constitutive means. Taken in either way, the example supports the view that in the perception of particular actions that are to be done, there is an implicit grasp of a general principle.[19]

That this is not a feature of every kind of perception can be seen from Aristotle's remarks in Bk. I that ethics lacks precision and is concerned with what is true for the most part (for example, 1094b12-22). John McDowell (1979) has provided an illuminating account of what Aristotle has in mind when he makes these remarks.[20] According to McDowell, what lies behind these remarks is a belief in an essential indeterminateness in the ends involved in moral behavior. For example, one may be able to give a rough, general characterization of what it is to be just, according to which actions in certain unproblematic cases can be seen to be just or unjust. But for every such specification there will be other cases in which the justice of the actions cannot be seen from the specification. The best one can do for these cases is to say that just actions are ones that are *like* those in the unproblematic cases. Exactly how they are alike, though, one cannot say. Whether an action is like such actions is something that has to be discovered by *perception,* but a perception based on *experience.*

McDowell likens the task of providing such content to moral ends to what Wittgenstein discusses when he discusses how to specify the correct way of continuing a given series of numbers. If one says, for instance, that the series is one which continues by increments of two because that's the way it has gone so far, there seems to be in principle no way of ruling out the possibility that instead it will change to increments of four when one reaches 1,000. The best general characterization one can give is to say that the rest of the series will be *like* what has gone on before. To understand exactly what this is one must learn from experience what our practice of counting such a series is. Similarly, one must learn from experience what our moral practice is.[21] This includes learning the content of moral ends by learning from experience what actions actions must be like to constitute that end.

This understanding of why it is that ethics lacks precision confirms what I have just been arguing about the grasp of a general principle being implicit in the perception of a particular action. More important, it provides a way of seeing why the same sort of thing isn't involved in every case of perception. Aristotle contrasts ethics with the theoretical sciences on the grounds that the latter do exhibit precision and are concerned with what is universally and necessarily true. For example, in NE Bk. VI he says,

> What has been said is confirmed by the fact that while young men become geometricians and mathematicians and wise in matters like these, it is thought that a young man of practical wisdom cannot be found. The cause is that such wisdom is concerned not only with universals but with particulars, which become familiar from experience, but a young man has no experience, for it is length of time that gives experience; indeed one might ask this question too, why a boy may become a mathematician, but not a philosopher or a physicist. Is it because the objects of mathematics exist by abstraction, while the first principles of these other subjects come from experience, and because young men have no conviction about the latter but merely use the proper language, while the essence of mathematical objects is plain enough to them? (1142a12-20)

In mathematics the basic concepts and principles can be given a precise content after contact with only a few instances that fall under them. In the perception of subsequent instances, thus, there will be no need for, and normally there will be no, implicit principle grasped in their perception. Universal principles can be given content independently of experience of a wide variety of particulars, and they can be applied to cases through the perception of particulars, which itself requires no such wide experience. Just the reverse is true in a subject like ethics. Content cannot be given to basic principles without a wide experience of particulars, and one cannot perceive particulars as falling under these principles without a wide variety of experience. It is only in the latter sorts of cases that the perception of particulars will involve an implicit grasp of general principles. As a result, it will only be in the latter sort of cases that one will have reason to say that *nous* is involved in the perception of particulars.

Thus, there is an interpretation of 1143a35-b5 that solves the major problems surrounding the passage and retains a reference to an inductive inference to universal ends. The contrast Aristotle draws in the passage is between *nous* in its theoretical employment and *nous* in its practical employment. In its theoretical employment *nous* grasps universal first principles. In its practical employment it grasps ultimate propositions in the other direction. These are not the minor premises of practical syllogisms; they are propositions indicating that particular actions are to be done.[22] These propositions provide all the starting points needed for the apprehension of a universal end. Not only can universal principles be inductively inferred from them, there is a sense in which a grasp of general principles is implicit in their grasp. Unlike theoretical first principles, universal practical principles can only be given content through experience of a wide variety of particulars. This experience allows one to see what an action must be like to constitute that end. That is why the perception of these particulars is said to be the work of *nous.* Unlike theoretical first principles, universal practical principles can only be grasped through the grasp of particular actions.

If one adds this interpretation to the presumptive grounds for thinking that there is a reference to induction in the passage, one has strong grounds for thinking that Aristotle is saying in 1143a35-b5 that universal ends are acquired through induction.

By contrast, the alternative interpretation set out above does not fare so well. In the first place, it must deal with the presumptive grounds for thinking that there is a reference to an inductive inference to universal ends in the passage. For example, how is it to explain Aristotle's going on to talk about those who have acquired an implicit grasp of general principles on the basis of experience? In the second place, it is not clear that it has a satsifactory solution to both of the major problems surrounding the passage. Although it has no difficulty in explaining how what *nous* is said to grasp at 1143a2-3 can provide starting points for a universal end, in what way is it to explain the fact that these propositions are said to be grasped by *nous*?[23] What marks off the perception involved in the grasp of these premises from other cases of perception where Aristotle would not want to say that *nous* was involved? On balance, it seems preferable to accept the interpretation I have argued for.

There is one final consideration which, I think, provides some additional confirmation for this result. That is the way the interpretation I have argued for solves a minor puzzle raised by Greenwood ([1909], pp. 163-64). Greenwood points out that with one exception, all of the practical faculties or virtues Aristotle has discussed up to this point in Bk. VI (*gnōmē, sunesis, phronēsis,* and *nous*) are explicitly mentioned in Ch. 11. The exception is *euboulia* (excellence in deliberation). This omission is remarkable, because all of the faculties mentioned are said to deal with ultimates (1143a28-29), and *euboulia* deals with ultimates as much as any of the others.[24] Although the omission may be due to carelessness, it has a simple explanation on the interpretation I have argued for. If in 1143a35-b5 Aristotle is talking about the way one grasps universal ends, he will quite naturally restrict himself to those faculties whose exercise involves the apprehension of universal ends. Although *euboulia* presupposes that one has the right ends, its exercise is concerned with the discovery of means. Thus, it would be quite natural for Aristotle to exclude it from consideration.

All in all, then, it does seem possible to defend the claim that in 1143a35-b5 Aristotle is saying that universal ends are acquired through induction. The passage does seem capable of bearing the weight I have put on it in my argument in Part One of this book.

Appendix II *De Anima* 434a12-15

That 434a12-15 is beset by a host of problems can be seen by looking at four different translations of the passage along with a summary
of it by Bywater.

> Sometimes it overpowers wish and sets it in movement; at times wish acts
> thus upon appetite, like one sphere imparting its movement to another, or
> appetite acts thus upon appetite, i.e. in the condition of moral weakness
> (though by *nature* the higher faculty is *always* more authoritative and gives
> rise to movement). Thus three modes of movement are possible. (J. A.
> Smith, in the Oxford translation)

> In fact it sometimes conquers and moves the will. But when one appetence
> controls another, as one celestial sphere controls another, is the occasion
> when incontinence occurs. But in nature the upper sphere always asserts
> the larger measure of control, so that there are three movements combined
> in one. (W. S. Hett, in the Loeb translation)

> At one time this desire conquers and drives out that, at another that con-
> quers and drives out this—like one ball hitting another—when incontinent
> action occurs; but by nature the higher desire is always more authoritative
> and determines action; so that three motions are already involved. (Ross
> [1961])

> But sometimes it overpowers rational wish and moves to action; at other
> times the latter, rational wish, overpowers the former, appetency. Thus,
> one appetency prevails over another appetency, like one sphere over
> another sphere, in the case where incontinence has supervened. But by
> nature the upper sphere always has the predominance and is a moving
> cause, so that action is actually the resultant of three orbits. (Hicks
> [1965])

But in the abnormal condition called incontinence (*hotan akrasia genētai*, 1. 14) the soul is in a state of anarchy, first one desire getting the upper hand then another, at one moment desire A overpowers desire B, at another desire B overpowers desire A (*hote d' ekeinē tautēn*, 1. 13)—the will being moved by whichever happens to have the mastery at the time (*nika kai kinei tēn boulēsin*), so that it is simply tossed to and fro like a shuttle-cock or ball (*hōsper sphaira*, 1. 13) instead of being moved. (Bywater (1888), p. 66)

Although it may not be possible to solve all of the problems that surround this passage, I think enough can be said to show that in it Aristotle does admit the existence of a genuine conflict of motives in *akrasia*.

A. Difficulties in Translation and Interpretation

In Greek the passage runs as follows.

> *nika d' eniote kai kinei tēn boulēsin (hote men hautē ekeinēn), hote d' ekeinē tautēn, hōsper sphaira (sphairan), hē orexis tēn orexin, hotan akrasia genētai. phusei de aei hē anō archikōtera kai kinei. hoste treis phoras ēdē kineisthai.*[1]

It is clear from the passage that Aristotle is talking about one or more situations in which one form of desire is in some sense opposed to another and in some sense emerges "over" it. It is also clear, I think, that Aristotle takes such a situation to occur in *akrasia*. What is not clear is the exact nature of this conflict. Its nature is given by the verbs *'nika'* and *'kinei'*, but at least three different ways of understanding them have been suggested. On the first they express a genuine state of conflict in which one form of desire overpowers the other and moves the agent. On the second, one form of desire overpowers the other in the sense that it drives it out. On the third, one form of desire "influences" the other in the sense of determining its content. On the latter two interpretations no genuine conflict of motives occurs.[2]

Of the difficulties that are relevant to determining which if any of these interpretations is correct, the following are the most important.

1) What are the objects of *'nika'* and *'kinei'*? Although it has been denied, it is clear from the context that the subject of these verbs is *'epithumia'*. Aristotle has just been talking about movement in animals that lack the faculty of deliberation (433b31ff). He says that this is why imagination does not involve opinion. Imagination is involved in the movement of such animals, but they have no opinions that result from calculation (434a10-11). Hence, appetite (*orexis*) contains no deliberative element (434a11-12). It is this nondeliberative form of *orexis*, *epithumia*, that is the subject of the sentence immediately preceding 434a12-15, and it continues as the subject of

the first sentence of this passage. But if *'epithumia'* is the subject of *'nika'* and *'kinei'*, what are their objects? Although many commentators take them both to have the same object, *'boulēsin'*, Hicks takes *'boulēsin'* to be the object of only *'nika'*, reading in *'zōon'* as the object of *'kinei'*. Bywater, on the other hand, takes *'boulēsin'* to be the object of only *'kinei'*, reading in *'epithumian'* as the object of *'nika'*. Taking *'boulēsin'* as the object of both verbs leaves open the possibility that one form of appetite drives out the other (*epithumia* "moves" *(kinei) boulēsis* by driving it from the scene). Hicks's reading fits naturally with an interpretation according to which a genuine conflict of motives is involved, while Bywater's reading fits his picture of *akrasia* according to which one appetite follows another, the person being at the mercy of whatever appetite is present.

2) How is one to translate *'hote d' ekeinē tautēn'* at line 13? Although *'ekeinē . . . tautēn'* is most naturally translated as 'the former . . . the latter', it can be translated as 'the latter . . . the former'. On the first translation Aristotle is repeating himself, and, so far, has mentioned only one situation in which one form of desire emerges out over another. On the second translation, at least two such situations are mentioned, and Aristotle is saying that the same kind of conflict occurs in both of them. This latter is important, for if it turns out to be correct, whatever one's understanding of this conflict is, it must fit all of the situations mentioned.

3) What is the illustration introduced by *'sphaira'*? Alexander and other ancient commentators took it to be drawn from astronomy, where the motion of a planet is determined by the motions of more than one celestial sphere. Each sphere has its own motion and exerts its own influence on the planet, but the outermost exerts the most influence and controls the direction of the planet. This illustrates a situation in which there is a genuine conflict of motives. Simplicius, however, suggested that the illustration should be taken as a game of ball. This in turn can be understood in one of three different ways. First, one ball strikes another, each one having its own motion, but one of them overpowering the other. Second, one ball drives another from the playing field. Third, a ball is moved by whatever player has control of it. The first of these illustrates a genuine conflict of motives, but the second and third do not.

4) How is one to understand *'hē orexis tēn orexin'* at line 14? Does it summarize the one or two situations that Aristotle has mentioned earlier, each one being a situation in which one form of desire *(orexis)* emerges out over another? Or does it introduce an additional situation of conflict? If it is the latter, then it is in this additional situation that *akrasia* occurs, for at line 14 Aristotle says *'hē orexis tēn orexin* when *akrasia* occurs. This is important, for it is this latter

reading that provides the main reason for understanding *'nika kai kinei'* as "influencing" in the sense of "determining the content of."

5) What are the "three movements" referred to by *'treis phoras'* at line 15? According to Hicks, line 15 is a continuation of the astronomical illustration, *'treis phoras'* referring to the three orbits into which the motion of a planet can be analyzed. According to Smith's translation, it refers to the three different actions that occur in the three different situations of conflict specifically mentioned earlier in the passage. Ross and Bywater take it to refer to three actions whose existence are implied by what has been said earlier, but not all of which were mentioned earlier. It will be much easier to take Aristotle to be talking about a genuine conflict of motives on some of these interpretations than it will be on others.

B. Alternative Interpretations

The answers that have been given to these and other questions suggest at least seven different interpretations of 434a12-15, three of which allow for genuine conflicts of motives in *akrasia* and four of which do not. Each one is suggested by one of the five translations or summaries listed at the beginning of this appendix. However, in saying this I am not saying that any of these authors would agree entirely with any one of the interpretations suggested by what they have said. In certain instances they would disagree with at least one of them. Furthermore, the interpretations I list do not exhaust the possible interpretations of 434a12-15. But I do think any other interpretation will contain elements similar to those that I do discuss, so that a discussion of these seven should serve as a basis for a discussion of any other interpretation.

I group the interpretations according to how many situations there are in which one form of desire conflicts with another, emerging over it.

I. Interpretations according to which Aristotle is talking about only one situation in which one form of desire conflicts with another and emerges over it.

A. (Suggested by Hett's translation) *'boulēsin'* is taken as the object of both *'nika'* and *'kinei'*. In *'hote d' ekeinē tautēn'*, *'hote'* is translated as 'when', and *'ekeinē'* and *'tautēn'* are translated as 'the former' and 'the latter', referring respectively to the subject and object of *'nika'* and *'kinei'*. Thus, *'hote d' ekeinē tautēn'* repeats what is said in *'nika d' . . . tēn boulēsin'*. *'hē orexis tēn orexin'* is a summary of the same situation, so that Aristotle is only talking about one situation in which one form of desire emerges over another, and that is the case of *akrasia*. *'nika kai kinei'* is taken to describe a situation in which two desires are in direct conflict with one another, one overpowering the other and moving the agent to act. The illustration introduced by *'sphaira'* is an astronomical one, with *'treis phoras'* occurring in a continuation of this illustration.

B. (Also suggested by Hett's translation) This interpretation differs from IA at three points. *'kinei'* is read as "drives out" in the sense that *boulēsis* is driven from the scene and rendered inoperative. The illustration is a game of ball in which one ball strikes another, driving it from the scene. The *treis phoras* are three forms of action whose existence is implied by what has been said earlier, but not all of which were specifically mentioned—action from *akrasia,* in which *epithumia* drives out *boulēsis,* action from *enkrateia,* in which *boulēsis* overcomes *epithumia,* and action from *sōphrosunē* (temperance), in which *epithumia* is not at odds with *boulēsis* and doesn't need to be overcome. On this interpretation there is no genuine conflict of motives in *akrasia.*

C. (Suggested by Bywater's summary) *'boulēsin'* is taken as the object of *'kinei',* and *'epithumian'* is understood as the object of *'nika'.* The passage refers to only one situation, *akrasia,* which is pictured as a state of anarchy. At one time one appetite *(epithumia)* overpowers (replaces) another appetite *(nika d' eniote)* and moves the will *(kinei tēn boulēsin)*; at a later time a second appetite overpowers (replaces) the first *(hote d' ekeinē tautēn),* and moves the will. *'hē orexis tēn orexin'* repeats the claim that one appetite is followed by another. The illustration is a game in which a ball is tossed about by a number of players. The will is pictured as a ball that is moved by whatever player (appetite) happens to have control of it at the time. The *treis phoras* are actions from the states of *akrasia, enkrateia,* and *sōphrosunē.* On this interpretation *akrasia* does not involve a genuine conflict of motives.

II. Interpretations according to which Aristotle is talking about two situations of "conflict."

A. (Suggested by Ross's translation) *'boulēsin'* is the object of both *'nika'* and *'kinei'.* *'nika . . . kinei tēn boulēsin'* refers to the state of *akrasia* in which *epithumia* and *boulēsis* are in direct conflict and epithumia overpowers *boulēsis,* moving the person to act. *'hote d' ekeinē tautēn'* refers to the state of *enkrateia,* in which *epithumia* and *boulēsis* are again in direct conflict, but this time *boulēsis* overcomes *epithumia.* *'hē orexis tēn orexin'* is a summary of what happens in both cases, one form of desire overpowering another. The illustration is a game of ball in which one ball strikes another determining the direction in which it moves. This illustrates a situation in which two forms of desire are in direct conflict and one overpowers the other. The *treis phoras* are the two actions that each of the conflicting desires moves the agent to do, together with the motion that results from the combination of these two motives.

B. (Also suggested by Ross's translation) This interpretation differs from IIA at three points. *'kinei'* is translated as 'drives out', making Aristotle say that *epithumia* drives *boulēsis* from the scene rendering it inoperative. The illustration is still a game of ball, but the point of it is that one ball drives another from the scene of action. The *treis phoras* are actions from the states of *akrasia, enkrateia,* and *sōphrosunē.* On this interpretation there is no genuine conflict of motives in *akrasia.*

C. (Suggested by Hicks' translation) *'boulēsin'* is taken as the object of *'nika',* but *'zōon'* is understood as the object of *'kinei'.* *'nika d' . . . tēn boulēsin'* refers to the case of *akrasia* and says that sometimes *epithumia* overpowers *boulēsis* and moves the agent. *'hote d' ekeinē tautēn'* refers to the case of *enkrateia* and says that at other times *boulēsis* overpowers *epithumia* and moves the agent. *'hē orexis tēn orexin'* is a summary of both situations, sayint that one form of desire overpowers another and moves the agent. The illustration is drawn from astronomy, illustrating a situation in which there is a genuine conflict of desires. The motions of each sphere associated with a planet each exert their influence on the planet at the same time, but one of them (the outermost) ultimately controls its direction. The *treis phoras* are the three orbits into which (then) current astronomy resolved the motions of the sun and moon.

III. Interpretations according to which Aristotle mentions three situations of "conflict."

A. (Suggested by Smith's translation) *'boulēsin'* is taken as the object of both *'nika'* and *'kinei'.* *'nika d' . . . tēn boulēsin'* refers to a situation in which *epithumia* "overpowers and moves" *boulēsis* in the sense of "influencing" or "determining the content of" *boulēsis.* It is, thus, a case of *akolasia,* in which appetite determines the content of whatever rational principles the agent has. *'hote d' ekeinē tautēn'* refers to the case of *sōphrosunē,* in which a person's appetite are determined by rational desire and do not run contrary to it. *'hē orexis tēn orexin'* refers to a third situation, one in which *epithumia* "overpowers and moves" *epithumia.* This is the state of *akrasia,* in which an agent is at the mercy of whatever appetite is present, each appetite overpowering and then being overpowered by another. The illustration is a game in which one ball strikes another, imparting its motion to the one it strikes. The *treis phoras* are the three actions that result from the three distinct situations mentioned in the passage, *akolasia, sōphrosunē,* and *akrasia.* On this interpretation there is no genuine conflict of motives in *akrasia.*

C. Akrasia as Involving a Conflict of Motives

Of the seven interpretations listed above, only three, IA, IIA, and IIC, allow for a genuine conflict of motives in *akrasia*. I shall argue that of these seven one must accept either IIA or IIC. Since both of these acknowledge a genuine conflict of motives in *akraisa*, 434a12-15 must be interpreted as acknowledging such a conflict. The form of this argument will be as follows. First, one must interpret 434a12-15 as mentioning two and only two situations of conflict. This limits the acceptable interpretations to IIA, IIB, and IIC. Both situations must be interpreted as acknowledging the same kind of conflict. This turns out to be enough to eliminate IIB. This leaves only IIA and IIC, both of which acknowledge a genuine conflict of motives in *akrasia*.

Let us begin with IIIA, the interpretation according to which 434a12-15 mentions three situations of conflict. There are at least three reasons for taking the passage to refer to three distinct situations. The first is the expression '*hē orexis tēn orexin*' itself. '*nika d'* . . . *tēn boulēsin*' refers to a situation in which *epithumia* emerges over *boulēsis*. '*hote d' ekeinē tautēn*' refers to a situation in which *boulēsis* emerges over *epithumia*. '*hē orexis tēn orexin*' might then be thought to bring in a third such situation. Since this is the case of *akrasia*, and since it is distinct from the previous two cases, *akrasia* must be a case in which one form of desire emerges over itself. That is, it is a state of anarchy in which the agent is moved by whatever desire happens to be present. The second reason is the mention of three motions *(treis phoras)* as line 15. These motions might naturally be taken as the motions of three actions mentioned earlier. Finally, there is the interpretation of '*nika kai kinei*' as "influencing" in the sense of "determining the content of." Since when *epithumia* determines the content of *boulēsis* one has a case of *akolasia*, and when *boulēsis* determines the content of *epithumia* one has a case of *sōphrosunē*, and since '*hē orexis tēn orexin*' refers to a case of *akrasia*, it must refer to a third situation of conflict, one in which *epithumia* emerges out over *epithumia*.

None of these reasons, slightly or jointly, is sufficient to show that '*hē orexis tēn orexin*' does introduce a third situation of conflict. In the first place, '*orexis*' is a general term that applies equally to the three more specific forms of desire—*epithumia, thumos,* and *boulēsis*. Without a special reason for taking it to refer to one of these three more specific forms of desire, it looks as if one should take it in this general sense.[3] So taking it, however, it is natural to take '*hē orexis tēn orexin*' as a summary of what has been said of the previous situations mentioned. One form of desire emerges out over another. More important, taking '*hē orexis tēn orexin*' to supply such a summary is necessary for the illustration introduced by '*sphaira*' to apply to all of the situations mentioned in the passage. What Aristotle says is that just as one sphere emerges out over another, so *hē orexis tēn orexin*. He couldn't say this and intend the illustration to cover the situations mentioned earlier unless '*hē orexis tēn orexin*' were a summary of those situations. '*hē orexis tēn orexin*', thus, seems better taken as a summary of what occurs in the situations mentioned earlier, rather than as introducing a new situation of conflict.

The occurrence of '*treis phoras*' at line 15 doesn't fare much better. Taken by itself it may suggest that there are three situations that Aristotle is talking about. But given the above reasons for thinking that '*hē orexis tēn orexin*' doesn't introduce a third situation, and given the possibility of understanding what these three motions are without there having to be three situations of conflict mentioned in the passage (see interpretations IA-IIC), the occurrence of this expression doesn't seem sufficient to show that three situations of conflict have been mentioned in the passage.

Finally, the main reason for reading '*nika kai kinei*' as "influences" in the sense of "determining the content" is that this reading fits best with Aristotle's mentioning three situations of conflict in the passage. Taken just by itself '*nika kai kinei*' would be more naturally understood as "overpowers and moves," whether in the sense in which one of two genuinely conflicting motives overpowers the other and moves the agent, or in the sense in which one of them overpowers the other, driving it from the scene. So understood, the two situations mentioned at the beginning of the passage would be most naturally taken to be *akrasia* and *enkrateia*. But if '*hē orexis tēn orexin*' introduces a third situation and this third situation is *akrasia*, then the first two situations cannot be *akrasia* and *enkrateia*. '*nika kai kinei*' must then be understood in such a way that it allows them to be something other than *akrasia* and *enkrateia*. Taking it as "influences" in the sense of "determining the content of" allows just this. So understood, the two situations turn out to be *akolasia* and *sōphrosunē*. But if this is the reason for adopting this interpretation of '*nika kai kinei*', then it cannot be used to support the existence of three situations of conflict in 434a12-15. There must already be evidence for three distinct situations for this interpretation to be plausible in the first place. And the two considerations already discussed don't seem strong enough to supply such reasons.

More important, even if this weren't so, there are grounds for thinking that it cannot both be the case that '*nika kai kinei*' means "influence" in the sense of "determine the content of," *and* that '*hē orexis tēn orexin*' refers to a third situation of conflict. '*nika*' and '*kinei*' describe not only a situation in which *epithumia* emerges out over *boulēsis;* they must also be understood as the verbs in '*hote d' ekeinē tautēn'*, *'hōsper sphaira'*, and in *'hē orexis tēn orexin'*. Without some special reason to the contrary, they should be understood in the same way in each one of these expressions. But this cannot be done if *'hē orexis tēn orexin'* is taken to refer to a third situation in which *epithumia nika kai kinei epithumian*. Whatever *'nika kai kinei'* could mean in this latter case, it could not mean "influences" in the sense of "determines the content of."

None of the above reasons, then, taken singly or collectively, provide sufficient grounds for taking 434a12-15 to mention three situations of conflict. Interpretations IIIA can be rejected.

Let us now turn to interpretations according to which 434a12-15 mentions only one situation of conflict, interpretations IA, IB, and IC. Let us begin with IC. There are a number of reasons why this interpretation cannot be correct. In the first place it translates *boulēsis'* as 'will' and treats it as though it were not a form of desire along with *epithumia* and *thumos*. Secondly, it takes *epithumia* to be both the subject and object of *'nika'* and this seems doubtful. Aristotle says that conflicts of desire are possible only when a rational desire is present (433b5-6). Given that *'nika'* presupposes some sort of conflict, one would expect *'epithumia nika boulēsin'* or *'boulēsis nika epithumian'*, but not *'epithumia nika epithumian'*. Finally, IC requires the illustration to be a game of ball in which a ball is tossed about by different players. But as Hicks points out, one should then have *'sphairan'* at line 13 rather than *'sphaira'* ([1965], p. 569).[4] Given *'sphaira'*, if Aristotle is talking about a game of ball, it is one in which a ball overpowers or moves something, not one in which something else overpowers or moves a ball. There appear to be too many problems with IC for it to be a correct interpretation of 434a12-15.

What then about IA and IB? Both of these take 434a12-15 to refer to only one situation of conflict, because they both translate *'ekeinē . . . tautēn'* as 'the former . . . the latter'. This makes *'hote d' ekeinē tautēn'* repeat what is said by *'nika d' . . . tēn boulēsin'*. But not only does this rob *'d''* at line 13 of its customary use of drawing a contrast, it makes what Aristotle says in the passage *doubly* redundant. *'hē orexis tēn orexin'* also goes on to say the same thing.[5] Not unsurprisingly, Hett, whose translation suggests both IA and IB, leaves *'hote d' ekeinē tautēn'* untranslated. But *'ekeinē . . . tautēn'* can also be translated as 'the latter . . . the former'. Given that it is unlikely that Aristotle would have used these terms if they made what he said doubly redundant, it looks as if they should be so translated. So translated *'hote d' ekeinē tautēn'* introduce a second situation.[6] Once this is accepted, interpretations IA and IB can be dismissed.[7]

What we are left with, then, are interpretations according to which

434a12-15 mentions two and only two situations of conflict, the situations of *akrasia* and *enkrateia*. That is, we are left with interpretations IIA, IIB, and IIC. However, I think we are also in a position to see that 434a12-15 does acknowledge a genuine conflict of motives in *akrasia*, for I think we are in a position to eliminate intepretation IIB. Since both of the remaining interpretations acknowledge a genuine conflict of motives in *akrasia*, we can see that 434a12-15 does countenance such a conflict without having to decide between them. In this way we can avoid such difficult issues as whether 'z̄oon' can be read in as the object of 'kinei', or whether the illustration introduced by 'sphaira' is an astronomical one or a game of ball.[8]

The key point here is one made in the discussion of interpretation IIIA. However the verbs 'nika' and 'kinei' are to be understood, they must be understood in the same way in all of the situations that Aristotle is talking about. If 'nika' and 'kinei' are understood in such a way that there is no genuine conflict of motives in *akrasia* (*epithumia* overpowering *boulēsis*, driving it from the scene), then they must be understood in the same way when they describe a case of *enkrateia*. *Boulēsis* would also have to drive *epithumia* from the scene. But that Aristotle should say this about *enkrateia* is highly implausible. If there is one thing that is clear, it is that Aristotle acknowledges a genuine conflict of motives in *enkrateia*.[9] Indeed, if there were no genuine conflicts of motives in *enkrateia*, it is not clear what would distinguish *enkrateia* from virtue. We have already seen that a virtuous man can have the kinds of appetites that can come in conflict with rational desire. It is just that when he recognizes what he ought to do, these appetites are "silenced." But this seems exactly what would happen if these appetites were driven from the scene. Thus, it looks as if in the case of *enkrateia* one will have to take 'nika' and 'kinei' to describe a genuine conflict of motives. Since they say the same thing about *akrasia* as they do about *enkrateia*, they must also describe a genuine conflict of motives in *akrasia*.[10]

Thus, even if one can't decipher all the details of 434a12-15, one can at least say that it acknowledges the existence of a genuine conflict of motives in *akrasia*.

Notes

Notes

Introduction

1. For a useful discussion of *internalism* and its denial, *externalism,* see Frankena (1958). (All references in this work will be made via the author's last name and date of publication. When possible, they will be incorporated into the text. For a full citation of the works referred to, see the Bibliography.)

2. In saying that judgments of obligation are objective, I mean that if any two people were to disagree over a specific answer to the question of what a person's obligation was in a particular situation, then one of them must be mistaken. For one illustration of how the "practical" side of morality threatens its objectivity, see Hare (1963).

3. Allan also gives a brief history of this controversy, from which I have borrowed in this introduction.

4. See also Hudson (1981), Irwin (1975) and (1978), McDowell (1979), Sorabji (1973-74), and Wiggins (1975-76).

5. See, e.g., Davidson (1970) and the essays in Mortimore (1971).

6. For a recent argument against this assumption see Kenny (1978). (See also Kenny [1979].)

7. For an argument for this assumption see Hardie (1980), Ch. V.

Chapter 1. A Statement of the Problem

1. See, for example, Hume (1964), p. 416 and p. 459.

2. But it is also difficult to distinguish exactly between conditions under which a desire for certain means provides a basis for the existence of practical reason from conditions that do not. See below, esp. n. 6.

3. It is important for Hume to deny that such a desire persists, for if it could, it would be a prime candidate for an irrational desire; and its irrationality could not be explained away as merely the irrationality of a false judgment accompanying it. When the falsity of the original judgment is discovered, there is no longer a false judgment accompanying it. It looks as if Hume would have to explain the irrationality of such a persistent desire either by

reason's contribution to its existence and hence its persistence, or to reason's failure to extinguish the desire. And if Hume admitted the latter, I think he would also admit that reason could (help) produce a desire.

4. Kant (1964) also seems to have thought that this was the appropriate condition for the existence of practical reason. See esp. Ch. 3.

5. This is the (alleged) Kantian doctrine that 'Whoever wills the end wills the means' is an analytic truth.

6. It may be difficult to decide in a case like this what the difference is between reason's being an initial condition and its being a causal condition of the desire for the means, but I think the most that this means is that it is difficult to distinguish between cases where the desire for means provides a basis for the existence of practical reason and cases where it does not. This is not as important as one might first think, for it turns out that what is important for the attempt to base ethics on practical reason is not whether practical reason is operative in a desire for means, but whether it is operative in a desire for ends.

7. It is not my purpose here to argue for one of these four possibilities; it is only to clarify the conditions under which practical reason might be said to exist, and to illustrate the use of (ii) as a statement of these conditions. However, for arguments for the fourth possibility and against a Humean position, see Nagel (1970), Ch. VI.

8. For a classical statement of the view that reasons are not causes, see A. I. Melden (1961). For a classical defense of the view that reasons are causes, see Donald Davidson (1963).

9. Two ends are incompatible if there are no occasions on which one can satisfy both of them.

10. The condition that the exercise of reason only lead to certain ends and not to incompatible ends *may* be too strong. If genuine moral dilemmas exist, then in some situations one ought both to do some action and to do some alternative to it. However, even if there are such dilemmas, there will have to be some restriction on the ends that one could acquire through the correct exercise of reason. Since it is not at all clear that there are such dilemmas, this is a complication that I shall ignore.

11. Two ends conflict with one another on a given occasion if on that occasion it is impossible to satisfy both of them.

12. I do not mean by this to rule out the possibility that situations exist in which more than one action is permissible no one of which one ought to do. What I mean is that if any two people disagree over a specific answer to the question of what one ought to do in a particular situation (whether the answer is that only one action ought to be done or that more than one action is permissible), one of the two people must be mistaken.

13. Such cases of conflict would not threaten the objectivity of morality if there were genuine moral dilemmas and every case of conflict turned out to be a moral dilemma. However, as I have said, it is none too clear that genuine moral dilemmas exist.

14. On one interpretation, the doctrine of the "unity of virtue" implies just such a harmony among the ends that make up moral virtue.

15. If one wants a term of Aristotle's that closely corresponds to my use of 'practical reason', I think it would be *'dianoia'* as it is used in practical matters.

Chapter 2. Aristotle and Hume: A Preliminary Contrast

1. See Nussbaum (1978), Essay V, for a helpful discussion of imagination (*phantasia*) in Aristotle as that which allows one to see something *as* something.

2. As far as *De Anima* is concerned it looks as if one could take this form of desire to be *boulēsis* (rational desire). But, as we shall see at the beginning of Chapter 3, Aristotle requires more for action from *boulēsis* than what is described here. If one wants a name for what is described here one can call it deliberative appetite.

3. That the object of such a desire is in the future allows Aristotle to account for conflicting desires, for a desire brought about by the perception of a present object may conflict with one brought about by the thought of some future object (433b5-8).

4. That action from a desire resting on calculative imagination also involves deliberation is not surprising, since, according to Aristotle, calculation and deliberation turn out to be essentially the same (NE 1139a13).

5. Given that at NE 1113a11-12 Aristotle defines choice *(prohairesis)* as deliberate desire of things in our own power, it looks as if action on the basis of a desire resting on calculative imagination will also be action on the basis of choice. However, as with the case of *boulēsis,* Aristotle requires more for action from *prohairesis* than a deliberate desire for means perceived to be at hand. (Again, see the beginning of Chapter 3).

6. For a list of Aristotle's examples of practical syllogisms, see Gerasimos Santas (1969), pp. 163-65.

7. *pace* D. J. Allan (1955), who takes the distinction between the good and the possible to be a distinction between two kinds of minor premises, one setting out actions as constituents of the end mentioned in the major premise, the other setting out actions as *means* to the end. Also, Aristotle says at NE 1146b35-1147a3 that two kinds of premise exist, one universal and the other particular, but his examples don't always include a universal major premise. These remarks, I think, are best taken as referring to the kind of syllogism involved in weakness of the will *(akrasia).*

8. On one occasion, though (*De Motu* 701a20), Aristotle seems to refer to the conclusion as a proposition or judgment. Whether the conclusion is an action or not will be of considerable importance for the discussion of Aristotle on weakness of the will in Part Two. It will be discussed in detail at that time.

9. One might argue that this is not an example of a practical syllogism because it contains no element of deliberation, and it is deliberation that provides the "syllogistic" part of the practical syllogism. One might even point to NE 1149b2 where Aristotle says that appetite does not obey argument, and argue that this is evidence that there is no syllogism of appetite. (See, for example, Kenny [1966], p. 180). However, the example does seem to be put forward as an example of a practical syllogism, and, as I shall argue later (Chapter 10, Section III, Part C, esp. n. 36), 1149b2 is not evidence that there is no syllogism of appetite. However, even if this is wrong, I think that one will have to admit that the example plays the same role as a practical syllogism, that of explaining an action on the basis of desire (in this case appetite). That the practical syllogism plays this role is all that I want to insist on at this time.

10. That Aristotle did require this is doubtful. See, for example, *De Motu* 701a25ff.

11. Santas (1969), p. 175, offers this as an explanation of Aristotle's ambivalent talk about the conclusion of the practical syllogism.

12. For example, it does not fit the example involving the coat given above. The minor premises in this example are not limited to pointing out that persons or objects of the kind mentioned in the major premise are at hand. Cooper is aware of this, but he thinks that this example is anomalous for other reasons. (See Cooper [1975], p. 25, n. 26.) However, this is not the only example. Aristotle's example involving dry foods at NE1147a5-7 also involves a minor premise that does not involve demonstratives or pronouns ('Such and such food is dry'), and so does the example at *De Motu* 701a17 ('A house is a good'). Furthermore, the major premises in three of the six examples in *De Motu* do contain demonstratives or personal pronouns, contrary to Cooper's claim that typically this is not the case. (The latter two points are noted by Burnyeat ([1978], p. 104).

13. One might argue that this passage is not about a decision as to which among competing ends is to be pursued, but rather a decision as to which among competing means is to be pursued, the expression 'that is pursued' (*'diokēi'*) being ambiguous between ends pursued and actions pursued for the sake of an end. However, it is doubtful that the action or means

that is pursued would be described as 'greater' ('to meizon'). This seems a more appropriate description to attach to pleasures or ends. But even if this passage is about means and not ends, essentially the same points can be made about it as I go on to make.

14. As is indicated by Aristotle's use of the term 'best' ('kallista').

Chapter 3. Reason and General Ends

1. Where this is not so, it will be explicitly noted.

2. Actually, there is a sense in which acting from desire, as it was described in Chapter 2, does involve acting for something universal. When, for example, a person makes a coat because she needs a covering, it is not the case that what she wants is some particular object. Any adequate coat or covering will do. Her object is, in this sense, universal. However, when, for example, a person eats dry food because dry food is good for any person, his object is universal not only because everything else being equal any dry food will do, but also because his principle makes reference to all people and not just to himself. Acting on what I am calling a general principle is acting from such a conception of what is good for human beings.

3. For a more detailed discussion of this question see Anscombe (1965).

4. In Chapter 5, Sections I and III, I provide such an examination.

5. My Humean critic would discount these remarks, arguing that they are unsupported by any particular account of the role that reason plays in the acquisition of ends. But *taking these remarks at face value,* I think they do balance off Aristotle's remarks that practical wisdom insures that one will take the right means.

6. One might wonder whether the antecedent of "the latter" isn't *'prohairesis'*. But reference to "the latter" requires a "former," and *'orexis'* is coupled with *'logos'* at 1. 24, while *'prohairesis'* is not coupled with anything.

7. This was suggested to me by Michael Woods.

8. Reading this more general account of *orexis* in to 1139a21-26 receives added confirmation from what Aristotle goes on to say at 1139a33 ff, where he links up *prohairesis* with moral character. What comes with moral character is a conception of ends worth aiming at in themselves. Aristotle goes on to say that good action *(eupraxia)* is just such an end, and that desire *(orexis)* aims at good action (1139b4-5). That is, the desire that is involved in *prohairesis* is not just a desire for means. It is a desire for means to ends desired as good in themselves.

9. One might think that incontinence is a case in which desire fails to pursue means that reason has discovered. But if it is, it is not a case in which the agent acts from a bad *prohairesis.* The incontinent man acts not from *prohairesis* (1111b14), but contrary to it (1141a6). His *prohairesis* is good, not bad (1152a17). Besides, incontinence will be a case in which desire fails to pursue means discovered by reason only if one includes in the determination of means what is overall best to do. This seems to concede the point at issue, since the determination of what is overall best will include a determination of what ends should be pursued.

It might also be thought that Aristotle allows desire to fail to pursue means that reason has discovered at NE 1110a29-31, where he says,

> It is difficult sometimes to determine what should be chosen at what cost, and what should be endured in return for what gain, and yet more difficult to abide by our decisions.

However, again it is not clear that a person who failed to abide by his decisions in such cases would be acting from *prohairesis* rather than contrary to it. It does seem clear, though, that if desire fails to pursue what reason asserts in such cases, reason will have determined which ends are best to pursue, for the cases are ones in which it has been determined "what should be endured for what gain." Again, it looks as if one can't find a case in which both reason discovers only means and desire's failure to pursue what reason has discovered results in a bad *prohairesis.*

One might suggest that desire's failure to pursue what reason has asserted is *not* being put forward as a condition of a bad *prohairesis;* rather it is a condition of there being any *prohairesis* at all. One won't have a deliberate desire for means if desire isn't for the means that have been discovered. (See, e.g., Kenny [1979], p. 93.) However, for Aristotle to be saying this at this point would surely be odd. It is already clear at line 24 that *prohairesis* is deliberate desire for means, and there is no reason to repeat the point at line 26. It seems preferable to treat line 26 as setting out a condition for a bad *prohairesis* rather than a condition for there being any *prohairesis* at all.

10. One might argue that even here one does not have a condition for a bad *prohairesis.* If *prohairesis* is a desire for means to ends desired as good in themselves, and if reason apprehends such ends, then the desire for any such end will be a desire for what reason has picked out as good. There seems to be no room for desire to fail to pursue what reason has asserted. However, this ignores an important possibility. According to Aristotle what one takes to be good is in part a function of the habits and dispositions one has acquired. One's moral character carries with it a certain conception of what is worth aiming at. If reason is capable of reflecting on the ends that come with one's character and of determining whether they are worth aiming at, then it will be possible for the ends that one pursues on the basis of one's character to fail to be what reason says they should be. Under these circumstances, continued pursuit of these ends would involve action from a bad *prohairesis.*

A large part of what I shall be arguing in the rest of this chapter is that Aristotle did allow reason to play such a reflective role in determining what ends are worth aiming at.

11. See, for example, n. *c,* p. 356 of Rackham's translation of the *Nicomachean Ethics* in the Loeb Classical Library edition.

12. However, this attitude begins to lose its plausibility the more passages one has to count as "just so much talk."

13. See Appendix I.

14. Even if one takes the final minor premise to be something that on another occasion could serve as the basis for an inductive inference to ends, Aristotle still will not have provided all the materials needed for such an inference. The final minor premise is of the form 'This is $\emptyset$'. Without an additional premise of the form 'This is good' or 'This is to be done', one will never get a universal principle of the form 'What is $\emptyset$ is good' or 'What is $\emptyset$ is to be done'.

15. Experience has provided them with a capacity to see in a particular situation that a particular action is to be done. However, since this capacity has been acquired through experience, it is not confined to this one situation. It is a capacity to pick out actions like this one in situations like this one. But this is an implicit grasp of the general principle that in situations like this one, actions like this one are to be done. Even though these people may not be able to articulate what it is for a situation or an action to be like this one, experience has provided them with a grasp of a general principle.

16. In describing the inference in this way I do not mean to say that this induction must have the form of simple enumerative induction. Speaking this way is only a graphic way of talking about one of the problems surrounding the passage that needs to be solved, that *nous* provide all of the starting points for an inductive inference to a universal end. Such an inference still might best be described as an inference to the best explanation, or as an inference in keeping with the Popperian notion of conjecture and refutation.

17. This will, perhaps, come out more clearly in the case of those whose undemonstrated sayings we should pay attention to. As I have already argued, these people do not just grasp that a particular action is to be done in a particular situation. Since their grasp is due to experience, it is a grasp that actions like this in situations like this are to be done. But this is just the implicit grasp of a general principle. Since their grasp that the particular action is

to be done is itself based on experience, it is the result of an (implicit) inductive inference. This shows up in the fact that what is grasped is not just that the action is to be done, but that actions like it are to be done.

18. More than this needs to be said for a fully satisfactory explanation of why *nous* is said to be involved in the grasp of these particulars. For additional considerations see Appendix I.

19. To acknowledge this point does not require Aristotle to give up the constrast he has drawn between *phronēsis* and *nous*. *Nous* will still be concerned with objects of scientific knowledge that *phronēsis* is not concerned with, and *phronēsis* will be concerned with some objects of deliberation that *nous* will not be concerned with in either of its theoretical or practical employment. (For a further discussion of this matter see Chapter 5 Section III.)

20. The theory builds on some suggestions made by Thomas Nagel in a series of lectures on Aristotle's ethics delivered at the University of California, Berkeley in 1965-66. I am not at all sure that he would approve of the use I have made of these suggestions.

21. For a justification of the use of 'self' in 'self-habituation', see the discussion of 1114b16-25 in Chapter 4 Section III.

22. For example, those whose undemonstrated sayings we ought to pay attention to referred to at 1143b6-14.

23. For evidence that Aristotle believed that in most cases a person will be provided with such cues, see NE Bk. IX Ch. 4 where Aristotle says that a good man feels good about himself and his life, while inferior men are "at variance with themselves," and do not feel good about themselves.

24. Aristotle has no explicit discussion of the existence and scope of practical reason, so that textual evidence will always come from passages where this is not the main topic of discussion. Although my Humean critic would point to passages like NE 1112b13 and 1144a6-9 as providing textual evidence for his view, I think that enough has been said in this chapter to show that the interpretation of these passages is not uncontroversial. Besides, he is willing to concede that what he thinks Aristotle should say may not be what Aristotle wants to say in passages like 1143a35ff. Although the theory I have sketched reads something into passages like 1143a35ff, the view that my Humean critic attributes to Aristotle reads something out of them.

25. Recall that the main reason for describing the inductive inference in 1143a35-b5 as a form of simple enumerative induction was to provide a graphic way of illustrating the problem of providing all of the materials needed for an inductive inference to general practical principles. Particular beliefs about what is good or what is to be done provide all the materials needed for a dialectical inference to general practical principles.

26. Recall that in the sense I am using the term 'objective', ethics is objective if for any particular ethical dispute there is a uniquely correct answer.

27. For a further discussion of this schema and the argument surrounding it, see Chapter 7 Sections II and III.

28. And Aristotle does say in Bk. VI Ch. 13 that one cannot have virtue in the strict sense without *phronēsis*. For a discussion of the exact way in which virtue in the strict sense requires the excellence of rational activity, see Chapter 5 Section III.

29. *ara phateon haplōs men kai kat' alētheian boulēton einai tagathon.*

30. See also 1113a25-26, where what Aristotle says (*to menou spoudaiō to kat' alētheian einai*) is translated as, "that which is in truth an object of wish is an object of wish to the good man" (Ross), or as, "the good man wishes for what is truly wished" (Rackham).

31. Especially if, as I have just argued, Aristotle is already committed to saying that the desires of a good person are rational in a way that the desires of a bad person are not.

32. See also NE 1140b4-6 and 1141a4-6.

33. For a more detailed discussion of this kind of means see Chapter 5 Section I.

Chapter 4. The Pervasiveness of Aristotle's Views on Practical Reason

1. To these one might want to add Aristotle's admission of mind as a source of motion at *De Anima* 433a9-10 and 433a18-20, his remark that calculation leads to a desire for the best among alternative ends at *De Anima* 434a6-9, and his claim at NE 1112b16-17 that deliberation provides a desire for the best among alternative ends. These were discussed in Chapter 2.

2. See also 1145a1-2 and 1146a8.

3. Particularly given the passages that my Humean critic takes as restricting practical wisdom to means and virtue to ends, but more will be said in Chapter 5 Section III.

4. Aristotle refuses to allow that an incontinent man who achieves what he is after by correctness of deliberation has exhibited *euboulia,* for he has arrived at something evil (1142b18-21).

5. That the addition of this conception of means is open to me can be seen by a quick glance back at Chapter 3. One way of seeing how the grasp of an end can be implicit in the perception of particular actions, is seeing the grasp of these actions as the grasp of means constitutive of the end implicit in them. However, the addition of this conception of means does not seem equally open to someone who adopts a Humean interpretation of Aristotle. An essential feature of such an interpretation is that reason plays no role in the acquisition of ends. But if a determination of means is sometimes a determination of ends, and if reason plays a role in the desire for means, then reason will also play a role in the acquisition of ends.

6. See also Hardie (1968), p. 276.

7. This is not to say that there may not be evidence elsewhere of Aristotle's adopting indeterminism, for example, *De Interpretatione,* Ch. 9. But the ethics itself does not seem to rest on any indeterministic assumptions. (Aristotle does say that ethics and practical thought are concerned with what can be otherwise, but this is not enough to guarantee indeterminism.) This absence of any such reference may account for what Mrs. Huby ([1967] , p. 357) finds puzzling, that Cicero should classify Aristotle along with Democritus, Heraclitus, and Empedocles as a determinist.

8. Joachim (1951) recognizes this. See pp. 106-7.

9. *kai gar tōn hexeōn sunaitioi pōs autoi esmen.* It has been argued that this remark need not be taken as an affirmation of (1) but can instead be viewed as an affirmation of (2). Using *De Anima* 416a9-18 as a parallel, Hardie argues that *'sunaitioi pōs'* can be taken to refer to a *subordinate cause* rather than a *co-cause* ([1980] , pp. 179-80, [1968] , p. 277). So understood, 1114b23-24 affirms the position that our ends come from nature, for even if nature gives us our ends, still it is through us that it works. We are subordinate causes if not *the* cause of our ends. Although this is a possible reading of *'sunaitioi pōs',* I do not think it is the most natural one. Given Aristotle's reference to "what depends on the man himself *(par auton estin)*" at 1114b17-18, a reading referring to a co-cause seems more natural. Hardie seems to acknowledge this himself, for his main reason for preferring the reading of "subordinate cause" is that otherwise Aristotle is affirming a position which he has not clearly stated, nor has he provided any grounds for it ([1980] , p. 179, [1968] , p. 277). Needless to say, as I understand (1), it is neither unclear nor groundless. Thus I think one should take *'sunaitioi pōs'* as referring to a co-cause and one should take 1114b23-24 as affirming (1).

10. The same point is repeated in Ch. 7 at 1098a25-34.

11. There is more to be said about the relationship between the lack of *akribeia* in ethics and Aristotle's position on practical reason than I say here. What more there is involves Aristotle's conception of the means-end relationship. It will be taken up in Chapter 5 Section I where the nature of Aristotle's conception of means is the main topic of discussion. Here all I want to note is that Aristotle's claim that ethics lacks *akribeia* is one of a series of remarks that taken together suggest that a fundamental part of ethics involves an inductive inquiry.

12. It is, perhaps, worth noting one possible objection to this suggestion. At 1098b3-4 Aristotle lists three ways in which one may arrive at first principles or starting points— induction *(epagōgē)*, perception *(aisthēsis)*, and habituation *(ethismos)*. In his note on this passage Burnet ([1904], p. 39) suggests that each of these three ways is appropriate to different inquiries. That is, they are mutually exclusive ways of arriving at first principles or starting points. He goes on to suggest that induction is the method appropriate to the physical sciences, perception to mathemathics, and habitatuion to ethics. If this is correct, then it looks as if it is a mistake to say that first principles in ethics are arrived at by induction.

However, there is no need to interpret the passage in this way. Nothing in the passage requires that these methods be exclusive of one another, and I think that it is clear that on at least some occasions what one perceives (especially what one takes to be relevant to the case at hand) is determined in part by the kinds of habits and experience that one has had. Grant ([1885], Vol. I, pp. 453-54) recognizes that each of these methods may apply to a number of inquiries, and even Burnet seems to recognize ([1904], p. xxxviii) that habituation is only *part* of the story of how one gets the *archai* of ethics. Perception is also needed. If these methods are not exclusive, then 1098b3-4 provides no objection to taking inductive inquiry to be an important part of ethics.   •

13. It may be that Aristotle would prefer to call this process *dialectic,* as Joachim suggests ([1951], pp. 29ff), but even so it will be inductive in character. This should not be surprising, since induction is one kind of dialectic *(Topics* 105a11).

14. See, for example, Chs. 4 and 5.

15. It should be clear from the preceding that I do not find as much discrepancy between Aristotle's explicit methodology in Bk. I and his actual practice as does J. Donald Monan (1968). (See esp. Ch. V.)

16. For similar remarks on how to proceed in political science see *Politics* 1260b27-35 and *Rhetoric* 1360a30-35.

Chapter 5. The Apparent Support for the Humean Position

1. See Chapter 2 Section II.

2. Chapter 2 Section IV.

3. Parts of the following discussion were, however, anticipated at the end of Chapter 3 Section V and in Chapter 4 Section II.

4. So much so that 'means' might be thought to be a misleading translation of it. It might be better to use a vaguer expression such as 'what is toward an end' (Wiggins) or 'contributor to an end' (Irwin). It doesn't seem out of place to say that in determining "what is toward an end" or "a contributor to an end" one is determining (in part) what the end is.

5. See, for example, Greenwood (1909), pp. 46-48. For more recent discussions of these two kinds of means and their relation to Aristotle and practical reason see Irwin (1975) and (1978), McDowell (1979), and Wiggins (1975-76). McDowell's paper is, I think, especially helpful.

6. See also NE 1094a2-6.

7. On one interpretation the same illustration occurs at 1142a24-29. (See Appendix I.)

8. For a discussion of some of the questions surrounding these issues see Chapter 7 Section I.

9. Of course, it has often been argued that in Bk. X of the *Nicohachean Ethics* Aristotle advocates an "intellectualist" view of *eudaimonia,* according to which a life is *eudaimon* only if it is devoted to contemplation. On such a view morally virtuous actions are at most instrumental means to *eudaimonia,* not parts of it. (See, for example, Cooper [1975], Ch. III, and Kenny [1978], Ch. 8.) However, it is just as common to note that if there is this intellectualism in Bk. X, it raises questions of consistency with other parts of Aristotle's

ethics, whether these be the rest of NE, Bks. II-IX, the "common books," or parts or all of EE. (Again, see Cooper [1975] and Kenny [1978]). For example, on such an intellectualist view it will be impossible for anyone who lives a life of *eudaimonia* to act virtuously in the way described in 1105a26-34 above. All I need for the point I make here is that somewhere Aristotle allows the morally virtuous man to act virtuously *and* for the sake of *eudaimonia*. On these occasions, morally virtuous actions will be means to *eudaimonia* in the sense of being parts of *eudaimonia*.

10. See also NE 1098a25-34.

11. See also NE 1142a24-29.

12. See esp. pp. 336-42. For others who embrace a similar view about the indeterminateness of ethical principles (and attribute it to Aristotle) see Anscombe (1958) and Wiggins (1975-76).

13. McDowell leaves it open whether what we learn is something fixed by human nature or by the society whose practice we learn. I think that Aristotle would say that it is, at least to a large extent, fixed by human nature.

14. If a given whole can exist with more than one set of parts, one can't infer the existence of the particular parts that make it up, but one can infer that there are some parts that make it up. (From the existence of a *eudaimon* life, one can't infer which particular virtuous acts made it up, but one can infer that virtuous acts made it up.) However, on Hume's conception of the means-end relationship, one can't infer even the existence of some means to that end. From the existence of an event, it doesn't follow that something caused it.

15. In Section V of Chapter 3.

16. One might argue that this too can be regarded as the grasp of some content of a yet more indeterminate end, for instance, "the good life." But the same question arises again here. How is it that the person has "the good life" as an end? To the extent to which this embodies the notion of an ordered life and rules out, for example, a life led "only for the moment," it is an end that the person might not have had. How then did the person come to have it? (For a discussion of questions related to this issue see Chapter 7 Section I.)

17. Not only can the kind of inductive inference I have argued for be taken to be an inference to means constitutive of less determinate general ends, taking it in this way allows one to see more clearly why the perception of such means should be said to be the work of *nous*. For an explanation of this see Appendix I.

18. See also NE 1151a20-26 and 1146b23-24.

19. That pleasure and pain lead one to make mistakes about what the good is is also suggested at 1113a35-b2.

It should be noted that there is one other passage in which Aristotle might be taken to say that a vicious person has no first principles.

> The first principles of action are the end to which our acts are means; but a man corrupted by a love of pleasure or fear of pain entirely fails to discern any first principle (*tō de diephtharmenō di' hēdonēn ē lupēn euthus ou phainetai archē*), and cannot see that he ought to choose and do everything as a means to this end, and for its own sake; for vice tends to destroy the sense of principle. (1140b16-20, Rackman's translation)

Again, however, I think that this passage should be taken as saying that pleasure and pain prevent one from having the *correct* first principles, not that they prevent one from having any first principles at all. What Aristotle has been talking about in the context surrounding this passage is the nature of *phronēsis*, something that involes the grasp of correct first principles. He is considering what corrupts *phronēsis*. Something that prevented one from having correct first principles would be as much a corruption of *phronēsis* as something that prevented one from having any first principles. Furthermore the passage can easily be taken as saying that pleasure and pain prevent one from having the correct first principles. As Rackham points out (n. b, p. 338), '*tō de diephtharmenō di' hēdonēn ē lupēn euthus ou phainetai archē'* can be translated as 'to one corrupted by pleasure or pain the end does not seem to be a first principle at all'. Finally, the many passages cited above in which Aristotle implies that the vicious person has first principles provide strong grounds for taking the passage in this way.

For a further discussion of whether a vicious person has first principles, see Walsh (1963), pp. 152-56.

20. Perhaps, it would be better to say that the habituation in virtue is not entirely responsible for the first principles of a good person. Since Aristotle says that one cannot have virtue without practical wisdom, virtue itself may involve or rest on the correct exercise of reasoning about ends. For an argument that virtue does rest on such reasoning see Section III below.

21. Terry Irwin (1978) argues that Aristotle's attempt to draw a parallel between the acquisition of first principles in ethics and the acquisition of theoretical first principles must be and was abandoned by Aristotle, for it does not leave room for what Irwin thinks must be acknowledged, that Aristotle does allow reason to play a role in the acquisition of first principles. Irwin argues that instead one must recognize that Aristotle took deliberation to play a broader role than is normally acknowledged, one not only broad enough to allow deliberation to play a role in the discovery of constitutive means of the sort discussed in Section I of this chapter, but broad enough to include the apprehension of first principles through dialectic. However, if what I have been arguing is correct, Irwin may have given up too soon on the attempt to use the parallel that Aristotle draws to provide a basis for Aristotle's recognition of practical reason. Certainly, an account that exploits a parallel explicitly drawn by Aristotle is, everything else being equal, preferable to one which attributes to deliberation a role never explicitly acknowledged by Aristotle (in particular, engaging in dialectic).

22. Literally "is not acquired" or "does not occur without" *phronēsis (ou ginetai aneu phronēsōs)*.

23. This objection was brought to my attention by Leslie Brown.

24. That Aristotle's view about the connection between natural virtue and the right ends is something like what follows was first suggested to me by David Pears.

25. Indeed, one will be able to distinguish between *phronēsis* and *aretē* simply in virtue of their being virtues of different parts of the soul. *Phronēsis* is a virtue of the intellectual part of the soul; *aretē* a virtue of the emotional part. Even if the emotional part of the soul won't be in its virtuous state unless the emotions are controlled by a correct exercise of reasoning, and even if one's practical intellect won't be in its virtuous state unless it leads to the right kind of control over the emotions, the two virtues will still be virtues of different parts of the soul. This will be sufficient for Aristotle to take them to be distinct.

Chapter 6. A Summary of the Argument

1. The full argument for this interpretation of 1143a35-b5 is given in Appendix I.

2. It might be thought that reason by itself does produce the desire for the end which one inductively infers one is aiming at by nature. But even here it might be argued that such an inductive inference wouldn't produce a desire for what one is aiming at by nature unless one were aiming at something by nature. As a result it is not something I shall insist upon.

Chapter 7. The Interest of Aristotle's Position on Practical Reason: Happiness and the Good Relative to Human Beings

1. In Part Two of this book I shall extend this discussion further by indicating the bearing Aristotle's position on practical reason has for his explanation of weakness of the will.

2. These questions have received a good deal of recent discussion, and I shall not try to

deal with all of the details connected with them. My main aim is to make plausible an answer suggested by the position on practical reason that I have attributed to Aristotle. For a sample of recent discussions of these questions see Ackrill (1974), Cooper (1975), Ch. II; Hardie (1980), Ch. II and Appended Notes; Kenny (1965-66) and (1978); McDowell (1980, and Wedin (1981).

3. Williams (1962) argues that the passage can be taken as setting out a condition under which one would be able to say what the chief good is (the first 'if'-clause). This in turn suggests the second 'if'-clause. Its parenthetical remark serves as a basis for it. (See also Hardie [1980], pp. 16-17).

Irwin (1978) argues that desires that are empty and vain are not impossible desires, but foolish or irrational desires. It is only the desires of a rational person that will be ordered according to a single end. Foolish people can fail to aim at a single end.

Wedin (1981) argues that the passage essentially argues for the uniqueness of a final good. It says that if something is desired for its own sake, everything else being desired for the sake of it, and if it is not the case that for everything desired there is something else for the sake of which it is desired, then there is a unique final good.

Sandra Peterson has called my attention to three other possible interpretations. First, one might take the passage to say

If, then, there is some end of the things we do which we *desire* for its own sake, the other things being desired for the sake of this, and if we do not *choose* everything for the sake of something else, then this would be the chief good.

On this interpretation what is said rests on a distinction between desire and choice, and the same thing is said about choice that is said about desire. However, since not everything a person does he does from choice (for example, an incontinent man does not act from choice), the passage does not say that there is some one thing for the sake of which everyone does what they do. Second, the passage might be taken as saying,

If in every action something is desired for its own sake, that is, if we don't choose to do everything for the sake of something else, then what is aimed at for its own sake will be the chief good.

'Kai' at line 20 is taken as 'that is' rather than 'and'; thus, the second 'if'-clause merely spells out what is said in the first 'if'-clause. Third, one might take the passage to say,

If *either* one and the same thing is aimed at for its own sake in all that we do, *or* if something or other is aimed at for its own sake whenever we act, then in either case the aimed at for its own sake will be the chief good.

On this interpretation 'kai' is taken to have the logical force of 'or' rather than 'and', and what is said parallels the opening remarks of Ch. 7,

If there is an end for all that we do, this will be the good achievable by action, and if there are more than one, these will be the goods achievable by action. (1097a23-24)

On each of these interpretations Aristotle is not making the fallacious inference that is often attributed to him, nor is he asserting that there is some one thing for the sake of which everyone does what they do.

4. Ackrill (1974) argues that it is not as easy to acquit Aristotle of such a fallacy as people like Williams and Hardie have thought.

5. That this is what Aristotle is arguing receives some confirmation from the opening remarks of Ch. 7. These can be taken as a summary of the general argument advanced in the first part of Bk. I. (See the passage cited at the end of n. 3 above.)

6. In Chs. 4 and 5 Aristotle seems to acknowledge more than one final end, listing pleasure, honor, and wealth as examples. These are things that, judging by their lives, people take to be good. That is, some people do things for the sake of pleasure, desiring it for its own sake, others act for the sake of honor, and still others for the sake of wealth.

7. Ackrill (1974) argues for just such a view.

8. In considering whether a person can act without acting for the sake of happiness (where this is taken to be the best arrangement of things desirable for their own sake), it is important to distinguish between the claim that everyone desires happiness for its own sake, and the claim that whatever anyone does is done for the sake of happiness. Even if no one would demur if asked whether he or she wants the best combination of things good in themselves, it still doesn't follow that when one acts, one can always fit what one does within such a conception of happiness.

Of course, what is ultimately at issue is not whether it is always possible for people to fit what they do within such a conception of happiness, but whether Aristotle *thought* it was possible. He may have thought it was possible when in fact it was not. However, if it isn't possible, and if what Aristotle says elsewhere seems to recognize that it isn't possible, then I think it is preferable not to saddle him with such a mistaken idea.

9. Both Hardie ([1980], pp. 17-18) and Kenny ([1965-66], p. 100) note the importance of this passage.

10. There is an objection that can be raised against drawing this conclusion. As Aristotle has traditionally been interpreted, the incontinent man does not recognize that he is acting contrary to his principles at the time that he acts. As a result one might think that he can still take what he does to fit his conception of the good. However, in Part Two of this book I argue that this interpretation is mistaken and that the incontinent man can recognize that he acts contrary to his principles at the time that he acts. Even if this is wrong, Aristotle still acknowledges the existence of impetuous incontinence (1150b19-22), in which people don't stop to think whether what they do falls under their principles. Like those who act impulsively, such a person does not seem always to act for the sake of some single conception of the good.

11. For example, taking happiness to be "the best arrangement of things desirable for their own sake" provides happiness with a minimal content and a mark to be aimed at, the kind of life organized by a single plan advocated in EE 1214b6ff. But then, as I argued above, there will be those who don't have such a plan as a mark in all that they do.

12. These last considerations would not carry much weight with someone who accepts an interpretation like Ackrill's. On such an interpretation Aristotle's task in Bk. I divides into two parts. The first is a conceptual inquiry designed to show just what is involved in the concept of happiness. It is in the course of this that it is supposed to emerge as a conceptual truth that everyone aims at happiness. The second part is to say what kind of life falls under this concept. It is the second part that is to provide a mark to be aimed at. This second part doesn't begin until after Aristotle has acknowledged the conceptual nature of the first part by saying at 1097b22-24 that to say that happiness is the good is a platitude.

However, given what I have argued earlier, not only is it not a conceptual truth that everyone aims at happiness in all that they do, what Aristotle says elsewhere is incompatible wih its being true. Thus, I think it is preferable not to take the two parts of Bk. I as falling into first just a conceptual inquiry about happiness and then an attempt to say what falls under this concept. Rather I think they should be taken to be the first two steps in an attempt to provide a successive refinement of what a good life is, something that will provide a mark to aim at.

13. Of course, more needs to be said before one would have a thorough-going defense of a reading of Bk. I in terms of the position I have attributed to Aristotle. For example, according to that position *eudaimonia* is an inclusive end constituted by morally virtuous activity. However, it has been argued that in Bk. I *eudaimonia* is not an inclusive end; rather it is a dominant end that Aristotle will go on to identify with contemplation. (See, for example, Kenny [1965], esp. p. 101, and [1978], especially pp. 203-5.) In explaining why *eudaimonia* is self-sufficient, Aristotle says that the self-sufficient is the

most desirable of all things, without being counted as one good thing among others—
if it were so counted it would clearly be made more desirable by the addition of even
the least of goods, (1097b16-19)

Kenny argues that this is incompatible with *eudaimonia*'s being an inclusive end. If it were an
inclusive end, there would be no goods additional to it. The addition of even the least of
goods wouldn't make it better, for it would already include them. Kenny also argues that
when Aristotle says that human good is a life in accordance with the best and most complete virtue (1098a17-18), Aristotle is not saying that it is a life in accordance with the most
comprehensive virtue (the sum total of all virtues); rather, it is a life in accord with the virtue that is better than the rest. This turns out to be the virtue of contemplation.

Since my main purpose is only to make plausible a reading of Bk. I in terms of the position I have attributed to Aristotle, I shall not go into these matters in the kind of detail
they deserve. Nevertheless, something can be said to show that Kenny's arguments do not
undermine what I have argued so far. Of course, Kenny's understanding of 1097b16-19 and
1098a17-18 can and has been called into question. (See for example Ackrill [1974], and
Cooper [1981].) But even granting Kenny's understanding of these passages, one can see
that the reading I have suggested is left untouched. Even if one grants Kenny his understanding of self-sufficiency, it doesn't follow that *eudaimonia* isn't an inclusive end. If *eudaimonia*
is *the best combination* of things good in themselves, then *eudaimonia* can still lack some
things that are good in themselves. Thus, there can be goods in addition to *eudaimonia*.
Besides, if *eudaimonia* is an inclusive end, there is no reason why it should include every
trivial good. A life might be made a little bit better by eating one more ice cream sundae,
but its exhibiting *eudaimonia* need not depend on this. In the second place, even if *eudaimonia* is a life in accord with the best virtue, there is as yet no reason why this virtue can't
be *phronēsis*. It is the best of all practical virtues, and it includes all of the moral virtues.
Finally, even if it should turn out that *eudaimonia* is to be identified with contemplation,
this would not require one to completely abandon the reading of Bk. I that I have suggested.
One could still maintain that in people's aiming at what they do in fact aim at, they are
really striving after a life of contemplation.

14. One might object that this criticism misrepresents Aristotle's conception of *eudaimonia*. In taking Aristotle to be talking about what benefits a person I have read too much
of our contemporary notion of happiness into *eudaimonia*. *Eudaimonia* involves "living
well" in the sense of "living nobly" at least as much as it involves "being well off" in the
sense of having benefited oneself. Once one recognizes this, it is not at all implausible to
say that a good person possesses *eudaimonia*, for a good person does live well (nobly). However, "being well off" is as much a part of *eudaimonia* as "living nobly." *Eudaimonia* includes both of these elements, and until Aristotle can show that one who lives nobly in the
sense that he or she is praiseworthy is thereby well off, he will not be entitled to the conclusion that the notion of human good based on the *ergon* of human beings provides one with
a clearer account of *eudaimonia*.

15. It is of course questions like this one raised in connection with the life of a just man
that Plato tried to answer in the *Republic*.

16. Virtue is discussed at 1098b30-1099a6, pleasure at 1099a7-21. Wealth is included in
the discussion of external goods at 1099a31-b8. Honor is not specifically mentioned, but it
is plausible to say that it falls either under virtue (if it is bestowed by the right sort of
people), or under political power, which is discussed under external goods (1099b23).

17. It is perhaps worth noting that given a connection between a person's fulfilling the
ergon of human beings well and something like moral goodness, the attempt to answer this
question is in effect the attempt to answer the question 'Why should I be moral?' in one of
its senses. One has some antecedent reason for believing that a certain kind of life is a moral
one, and one is asking what motives a person has or should have for leading this kind of
life. That an attempt to draw the connection between Aristotle's two discussions of the good

in Bk. I can be understood as an answer 'Why should I be moral?' was first brought to my attention by Thomas Nagel.

18. If there is anything that can be salvaged from the connection between desire and a good X, it appears to be that it is *rational* to want to be a human being, and, thus, it is rational to want to be a good human being. It is at least plausible to say that the desire to cease to be a human being is an *irrational* desire. However, even this requires further argument. The suggestion drawn from above that such a desire is irrational because it is a desire both to be and not to be a human being won't work, for on Aristotle's view the desire not to be a human being only seems to require the desire not to be. I shall go on to give an argument that could be used to show that it is rational to want to be a human being, but since the argument is capable on its own of connecting Aristotle's two discussions of the good, it makes an appeal to the general connection between desire and a good X unnecessary.

19. There is, in fact, textual evidence that Aristotle acknowledged this. Cooper ([1975], pp. 123ff) argues that when Aristotle distinguishes his conception of *eudaimonia* from ones that would identify it with external goods or with gifts of chance (for example, *Politics* 1323b24-29, EE 1215a12-19, NE 1099b18-25), he is saying that something cannot be a part of *eudaimonia* unless it is a result of one's own efforts.

20. In arguing this, I am not claiming that Aristotle actually connected his two notions of human good in this way. Aristotle may have confused the two notions, not recognizing the need to connect them. I am only claiming that Aristotle's position on practical reason allows him to make the connection, and, thus, makes his discussion of the human good in Bk. I that much more interesting.

For a different way of connecting these two notions of human good than I have suggested, see Wilkes (1978).

Chapter 8. Does Aristotle's Position on Practical Reason Provide An Adequate Basis for Ethics ?

1. For example, the answer to the question "Why should I be moral?" suggested by the connection between the two notions of human good drawn in the last chapter.

2. In fact, a real question exists as to how extensive a teleology Aristotle did embrace, and to what extent it has been discredited. For a discussion of these issues, see Essay 1 in Nussbaum (1978). I have not gone into these issues, since I think Aristotle's position can be defended without resting it on a teleological conception of nature.

3. There is even some reason for thinking that the kind of ethical theory that would result from Aristotle's position on practical reason would be more plausible if it were separated from Aristotle's teleological picture of nature than if it were based on it. According to Aristotle the organism that fails to achieve its end is the exception rather than the rule. Thus, to see just what the end of a species is, one has only to look at what conditions the majority of the species realize. Although this may have an advantage in trying to determine just what it is that some organism is aiming at, in ethics it has the disadvantage of having the behavior of the average man set the standards of ethical performance. If Aristotle's position on practical reason were divorced from his teleological picture of nature, there would be less risk of having ethical standards dragged down by the performance of the average person.

4. This problem was brought to my attention by Henry West.

5. In the case of the second criteria one could argue that self-consciousness of what one is aiming at is possible only if an organism is capable of self-consciousness and generalization. Again, these features could be used to mark off the relevant sample, and neither of them implies the existence of practical reason.

6. There isn't sufficient space to consider all of the arguments that have been raised against naturalism as they might be applied to Aristotle's position. But it should be noted

that one of the strongest and most persistent arguments against naturalism is that it fails to account for the "practical" side of moral judgments. (See, for example, Hare [1952].) If I am right in thinking that basing ethics on practical reason does account for the "practical" side of moral judgments, then Aristotle's position has an answer to at least this objection.

7. Aristotle's main discussion of justice occurs in NE Bk. V.

8. For Aristotle's main discussion of friendship, see NE Bks. VIII and IX. For useful recent discussions of Aristotle on friendship see Cooper (1977a) and 1977b), and Kraut (1975).

9. Here and in the rest of this chapter all page references to Kant's *Groundwork of the Metaphysics of Morals* will be to the Royal Prussian Academy edition.

10. This is not the only reason for concentrating on what is involved in a contradiction of the will. By itself, Kant's conceivability test does not seem sufficient to pick out maxims that ought not to be acted on.

The conceivability test is susceptible of at least two interpretations. According to the first, a maxim fails the test if its universalization leads to a contradiction. Applying this interpretation to the case of false promising (422), what emerges is the following. If acting on a maxim is made possible by the existence of an institution and if universalization of this maxim would lead to the nonexistence of the institution, then acting on this maxim would be wrong. (It is wrong to make a false promise to further one's interest, because if everyone were to do so, the institution of promising would cease to exist and everyone couldn't make a false promise when it was in their interest to do so.) But then all one needs for counter-examples to the categorical imperative are maxims involving immoral institutions whose universalizations would lead to the nonexistence of those institutions. For example, according to this interpretation it would be wrong to act on the maxim 'Refuse a bribe' for if everyone were to do so, bribery would cease and no one could refuse a bribe. The only way of rescuing the categorical imperative would seem to be either to jettison the conceivability test in favor of the contradiction of the will test, or to supplement the conceivability test with the contradiction of the will test. For example, one applies the conceivability test only to cases that do not involve immoral institutions, where an immoral institution is one whose existence can't be willed without the will being in contradiction with itself.

According to the second interpretation, a maxim fails the conceivability test if its universalization is incompatible with fulfilling the purpose or intention of the original maxim. (One ought not to make a false promise to further one's own interest, for everyone's making false promises under similar circumstances would be incompatible with the intent of one's original maxim, to further one's interest.) This allows one to avoid drawing the conclusion that it is wrong to refuse a bribe, because the nonexistence of bribery may have been part of the original purpose in refusing the bribe. However, this interpretation is not without its own problems. Not only is there some question as to how the conceivability test will differ from the contradiction of the will test, there will be no way of showing through the conceivability test what is wrong with someone who exploits a perfectly legitimate institution with the purpose of undermining it. (Consider, for example, someone who makes a false promise whenever it would be in his interest to do so, in order to undermine the institution of promising.) Again, it looks as if one will have to fall back on the contradiction of the will test to deal with such cases.

On either interpretation it looks as if the contradiction of the will test is the more fundamental test in applying the categorical imperative.

11. The interpretation of the categorical imperative that follows is not idiosyncratic. See, for example, Buchanan (1977).

12. Presumably the argument would be parallel to that involving the development of one's talents. No matter what ends one has there will always be circumstances in which the help of others will be necessary as a means for achieving those ends. For even the "self-reliance fanatic" there will be circumstances in which he will need the help of others just to maintain a measure of self-reliance.

13. Strictly speaking the categorical imperative is more complicated than this. It can be rational to act in ways that when universalized do conflict with a person's rational ends. Just as it can be rational to sacrifice one's ends on one occasion in return for a greater ability to secure those ends on other occasions, so it can be rational to act in a way that when universalized conflicts with a person's rational ends if such a universalization also carries with it an increased ability for all people to secure their rational ends.

14. The most one gets is the argument noted above that it is rational to want whatever is necessary for any end that one might happen to have. However, such an argument doesn't seem strong enough to secure as rational ends ends such as freedom, happiness, or perfection. However, Kant needs something like the latter if he is to derive all of the duties that he thinks follow from the categorical imperative.

15. Nagel's formal definitions of subjective and objective reasons rest on the technical notion of a reason predicate. According to Nagel, a reason can always be understood in terms of a predicate that, when it applies, provides a person with a reason. A reason whose reason predicate contains a free occurrence of an agent variable is a *subjective reason*. A reason whose reason predicate contains no free occurrences of an agent variable is an *objective reason*. If a person has a reason to promote A because A is in *his* interest, then the reason can be expressed in terms of the predicate 'A is in p's interest'. The reason turns out to be a subjective reason because this predicate contains a free occurrence of the agent variable 'p'. If a person has a reason to promote A because it is a case of promoting *someone's* interest, then the reason can be expressed in terms of the predicate, '($\exists$q) (A is in q's interest)'. This reason turns out to be objective, because its predicate contains no free occurrences of the agent variable 'q'.

16. A judgment with motivational content can and usually does motivate a person to act ([1970], p. 66).

17. It might be thought that the mere recognition of objective reasons will be sufficient for the reduction of interpersonal conflicts, because the existence of objective reasons always seems to provide the possibility of a countervailing factor to a person's pursuit of his or her own ends. However, whether it does provide such a basis or not depends on what one has primary reasons to promote. If, for example, one has a primary reason to promote a state of fierce competition, then the recognition of the existence of objective reasons would seem to promote rather than reduce interpersonal conflict.

18. Of course, one will still need a theory of practical rationality to see whether this suggestion is correct, and Rawls provides no such theory. Among other things, Darwall (1983) tries to supply such a theory.

19. One might wonder whether Aristotle's position on practical reason fits as neatly with the views of Kant, Nagel, and Rawls as I have suggested. For example, Rawls countenances people acting from a variety of conceptions of the good, whereas Aristotle seems to think that there is a single conception of the good that everyone must pursue. I admit that not all of the details of Aristotle's ethics will fit neatly with the position of Kant, Nagel, or Rawls. But I do not think that this affects the main point I am making. Even if Rawls does countenance people acting on a variety of conceptions of the good, he still maintains that a common core of everyone's good will be maintaining the ability to form, revise, and act on his or her own conception of the good. If this is to be part of a theory that bases how one ought to act on principles of practical rationality, then Rawls must be able to argue that it is rational for anyone to have this as part of his conception of the good. The kind of position I have attributed to Aristotle provides for the possibility of one such argument. Of course, using it might force some revisions in Rawl's position. But, then, we have yet to see that what follows from this argument is Aristotle's ethics in all of its detail.

20. This is essentially the same point made in discussion of NE 1113a13-23 in Chapter 3 Section V. It is noted there that this feature of Aristotle's position also threatens the existence of practical reason in the acquisition of ends.

Chapter 9. The Traditional Interpretation: Some Problems and Preliminaries

1. The Socratic position that Aristotle is referring to is the position that knowledge cannot be dragged about like a slave by passion. But it seems to follow from this position that action contrary to full and complete knowledge is impossible. If a person did act from passion contrary to full and complete knowledge, then it looks as if passion would be overpowering knowledge and dragging it about like a slave.

2. Among those who accept the above outline, although with considerable variation in the way they fill out the details, are Ando (1971), Burnet (1904), Cooper (1975), Hardie (1980), Joachim (1951), Milo (1966), Santas (1969), Stewart (1892), Walsh (1963), and Wiggins (1978-79). Among exceptions to this tradition are Kenny (1966) and (1979), McConnell (1975), and Mele (1981).

3. Its solution has been provided for by Owen (1967). (See also Hardie [1980], pp. 264-271).

4. See Chapter 4 Section IV and Chapter 7 Section III.

5. The Socratic position is set out and argued for in *Protagoras* 352a-360d, *Meno* 77b-78b, and Gorgias 467c-479d, 492c-509d.

6. See, for example, *Progatoras* 356c-357c.

7. The foregoing rests on an oversimplification of the Socratic position, but it is close enough to allow one to see why Aristotle would have thought that it was contrary to the *phainomena*. For an introduction to some of the subtleties of the Socratic position see Santas (1964) and (1966).

8. This is essentially Ross's explanation of how incontinence can be blameworthy ([1963], p. 216). (See also Kenny [1979], pp. 162-63.) Jackson (1942) argues against Ross, but I think that he can be shown to be mistaken. (See, e.g., Walsh [1963], pp. 115-16, and Hardie [1980], pp. 277-78).

This is not to say that this explanation is free from difficulty. If acting in ignorance is blameworthy only if the agent is responsible for his ignorance, then an incontinent man will be blameworthy only if he is responsible for the ignorance involved in his incontinence. I think it is likely that an incontinent man will be responsible for his ignorance only if what led to his ignorance was itself a case of incontinence. *If* this is right, then the above explanation begs the question. (For other possible problems in explaining on the traditional interpretation how incontinence can be blameworthy, see Reilly [1976].) Nevertheless, it is not necessary for present purposes to show that Aristotle could have provided a *successful* explanation of how incontinence can be blameworthy. All that is needed is to show how Aristotle could have *thought* that incontinence is blameworthy, and, thus, that his own view fits the *phainomena* in a way that Socrates' does not. This the above explanation does.

9. Aristotle also seems to allow the possibility of failing to abide by the conclusions of one's deliberations at 1110a29-31, where he says,

> It is difficult sometimes to determine what should be chosen at what cost, and yet more more difficult to abide by our decisions.

10. This is important because 1150b19-22 has been taken as evidence that the conclusion of a practical syllogism is not an action. (See, for example, Santas [1969], p. 176).

11. I do not take this to be a decisive reason for adopting the first reading I suggested. It is not my purpose here to provide such a reason. I only want to point out that there is a natural enough reading of this and other passages to provide grounds for questioning and reexamining the traditional interpretation. One could admit this, and still maintain that the traditional interpretation holds up under reexamination. One could even go on to use this as a basis for rejecting the reading of this passage that I suggested. Nothing I have argued here rules this out.

12. This is not to say that the *phronimos* is incapable of having the kind of desires that can come in conflict with what he ought to do. If, for example, pursuing the good sometimes requires refraining from eating sweets, it does not follow that a *phronimos* can't have desires for sweets. He can. It is that when he recognizes what virtue demands he is not moved by the fact that something is sweet. To use the terminology of McDowell (1978) the truly virtuous man has the capacity to "silence" considerations that on other occasions would provide him with reasons to act. He has acquired the capacity to keep this potential source of motivation just that, a potential source of motivation. On other occasions, though, it can be an actual source of motivation.

13. For a discussion of Aristotle's views on moral development that at least in its general outlines is compatible with the continuum I have just sketched and the interpretation of *akrasia* that I go on to argue for, see Burnyeat (1980).

14. I am not the only one who sees this as a problem. Wiggins ([1978-79], pp. 262-66) also attributes to Aristotle a position on practical reason that would allow the *akratēs* to recognize that the particular action that he does is wrong. He too agrees that Aristotle's failure to allow this positibility requires an explanation. Being an advocate of the traditional interpretation, he tries to provide one.

15. For a brief summary of the problems surrounding the texts of Aristotle's ethical writings, see Hardie (1980), pp. 1-10.

16. Cook Wilson (1912) has argued that Ch. 3 was not written by Aristotle. But for arguments against Cook Wilson, see Stewart (1892), Vol. 2, pp. 141ff, and Walsh (1963), p. 65 and pp. 183-88.

17. The evidence for this claim will be examined in greater detail in Chapter 10 Sections I and III.

18. Kenny ([1966], pp. 179-83) denies that there are two syllogisms in Aristotle's explanation of *akrasia*. This too will be taken up in Chapter 10. For the present, however, I shall state the various forms of the traditional interpretation in terms close to those which their advocates would use.

19. Ross (1963) is, I think, committed to this form of the traditional interpretation. Owen (1967) says that this may be the view that Aristotle held.

20. Joachim (1951) is the best example of someone who holds this second version of the traditional interpretation.

21. Ando (1971) and Walsh (1963) hold this third version of the traditional interpretation. Sorabji (1973-74) also seems to accept it.

Chapter 10. An Argument for the Traditional Interpretation

1. Part of the argument is based on an argument in Gregory Zeigler, "Aristotle's Analysis of *Akrasia*," presented at the Western Division Meetings of the American Philosophical Association in the spring of 1974.

2. If Aristotle maintained, as he seems to have, that one who believes the premises of a valid theoretical syllogism must also believe the conclusion, then it looks as if he didn't always keep this distinction firmly in mind.

3. Kenny puts forward the suggestion in connection with the view that the conclusion of the practical syllogism is (at least sometimes) a decision. However, the same considerations can be used to explain how the conclusion could be an action.

Since Kenny's arguments in (1966) and (1979) provide one of the few sustained attempts at providing an alternative to the traditional interpretation, they will be a major source of the objections raised against the argument being set out in this chapter.

4. As further support for the possibility of an action's occurring *after* the conclusion of a practical syllogism has been drawn, Kenny points to 702a17 where Aristotle says, "thinking that one ought to go and going are virtually simultaneous." ([1979], p. 143).

5. The interpretation of 701a18-22 that follows is essentially the same as Martha Nussbaum's ([1978], pp. 344-45).

6. One might object that it still isn't clear, because after all Aristotle has said that the conclusion *I must make a coat* is an action. There seems to be no action for 'I must make a coat' to express. It should be noted, though, that what Aristotle says here poses a problem whether one takes the conclusion of a practical syllogism to be an action or not. (If 'I must make a coat' doesn't express an action, then why does Aristotle say that the conclusion I must make a coat *is* an action?) Kenny says that Aristotle is willing to call a decision to act an action ([1979], p. 143). Another possibility is to take this intermediate conclusion to be the action of setting out to take steps to make a coat, including deliberating about what those steps should be. (See Nussbaum [1978], pp. 194-95.) In engaging in this further deliberation one is drawing this intermediate conclusion. This would explain why what follows is further deliberation.

7. Nor does 702a17 provide sufficient grounds for thinking that drawing the conclusion can antedate action. Nussbaum argues that 'One ought to go' more than likely refers to a major premise rather than a conclusion ([1978], p. 358).

8. Kenny ([1968], p. 178) suggests this in conjunction with the parallel NE passage, 1147a26ff. However, it might just as well be raised here.

9. In the previous lines, 701a14-15, Aristotle implicitly distinguishes between syllogisms involving positive and negative actions. One *might* take '*kōluē*' and '*anagkazē*' to be saying the same thing of each of these two cases. Thus, Farquharson translates 11. 15-16 as,

And one so acts in the two cases provided that there is nothing in the one case to compel or in the other to prevent.

So understood, redundancy is just what one would expect.

10. Whether this claim turns out to be trivial or not depends on whether and how strong a motivation goes along with possession and combination of the premises of a practical syllogism. According to the traditional interpretation the motivation is so strong that only something like external compulsion will prevent a person from acting. The question is whether on an alternative interpretation one can show that there will be sufficient motivation to avoid a charge of triviality.

11. Taking '*pōs*' with *hypolembanōn orthōs*'.

12. For example, Joachim (1951), p. 223, Ross (1963), pp. 216-17. For a more detailed discussion of this way of understanding this distinction, see Mele (1981).

13. E.g., by drawing an intermediate conclusion.

14. The objections can all be found in Kenny (1966) and (1979), although arguments for them will also be drawn from elsewhere.

15. To these one could add the problems I raised in Chapter 9. These problems will be given separate attention in Section IV.

16. The contrast is between '*anagkē to sumperanthen entha men phainai tēn psuchēn*' and '*en de tais poiētikais prattein euthos*'.

17. For a brief description of this distinction see Chapter 5 Section I.

18. One might also note that here there is no way of explaining the redundancy of '*kōluomenon*' as there was in De Motu 701a8ff. (See n. 9 above.)

19. To this one might add a consideration based on points noted by Cooper and Nussbaum. If at 1147a27 one takes '*sumperanthen*' ('conclusion') with '*prattein*' as well as with '*phainai*', what Aristotle says suggests that something proposition-like occurs in cases of *poiētikais* where action immediately results (Cooper [1975], n. 61, p. 48, Nussbaum [1978], n. 50, p. 204). That something proposition-like results from combining the premises of a practical syllogism is also suggested at 1147a31. Instead of saying that one who is able and not prevented *straightway* acts, Aristotle says that he must *also* act *(hama touto kai prattein)* (Nussbaum [1978], n. 50, p. 204). One might argue that it is this proposition-like entity that is the conclusion of a practical syllogism, not an action.

20. Kenny also says that if there were a syllogism of desire, the *akratēs* would act from *prohairesis*. But Aristotle says that the *akratēs* does not act from *prohairesis* (1111b14-15) ([1966], p. 180).

21. One could also argue from the activity of 'This is sweet' to the drawing of this conclusion even if one acknowledged two syllogisms in Aristotle's explanation of *akrasia*. If one reconstructed both syllogisms as having 'This is sweet' as their final minor premise, then its activity would seem to imply that the conclusion 'Don't taste this' is drawn. Santas (1969) and Bogen and Moravcsik (1982) argue in this way for the drawing of this conclusion.

22. Kenny also argues that unless the *akratēs* did draw this conclusion, his *prohairesis* could not be said to be virtuous (1152a17), for one cannot have a *prohairesis* unless a conclusion is drawn ([1966], p. 182).

23. One could give essentially the same argument if one admitted the existence of two syllogisms in Aristotle's explanation of *akrasia* but reconstructed them so that they shared the same final minor premise. Santas (1969) argues in this way.

24. The interpretation is essentially Kenny's in (1966). With one addition it could also serve as a summary of his interpretation in (1979). The addition is that the conclusion on which the *akratēs* ought to act is "half-had" (Kenny's term for knowledge which a person in a sense has and in a sense does not have).

25. Thus, the explanation in 1147a24-1147b19 is an explanation of weak incontinence. The explanation of impetuous incontinence is hinted at in 1147a4-10 ([1979], p. 161).

26. Given the parallel that exists between the two passages, if Kenny were right about 1147a24-32, one should be able to read the same distinction into *De Motu* 701a8ff that Kenny finds in 1147a24-32. But one will be hard-pressed to find in 701a8ff a distinction between all cases of practical reasoning and straightforward cases of technical reasoning where there is no conflicting desire to prevent action in accord with it.

27. Kenny might argue that the qualification occurs at 1147a30-31 where it is said that a person who combines the premises of a practical syllogism will act if he is able and not prevented *(dunamenon kai mē kōluomenon)*. However, we shall see that there are difficulties in taking this qualification to allow that a person can be prevented from acting by a conflicting internal desire.

28. Again, whether this claim is trivial or not depends on whether and how much motivation results from possession and combination of the premises. As we shall see, on Kenny's interpretation no such motivation need result. This would make the claim trivial.

29. One can argue that this will be true even if one acknowledges the existence of something proposition-like that results from the combination of the premises of a practical syllogism. (See n. 19 above.) One might argue that Aristotle's repeated insistence elsewhere that the conclusion of a practical syllogism is an action is a reason for thinking that one hasn't drawn the conclusion unless one has acted on this proposition-like thing. See, for example, Cooper (1975), n. 61, p. 48.

30. Again, for a list of Aristotle's examples see Santas (1969), pp. 163-65.

31. For example, the coat example at *De Motu* 701a18-22 can be read as setting out something needed to keep warm during cold weather, something which in turn is necessary for health. The example involving walking at 701a13-15 is quite naturally taken to refer to a form of exercise that is necessary for health.

32. This latter example can be taken as a medical example (applicable, for example, to someone on a special diet), as a nonmedical "culinary" example (applicable to someone like a dessert taster who works in a kitchen), or as an ethical example, setting out one of the principles of an intemperate man (tasting sweet things being one way of acquiring pleasure).

33. It might be more plausible to take the major premise of this second syllogism to be 'I want to taste something pleasant', rather than as 'Everything sweet is pleasant'. This would have the virtue of making explicit that it was a syllogism of desire. 'Everything sweet is pleasant' and 'This is sweet' would then be parts of its composite minor premise.

34. It turns out that one *can* construe 'Everything sweet is pleasant' and 'This is sweet' as

parts of the minor premise with 'Don't taste an excessive number of sweets' as the major premise. But, as I shall point out below, taking the example this way is still compatible with the traditional interpretation.

35. As n. 33 above shows, one could even grant that 'Everything sweet is pleasant' and 'This is sweet' are parts of a composite minor premise and still maintain that they are parts of a second syllogism.

36. The key to understanding 1149a32-b2 is Aristotle's reference to argument *or imagination (logos ē hē phantasia)* at line 32. In *De Anima* Aristotle marks off *boulēsis* from *epithumia* in terms of the way imagination *(phantasia)* works. Sometimes one calculates by means of images what is to come and pronounces some future object as pleasant or painful (431b7-9). Calculative imagination is also involved in determining according to a single standard which among competing ends is to be pursued (434a6-9). This kind of calculation is not present in *epithumia* (at least not in its most primitive form) (434a11-12). It is in terms of this kind of calculation that Aristotle distinguishes *thumos* from *epithumia* in 1149a32-b2. This kind of calculation is operative in acquiring a desire for something as an *end*. In this respect *thumos* falls together with *boulēsis* in contrast to *epithumia*. The distinction drawn in 1149a32-b2 has nothing to do with whether there is a syllogism of desire or not. The most that follows is that if there is a syllogism of *epithumia*, its major premise is not arrived at by the same kind of calculative imagination that is involved in *boulēsis* and *thumos*. This is not contradicted by Aristotle's saying, "while appetite, if *argument* or perception *(ho logos ē hē aisthesis)* merely says that an object is pleasant, springs to the enjoyment of it" (lines 34-b1, emphasis mine). If 'Everything sweet is pleasant' and 'This is sweet' are parts of a syllogism of desire, then this would be a case where argument says that an object is pleasant, but the existence of the desire to taste something pleasant would still not be based on the kind of calculative imagination discussed at *De Anima* 434a6-9. (Note that the reference to argument here does suggest the existence of syllogism of desire, although it may turn out, as Rackham suggests, *'ho logos ē'* is a later interpolation.)

In fact, at *De Motu* 701a32-33 Aristotle seems to provide an example of a syllogism of desire, "I want to drink, says appetite; this is drink says sense or imagination or mind; straightway I drink." Although one might want to refrain from calling this a practical *syllogism* since it contains no deliberative reasoning, it still provides a model for explaining certain actions in the way that a practical syllogism does. This is all that really matters. Besides, one can easily imagine another example in which deliberative reasoning is used to allow a person to quench his thirst. Aristotle's admission at NE 1142b17-19 that an incontinent man can act on the basis of deliberation implies that there are such examples.

37. In addition, the admission that there is a syllogism of desire does *not* entail that the *akratēs* acts from *prohairesis*. The most that follows is that the *akratēs* acts from deliberation. As I pointed out at the beginning of Chapter 3, there is more to acting on *prohairesis* than acting on a desire based on deliberation.

38. Nor are the prospects any brighter for arguing for this conclusion from the activity of 'This is sweet' and a reconstruction of the two syllogisms as containing the same final minor premise. Not only does such a reconstruction require argument, but someone who held the second form of the traditional interpretation could argue that even if both syllogisms did share 'This is sweet', its activity is confined to drawing the conclusion of the syllogism of desire. Relative to the syllogism of reason it is possessed but not exercised.

39. Nor will it do to argue that the *akratēs* must draw the conclusion of the syllogism on which he ought to act on the grounds that Aristotle says that the *prohairesis* of the *akratēs* is virtuous (NE 1152a17) and that the *akratēs* wouldn't have a *prohairesis* if he didn't draw the conclusion. Relying either on an account of deliberation and the practical syllogism like that of Cooper (1975) or on arguments like those of Anscombe (1965), a proponent of the traditional interpretation can argue that a *prohairesis* is a reasoned desire included in a relatively specific decision, one which may or may not be implemented on a particular occasion. This is not the way I have understood *prohairesis*, but as I said earlier

in a comment on Cooper's views, they are best compared with mine in terms of how well they account for a whole range of issues. One of these is the relation between Aristotle's explanation of *akrasia* and his conception of *prohairesis*. If one couldn't make the details of Aristotle's explanation of *akrasia* fit what he says about *prohairesis* without attributing to him a conception of *prohairesis* of the sort that Cooper suggests, then that is certainly a mark in favor of that conception of *prohairesis*.

40. Aristotle seems to say of *hē teleutaia protasis* that it is either not possessed or not exercised. If it were the final minor premise, then either one of these would prevent it from being combined with the other premises to yield something expressing what ought to be done in the situation at hand.

41. This suggestion is reinforced if Aristotle's division of the soul into parts in NE I, 13 is based ultimately on Plato's tripart division of the soul in the *Republic* (435-440), (for example, if the "exoteric works," on which Aristotle's division is based, espouse an essentially Platonic view.) Plato's argument requires the existence of genuine conflicts of motive. That Aristotle's division of the soul in NE I, 13 may be based on Plato's arguments for the division of the soul was suggested to me by Sandra Peterson.

42. Thus, one won't be able to argue that the responses offered in Part C ignore important evidence against the traditional interpretation, the problems raised in Chapter 9. Without some other way of understanding 1147b9-13, the proposed alternative to the traditional interpretation can't solve these problems either.

43. Part of what I have been arguing is that Kenny's interpretation in (1966) fails to acknowledge the force of what Aristotle seems to be saying in 1147b9-13. An important difference between (1966) and (1979) is that in (1979) Kenny does admit that the conclusion on which the *akratēs* ought to act is "half-had" (Kenny's term for knowledge that a person in a sense has and in a sense does not have) ([1979], p. 162). However, Kenny still doesn't seem to recognize the problem that this raises for his interpretation. In discussing criteria for acceptance of propositions, Kenny says,

> It is only when we reach a decision like 'Avoid this now' where (sic) there is only one single behavioural criterion for sincerity in the utterance; and this in the case of the incontinent is *ex hypothesi* lacking. ([1979], p. 166)

Even though this behavioral criterion is lacking in *akrasia*, Kenny seems to think that there are still grounds for taking the *akratēs'* utterance of such a conclusion to be sincere.

> Here we have the clash between the verbal criterion for what the person believes (he says he is not to do it) and the behavioural criterion (he goes on to do it) which was precisely what Aristotle's distinction between having and half-having was introduced to take account of. ([1979], p. 166)

However, it is hard to see how the verbal criterion can be given any weight when Aristotle says of people who half-have knowledge that their using the language of knowledge proves nothing (1147a18-19) and that they have knowledge in the sense in which it does not mean knowing but only talking (1147b11-12). Without further argument to show how people who half-have knowledge can believe and understand what they are saying at the time they are saying it, it looks as if Kenny is not entitled to the claim that the *akratēs* can recognize what he ought to do in the situation that faces him.

44. Reading in a time-lag will be even more natural if one accepts Cooper's account of deliberation and its relation to the practical syllogism.

45. For references to topics that Aristotle approaches in this way, see Owen (1965).

46. At least I think that this is what the Socrates of the *Protagoras* would say, and it is the saying of the Socrates of the *Protagoras* that is supposed to turn out to be right.

47. Wiggins (1978-79) suggests a different explanation. He thinks that if an *akratēs* were allowed to recognize a particular action as falling under humanity's good and yet prefer something else, Aristotle's notions of *eudaimonia* and practical reason would be subverted (pp. 264-66). Once one has understood *eudaimonia*, how could one prefer something

less important? "How could he prefer a smaller good·when there was an overwhelming-ly larger one staring him in the face and he understood what made it overwhelming?" (p. 265).

Chapter 11. An Argument for an Alternative Interpretation

1. See Chapter 10, Section II, Part D.

2. There is an objection that might be raised against the way I have taken these passages. At 1224b9 where I have 'it is *a* present *internal* tendency,' the Oxford translation has 'it is *the* present *internal* tendency.' And immediately after 1224b5-21, Aristotle says,

> So to say that both act from compulsion is not without reason, the one sometimes acting involuntarily owing to his desire, the other owing to his reason; *kechōrismena gar onto hekatera ekkrouetai hup' allēlōn.* (1224b21-24)

The Oxford edition translates this last sentence as 'these two, being separated, are thrust out by one another.' In both cases the Oxford translation suggests that at any given time only one of the two opposing tendencies (*the* present internal tendency) is present. The other has been "thrust out." If this is correct, then it looks as if these passages do not acknowledge a genuine conflict of motives in *akrasia*.

The general reply to this objection is as follows. Taking the two lines just by themselves, there is an alternative translation that is just as plausible as the Oxford translation. Taken with what else is said in the passages, this alternative is preferable to the Oxford translation.

'*A* present internal tendency' is as good a translation of '*bē kath hauton horme*' as is '*the* present internal tendency.' But the former fits better with Aristotle's saying that the *akratēs* drags himself against the resistance of an opposing desire and that he feels pain when he acts than does the latter. Furthermore, rather than translating '*kechōrismena . . . ontoa*' as 'being separated,' thus providing grounds for taking '*ekkroutai*' as 'thrust out' or 'driven out,' one can read it as 'being at variance,' allowing one to read '*ekkrouetai*' as 'repulsed' or 'driven back.' This also seems to make better sense of '*gar*', for what Aristotle is trying to explain is why the *akratēs* and *enkratēs* have been thought to act from compulsion. The mark of the compulsory is that it is painful (1224a30-31), and both the *akratēs* and *enkratēs* are said to feel pain when they act. As I pointed out above, the reason they are pained is that they act contrary to a present desire. This requires the presence of a conflicting desire.

Thus, these passages should be taken as acknowledging the existence of a genuine conflict of motives in *akrasia*.

For a translation and interpretation that supports a similar conclusion about these passages see Woods (1982), pp. 27-28, pp. 140-41.

3. A proponent of the traditional interpretation will be quick to point out that at 1166b22-23 Aristotle says, "If a man cannot at the same time be pained and pleased, at all events after a short time he is pained because he was pleased," noting that this suggests that the two opposing elements in the soul are not both operative at the same time. However, this runs directly in the face of what I have just pointed out, the rather strong language in terms of which Aristotle says that an *akratēs* is torn apart by conflicting desires. Given this language, I think that one should take these lines as a concession to those who would not accept that these conflicting elements can be present at the same time. This is a concession Aristotle can make because the conclusion he is arguing for doesn't turn on it. (The conclu-sion is that inferior men (including the *akratēs*) do not love themselves.) Lines 22-23 should be taken as saying that this conclusion will follow even if these people are not pleased and pained at the same time. I do not think it should be taken as indicating that Aristotle doesn't think that they can be pleased and pained at the same time.

4. To these sets of passages in EE and NE one might also add *Metaphysics* 1048a21-22.

5. For example, compare 1219b26-1220a12 in EE, II, 1 with what Aristotle says in NE, I, 13.

6. There is, however, a reading of this passage according to which it does not acknowledge a genuine conflict of motives. If one reads *'enantiai'* as 'contradictory', one might think that what Aristotle says provides grounds for thinking that contradictory desires *cannot* be present at the same time. When Aristotle says that desire, influenced by what is just at hand, presents an object as pleasant and good without condition *(haplōs hēdu kai agathon haplōs)*, it is natural to take him to be saying that *un*influenced by considerations about the future, *epithumia* presents the object as the pleasantest and best to pursue. However, when mind bids the agent to hold back because of what is future, the object is viewed as *not* being the pleasantest and best. It is this that makes reason and appetite *contradictory*. But since Aristotle only says that *epithumia* presents the object as pleasantest and best when *un*influenced by considerations about the future, one might think that when *epithumia is* influenced by considerations about the future, it will no longer present the object as pleasantest and best. That is, when mind bids the agent to hold back, *epithumia* will no longer be a contradictory desire. A rational desire and an appetite will be contradictory only if they are had at different times.

A number of things can be said against this as a ground for denying that the passage affirms a genuine conflict of motives.

i) There is no good reason for translating *'enantiai'* in the narrower sense of 'contradictory rather than in the broader sense of 'contrary' or 'opposed'.

ii) *Epithumia* may actually be something that *cannot* be influenced by considerations about the future. Aristotle says at 434a12 that *epithumia* contains no deliberative element. The distinction between *epithumia* and rational desire in 433b5-10, thus, may be a distinction between desires that are not and desires that are based on considerations about the future. If this is right, then one won't be able to say that when *epithumia* is influenced by considerations about the future, it no longer presents the object as pleasantest and best. *Epithumia* will not be the kind of desire that can be influenced by considerations about the future.

iii) Aristotle's distinction between the three forms of desire, *epithumia, thumos,* and *boulēsis,* seems in part designed to allow a person to be in opposing states at one and the same time (including ones involving contradictory judgments). (Cf. Plato's argument for the tripart division of the soul at *Republic,* 436-41.)

iv) Even if one can't have two *contradictory* desires at the same time, it doesn't follow that one can't have two conflicting desires at the same time. Even if influenced by considerations about the future *epithumia* no longer presents the object as pleasantest and best, it can still present it as pleasant. And this is enough to move a person to pursue it. Nothing Aristotle says in the passage suggests that *epithumia* is *extinguished* when considerations about the future are brought in. If it isn't extinguished, then a genuine conflict of motives can still occur, even if the desires in question can't be properly described as *contradictory.*

Thus, the passage does seem best taken as acknowledging the existence of a genuine conflict of motives.

7. See, for example, the objection in n. 6 above.

8. See especially his "value-strength principle," pp. 187-88.

9. What this means is that the interpretation of this and other passages considered in this section is subject to revision pending a reexamination of the details of Aristotle's explanation of *akrasia*. But, given the nature of the present argument, that is only to be expected.

10. The existence of a genuine conflict of motives in *enkrateia* also seems to be acknowledged at *De Anima* 433a7-8.

11. A proponent of the traditional interpretation might resist this conclusion, arguing that there is no conclusive proof that the person who acts from desire acts *at the same time* that mind commands him to act otherwise. For example, there is no specific language referring to a struggle of the sort that occurs in NE 1102b13-19, NE 1166b7ff, or EE 1224b5ff. In the absence of such language, it might be argued, one can always take the kind of case mentioned to be one in which an *akratēs* is first moved to do what he ought to do,

but then passion arises, preventing him from recognizing what he ought to do and extinguishing the motive to do it. It is only then that he acts from desire instead.

Given the present context of argument, though, this does seem to be grasping at straws. Considered apart from Aristotle's explanation of *akrasia*, there is no reason whatsoever for reading in a time differnce between the time the *akratēs* is moved by mind's command and the time he acts from desire. Taken at face value, the passage seems to acknowledge the existence of a genuine conflict of desires in *akrasia*.

12. See Appendix II. Given the difficulties that surround this passage, it might be thought unfortunate if anything of consequence rests on its interpretation. How much importance the passage has depends on how strong a case one takes 433b5-10 and 432b26-433a3 to provide for the acknowledgement of a genuine conflict of motives in *akrasia*. If one reads these passages in the way I have suggested, then 434a12-15 simply provides an opportunity for some welcome confirmation. However, if one resists my readings of these passages, arguing, for example, that at most they acknowledge a genuine conflict of motives in *enkrateia*, then 434a12-15 takes on greater importance. Fortunately, I think the passage can bear this added importance. Properly understood, it says that the same kind of conflict occurs in *akrasia* as occurs in *enkrateia*. The argument of Appendix II, I hope, will bear this out.

13. Indeed there is textual evidence in the NE passage for something proposition-like that expresses this recognition. See Chapter 10 n. 19.

14. See, for example, the argument in Chapter 10 Section I.

15. For the exception see n. 38 below.

16. '*koluē ē anagkazē*' (*De Motu* 701a16-17), '*dunamenon kai mē kōluomenon*' (NE 1147a31-32). See Section I and Section III Part B.

17. In Chapter 10 it was noted that at least in the *De Motu* passage this redundancy might be explicable. (See n. 9.) However, in Chapter 10 it was also argued that the *De Motu* and NE passages are parallel passages. (See Section III Part C.) If this is right, then I think the explanation of the redundancy in the *De Motu* passage can be discounted. There is no corresponding way of explaining the redundancy in the NE passage.

18. Nor will it be enough to overthrow these general considerations to point to Aristotle's use of '*kōluō*' at NE 1147a32 to refer to an internal factor. At 1.32 the verb means 'prohibit'. What is needed is a case where the verb refers to an internal factor and means 'prevent'.

19. See also *Politics* 1300a3-6. It is worth noting that although the case mentioned in 1309a17-19 concerns a matter for possible legislation, the question is not how to *prohibit* the behavior in question. The way to pass the relevant legislation would be clear enough. The question is how to *prevent* the behavior.

20. As I have said before, whether this claim turns out to be trivial depends on how strong a motivation to act goes along with the possession and combination of the premises of a practical syllogism. The claim is not trivial on the traditional interpretation because the motivation in question is so strong that only external compulsion can prevent a person from acting on it. On the alternative interpretation considered in Chapter 10, the claim does turn out to be trivial, for as I argued there, that interpretation is committed to saying that one can possess and combine the premises of a practical syllogism without being motivated at all. However, this does not turn out to be true on the interpretation I am arguing for. This is underscored by the fact that the relevant notion of prevention is prevention "contrary to impulse or choice." This implies that a motive exists to do what one is prevented from doing.

21. See esp. *Politics* 1300a3-6 and 1309a17-19.

22. For arguments in defense of the existence of a syllogism of desire see Chapter 10 Section III Part C.

23. A proponent of the traditional interpretation might respond by arguing for only a restricted version of this claim. The practical syllogism contains all of the elements needed for explaining action except for the presence or absence of external compulsion. But what

are the arguments for limiting the exceptions just to external compulsion? To point to *De Motu* 701a16-17 and NE 1147a31-32 would simply reintroduce the arguments already given that exceptions to this claim should include more than external compulsion.

24. Again, see his "value-strength principle" (1969), pp. 187-88.

25. Of course, if one had some independent reason for attributing to Aristotle Santas's "value-strength principle," one would have a reason for attributing the revised thesis to Aristotle. But Santas's attribution of this thesis to Aristotle seems based entirely on Aristotle's explanation of *akrasia*. We are considering the matter here independently of that explanation.

26. Even if it is already understood that the *akratēs* operates with a kind of practical knowledge that is liable to break down, there is still a question that arises for *akrasia* that does not arise in the case of *enkrateia*—what happens on those occasions on which it does break down that makes it break down. (The answer to this question is discussed in Section V below.)

27. "Within the case of having knowledge but not using it we see a difference of state, admitting of the possibility of having knowledge in a sense and yet not having it" (1147a11-13).

28. This is only reinforced if one takes exercising such a premise to be combining it with other premises. As the second version of the traditional interpretation acknowledges, one can have occurrent knowledge of a final minor premise of a practical syllogism without combining it with the major premise.

29. See n. 27 above.

30. For additional arguments for taking unexercised knowledge to include more than mere dispositional knowledge, see Mele (1981), pp. 141-44.

31. See the discussion of 1147b9-12 in Section IV below.

32. Especially if, as it turns out, Aristotle's main focus of attention in his detailed explanation is on weak rather than impetuous *akrasia.*

33. The *akratēs* is said to be blameworthy (1145b10), and inability to act would provide him with an excuse. (It is true that at 1152a9-10 Aristotle says that in contrast to the *phronimos*, *'ho d' akratēs ou praktikos.''* But rather than translating this as "the incontinent man is unable to act," as Ross does, I think it should be translated as, "the incontinent man does not act.")

34. Aristotle has already (implicitly) acknowledged at 1147a1-10 that an *akratēs* can fail to possess or combine the premises of the syllogism of reason. This provides an explanation of impetuous *akrasia*. What he goes on to explain is weak *akrasia.*

35. We have already seen that there is evidence for something proposition-like that expresses this recognition in cases where a person has been prevented from acting (Chapter 10, n. 19). We have also seen that there is reason for thinking that *akrasia* is included in such cases (Section II above).

36. For a discussion of 433b5ff and 432b26ff see Section I above. For a discussion of 434a12-15 see Appendix II.

37. This will be something that expresses his *prohairesis*. Again, for some textual evidence for this proposition-like entity, see Chapter 10, n. 19.

38. It is in providing a basis for a reply to the objections raised above that my assumption that the conclusion of a practical syllogism is an action makes it easier for me to argue for my alternative interpretation. Because of this, it is important that independent arguments were offered in Chapter 10 for taking the conclusion of a practical syllogism to be an action.

39. There is one other objection that might be raised against the way I have taken *'hē teleutaia protasis'*. Aristotle says that *hē teleutaia protasis* is about a perceptible object, and that it determines action (1147b9-10). Not only is it the mark of the minor premise to be discovered by perception, at *De Anima* 434a19-20 Aristotle says that it is the minor premise that originates movement. However, we have seen in Chapter 3 Section II that Aristotle

allows what is to be done to be a matter of perception, and the recognition of what one is to do is as good or better candidate for what determines action than the minor premise. Furthermore, even though Aristotle says at *De Anima* 434a19-20 that it is the minor premise that originates movement, the issue in *De Anima* is restricted to which of the two premises of the practical syllogism, universal or minor, originates movement. There is no reason for thinking that when the issue includes something else (for instance, something that expresses the agent's *prohairesis*), that Aristotle's answer wouldn't be different.

40. This is confirmed by Aristotle's saying that the *akratēs* is in a situation that is *similar* to *(homoiōs)* these (1147a18). He does not say that *akrasia* is such a case.

41. See, for example, 1143b11-14, where Aristotle talks about people whom experience has given an eye "to see aright." Even though such people may not be able to articulate their general principles, they are able to spot cases that fall under them.

42. Mele (1981) argues for a similar interpretation of this range of cases, but for different reasons than I have given. It is also not clear to me that he takes these examples to leave open all of the possibilities that I think they leave open. (See pp. 154-55.)

43. The above also provides the argument for the proviso promised in Section III above.

44. It is true that on the second version of the traditional interpretation the *akratēs* can possess the final minor premise of the syllogism of reason. He just doesn't exercise it in connection with the major premise of the syllogism of reason. On this view it looks as if *akrasia* can occur in the presence of the knowledge expressed by *hē teleutaia protasis*. However, the proponent of this version still owes us an explanation of how this knowledge can be present if it is known only in the way a drunk muttering the verses of Empedocles knows what he is talking about. If he resorts to an account like that given above, there is no reason why the same account won't extend to knowledge of what the *akratēs* ought to do. There is no reason that the *akratēs'* use of the "language of knowledge" can't include an expression of what he ought to do.

45. There are two objections that might be raised against the way I have taken 1147b12-17. The first is that there is evidence of corruption in the text at just the point that I rely on it. As Stewart points out ([1892], Vol. II, p. 163), *'dokousēs parousēs'* at 1.15 is an instance of a rhyming construction that Greek authors tried to avoid. Also, as the text stands, *'to pathos'* occurs twice within the space of a line, with each occurrence having to be taken in a different sense. This is awkward. Stewart suggests *'periginetai'* instead of *'parousēs ginetai'*. This eliminates the rhyming *'parousēs'* and allows one to read both occurrences of *'to pathos'* as referring to the passion present in *akrasia*. On this reading, what Aristotle says at 11.15-17 is

for it is not knowledge proper that is overcome by passion, nor is it this that is 'dragged about' by passion.

This in turn leaves it open to be argued that the perceptual knowledge expressed by *'ton eschaton horon'* is *not* present in *akrasia*, and that its not being present is just what is involved in its being overcome and dragged about by passion.

Two things can be said in reply to this alternative way of taking 1147b12-17.

i) Despite the awkwardness of the text as it stands, there is some reason to prefer it to Stewart's emandation. Stewart's explanation of how the text became corrupt involves a series of three mistakes ([1892], Vol. II, p. 163). With each additional mistake required, the probability that this is what occurred decreases. Furthermore, in an earlier reference to the Socratic position Aristotle says,

for it would be strange—so Socrates thought—if when knowledge was in a man *(enousēs)* something else could master it and drag it about like a slave. (1145b23-24)

As Burnet points out ([1904], p. 305), the occurrence of *'enousēs'* in this earlier passage is evidence that *'parousēs'* belongs at 1147b15.

ii) Even if one accepts Stewart's emandation, the passage should be understood in the same way it would be understood if *'parousēs'* were in the text. On Stewart's reading 'nor is it this that is 'dragged about by passion' at 1. 17 would be redundant except for Aristotle's use of the same verb, *'perielkō'* ('to drag about') that Plato uses in his statement of the Socratic position at *Protagoras* 352b. In this way Aristotle emphasizes that it really is Socrates' position that seems to result. But not only is it part of Plato's statement of Socrates' position that knowledge that is present cannot be dragged about like a slave, we have just seen that in Aristotle's own earlier statement of the Socratic position, he says the same thing. Thus, one *should* take Aristotle to be saying at 1147b15-17 that knowledge proper is not present and dragged about like a slave. So understood, 1147b12-17 says by implication that perceptual knowledge *is* present *and* dragged about like a slave. That is, 1147b12-17 says just what I have taken it to say.

The second objection is that on the reading I have given of 1147b12-17 it is hard to see how the Socratic position does turn out to be true. If the *akratēs* knows what he ought to do in the situation that faces him and this knowledge is dragged about by passion, then knowledge *is* being dragged about like a slave. But the Socratic position is that knowledge *cannot* be dragged about like a slave.

The obvious response to this is that Aristotle's explanation of why the Socratic position seems to result is that the knowledge expressed by *ton eschaton horon* is not universal, whereas knowledge proper is universal. Thus, *knowledge proper* is not present and dragged about like a slave. However, as we saw in Chapter 10 Section IV, it can be maintained that universal knowledge is present to the extent that it is applied to the case at hand. If this is right, then the fact that the knowledge expressed in *ton eschaton horon* is particular can't be all there is to the explanation of why the Socratic position seems to result.

However, even if this is right, there is still a way of showing that on my interpretation knowledge proper is *not* present and dragged about like a slave in *akrasia*. On my interpretation, knowledge proper in practical matters is *phronēsis*, and *phronēsis* is so fully integrated into a person's character that *akrasia* in the face of it is impossible. That is, the knowledge that the *akratēs* has of what he ought to do is not *phronēsis*. Thus, even if one grants that universal knowledge is present to the extent to which it is applied, *knowledge proper* is still not present and dragged about like a slave in *akrasia*.

If one objects that on this way of understanding why the Socratic position seems to result, it doesn't turn out to be true in the way that Socrates thought it was true, it can be replied that when Aristotle "saves" *phainomena* they don't always turn out to be true in the way that people who believed them thought they were true.

46. One further advantage of my interpretation might perhaps be mentioned. On the traditional interpretation Aristotle fails to provide a crucial part of his explanation of *akrasia*—the details of the syllogism of reason. Without knowing what its major and minor premises are, one won't know, for example, which of the three versions of the traditional interpretation to adopt. However, on my interpretation, this is not an oversight at all. According to it, no matter what exactly the major and minor premises of the syllogism of reason are, the *akratēs* can possess and combine them, recognizing that he ought not to taste the object in front of him. What is important is that the *akratēs* can have this recognition. It is not important what the particular premises are that give it to him. Thus, on my interpretation the omission of these details is just what Aristotle's failure to mention them makes it look like, an omission of unnecessary detail.

47. Aristotle regards those who are mastered by a weak desire as self-indulgent, not incontinent; only those mastered by a strong desire deserve the name 'incontinent' (1148a18-22, 1150a27-31).

48. What follows is due to a suggestion by Troels Engberg-Pedersen, although I am not sure that he would approve of the use to which I have put it.

Concluding Remarks

1. One might expect to find a Humean position among the Sophists, but even if this turns out to be so, the Sophists do not appear to be in the forefront of Aristotle's thinking on ethics and politics in the way that they were for Socrates and Plato.

2. Perhaps it would be better to describe this as an explanation of why people fail to develop beyond incontinence into continent or virtuous people, as Burnyeat (1980) suggests.

3. To this one might want to add a more detailed account of the nature of pleasure and its relation to incontinence. Rorty (1980) provides the beginning of such a discussion for an interpretation of Aristotle along traditional lines. The question is whether something similar can't be done for the kind of interpretation I have argued for.

4. David Charles has undertaken such an investigation in an as yet unpublished manuscript on Aristotle on action. My recollection is that what he says is compatible with the main lines of what I have argued for.

Appendix I. NE 1143a35-b5

1. *Nous* is said to grasp the first and unchangeable terms of demonstrations (*apodeixeis*) (1143b1-2), and it is scientific knowledge, knowledge expressed in theoretical syllogisms, that deals with what is unchangeable (See, for example, NE 1139b20-21).

2. This problem is further complicated by an uncertainty over the antecedent of *'tais praktikais'*. Initially it would seem to be *'apodeixesin'*, for the latter is feminine as is *'tais praktikais'*, and *'apodeixais'* is the noun in the contrasting clause. This suggests that the contrast is between the way *nous* operates in theoretical syllogisms and the way in which *nous* operates in practical syllogisms. However, as Burnet points out ([1904]), p. 280), *'praktikais apodeixesin'* appears to be a contradiction, *'apodeixeis'* apparently being reserved for demonstrations in a theoretical syllogism. One could not take the antecedent to be *'sullogismoi'*, the genus under which *apodeixeis* falls, for *'sullogismoi'* is masculine and *'tais praktikais'* is feminine. Burnet suggests *'protasesi'* (premises) as the antecedent, citing *'en de tais poiētikais'* at 1147a28 as a parallel. Another possibility (suggested to me by Vicki Harper) is *'dunamesin'* (faculties), referring back to *'dunameis'* at 1143a38. Both of these latter suggestions allow *tais praktikais* to be an inductive form of practical reasoning of the sort suggested at 1143b3-5.

3. It is for this reason that Ross ([1963]), p. 213) suggests that the passage contains a confusion between the minor premise and the conclusion of a practical syllogism.

4. One answer might be that it is the mark of *nous* that it involves the immediate grasp of something, and the perception of particulars referred to in 1143a35-b5 is immediate. However, Aristotle had this move open to him at 1142a24-31 and he did not make it. Just as important, this would provide grounds for saying that *nous* is operative whenever perception is operative, whether it is a practical matter that is involved or not. This does not seem to be something that Aristotle would say.

It might be suggested that in 1143a35-b5 Aristotle is using *'nous'* in a looser, more common sense than he would ordinarily use it. The whole of Bk VI Ch. 11 is concerned with the virtue *gnōmē* (judgment), where the term *'gnōmē'* is being used more broadly than Aristotle would ordinarily use it. However, I think that this can be at most part of the answer, for I think Aristotle wants to allow that there is something correct about the common use of *'nous'* in connection with practical affairs. This is not explained by pointing out that it is a different use from Aristotle's normal one.

5. For a summary of most of the different intepretations offered of 1143a35-b5 see

Ando (1971), pp. 193-208. (See also Michelakis (1961), pp. 25-38.) For three interpretations not summarized in these works see Cooper (1975), pp. 41-45, Sorabji (1973-74), p. 117, pp. 124-25, and Wiggins (1975-76), pp. 47-48).

6. The considerations that follow were drawn from some suggestions made by Jonathan Barnes.

7. Two other interpretations are worth mentioning at this time. The first is Cooper's (1975), esp. n. 52, p. 42. It resembles the interpretation set out just above in that it also takes '*ek ton* . . . ' at 1143b4-5 to say that universal ends are achieved through particular actions. However, it does not take '*tou eschatou kai endechomenou kai tēs heteras protaseōs*' to refer just to the minor premise of a practical syllogism. According to Cooper, '*tou eschatou kai endechomenou*' ("the last and variable") refers to the last judgment resulting from deliberation, a judgment that a specific *kind* of action is to be done. This judgment serves as the major premise of a practical syllogism, for according to Cooper, the practical syllogism applies the results of deliberation to action. He takes '*tēs heteras protaseōs*' ("the other premise [proposition]") to refer to the minor premise of a practical syllogism, the other premise needed to apply the results of deliberation to action. To the extent that Cooper's interpretation resembles the interpretation just set out above, the argument I provide against it will also provide an argument against Cooper's interpretation. Additional considerations against Cooper's interpretation will be noted in footnotes.

The second interpretation worth noting is what I will call the "minimalist" interpretation. It agrees with the interpretation set out above that what *nous* grasps are means to ends. However, unlike this interpretation, it takes the grasp of these means to provide a person with a grasp of ends. Aristotle acknowledges not only means that instrumentally secure their ends, he also acknowledges means that are *constitutive* of their ends. (See, for example, Chapter 6 Section I.) According to the "minimalist" interpretation, it is the perception of these latter means that Aristotle is talking about in 1143a35-b5. To the extent to which these means are constitutive of their ends, to that extent a grasp of them is a grasp of universal ends. The importance of this interpretation is that it seems to provide a role for reason in the acquisition of ends without having to read into 1143a35-b5 the kind of inductive inference I have read into it. The only "induction" it requires is the minimal "induction" involved in revising previously held ends in the light of newly perceived constitutive means. No other induction needs to be brought in. Part of the argument I shall give against the above alternative interpretation also serves as an argument against this "minimalist" interpretation. Where it does, I shall note it in a footnote.

8. *Nous* and these other faculties are thought to come by nature because they come at a certain age. But these faculties come at a certain age because they deal with what is ultimate or particular (1143a25-29). Particulars become familiar only through experience (1142a14). Thus, *nous* and these other faculties come at a certain age because they come through experience. Indeed, if this were not so, Aristotle could not go on to conclude that we ought to pay attention to the undemonstrated sayings of older people because of what they have acquired through experience.

9. This capacity is a capacity to see in a particular situation that a particular action is to be done. Since this capacity has been acquired through experience, it is not confined to this one situation. It is a capacity to pick out actions like this one in situations like this one. But this is to say that people who have this capacity have an implicit grasp of the general principle that in situations like this one, actions like this one are to be done. Even though they may not be able to articulate what it is for a situation or an action to be like this one, experience has provided them with a grasp of a general principle.

One might object that what experience provides these people is not a particular evaluative proposition, something the grasp of which would be part of an implicit grasp of a general principle. Rather experience provides these people with particular *facts* relevant to drawing particular evaluative conclusions. That is why experience allows a person to see what to do on a particular occasion. In support of this one might cite Aristotle's discussion at 1141b16-20 of those who as a result of experience are more successful than those who have knowledge. One who has knowledge without being successful knows, for example, that light meats are digestible and wholesome, but one does not know what sorts of meat are light. A person who has experience, thus, would seem to be one who has what such a person lacks, for instance, knowledge that chicken is light meat. But this is knowledge of a fact needed to draw an evaluative conclusion, not knowledge of that conclusion itself. However, Aristotle says at 1141b16-20 that what the experienced man knows is *not* that chicken is light meat, but that chicken is *wholesome*. This *is* an evaluative proposition, the grasp of which would be involved in the implicit grasp of the more general principle that light meats are wholesome.

10. This also provides grounds against the "minimalist" interpretation noted in n. 7. To the extent to which Aristotle is talking about constitutive means in 1143b6-14, he is not just saying that one will revise previously held ends in the light of newly discovered constitutive means. He is saying that the grasp of these constitutive means is itself based on experience, and hence on induction. This is an induction not recognized by the "minimalist" interpretation.

11. Also, at 1141b27-28 Aristotle says that a political enactment is a thing to be done, for it is a last step (*to eschaton*) in a deliberative process (again, relying on Rackham's translation).

12. There is some question as to whether this can refer to a particular action. Cooper ([1975]), Ch. 2 and Appendix) has argued that what is *eschaton* is the last step in the process of deliberation, where this is a judgment about a specific kind of action. (For example, a political enactment of the sort mentioned at 1141b27-28 is something that will require or permit a specific *kind* of action, not a particular action on a particular occasion.) However, the present passage appears to be a stumbling block for Cooper's interpretation, for '*tou eschatou kai endechomenou*' is said to be grasped by *nous,* and what *nous* grasps it grasps through perception (1143b5). Since perception is of particulars, it looks as if *tou eschatou kai endechomenou* will also be about particulars.

Cooper is aware of this and tries to explain how *tou eschatou* . . . can be grasped by perception without its being a particular action ([1975]), pp. 42-44). But even if his explanation works, the question is whether it is needed. I agree with Cooper that '*eschaton*' needn't refer to a particular action, but I don't see why it can't sometimes refer to a particular action. (For instance, why can't a political enactment be about a particular action? Congress deliberated over whether to loan Chrysler Corporation a certain sum of money on a particular occasion. Why couldn't an Athenian legislative body do the same?) Since I also think that there are other problems with Cooper's view (see Chapter 2, n. 12, as well as ns. 14 and 23 below), I prefer to read the passage as not requiring such an explanation, thus taking '*tou eschatou* . . . ' to refer to a particular action.

It may not seem crucial to the argument for this appendix that '*tou eschatou* . . . ' refer to a particular action, since it looks as if essentially the same interpretation could be given if it were taken to refer to a specific kind of action. (See Sorabji (1973-74), pp. 124-25.) (However, see n. 23 below.) It does make a difference, though, to my discussion of Aristotle on weakness of the will (see, for example, Chapter 11 n. 39), and that is one of the reasons why I take time to argue for it here.

13. As Stewart points out ([1892], Vol. II, p. 92), the expression '*heteras protaseōs*' does not occur elsewhere in Aristotle, so it cannot automatically be assumed to refer to the minor premise of a practical syllogism. Aristotle does refer to the minor premise of a practical syllogism by '*heteras*' (with '*protaseōs*' understood) at 1147a26, but here it carries its literal meaning of 'the other', and its reference to the minor premise is given by what is it contrasted with as other, *katholou,* the universal premise. The safest way to treat '*tēs heteras protaseōs*' is, thus, to give it its literal meaning of 'the other premise' or 'the other proposition'.

14. The other natural point of contrast is with '*tou eschatou kai endechomenou*' itself, and there are at least three ways of drawing the contrast when it is understood in this way.

i) '*tou eschatou* . . . ' is taken to refer to a particular action that is to be done, and '*tēs heteras protaseōs*' is taken to refer to the other premise needed to provide starting points for an inductive inference to a universal practical principle. According to this interpretation, '*tou eschatou* . . . ' provides one with a premise of the form 'This is to be done'. '*tēs heteras protaseōs*' provides one with a premise of the form 'This is ∅'. This is the other premise needed to infer a general principle of the form 'What is ∅ is to be done'.

Two things recommend this interpretation. First, the major problems surrounding 1143a35-b5 seem to have a solution. The contrast is between *nous* as it grasps ultimate first principles for theoretical reasoning, and *nous* as it grasps ultimate premises for a form of practical reasoning, reasoning toward universal practical principles. In both cases what is grasped can be described as the work of *nous* because it is the job of *nous* to grasp universal first principles. Second, taking the contrast in this way takes the '*kai*' that precedes '*tēs heteras protaseōs*' to be the conjunctive 'and' rather than the explicative 'i.e.'. This fits Aristotle's use of the plural '*hautai*' ('these') at b4.

However, as I shall point out below, not only can the interpretation I suggest give essentially the same solutions to the problems surrounding 1143a35-b5, for the second problem to be solved, the interpretation under consideration here must take the perception of these two different premises to be part of a single perception (see n. 18 below). This seems to remove the need to regard them as two. Indeed, treating 1143b2-3 as a conjunction introduces an unnatural asymmetry into the contrast Aristotle is drawing. *Nous* as it operates in theoretical reasoning grasps only one sort of ultimate proposition. It would be odd if in contrast *nous* were to grasp two sorts of ultimates in practical reasoning. Besides, the plural '*hautai*' can be explained by its agreement with '*archai*' at b4, rather than by the occurrence of a conjunction at b2-3.

Thus, it seems preferable to take '*tou eschatou* . . . *heteras protaseōs*' to refer to a single proposition indicating what is to be done in a specific situation, rather than to the two particular propositions that the above interpretation takes it to refer to.

ii) '*tou eschatou* . . . ' is taken to refer to a particular action that is to be done and *tēs heteras protaseōs*' is taken to refer to the other ultimate proposition in a practical syllogism, the major premise. This is essentially Kenny's interpretation ([1978] , pp. 170-72). Kenny argues that without taking '*tēs heteras protaseōs*' to refer to the major premise, Aristotle's introductory sentence in 1143a35-b5, (that *nous* is concerned with ultimates in both directions), will be irrelevant, and the use of plural '*hautai*' will be inexplicable. Three things can be said in response to this.

First, as I have already indicated, the use of the plural '*hautai*' can be explained by its agreement with '*archai*', rather than by the occurrence of a conjunction at b2-3. Indeed, taking '*archai*' to refer to the two kinds of propositions that Kenny suggests is odd, since it looks as if only one of them will provide starting points for a universal end.

Second, Kenny's reason for thinking that Aristotle's introductory sentence will be irrelevant is not a good one. Kenny things it will be irrelevant because he thinks that *nous* in its theoretical employment grasps two different extremes, one the grasp of something universal, the other the perception of a particular as an instance of a general kind. He takes the latter to be referred to at 1142a29. Now the passage in which this occurs is normally taken to *deny* that *nous* in its theoretical employment grasps particulars, for it is normally taken to contrast *nous* with *phronēsis* on the grounds that the latter deals with particulars, but the former does not. However, Kenny amends the text (suggesting '*antilēptikon*' at 1142a25 rather than '*autikatei*'), making 1142a24-31 say that *phronēsis* perceives by *nous,* not that it is opposed to *nous.* Kenny's reason for this emendation is that so understood, 1142a24-31 agrees with rather than contradicts 1143a35-b5. However, as I argue elsewhere (see Chapter 5 Section III and n. 19 below), 1142a24-31 is compatible with 1143a35-b5 without making such an emendation. Thus, there is as yet no good reason for thinking that in its theoretical employment *nous* is involved with the perception of particulars. Indeed, as I shall argue below, there is a good reason for restricting the grasp of particulars by *nous* to its practical employment, for this preserves an important distinction that Aristotle draws between ethics and the theoretical sciences.

Finally, Aristotle's introductory sentence is relevant on the interpretation I suggest. *Nous* is concerned with ultimates in both directions, because it is concerned with ultimates in one direction in its theoretical employment (universal first principles), and ultimates in the other direction in its practical employment (particular actions that are to be done).

Again, it seems preferable to take '*tēs heteras protaseōs*' to refer to the same proposition as does '*tou eschatou . . .* '

iii) The third way of understanding the contrast by reference to '*tou eschatou . . .*' is the reverse of Kenny's interpretation. It turns out to be Cooper's interpretation. '*tou eschatou . . .* ' is taken to refer to the major premise of a practical syllogism, and '*tēs heteras protaseōs*' is taken to refer to the other ultimate premise in a practical syllogism, the minor premise.

I have already raised one problem for Cooper's interpretation, but the discussion of the above two interpretations suggests two more. First, Cooper also treats '*tou eschatou . . . heteras protaseōs*' as a conjunction, and this introduces an unnatural asymmetry into the contrast Aristotle is drawing. Second, on Cooper's interpretation it is not these two kinds of proposition that are starting points for a universal end, but rather the actions that result from them. It is by performing particular actions that universal ends are secured.

Again, it seems preferable to take '*tou eschatou . . . heteras protaseōs*' to refer to a single kind of proposition indicating that a particular action is to be done, thus making the point of contrast what *nous* grasps in the other direction in its theoretical employment.

15. Accordingly I take the antecedent of '*tais praktikais*' to be *protasesi*' (or, if need be, '*dunamesin*') rather than '*apodeixesin*'. It turns out that one can give an interpretation similar to the one I argue for and still take '*apodeixesin*' to be the antecedent of '*tais praktikais*', but doing so introduces some problems that, I think, are best solved by avoiding them. (See n. 22 below.)

16. In describing the inductive inference as proceeding from instances of the form 'This Ø is to be done' to 'What Ø is to be done', I do not mean to say that the induction in question must have the form of simple enumerative induction. Speaking this way is only a graphic way of talking about one of the problems surrounding the passage that needs to be solved, that *nous* provide all of the starting points for an inductive inference to a universal end. Such an inference might still best be described as an inference to the best explanation, or as an inference in keeping with the Popperian notion of conjecture and refutation.

17. This explanation will seem more plausible if what Lesher (1973) argues is correct. According to Lesher, *nous* is not restricted to the apprehension of ultimate first principles, but is operative whenever a person arrives at a generalization from statements of a less general sort.

18. It looks as if it would be just this kind of explanation that interpretation (i) in n. 14 above would have to give of why it is that *nous* is said to grasp practical particulars. But then there is no reason for thinking that there are two kinds of particular propositions that *nous* grasps, one of the form 'This is to be done' and the other of the form 'This is Ø'. What in effect *nous* grasps is a single proposition of the form 'This Ø is to be done'. It, thus, seems best to treat 1143a2-3 as referring to just this kind of proposition.

19. It should be noted that saying this does not require Aristotle to give up the contrast he has drawn between *phronēsis* and *nous*. *Nous* will still be concerned with objects of scientific knowledge that *phronēsis* is not concerned with, and *phronēsis* will be concerned with some objects of deliberation that *nous* will not be concerned with in either its theoretical or practical employment. (For more on this see Chapter 5 Section III.)

20. See esp. pp. 336-42. For a further discussion of these matters see Chapter 6 Section I.

21. McDowell leaves it open whether what we learn is something fixed by human nature or something determined by the features of the society of which it is the practice. That is,

he leaves it open whether ethics is objective or socially relative. I would argue that Aristotle would say that it is fixed by human nature.

22. It turns out that it is possible to provide an interpretation that allows *nous* to grasp propositions about what is to be done *and* to grasp minor premises of a practical syllogism. One way (adopted by Sorabji) is to take *'tou eschatou kai endechomenou'* to refer to the last minor premise indicating what is to be done. Like Cooper's interpretation, this takes *'tou eschatou . . . '* to refer to a proposition of the form 'What is Ø is to be done', where Ø is a specific kind of action. One might argue that propositions of this form can provide the basis for an inductive inference to a more general practical principle. A second way (adopted by Ando [1971], p. 207), pp. 254-55) involves taking the final minor premise of a practical syllogism to refer to a particular fact under an evaluative description whenever ethical questions are at issue, for instance, 'Drinking this would be drinking to excess'. Again, one might argue that propositions of this sort can provide the basis for an inductive inference to a more general practical principle.

However, both of these interpretations introduce an unnecessary complexity into the passage. Aristotle will be referring to premises of a practical syllogism, not because of their use in a practical syllogism, but because of their use in another form of reasoning. Why not simply take him to be referring to the propositions in this other form of reasoning? Second, it is not at all clear that these interpretations can give a fully satisfactory answer to why it is that *nous* is said to be involved in the grasp of these premises. For example, what marks off the perception of these premises from the perception of other premises where Aristotle wouldn't say that *nous* is involved? We have also seen that there is some reason for thinking that *'tou eschatou . . . '* is about particulars and not just about a specific kind of action (see n. 12 above). And although I agree with Ando that a final minor premise can be evaluative in the way he says that it is, I see no reason for saying that it will always be evaluative in this way whenever ethical questions are at issue. All in all, it seems preferable to adopt the interpretation I have argued for.

23. To be fair, the parallel that Cooper draws between the role of *nous* in scientific demonstrations and the role that he takes *nous* to play with respect to the ultimates of practical reasons ([1975], n. 54, p. 44) would be the beginning of such an explanation, but I think more will have to be said for the explanation to be fully satisfactory.

24. The omission would be even more remarkable if in 1143a35-b5 Aristotle were only talking about the way in which securing universal ends depends on pursing particular means, for the exercise of *euboulia* lies precisely in the discovery of the right means for the right ends. Burnet's explanation that all the faculties mentioned grasp their objects immediately whereas *euboulia* grasps its objects through a process of reasoning is inadequate, for, as Greenwood points out, this would also require the omission of *phronēsis*.

Appendix II. De Anima 434a12-15

1. Of the emendations that have been suggested, the two most important are indicated in parentheses. I shall adopt neither of them. *'hote men hautē ekeinēn'* has been suggested at lines 12-13 instead of *'tēn boulēsin'*, but it has no support in the manuscripts, and, by and large, the same difficulties arise on its adoption as arise on taking *'tēn boulēsin'* to be in the text. If anything, the adoption of *'hote men hautē ekeinēn'* makes the argument I want to give easier (see n. 6 below), so the adoption of *'tēn boulēsin'* does not beg any questions in my favor. Two manuscripts have *'sphairan'* instead of *'sphaira'*. Although this is of some importance, since it is not clear that these manuscripts are as reliable as the others, this is an emendation that I reject. (*'sphairan'* has also been suggested in addition to *'sphaira'*, but this doesn't make any difference. If it isn't added, it will have to be understood.)

2. To these one might want to add another interpretation suggested by the traditional interpretation of Aristotle's explanation of *akrasia*. (Strictly speaking, though, this is out of place in this discussion.) *'boulēsis'* is a desire for a general end expressed in the major premise

of a practical syllogism. It is at odds with *epithumia* in the sense that if applied to the situation at hand it would move the agent to act contrary to the way he is moved by *epithumia*. *Epithumia*, however, pushes aside *(kinei)* or overcomes *(nika)* *boulēsis*, preventing it from being applied to the case at hand. On this interpretation, there is also no genuine conflict of motives in *akrasia*.

3. One might think that there is a special reason for taking *'orexis'* in a more specific sense. In the sentence immediately preceding 434a12-15 *'orexis'* is used to refer to *epithumia*. One might think that this same use is carried over to line 14. However, for reasons I give just below, the context has changed by the time one reaches line 14.

4. It is true that two manuscripts have *'sphairan'* rather than *'sphaira'*, but it is not clear how reliable they are. Bywater, whose summary suggested IC, takes the text to contain *'sphaira'*.

5. One might think that *'hote d' ekeinē tautēn'* at least has the function of introducing the illustration brought in by *'sphaira'*, but in fact *'hē orexis tēn orexin'* does this.

6. It is in connection with just this issue that the emendation of *'hote men hautē ekeinēn'* for *tēn boulēsin'* would make my argument easier. If one were to accept it, then I think one would have to grant that Aristotle is talking about two situations of conflict.

7. I should mention one other reason that might mistakenly lead one to think that there is only one situation of conflict mentioned in 434a12-15. That is the occurrence of *'hotan akrasia genētai'* immediately after *'hē orexis tēn orexin'*. Hicks takes this to say that whenever one form of desire is in conflict with and emerges out over another, *akrasia* occurs. Since Hicks believes that Aristotle has previously referred to two such situations of conflict, *akrasia* and *enkrateia*, he is led to the implausible suggestion that in *'hotan akrasia genētai'* Aristotle is using *'akrasia'* in a special broad sense, covering both *enkrateia* and *akrasia*. Since this is an implausible suggestion, one might think that this provides one with a reason for taking Aristotle to have mentioned only one situation of conflict in the passage, *akrasia*. This, I think, would be a mistake. *'hē orexis tēn orexin, hotan akrasia genētai'* can be perfectly well understood as saying that one desire emerges out over another *when akrasia* occurs, and *not* as saying *whenever* one desire merges out over another, *akrasia* occurs. Understanding it in this way eliminates the need for Hicks' implausible reading of *'akrasia'*. With it goes any reason for taking its implausibility as grounds for thinking that Aristotle mentions only one situation of conflict.

8. For an indication of some of the difficulties surrounding these issues, see Hicks (1965), pp. 568-569.

9. As I have argued in Chapter 11, I think one will have to grant that at 433b5-10 Aristotle is at least saying that there are genuine conflicts of motives in *enkrateia*. See also NE 1102b13-19 and EE 1224a30ff. (For evidence of Aristotle's admission of a genuine conflict of motives in *enkrateia* in his discussion of *akrasia*, see NE 1146a10-17, 1150a33-b1, 1150b22-25, and 1151b35-1152a4.)

10. This same line of reasoning, I think, will also handle the interpretation suggested in n. 2 above. It is doubtful that Aristotle would be saying that in the case of *enkrateia boulēsis* thrusts *epithumia* aside, preventing it from being applied to the situation at hand. Among other things, this too would prevent *enkrateia* from exhibiting a genuine conflict of motives.

Bibliography

Bibliography

(Works cited in the text and notes.)

Works of Aristotle

De Anima. Translated by J. A. Smith. Oxford. The Clarendon Press, 1931.
De Anima. Translated W. S. Hett (Loeb Classical Library). London: William Heineman Ltd., 1935.
De Interpretatione. Translated by E. M. Edghill. Oxford: The Clarendon Press, 1928.
De Motu Animalium. Translated by A. S. L. Farquharson. Oxford: The Clarendon Press, 1912.
Eudemian Ethics. Translated by J. Soloman. Oxford: The Clarendon Press, 1925.
Eudemian Ethics. Translated by H. Rackham (Loeb Classical Library). London: William Heineman Ltd., 1935.
Metaphysics. Translated by W. D. Ross. Oxford: The Clarendon Press, 1908.
Nicomachean Ethics. Translated by W. D. Ross. Oxford: The Clarendon Press, 1925.
Nicomachean Ethics. Translated by H. Rackham (Loeb Classical Library). London: William Heineman Ltd., 1926.
Physics. Translated by R. P. Hardie and R. K. Gaye. Oxford: The Clarendon Press, 1930.
Politics. Translated by Benjamin Jowett. Oxford: The Clarendon Press, 1921.
Posterior Analytics. Translated by G. R. G. Mure. Oxford: The Clarendon Press, 1928.
Rhetoric. Translated by W. Rhys Roberts. Oxford: The Clarendon Press, 1924.
Topics: Translated by W. A. Pickard-Cambridge. Oxford: The Clarendon Press, 1928.

Other Works

Ackrill, J. L.
1974   "Aristotle on *Eudaimonia*," *Proceedings of the British Academy* 60: 1-23.
Allan, D. J.
1953   "Aristotle's Account of the Origin of Moral Principles." *Proceeding of the XIth*

Congress of Philosophy, Vol. XII, pp. 120-27. Amsterdam: North-Holland Publishing Co.

1955 "The Practical Syllogism," *Autour D'Aristote*, pp. 325-40. Louvain: Publication's Universitaires de Louvain.

Ando Takatura

1971 *Aristotle's Theory of Practical Cognition*. 3rd ed. The Hague: Martinus Nijhoff.

Anscombe, G. E. M.

1958 "Modern Moral Philosophy." *Philosophy* 31: 1-19.

1965 "Thought and Action in Aristotle." *New Essays on Plato and Aristotle*, edited by Renford Bambrough, pp. 143-58. New York: Routledge & Kegan Paul Ltd.

Bogen, James and Moravcsik, Julius

1982 "Aristotle's Forbidden Sweets." *Journal of the History of Philosophy* 20: 111-127.

Buchanan, Allen

1977 "Categorical Imperatives and Moral Principles." *Philosphical Studies* 31: 249-60.

Burnet, John

1904 *The Ethics of Aristotle*. London: Methuen and Co.

Burnyeat, Myles

1978 Review of John Cooper, *Reason and Human Good in Aristotle. Philosophical Review* 87: 102-5.

1980 "Aristotle on Learning to be Good." *Essays on Aristotle's Ethics*, edited by Amelie Oksenberg Rorty, pp. 69-92. Berkeley: University of California Press.

Bywater, Ingram

1888 "Aristotelia. III." *Journal of Philology* 17: 53-74.

Cook Wilson, J.

1912 "On the Structure of the Seventh Book of the *Nicomachean Ethics*, Chs. I-X." *Aristotelian Studies*. Oxford: The Clarendon Press.

Cooper, John

1975 *Reason and Human Good in Aristotle*. Cambridge, Mass.: Harvard University Press.

1977a "Aristotle on the Forms of Friendship." *Review of Metaphysics* 30: 619-48.

1977b "Friendship and the Good in Aristotle." *Philosophical Review* 68: 290-315.

1981 Review of Anthony Kenny, *The Aristotelian Ethics. Nous* 15: 381-92.

Darwall, Stephan

1983 *Impartial Reason*. Ithaca, N. Y.: Cornell University Press.

Davidson, Donald

1963 "Actions, Reasons, and Causes." *Journal of Philosophy* 60: 685-700.

1970 "How is Weakness of the Will Possible?" *Moral Concepts*, edited by Joel Feinberg, pp. 93-113. Oxford: Oxford University Press.

Frankena, William

1958 "Obligation and Motivation in Recent Moral Philosophy." *Essays in Moral Philosophy*, edited by A. I. Melden, pp. 40-81. Seattle: University of Washington Press.

Fortenbaugh, W. W.

1975 *Aristotle on Emotions*. London: Gerald Duckworth & Co. Ltd.

Gauthier, R. A.

1958 *La Morale d'Aristote*. Paris: Presses Universitaires de France.

Grant, Alexander

1885 *Aristotle's Ethics*. 2 vols. London: Longmans, Green and Co.

Greenwood, L. H. G.

1909 *Aristotle, Nicomachean Ethics, Bk. VI*. Cambridge: Cambridge University Press.

Hardie, W. F. R.

1968 "Aristotle and the Freewill Problem." *Philosophy* 43: 274-77.

1980   *Aristotle's Ethical Theory.* 2nd ed. Oxford: The Clarendon Press.
Hare, Richard
    1952   *The Language of Morals.* Oxford: The Clarendon Press.
    1963   *Freedom and Reason.* New York: Oxford University Press.
Hicks, R. D.
    1965   *Aristotle, De Anima.* Amsterdam: Adolf M. Hakkent.
Huby, Pamela
    1967   "The First Discovery of the Freewill Problem." *Philosophy* 42: 353-62.
Hudson, Stephen D.
    1981   "Reason and Motivation in Aristotle." *Canadian Journal of Philosophy* 11:
            111-35.
Hume, David
    1964   *A Treatise on Human Nature.* Selby-Bigge edition. Oxford: The Clarendon Press.
Irwin, Terry
    1975   "Aristotle on Reason, Desire, and Virtue." *Journal of Philosophy* 72: 567-78.
    1978   "First Principles in Aristotle's Ethics." *Midwest Studies in Philosophy* 3: 252-78.
Jackson, Reginald
    1942   "Rationalism and Intellectualism in the Ethics of Aristotle." *Mind* 51: 343-60.
Jaeger, Werner
    1948   *Aristotle, Fundamentals of the History of his Development.* Oxford: The Clar-
            endon Press.
Joachim, H. H.
    1951   *The Nicomachean Ethics.* Oxford: The Clarendon Press.
Kant, Immanuel
    1964   *Groundwork of the Metaphysics of Morals.* New York: Harper Torchbooks.
Kenny, Anthony
    1965-66 "Happiness." *Proceedings of the Aristotelian Society* 66: 93-102.
    1966   "The Practical Syllogism and Incontinence." *Phronesis* 11: 163-84.
    1978   *The Aristotelian Ethics.* Oxford: Oxford University Press.
    1979   *Aristotle's Theory of the Will.* New Haven, Conn.: Yale University Press.
Kraut, Richard
    1975   "The Importance of Love in Aristotle's Ethics." *Philosophy Research Archives*
            1, no. 1060.
Lesher, James
    1973   ''The Meaning of *Nous* in the *Posterior Analytics.*" *Phronesis* 18: 44-68.
Loening, Richard
    1903   *Die Zurechnungslehre des Aristotles.* Jena: G. Fischer.
McConnell, Terrance
    1975   "Is Aristotle's Account of Incontinence Inconsistent?" *Canadian Journal of
            Philosophy* 4: 635-51.
McDowell, John
    1978   "Are Moral Requirements Hypothetical Imperatives?" *Proceedings of the Aris-
            totelian Society,* Supplementary Vol. 52: 13-29.
    1979   "Virtue and Reason." *The Monist* 62: 331-50.
    1980   "The Role of *Eudaimonia* in Aristotle's Ethics." *The Proceedings of the African
            Classical Association* 15. Reprinted in *Essays on Aristotle's Ethics,* edited by
            Amelie Oksenberg Rorty, pp. 359-76. Berkeley: University of California Press.
Melden, A. I.
    1961   *Free Action.* London: Routledge & Kegan Paul Ltd.
Mele, Alfred
    1981   "Aristotle on *Akrasia* and Knowledge." *The Modern Schoolman* 58: 137-57.
Michelakis, Emmanuel M.
    1961   *Aristotle's Theory of Practical Principles.* Athens: Cleisiounis Press.

Milo, Ronald
    1966   *Aristotle on Practical Knowledge and Weakness.* The Hague: Mouton & Co.
Monan, J. Donald
    1968   *Moral Knowledge and Its Methodology in Aristotle.* Oxford: The Clarendon
            Press.
Moravcsik, Julius and Bogen, James
    1982   See Bogen, James and Moravcsik, Julius.
Mortimore, G. W., editor
    1971   *Weakness of the Will.* London, Macmillan and Co. Ltd.
Nagel, Thomas
    1970   *The Possibility of Altruism.* Oxford: The Clarendon Press.
Nussbaum, Martha
    1978   *Aristotle's De Motu Animalium.* Princeton, N. J.: Princeton University Press.
Owen, G. E. L.
    1965   "The Platonism of Aristotle." *Proceedings of the British Academy* 51: 125-50.
    1967   *"Tithenai Ta Phainomena."* Aristotle, edited by J. M. E. Moravcsik, pp. 167-90.
            Garden City, N. Y.: Doubleday and Company, Inc.
Rawls, John
    1971   *A Theory of Justice.* Cambridge, Mass.: Harvard University Press.
    1980   "Kantian Constructivism in Moral Theory." *Journal of Philosophy* 77: 515-72.
Reilly, Richard
    1976   "Weakness and Blameworthiness: The Aristotelian Predicament." *Philosophical
            Studies* (Ireland) 24: 148-65.
Rorty, Amelie Oksenberg
    1980   *"Akrasia* and Pleasure: *Nicomachean Ethics,* Bk. 7." *Essays on Aristotle's Ethics,*
            edited by Amelie Oksenberg Rorty, pp. 267-84. Berkeley: University of Califor-
            nia Press.
Ross, W. D.
    1961   *Aristotle, De Anima.* Oxford: The Clarendon Press.
    1963   *Aristotle.* Cleveland: The World Publishing Company.
Santas, Gerasimos
    1964   "The Socratic Paradoxes." *Philosophical Review* 73: 147-64.
    1966   "Plato's *Protagoras* and Explanation of Weakness." *Philosophical Review* 75: 3-33.
    1969   "Aristotle on Practical Inference, the Explanation of Action, and *Akrasia."*
            Phronesis 14: 162-89.
Siegler, Frederick
    1967   "Reason, Happiness, and Goodness." *Aristotle's Ethics,* edited by James J.
            Walsh and Henry L. Shapiro, pp. 40-46. Belmont, Calif.: Wadsworth Publishing
            Company, Inc.
Sorabji, Richard
    1973-74 "Aristotle on the Role of Intellect in Virtue." *Proceedings of the Aristotelian
            Society* 74: 107-29.
Stewart, J. A.
    1892   *Notes on the Nicomachean Ethics of Aristotle.* 2 vols. Oxford: The Clarendon
            Press.
Walsh, James J.
    1963   *Aristotle's Conception of Moral Weakness.* New York: Columbia University
            Press.
Walter, Julius
    1874   *Die Lehre von der praktischen Vernunft in der griechischen Philosophie.* Jena:
            Mauke.
Wedin, Michael V.
    1981   "Aristotle on the Good for Man." *Mind* 90: 243-62.

Wiggins, David
    1975-76 "Deliberation and Practical Reason." *Proceedings of the Aristotelian Society* 76: 29-51.
    1978-79 "Weakness of Will, Commensurability, and the Objects of Deliberation and Desire." *Proceedings of the Aristotelian Society* 79: 251-77.
Wilkes, Kathleen V.
    1978   "The Good Man and the Good for Man in Aristotle's Ethics." *Mind* 87: 553-71.
Williams, Bernard
    1962   "Aristotle on the Good: a Formal Sketch." *Philosophical Quarterly* 12: 289-96.
Woods, Michael
    1982   *Aristotle's Eudemian Ethics, Bks. I, II, and VIII.* Oxford: Oxford University Press.

Indexes

General Index

Index of Aristotelian Passages

1147a32ff	151-52, 170	1151a17-18	84
147a32-33	166	1151a18-19	84
147a32-35	205	1151a20-26	105, 157, 257n18
1147a33	216	1151b35-1152a4	283n9
1147a33-34	167, 170	1152a4-7	170
1147a34	167, 168, 170-71, 178, 179, 186, 205, 216	1152a9	47
		1152a9-10	274n33
1147a34-35	205, 207, 216, 218	1152a15-17	224
1147a34-36	167	1152a17	252n9, 268n22, 269n39
1147a35	205, 216		
1147b1	171	1152a20-24	105
1147b3-5	205-6	1152a28-29	212, 214
1147b4-6	216	1156b7-8	125
1147b6-9	212	1156b19-21	125
1147b9	168, 178-79, 186	1158a10-12	125
1147b9-10	274n39	1158b3-35	125
1147b9-12	167, 206-7, 207-11, 274n31	1165b22-30	125
		1166a29-31	125
1147b9-13	171, 270n43	1166b7ff	273n11
1147b11-12	179, 270n43	1166b7-11	190-91
1147b12-17	210-11, 216, 275-76n45	1166b18-26	191
		1166b22-23	271n3
1147b12-19	206	1181b7-13	73
1147b13-17	183-84	1181b16-23	73
1147b15-16	141		
1147b17	276n45	*Eudemian Ethics*	
1147b23-35	213	1214b6ff	105, 260n11
1148a4-10	170	1215a12-19	262n19
1148a13-15	143	1219b26-1220a12	271n5
1148a16-17	143	1224a30ff	283n9
1148a18-22	276n47	1224a30-31	271n2
1149a32-b2	170, 176, 269n36	1224a30-36	190
1149b2	251n9	1224b5ff	273n11
1150a27-31	276n47	1224b5-21	190, 271n2
1150a33-b1	283n9	1224b9	271n2
1150b19-22	144, 154, 181-82, 260n10, 265n10	1224b21-24	271n2
1150b22-25	283n9	*Politics*	
1150b29-30	143	1260b27-35	256n16
1150b30	197	1300a3-6	273n19, 273n21
1150b33-35	212	1309a17-19	197, 273n19, 273n21
1150b36	181, 182		
1150b37	145	1323b24-29	262n19
1151a1-3	145		
1151a6	197	*Rhetoric*	
1151a11-13	83	1360a30-35	256n16
1151a11-15	170, 197	1360b27-35	256n16
1151a15-19	82-85, 90, 96		

Norman Dahl earned his B.A. in mathematics at Pacific Lutheran University and his doctorate in philosophy at the University of California, Berkeley. Now professor of philosophy at the University of Minnesota, he has taught at Minnesota since 1967 and served as chair of the department of philosophy from 1978 till 1980.